The Idea of the Book

in the Middle Ages

The Idea of the Book
in the Middle Ages

LANGUAGE THEORY,
MYTHOLOGY, AND FICTION

JESSE M. GELLRICH

Cornell University Press

ITHACA AND LONDON

Cornell University Press gratefully acknowledges a grant
from the Andrew W. Mellon Foundation that
aided in bringing this book to publication.

First published 1985 by Cornell University Press.

Excerpts from Dante Alighieri, *The Divine Comedy*, translated, with a commentary by
Charles Singleton, Bollingen Series 80, Volume 1: *Inferno*, copyright © 1970 by
Princeton University Press; Volume 2: *Purgatorio*, copyright © 1973 by Princeton
University Press; Volume 3: *Paradiso*, copyright © 1975 by Princeton University
Press, are reprinted by permission of Princeton University Press.

International Standard Book Number 0-8014-1722-8
Library of Congress Catalog Card Number 84-23814
Printed in the United States of America
*Librarians: Library of Congress cataloging information appears
on the last page of the book.*

*The paper in this book is acid-free, and meets the guidelines for permanence and
durability of the Committee on Production Guidelines for Book Longevity
of the Council on Library Resources.*

219130

For my family

and in memory of my father

1901–1970

Letters are indeed the indices of things, the signs of words, in which there is such power that they speak to us without voice the discourse of the absent.

Isidore of Seville, *Etymologiarum*

But the *Idols of the Market-place* are the most troublesome of all: idols which have crept into the understanding through the alliance of words and names. For men believe that their reason governs words; but it is also true that words react on the understanding; and this it is that has rendered philosophy and the sciences sophistical and inactive.

Francis Bacon, *Novum organum*

CONTENTS

[7]

Contents

ILLUSTRATIONS

[9]

Illustrations

[7]
David with beast musicians.
Psalter. Manuscript illumination (ca. 1300).
89

[8]
Harp (detail). Right wing triptych. *Garden of Earthly
Delights*. Hieronymus Bosch (fifteenth century).
90

[9]
Grammar with two children.
Wooden statue. Souabe (ca. 1330).
97

ACKNOWLEDGMENTS

I wish to express my warmest thanks to all the people who have given me support of various kinds during the development of this book. First of all, to Herbert N. Schneidau, whose work in related areas of scholarship inspired my own, I owe a special debt for encouragement all along the way, for reading the entire manuscript, and for offering many valuable comments. I am also grateful to James McMichael, not only for reading each of the chapters, but also for being an important influence on my work throughout its several stages. Henry A. Kelly has also been a dependable reader and supporter. So too has Harold E. Toliver, who read and responded to early sections of this book, shaping its course significantly. Hayden White has helped me in countless ways with his generous advice on chapter 1 and on the major themes of succeeding chapters. At Cornell University Press, Bernhard Kendler has taken particular care in handling this manuscript, and I am grateful to him and to the anonymous readers for their extensive responses. I also thank James L. Calderwood, Robin McAllister, Eugene Kaelin, R. Howard Bloch, John Ahern, Francis Duggan, and Barbara Pavlock for their help during the past several years.

Many students have participated in the genesis of this book, too many to name. Their questions and eagerness have been continuously inspiring. To the three students who worked directly on the manuscript, I express my appreciation: to Margaret Ward for help with footnotes in chapters 1, 2, and 3; to Richard Divozzo and Phylis Floyd for assistance with the Bibliography. The librarians at the University of California at Berkeley and Santa Cruz have offered resource materials; and the reference and art librarians at the University of Michigan, Ann Arbor, have worked with me tirelessly on sources and addresses for permissions. Thanks, too, go to Elizabeth Beatson of the Index of Christian Art at Princeton University for research on one of the illustrations.

The editors of *Clio* have kindly granted me permission to publish as chapter 1 a revised version of an essay that originally appeared in *Clio* 10, 3 (1981):245–263. D. Reidel Publishing Company has allowed me to adopt for chapter 3 a few pages that appeared in *Analecta Husserliana* 18 (1984):186–189. I am also grateful to the following museums and libraries, which have supplied photographs for the illustrations and granted me permission to reproduce them: the Metropolitan Museum of Art, the Curators of Karlstejn Castle, the Putnam Foundation, the Timken Art Gallery, the Department of Manuscripts in the British Library, the Dean and Chapter of Hereford Cathedral, the Austrian National Library, the Prado Museum, and the Bavarian National Museum.

Finally, the assistance of my mother and the presence of my children have been sources of renewed encouragement, especially toward the end. But I thank, more than anyone else, my wife, Michelle, for her continuing interest in the ideas of this book, her deep insight into them, and her many thoughtful suggestions. Without her excellent intelligence about literary matters and her devoted support of my daily efforts, the development of this volume would have been very different.

JESSE M. GELLRICH

Ann Arbor, Michigan

ABBREVIATIONS

Actes 4	*Arts Libéraux et Philosophie au Moyen Age. Actes du 4me Congrès International de Philosophie Médiévale*
ALMA	*Archivum Latinitatis Medii Aevi*
CI	*Critical Inquiry*
CIMAGL	*Cahiers de l'Institut du Moyen-Age Grec et Latin*
CJL	*Canadian Journal of Linguistics*
CPDMA	*Corpus Philosophorum Danicorum Medii Aevi*
EIC	*Essays in Criticism*
ELH	*English Literary History*
ES	*English Studies*
FL	*Foundations of Language*
HL	*Historiographia Linguistica: International Journal for the History of Linguistics*
JEGP	*Journal of English and Germanic Philology*
JHI	*Journal of the History of Ideas*
Lg	*Language*
MLN	*Modern Language Notes*
MLQ	*Modern Language Quarterly*
MLR	*Modern Language Review*
MP	*Modern Philology*
MS	*Mediaeval Studies*
MSLL	*Monograph Series on Languages and Linguistics*
NLH	*New Literary History*
NM	*Neuphilologische Mitteilungen*
PBA	*Proceedings of the British Academy*
PL	*Patrologia Latina*
PQ	*Philological Quarterly*
REL	*Review of English Literature*
SiHoL	*Studies in the History of Linguistics*
SPh	*Studia Phonetica*
UCSLL	*University of Colorado Studies in Language and Literature*
UTQ	*University of Toronto Quarterly*

The Idea of the Book

in the Middle Ages

Plate 1. John eats the book. Apocalypse 10.9–10 (early fourteenth century). Metropolitan Museum of Art, Cloisters Collection, 1968. MS 68.174, fol. 16ᵛ.

And I went to the angel, saying unto him that he should give me the book. And he said to me: Take the book and eat it up. . . . And I took the book from the hand of the angel and ate it up; and it was in my mouth, sweet as honey; and when I had eaten it my belly was bitter.

Apocalypse 10.9–10

INTRODUCTION

> For Christ is a sort of book written into the skin of the virgin. . . .
> That book was spoken in the disposition of the Father, written in
> the conception of the mother, exposited in the clarification of the
> nativity, corrected in the passion, erased in the flagellation, punc-
> tuated in the imprint of the wounds, adorned in the crucifixion
> above the pulpit, illuminated in the outpouring of blood, bound
> in the resurrection, and examined in the ascension.
>
> Pierre Bersuire, *Repertorium morale*

This book is intended, first of all, to carry on the work of
such scholars as Johan Huizinga, Erich Auerbach, Ernst Curtius,
Charles Singleton, and D. W. Robertson, Jr., who have helped to
assess the place of literature among the various cultural forms
of the middle ages.[1] But it is also devoted to reconsidering the
grounds on which this place may be established in light of proposals in critical theory that have emerged since structuralism. I
attempt to develop a systematic approach to the continuity of medieval ideas about speaking, writing, and texts—the history of *auctores* ("authors") and *auctoritates* ("sources"); this history is studied
in theological and philosophical traditions as well as in medieval
fictional writing. Through close readings of poems by Dante and
Chaucer, I analyze the extent to which fiction becomes the ground
for departures in the modes of signifying meaning that were dif-

---

[1] Johan Huizinga, *The Waning of the Middle Ages: A Study of the Forms of Life, Thought
and Art in France and the Netherlands in the Fourteenth and Fifteenth Centuries* (1924; re-
print, New York: Doubleday, 1954); Erich Auerbach, *Mimesis: The Representation of
Reality in Western Literature*, trans. Willard Trask (1946; reprint, Garden City, N.Y.:
Doubleday, 1957); Ernst Robert Curtius, *European Literature and the Latin Middle
Ages*, trans. Willard Trask (New York: Harper & Row, 1963); Charles S. Singleton,
Dante Studies I: "Commedia," Elements of Structure (Cambridge: Harvard University
Press, 1954; D. W. Robertson, Jr., *A Preface to Chaucer: Studies in Medieval Perspec-
tives* (Princeton: Princeton University Press, 1962).

ferent from and more consequential than developments in the history of thinking about language in other areas of learning, such as the trivium (grammar, dialectic, and logic). My overall aim is to examine the nature of historical change insofar as it may be reflected in linguistic change, and thus to use language as a model for rethinking the nature of the conceptual boundary lines at each end of the so-called middle ages—the archaic or mythological societies opposed by cultural traditions after Augustine and the "Renaissance" that emerged after Chaucer.

The approach to continuity in this book arises from medieval ideas themselves, principally from the commonplace attempt to gather all strands of learning together into an enormous Text, an encyclopedia or summa, that would mirror the historical and transcendental orders just as the Book of God's Word (the Bible) was a speculum of the Book of his Work (nature). The function of the Bible as mirror has limits that are well established within medieval hermeneutics, and heretofore those limits have controlled to a great extent how the much broader idea of the Book as a reflection of cultural traditions has been analyzed. But in light of the vast and diverse attention that this topic has received in modern theory— for example, by Ferdinand de Saussure, Claude Lévi-Strauss, Michel Foucault, and Jacques Derrida—the medieval image may be reopened for a new look at its role in the origin and development of cultural forms.[2]

One of the most seminal of recent proposals is that the Text fulfills certain expectations that mythology supplied in archaic cultures. In arguing this position with reference to various societies, Lévi-Strauss emphasizes a principle about the totalizing and classifying determinations of mythological thought that not only has been suggested in other areas of scholarship—such as prehistory—but has unusual bearing on the classifying forms of the medieval world. This conception of myth as a storehouse of a culture's lore will, to begin with, subsume customary notions of medieval "mythography"; yet it has the capacity to offer a much wider explanation for the "encyclopedia" of culture. In attempting to read myth as the *langue* of a society, Lévi-Strauss (following Saussure) sees a distinction between the unexpressed system of cultural norms or rules and the many veiled manifestations in the individ-

---

[2]Ferdinand de Saussure, *Cours de linguistique générale*, ed. Charles Bally and Albert Sechehaye (1916; reprint, Paris: Payot, 1973); Claude Lévi-Strauss, *La Pensée sauvage* (Paris: Plon, 1962); Michel Foucault, *Les Mots et les choses* (Paris: Gallimard, 1971); Jacques Derrida, *De la grammatologie* (Paris: Minuit, 1967).

ual *parole* of speaking and writing, the specific and idiosyncratic ways a people may act.[3] Since this conception of a societal *langue* also has a parallel in Foucault's idea of cultural "episteme," both he and Lévi-Strauss have made available a systematic approach to studying seemingly diverse societies or historical eras in terms of their common "grammar."[4]

The following chapters maintain that in the middle ages the Text is the metaphor of such a structuring process or grammar; therefore, this study is not an encyclopedic survey of what medieval thinkers wrote about books, nor is it an effort to treat this metaphor as a container enclosing a defining content. It is rather a consideration of the conditions of signifying that produced the great books of the middle ages, an exploration of the "textuality" of traditions at work not only in writing but, just as important, in several cultural forms from the fourth century to the fourteenth. If the totalizing foundation of myth informs the model of a cultural Book, then it is worthwhile to consider whether medieval forms have roots in more archaic prototypes, those that supposedly were displaced by the development of traditions after Augustine and Jerome. For example, the treatment of space (taken up in chapter 2), specifically its sacralization in the ancient world, where volume, height, and density were considered to be attributes of holiness, is a compelling instance of the presence of divinity in visual forms. Medieval representations of the divine begin from a manifestly different grounding in the second commandment (Exod. 20.4) against making "likenesses" of God and in the continuing repudiation of idol worship throughout the prophetic books of the Bible. The pulpits of medieval Christendom surely thundered with these pronouncements, but the sacrality of stone and volume as well as the association of divinity with towering visible forms prevails over any diatribe against the "idols of the Market-place" and the "Theater," as Francis Bacon would later call them.[5] Space is radiant with meaning in these forms; it replicates a supernatural order; it is imbued with the presence of significance that is of a piece with the stress on heavy outlines and sharp borders. Accordingly, the effort to contain all within sacred confines becomes a determinant of structure: we see it perhaps most graphically in certain miniatures of manu-

[3]See Lévi-Strauss, *Pensée*, chap. 1.
[4]See Foucault, *Mots*, chap. 2.
[5]*Novum organum*, in *Seventeenth-Century Prose and Poetry*, ed. Alexander M. Witherspoon and Frank J. Warnke, 2d ed. (New York: Harcourt, Brace, & World, 1963), pp. 56–57.

script painting that show an attempt to reduce to manageable size the meaning of an elusive biblical passage, to contain and stabilize its significance. And similar totalizing efforts are, to some degree, commonplace by the time of late Gothic architecture, especially in the ribbed column, vault, and window.

Insofar as these are forms of replicating a divine ordo, of revealing or illuminating its structural principles, they reflect the textual properties of the Book of nature and the Book of Scripture, where all of God's plan is set forth. Any number of chapters in the medieval Text of cultural forms may be probed for their mythologizing structure, and among those treated in the following pages, musical theory offers especially rich evidence. It indicates how a metaphor can be fixed so firmly that its capacity as a mere analogy of apprehending a transcendent meaning becomes fascinating in its own right and is treated as a structure of reality itself: the music of the spheres determines the *musica* in the physical world and in the heart of man. The bond between image and referent, signifier and signified is highly motivated or natural in these examples, and they suggest that the structure of the summa or encyclopedia is continuous with the larger Book of medieval culture. It is a continuity motivated by the firm belief that the books of man's making would never come into existence without the Logos spoken by God.

The "idea" of the Book presented here, therefore, is not a specific abstraction that descended into writing, but rather is a structuring principle of far-reaching potential. It is an "idea" in the broad sense of an inherited or received supposition about the ordo radiating throughout the physical universe and the language composed in explanation of it. While it prevails in learned traditions from Augustine to Chaucer, it is not a transhistorical concept but is determined and stabilized by the unique homogeneity of medieval learning. It represents an "episteme" that changed radically by the time of Francis Bacon, and consequently the Book studied in these pages is a definite medieval idea. Yet the Text cannot be situated so simply, since the totality and presence of meaning represented by it have obviously corresponding forms in mythological cultures both antedating and postdating the middle ages. As a result, the medieval idea of the Book is a particular form of this larger, mythologizing phenomenon of Western tradition.

Although the effort to establish the grounds of this idea touches on several cultural forms—manuscript painting, sacred architecture, Scholasticism, and musical theory—the intention of these chapters can only be to assemble suggestive evidence, rather than to write a prescription for how the culture made itself. Much more work can be done on the textuality of any of these forms. One of the most challenging areas of its manifestation is grammatical and hermeneutic theory, which is given separate and extensive treatment (in chapter 3). A tradition full of potential comparisons for modern theoretical interests in the *abecedarium culturae*, medieval sign theory has recently attracted several engaging studies.[6] An increasing section of this scholarship regards the subtle treatment of signs in the middle ages as on a par with the strategies of signifying that have become commonplace in the wake of structuralism and especially in "deconstruction." When the medieval sign is defined as a tripartite structure—a *signum* ("sign") that is divided into a *signans* ("signifying") and a *signatum* ("signified")—the work of Saussure comes to mind; and when Augustine imagines the cosmos as a vast "script" written by the hand of God, in contrast to his own pale, flawed imitation of it, modern readers may see the deconstructive project of Derrida "prefigured." Indeed, a fourteenth-century illumination of Apocalypse 10.9, in which the visionary is told, "Take this book and eat it," might appear to suggest an unusually vivid instance of the deconstruction of textuality in this digestion of the Word.[7]

Although these possibilities may be intriguing, they should be pursued only in full appreciation of the extent to which signs and signification, as they were explored in *grammatica* (the first discipline of the seven liberal arts) and in the hermeneutics of Scripture, remained committed to a larger intellectual preoccupation with stabilizing the sign, moving it out of the realm of potential arbitrariness, and tracing utterance back to a fixed origin, such as the primal Word spoken by God the Father. There can be no doubt that grammar in the middle ages makes tremendous strides in exploring the "ways of signifying" through spoken and written discourse, particularly among the speculative grammarians (or *mo-*

[6]Edward Said, *Abecedarium Culturae: Structuralism, Absence, Writing, Modern French Criticism* (Chicago: University of Chicago Press, 1972). Full documentation for medieval sign theory is provided in the notes to chapters 1 and 3 below. A few recent and important items came to my attention after completing this book, but revisions allowed for some references to them: R. Howard Bloch, *Etymologies and Genealogies: A Literary Anthropology of the French Middle Ages* (Chicago: University of Chicago Press, 1983); Brian Stock, *The Implications of Literacy: Written Language and Models of Interpretation in the Eleventh and Twelfth Centuries* (Princeton: Princeton University Press, 1983); Eugene Vance, "Saint Augustine: Lanugage as Temporality," in *Mimesis: From Mirror to Method, Augustine to Descartes,* ed. John D. Lyons and Stephen G. Nichols, Jr. (Hanover, N.H.: University Press of New England, 1982).

[7]See plate 1.

distae) of the thirteenth and fourteenth centuries. But it is also true
that the *end* of learning about language was ingrained profoundly
in education, and that end was to carry out the well-known instructions for finding the "right reading"—the correct historical, moral,
and anagogical interpretation—of the pages in the Book of nature
and Scripture. Eating the Book, such as we find it glossed by Hugh
of St. Cher and Pierre Bersuire, was an act of reconstructing the
life of Christ through the proper understanding of the Old and
New Testaments;[8] and the illuminator of Apocalypse 10 makes a
connection predicted by such glosses as he represents the scene in
the familiar gesture of taking the Eucharist, through which the
"Word made flesh" becomes "bread" by the words of the priest (as
Aquinas says), and the Logos of Christ's life is truly ingested. When
a theological idea is represented so literally in visible things, as in
this painting, word and thing are interchangeable; nature and
Scripture constitute a transparent Text whose digestion is simultaneously a reconstruction; it is maintained by validating learning in
a source or end; it is intensely teleological and organic; and it is accordingly dominated by motifs of deliberate causality and sequentiality: the "narrative" of the Book is the "history" of mankind from
creation to the ascent into the celestial city. Narrative as a structure
of moralizing never had better illustration than in the medieval
Text of culture.[9]

Against such "logocentric" structures of language and meaning,
the analysis of signs in the middle ages does not appear to establish
a significant subversion. Consequently, in distinction to that branch
of scholarship that sees medieval sign theory as inclining toward, if
not prefiguring, modern concerns with arbitrary signs, deferred
meaning, postponed ends, and textual indeterminacy, the study
of linguistic disciplines in these chapters moves in a different direction—toward the larger received idea of post-Augustinian tradition that found a place for everything (as C. S. Lewis has re-
marked) and kept everything in its right place, even the errant

---

[8]Bersuire's remark is the epigraph of this Introduction. Hugh of St. Cher's gloss
is: "Indeed this book is the life of Christ . . . the sacraments and mysteries of the
Church"; *Opera omnia*, 8 vols. (Venice, 1732), 7.397. Aquinas meditates on these images in his *Corpus Christi* hymn for Vespers, especially the untranslatable verses:
"Verbum caro panem verum / verbo carnem efficit"; *The Oxford Book of Medieval
Latin Verse*, ed. F. J. E. Raby (Oxford: Clarendon Press, 1959), p. 401. Translations
from Latin throughout this book are mine unless otherwise noted.
[9]Cf. Hayden White, "The Value of Narrativity in the Representation of Reality,"
CI 7 (1980): 5–27.

potential of the written or spoken sign.[10] Thus does the end determine the beginning of the idea of the Book in the middle ages. It remained a determinant of cultural growth from the time of Augustine's emphasis on it and continued at least until its magnificent illustrations in late Gothic art, when the "unbinding" of the Book became inevitable in the ornamentality and artificiality that eventually flowered in Baroque styles of the seventeenth century.

But the idea of the Book after Augustine is also analyzed in these chapters with attention to writings that were composed outside the formal institution of language study taught by the church. This writing, medieval poetic fiction, surely inherited models of textuality along with basic conceptions from the trivium about the ways that signs signify. Whether or not fictional discourse carries out the prevailing commitment of the inherited structure to imitate past models and thus contribute to the stabilization of tradition cannot be affirmed as unilaterally as, for example, Singleton and Robertson once assumed. The chapters on the poetry of Dante and Chaucer in this book take a new look at the place of fiction within the encompassing Text of medieval cultural forms; they suggest that the customary view of medieval fiction as an affirmation of inherited linguistic and textual models needs to be renovated. Dante's *Commedia* (taken up in chapter 4) is perhaps the most prominent and engaging test case for this claim, since the poem represents the fiction of the poet as a *scriba* ("scribe") who is copying from the "book of memory" his experience of religious conversion. All the trappings of medieval textuality are here: the determinate origin in a book, the progress of the journey as a narrative with deep moral commitments, the comparison between the poem and the "art" of nature, and the encyclopedic scope of the work. The language of the poem, as Singleton and others have maintained, is an imitation of the writing of God etched in the rock over the hellgate in *Inferno* 3.

And yet the evidence of textuality in the poem does not function simply according to a principle of mimesis. A close look shows that Dante read Augustine very carefully on the notion of the separation between divine language and human writing and established that separation or departure in terms that were fundamentally resisted within the formal confines of reading and writing that

[10]C. S. Lewis, *The Discarded Image: An Introduction to Medieval and Renaissance Literature* (Cambridge: Cambridge University Press, 1964), pp. 10–11.

composed the Text of the past. As one modern study has argued, Dante's poem is less an allegory of history than a reflection of the reading process, with all its limitations in the uncertainty of meaning and the temporality of understanding.[11] It may be true that one of Dante's most important sources was the Bible; but it is also worthwhile to consider the degree to which his *Commedia* responds to the style of biblical writing per se, that is, to the discourse of Scripture stripped of the medieval mythology that was made of it from the ways of signifying taught in the tradition of the Text. In this way we are invited to reflect on the separation or split between the Book of tradition and the text of fictional writing and to consider this writing as the ground for changes in the modes of signification that were only foreshortened in the disciplines of grammar and hermeneutics. Fictional signifying introduces a galaxy of possibilities for meaning that could not be encouraged within the fixed "geocentric" cosmos of the Book of culture.

What Dante's poem introduces, *The House of Fame*—in a certain respect Chaucer's "Dante"—explores much more boldly. In this poem (the subject of chapter 5) the foundational principle of the Text, its insistence on the fixed origin of language, is confronted in no uncertain terms as a plot that makes little if any sense. As the quest for the source of "fame" in writing is submitted to the outrageous parody of discovering the garrulous goddess of discourse and the windy house of sticks, the whole idea of containment, narrative order, and determinate meaning loosens with such humor that the sacrality of the medieval myth can no longer be taken for granted: signification destabilizes as it never had before in the pages of the grammarians and exegetes, and the question about locating the authority of meaning in an origin or text is postponed indefinitely in this poem of uncertain ending and dubious figures of "auctoritee." The questions Dante asked about the textuality of history and nature are taken up so fully by Chaucer that two more of his works are considered separately.

In the "Prologue" to *The Legend of Good Women* (examined in chapter 6), a work that follows directly from the convention of the dream vision in *The House of Fame*, the disjunction between the myth of the Text and the discourse of poetry corresponds to the opposition in the work between narrative order and textual matters with hardly any interest in it. The question of the reliability of

---

[11]Giuseppe Mazzotta, *Dante, Poet of the Desert: History and Allegory in the "Divine Comedy"* (Princeton: Princeton University Press, 1979).

the narrator's voice, which Chaucer exploits thoroughly in later poems, is sharply figured in this early work as a construct that does not completely prevail over the meaning of the text, and consequently the question of the determinacy of signification is confronted outright. As the voice of the text plays with the insistence of the speaker, complaining against the way he and his narrative are inviting us to read, the location of the authority for meaning has shifted clearly away from a source and its author, where it had been so well protected in the tradition of the Book; instead, it has been set loose in the play of plurivalent senses allowed by the hypothetical boundary lines of fictive response. The causality and sequentiality of storial sense give place to the more abiding interests of the poem in how, for example, the participants in the court scene, even Queen Alceste, speak without full control of the errancy and distraction in their discourse. The narrator promises to give us the "naked text," to make present the plain sense of things, but the play of the text with his voice proves a far more alluring and pleasant experience. In short, this poem in self-defense of "Chaucer's" poetry and in preface to his tales of good women turns out to engage some of the most compelling arguments about the order and validation of signification in language that had come down through the hierarchy of the textual tradition of the middle ages. The "Prologue" amounts to a subversion of that hierarchy long before such a critique took over all branches of learning in the sixteenth and seventeenth centuries;[12] and thus the poem is, contrary to the opinion of those who count it as one of Chaucer's incidental pieces, a crucial stage in his reflection on the problems of reading and writing: it looks forward immediately to the staging of these matters in his subsequent poetic efforts, notably *The Canterbury Tales.*

To a significant extent, Chaucer's dream visions and Dante's *Commedia* demonstrate an alternative to one of the basic premises of the idea of the Book in the middle ages—its firm grounding in the Platonic and Augustinian concept of imitation. This premise is at work most obviously as one medieval reader of Scripture after another copies precedent *auctores* on the interpretation of a passage. Interpretation in the grammatical and hermeneutic traditions is a form of imitation under definite control of a poetics in which the pages of nature and Scripture are imagined as copies of God's *Verbum.* But in Chaucer and Dante the idea of copying or

[12]Cf. Patricia Parker's suggestive study of "error" and "fictional deviance" within the genre of romance (Ariosto and Spenser): *Inescapable Romance: Studies in the Poetics of a Mode* (Princeton: Princeton University Press, 1979), chaps. 1 and 2.

rewriting is displaced by a new kind of interpreting, one that no longer allows for the straightforward validation of meaning in an "old book," the sequence of events, or the voice of a speaker. This movement from imitation to interpretation—"from mirror to method"—is an unmistakable concern of fictional writing in the late middle ages, and nowhere more provocatively than in *The Canterbury Tales.*[13] The whole work could be studied for its analysis of this problem, but Chaucer gives enough attention to it in the "General Prologue" that a consideration of this poem (in chapter 7) may serve as a preface.

The work begins with undermining the convention of imitation by casting the narrator in the role of copyist or reporter. If the rich and complex suggestions that have been made about this pose have anything in common, it is that the narrative strategy of the "General Prologue" is an instance of Chaucerian "irony" or "paradox"; this idea is more conventional than it may appear, since it still holds firmly to the validation of meaning in an authorial voice of which the fictive expression is an inversion or opposition. But the text of the "General Prologue" invites us to construe its speaking in many ways and through many voices whose structural order cannot be explained by appeal to an organic principle of ironic language. Yet the question of voice is only one example of a much more complex set of issues about structure in the poem. Of the major principles of form that have been set forth in scholarship, each has been taken from the more encompassing Book of tradition according to its preferences for understanding influence and order in terms of mimesis. Whether the model of the poem is regarded as the narrative of pilgrimage, the architecture of Gothic building, or the art of memory—all of which have been proposed—a poetics of imitation controls the understanding of the poem.[14] These are strong suggestions offering deep insights into medieval poetry and the relation of language to other cultural forms; but they all testify to the prevailing influence of the medieval idea of the Book on the ways we read the books of the poets. If, by contrast, the suggestions from Dante's *Commedia* and Chaucer's early poetry have bearing on the *Tales*, then we have occasion to see a correspondence between customary models of the Text and Chaucer's narrative

[13]Cf. the essays collected by Lyons and Nichols in *Mimesis: From Mirror to Method.*
[14]These proposals, documented fully in chapter 7, are associated with the work of D. W. Robertson, Robert Jordan, and Donald Howard.

and at the same time to recognize narrative signifying as only one strand among several created by the poem. A divergence or disassociation is established between Chaucer's treatment of narrative and other conditions of signifying in the "General Prologue." Speaking, sequence, and validation no longer have convenient roots in the old form of the Text by the time we reach the palinode at the end of this poem. In little, the problem of textual meaning in the "General Prologue" identifies the much more comprehensive issue Dante and Chaucer confront as they situate fictional writing next to the broader and more dominant discourse of the past.

It would be incomplete or at least oversimplified to continue to regard the relation of fictional voices to the *auctores* of tradition as an instance of "irony" and the writing of poetry as a "language of paradox." For these medieval poems become the grounds for new ventures in the ways of signifying meaning that expand the limits of irony by deferring the boundaries of proper response. Augustine's fear of the pleasure of reading poetry, recorded in the *Confessions,* issues from the potential erosion of such limits, and his advice on how to protect them by reading correctly was taken seriously for at least one thousand years. So too were the powerful commitments of the idea of the Book, its grounding in fixed meanings validated in a definite origin—the Bible, nature, tradition, God. Chaucer and Dante embraced those commitments firmly, but at the same time they emphasized what linguistic disciplines tried to suppress—a discourse that recognizes its own impossibilities and proceeds by locating the authority for making sense no longer in the pages of the past, but in the hands of the reader.

A shift is under way in the writings of the poets, one that was forestalled or prevented from surfacing in any dominant way in the tradition of the Text. Reflection on this development invites a reconsideration of the extent to which linguistic change may initiate historical change during the middle ages of Western tradition. While it is customary to mark such shifts in seventeenth-century writers like Bacon, the following chapters carry out a suggestion, forthcoming from various areas of medieval and renaissance studies, that the notion of a "rebirth" or "epistemic break" needs to be rethought. I suggest that the language of poetry is an essential area in which this historical change was taking place. If the discourse of history writing that has taken its form from the emphasis on sharp demarcations in sequential and causal models bears a certain resemblance to the medieval idea of the Book, then I would offer the writing of critical commentary on poetry as an alternative discourse that can move closer to explaining historical consciousness because it responds to the writers who demythologized its medieval forms to begin with.

[1]

The Argument of the Book:

Medieval Writing and Modern Theory

> You have extended like a skin the firmament of your Book [*Liber*], your harmonious discourses, over us by the ministry of mortals. . . . Let the angels, your supercelestial people, praise your name. They have no need to look upon this firmament, to know through reading your word. For they always see your face, and read there without the syllables of time your eternal will. They read, they choose, they love. They are always reading . . . the changelessness of your counsel.
>
> Augustine, *Confessiones*

1

Reading "without the syllables of time" from a heavenly Book may have been recognized by most medieval students as an exclusively angelic privilege, one that contrasted rather obviously with the human activity of poring over the texts of the everyday world. Yet as Augustine assumes a distinction between heavenly and worldly books, his own passage illustrates the value of meditating on their similitude, and his procedure corresponds perfectly with the broad exhortation of the fathers of the church who instructed medieval readers to clarify and explain the mysterious purpose of the divine Word within the revealed words of this world, such as the Bible and the Book of nature. A far more vivid sense of the gap between human writing and transcendent language is customarily noticed in the works of writers many centuries after Augustine, for instance, in seventeenth-century authors like Sir Thomas Browne:

> Thus there are two bookes from whence I collect my Divinity; besides that written one of God, another of his servant Nature, that universall

and publik Manuscript, that lies expans'd unto the eyes of all; those
that never saw him in the one, have discovered him in the other. . . .
Surely the Heathens knew better how to joyne and read these mysti-
call letters, than wee Christians, who cast a more carelesse eye on these
common Hieroglyphicks, and disdain to suck Divinity from the flowers of nature.[1]

While the divine plan is rather less accessible to Browne's audience
than it was to Augustine's, the exhortation is still to apprehend that
order by reading it "as a book"—"that universall and publik Manuscript."

Both Augustine and Browne, notwithstanding their separation
by many centuries, illustrate a similar problem: on the one hand
they recognize the limitations of writing and reading within the
"syllables of time," and on the other they conceive of nature and
history as an order summarized in the metaphor of the perfect
Text or Book. Although these examples manifest a clear distinction, the consequences of blurring or erasing it would eventually
attract theoretical speculation in the history of discussions about
writing—and rarely with more intensity than in recent theoretical
debate about reading the institutions of culture "as a book." Not
unlike Augustine, the father of modern semiology—Ferdinand de
Saussure—recommends reflecting on the linguistic sign as a model
for analyzing the structure of cultural forms, and his program for
explaining the "language" of culture, at least as it has influenced
Claude Lévi-Strauss's study of archaic societies, is no less expansive
in theory than some of the medieval efforts to explain the semiology of the Book of nature. But against the structuralist request to
study culture "as a book," the reminder of its abiding difference
from the more limited written means of its construction has also
been unmistakable in a number of poststructuralist works. For instance, with this difference in mind, the problem of periodization
in history has been reopened, and modern conceptions of eight-
eenth- and nineteenth-century Europe have been shown to be
modeled on the organicism of a text unified by singleness of purpose or ideology.[2] And what may be true of a historical period, it is
suggested, may also apply to the history of an entire discipline, like
the history of Western literature or philosophy or art. The expo-

---

[1]Sir Thomas Browne, *Religio Medici and Other Works*, ed. L. C. Martin (Oxford:
Clarendon Press, 1964), p. 15.

[2]See Hayden White, *Metahistory: The Historical Imagination in Nineteenth-Century
Europe* (Baltimore: Johns Hopkins University Press, 1973); and idem, *Tropics of Discourse: Essays in Cultural Criticism* (Baltimore: Johns Hopkins University Press, 1978).

sure of the organicism and teleology underlying such formulations of the past—their "textuality"—is too far removed from medieval and renaissance approaches to the problem to justify an attempt at demonstrating historical influence or continuity.

But while the problem of textuality in modern theory is involved with historical forces specific to the twentieth century, the debate about the ambiguity of the fading boundary line between text and written discourse has bearing on Augustine and his immediate intellectual heirs during the middle ages. For it is not at all clear that Augustine's separation of transcendent writing from the "syllables of time" was always preserved in his own works or in those of the writers who followed him. Nor is it obvious how the tradition of ideas concerning writing in the middle ages established the grounds for its own continuity or why departures from the tradition have customarily been located long after the waning of the middle ages in authors like Sir Thomas Browne or still later in modern criticism interested in "deconstructing" textuality. The project of deconstruction, to be sure, offers a graphic departure from the medieval evidence of textuality; but if a poststructuralist perspective may help us see medieval ideas in a way that has not heretofore been possible, the discussions about writing in the middle ages may very well turn out to confront modern deconstruction with its own history.

However, before considering any changes in the history of medieval textuality, it will be worthwhile first to turn to the grounds of its continuity. A useful starting point is provided by Jacques Derrida, since his distinction between "writing" (*écriture*) and the "idea of the book" suggests a certain resemblence to medieval discussions of writing and the Bible. Whereas the Text or Book has been regarded as a fact of literary history or a container of information and signs, Derrida has called attention to its function as a sign itself of a sense of meaning as homogeneous, present as a totality. On the other hand, as the means that strives to render that totality of meaning intelligible, "writing" (*écriture*) does not embody this conception of the Book and is essentially different from it: "the idea of the book, which always refers to a natural totality, is profoundly alien to the sense of writing. It is the encyclopedic protection of theology . . . against the disruption of writing, against its aphoristic energy, and . . . against difference in general."[3] The idea of the

---

[3]*De la grammatologie* (Paris: Minuit, 1967), pp. 30–31; trans. Gayatri C. Spivak as *Of Grammatology* (Baltimore: Johns Hopkins University Press, 1976), p. 18. Paul Zumthor has traced a similar distinction between *écriture* and textual models in medieval French literature in his *Essai de poétique médiévale* (Paris: Seuil, 1972), and

Book readily corresponds to the medieval conception of the Bible, the book that revealed or made present God's transcendent and absolute will, law, and wisdom, a container of the divine plan and itself a sign of the totality of that plan in the world. This idea of the Bible was composed from the familiar practice of reading "allegorically" for historical continuities between various scriptural books, such as King David as a type in the Old Testament of Christ in the New; of reading "tropologically" for moral significance, for example, David's adultery as representative of lechery and other deadly sins; and of interpreting "anagogically" for revelation of divine mysteries, such as David playing the psaltery as a prefiguration of the music accompanying the songs of the heavenly host in praise of the celestial lamb.[4] Such assumptions of continuity and unity gradually led to the conception that any book of the Bible, or all of them together, constitutes a totality, not a loose collection of texts, but a book bound by a single purpose, which Saint Augustine called "the New Law of Charity." What Thomas of Celano said in the thirteenth century of the Book of Apocalypse was the implied understanding of the Bible from writings of the earliest fathers of the church. Apocalypse, said Thomas, "is the book in which the total is contained" ("Liber . . . in quo totum continetur").[5] In its simplest form, the idea of the Book begins in medieval readings of the Bible.

On the other hand, "writing" as *écriture* in the sense described by Derrida appears to have little place in medieval theories of language, since education was devoted to teaching that writing was not an arbitrary collection of words, but special, "divine" words whose "signifying" (*signans*) was not truncated from "signified" (*signatum*)

Eugene Vance has traced it in Augustine's works; see "Augustine's *Confessions* and the Grammar of Selfhood," *Genre* 6 (1973):1–28; "Augustine's *Confessions* and the Poetics of the Law," *MLN* 93 (1978):618–634; "Saint Augustine: Language as Temporality," in *Mimesis: From Mirror to Method, Augustine to Descartes,* ed. John D. Lyons and Stephen G. Nichols, Jr. (Hanover, N.H.: University Press of New England, 1982), pp. 20–35.

[4] For example, see Hugh of St. Cher, *Opera omnia,* 8 vols. (Venice, 1732): type of Christ (1 Kings 16), 1.231; adultery (2 Kings 11), 1.250; music ("Prologue" to Psalms), 2.2.

[5] Augustine, *De doctrine Christiana* 3.10; trans. D. W. Robertson, Jr., as *On Christian Doctrine* (New York: Bobbs-Merrill, 1958) , pp. 87–89; Thomas of Celano *Dies irae,* in *Hymns of the Roman Liturgy,* ed. Joseph Connelly (Westminister, Md.: Newman Press, 1957), p. 254, lines 13–15. Abundant references to the book are available in Ernst Robert Curtius's "The Book as Symbol," in *European Literature and the Latin Middle Ages,* trans. Willard R. Trask (New York: Harper & Row, 1963), pp. 302–347.

allegorical, tropological, and anagogical truth. The "aphoristic energy" of writing did not oppose these correspondences, but linked
them in an intricate system of revealing divine truth. What looked
"different" in the Old Testament was simply a "prefiguration" of
the New. From the medieval point of view, in other words, the literal sense of Scripture was hardly *écriture*, particularly as this term
has been explained in recent critical debate with reference to the
story of the discovery of writing told in Plato's *Phaedrus*. As Socra-
tes relates the story, King Thamus repudiates Thoth's invention of
writing because it is merely a "semblance" of truth that would im-
pede the capacity to know and recall. "For this discovery of yours
[writing] will create forgetfulness in the learner's souls, because
they will not use their memories. . . . As for wisdom, it is the reputation [semblance], not the reality, that you have to offer to those
who learn from you."[6] While medieval instructors surely appreciated the distinction between "reality" and "semblance"—between
Augustine's eternal Text and temporal writing—they nonetheless
tried rigorously to locate divine wisdom within the letters of the *sacra pagina*. Instead of a stumbling block to truth, the "semblance"
was its "revelation" in the Bible, the "veil" (*integumentum*) or "mirror" (*speculum*) in which divine wisdom was present, if only readers
had "eyes to see." Writing in the middle ages corresponded closely
to what Plato said about the "writing" in the soul. Derrida has commented on this point: "As was the case with the Platonic writing of
the truth in the soul, in the Middle Ages too it is a writing understood in the metaphoric sense, that is to say a *natural*, eternal, and
universal writing, the system of signified truth. . . . As in the *Phaedrus*, a certain fallen writing continues to be opposed to it. There
remains to be written a history of this metaphor, a metaphor that
systematically contrasts divine or natural writing and the human
and laborious, finite and artificial inscription."[7]

In this remark the "divine or natural" writing of the middle ages
is *itself* a metaphor of the "system of signified truth." Sir Thomas
Browne's "publik Manuscript" and "letters" of nature repeat metaphors familiar in medieval books; he invites reading in the old medieval way the "letters," written or natural, as metaphors of divinity: the biblical tablets are "written with the finger of God" (Exod.

---

[6]*Phaedrus*, 275AB, in *The Dialogues of Plato*, trans. Benjamin Jowett, 4th ed. (Oxford: Clarendon Press, 1953), 3:184. See Jacques Derrida, "La Pharmacie de Platon," in *La Dissémination* (Paris: Seuil, 1972). Medieval sign theory is treated in detail
below, chapter 3.
[7]*De la grammatologie*, p. 27; trans. p. 15.

31.18), his "tongue" is a "pen" (Ps. 45.2), and the "heavens" are a "book" (Apoc. 6.14). Metaphorical transforming of eternal into natural is nowhere more vivid than in Isidore's metaphor of "plow-share" (*vomer*) for "stylus" (*stilus*) in the *Etymologiarum:*

> Vertamus vomerem
> In ceram mucroneque osseo.
>
> [We turn the plowshare upon the wax,
> and plow with a point of bone.][8]

In other writers the field is a parchment, thorns are the scribes' errors, the plow is a pen, and letters are seeds. "Se pareva boves alba pratalia araba et albo versario teneba et negro semen seminaba" ("He urged on the oxen, plowed white fields, held a white plow, and sowed black seeds").[9] The "naturalizing" that turned a stylus into a plow and a line of writing into a furrow is only prefatory to the more elaborate exercises of the various books of beasts (bestiaries) in which any member of the animal world was "read" as a "sentence" or moral and eschatological truth. From the animal kingdom to the world of men, that naturalizing was carried over massively; as Alanus de Insulis observes, "every creature is a book":

> Omnis mundi creatura
> Quasi liber et pictura
> Nobis est et speculum.

Universal history is a book of three stages for Hugh of St. Victor (*lex naturalis; lex scripta; tempus gratiae*); and all of nature is God's script—the Book of nature.[10] Learning to read the signs of that Book was a process not of "inventing" or "creating" *sententia* for the "sentences" in the Bible or nature, but of coming to comprehend a writing that exists "within a nature or a natural law, created or not, but first thought within an eternal presence. Comprehended, therefore, within a totality, and enveloped in a volume or a book. The idea of the book is the idea of a totality, finite or infinite, of the signifier; this totality of the signifier cannot be a totality, unless a totality constituted by the signified preexists it, supervises its inscriptions and its signs, and is independent of it in its ideality."[11]

---

[8]*Etym.* 6.9.2 (*PL* 82, 239 D).

[9]Gerolamo Lazzeri, *Antologia dei primi secoli della litteratura italiana* (Milan: U. Hoepli, 1942), p. 1; cited in Curtius, p. 314.

[10]Alanus, *PL* 210, 579A; Hugh, *PL* 176, 32B, 343, 347, 371, 644.

[11]*De la grammatologie*, p. 30; trans. p. 18.

This summary by Derrida points to the inevitability of the "idea of the Book" in the middle ages as soon as a signifying system—words in Scripture, things in nature—became a metaphor for divinity: the entire preexistent "totality" of God's plan was potential in the signifying means. Although Augustine began with a distinction between writing and the celestial Book, medieval reflections on the boundary line between them seem fascinated by the presence of one in the other. Master Theodoric, many centuries following Augustine, illustrates this fascination vividly in his painting of Matthew receiving the Divine Logos as a physical text; and Dante obviously meditated long and hard on this paradigm of writing, since he opened *La vita nuova* with the phrase "in that part of the book of my memory" and ended the *Commedia* with a vision of the cosmos as a magnificent volume whose "leaves are bound by love."[12] The cosmic Book was the ideal *sine qua non* of medieval architects, who imagined that they were copying it as vast encyclopedias in stone when they designed cathedrals across Europe and Britain from the eleventh century to the fourteenth. Like the relics of a saint in the cathedral, letters themselves were intrinsically sacred to Saint Francis of Assisi, who is said to have collected and saved every shred of parchment that he found during his travels because "litterae sunt quibus componitur gloriosissimum domini Dei nomen" ("letters are the things from which the most glorious name of God is composed").[13]

2

Insofar as medieval evidence demonstrates that the metaphor of the Text, such as we find it in Augustine's *Confessions* (book 13), was extended throughout many aspects of the orders of nature and history, another important connection with modern theoretical dis-

[12]See plate 2. *La vita nuova*, in *Le opere di Dante Alighieri*, ed. E. Moore and P. Toynbee (Oxford: Oxford University Press, 1924), p. 205. *La divina commedia*, vol. 3, *Paradiso* (Firenze: Nuova Italia, 1957), 33.85–87, pp. 411–12.

[13]Thomas of Celano, *Legenda prima*, in *S. Francisci Assisiensis vita et miracula* (Rome: Desclée, Lefebure, 1906), p. 83. As will be discussed at greater length in chapters 2 and 3, these kinds of examples suggest that medieval language theory leans much more heavily toward "logocentrism" than toward the deconstructive strategies that have been claimed for it, for example, by: Eugene Vance (note 3 above); Margaret W. Ferguson, "Saint Augustine's Region of Unlikeness: The Crossing of Exile and Language," *Georgia Review* 29 (1975):842–864; and Peter Haidu, "Repetition: Modern Reflections on Medieval Aesthetics," *MLN* 92 (1977):875–887.

Plate 2. Matthew receiving the Word of God. Wooden panel. Master Theodoric (ca. 1360). Chapel of the Holy Cross, Karlstejn Castle.

cussion of textuality presents itself for consideration—the relationship of the Book of culture and "myth." While this relationship may be noted in various quarters of scholarship, it has perhaps drawn most attention in studies of "mythological" cultures, for example, the primitive tribes analyzed by anthropologists or the societies of the archaic world (Ancient Egypt, Mesopotamia, Canaan, and Neolithic Europe). Initially it may appear that reference to a textual model for a culture in which writing was undeveloped or even unknown amounts to a rather willful use of terms. Yet the idea of the Book has served as an instructive model for reflecting on the nature of mythological forms, and it will also provide a helpful comparison in understanding patterns of thought in the middle ages. But, first, the term "myth" should not be confused with legends concerning special kinds of heroes, conflicts, settings, images, motifs, or themes. The term is used here in the anthropological sense defined by Georges Dumézil: "The function of that particular class of legends known as myths is to express dramatically the ideology under which a society lives; not only to hold out to its conscience the values it recognizes and the ideals it pursues from generation to generation, but above all to express its very being and structure, the elements, the connections, the balances, the tensions that contribute to it; to justify the rules and traditional practices without which everything within a society would disintegrate."[14]

In the *Phaedrus*, Thoth's invention of writing is repudiated by King Thamus because he fears it will disintegrate "the very being and structure, the elements, the connections, the balances, the tensions" that constitute the culture. His mode of thought is "mythological" exactly because he fears that the "semblance" of writing will destroy wisdom and truth. That fear and his prohibition are indications of the determinations of mythological thought and its most distinguishing qualities: to identify a thought with a thing, to perceive the supernatural as immanent in the natural (a deity in a tree or stone), and to conceive of the divine realm as a replica of the physical order. In other words, as Sigfried Giedion has described Egyptian culture and its roots in prehistoric societies, mythological thought knows no "transcendent" world because it "sees" the eternal emanating throughout known and familiar things; stars, mountains, rivers, trees, caves, animals, and the elements of the earth are

---

[14]*The Destiny of the Warrior*, trans. Alf Hiltebeitel (Chicago: University of Chicago Press, 1970), p. 3.

intrinsically sacred, imbued with eternal truth and wisdom.[15]
Charting the continuities throughout the physical universe created
elaborate systems of classification, such as those recorded in Lévi-
Strauss's recent scholarship on South American mythology. Fire,
thunder, stones, tools, crockery—any item or any event past or
present could be connected in an elaborate network of related
meanings. Myth was the comprehensive "encyclopedia" of a culture's several volumes—history, religion, physical science, and domestic lore—the unwritten Book of culture that was sacred by virtue of its embodiment of the eternal present in all things.

In such a world, writing is predictably received with suspicion or
even hostility as a kind of trick, as King Thamus feared. For to represent truth by a written artificial means was to obscure its presence, if not offend the spirits of place, and to set up a barrier to
the "true self" of wisdom emanating from stars to stones. Writing
therefore not only was artificial, but even threatened to erode
knowledge and desacralize divinity. King Thamus's prohibition
was nothing less than a defense of the mythological consciousness.
It may be compared with a more recent defense of mythological
habits by a tribesman who also associates writing with forgetfulness
and false knowledge. In contrast, his own learning is a direct participation in the continuity that simply knows no distinction between animal and human but assumes the natural oneness of the
universe.

> We know what the animals do, what are the needs of the beaver, the
> bear, the salmon, and other creatures, because long ago men married
> them and acquired this knowledge from their animal wives. Today the
> priests say we lie, but we know better. The white man has been only a
> short time in this country and knows very little about the animals; we
> have lived here thousands of years and were taught long ago by the
> animals themselves. The white man writes everything down in a book
> so that it will not be forgotten; but our ancestors married the animals,
> learned all their ways, and passed on the knowledge from one genera-
> tion to another.[16]

Although this world may be appreciated conceptually, it seems
very difficult to enter. From an alien viewpoint its knowledge is a

---

[15]*The Eternal Present*, vol. 2, *The Beginnings of Architecture* (New York: Bollingen
Foundation, 1964), pp. 30–31, passim. See Henri Frankfort, "Myth and Reality," in
Before Philosophy: The Intellectual Adventure of Ancient Man, ed. H. Frankfort, J. A.
Wilson, and T. Jacobsen (Baltimore: Penguin Books, 1973).

[16]Cited in Claude Lévi-Strauss, *The Savage Mind* (Chicago: University of Chicago
Press, 1969), p. 37.

"lie"; yet from the mythological point of view the knowledge set down in writing is a dissembling aspect of a weak memory. But an understanding of writing as a metaphor of "divine or natural" perceiving, a "system of signified truth"—which is the writing that composed the medieval summa—resolves the opposition and establishes a direct link between myth and the Book. For the metaphor of writing does not get in the way of the truth with its "artificial inscription" and "difference" but reveals divine wisdom like a brilliant mirror (speculum). Writing is not conceived of as an invention superimposed on things; it is perceived "within a nature or a natural law, created or not, but first thought within an eternal presence. Comprehended, therefore within a totality, and enveloped in a volume or a book." Such a mode of "writing" is not *écriture*, but a system of supernatural knowledge determined by the preexistent assumption of the unity and totality—the eternal presence—of meaning. The metaphor of writing is the language of mythology, and the idea of the Book, like myth, is preoccupied with a oneness and continuity that it conceives of as natural. Insofar as the medieval conception of the Bible and the Book of culture illustrates the metaphor of writing, the two Books and the encyclopedias about them did not finally cut their ties with the mythological world they sought to repudiate. For the new activities of writing and reading carried with them traces of older mythological ways of perceiving: the idea of the Book that determined medieval writings was a new mythology.

3

In a certain respect, that the middle ages preserved ancient mythologies has been well known ever since sixteenth- and seventeenth-century scholarship undermined archaic notions of the geocentric cosmos, the flat earth, the animism of nature, and attendant myths like magic, witchcraft, and demonology. "Mythography," more than any other discipline, preserved the few Greek and Roman legends, heroes, and motifs that were known, though not without changing them radically through Christian, most frequently tropological, interpretations in such works as Bernard Sylvester's *Cosmographia* (a commentary on Plato's *Timaeus*) and Pierre Bersuire's *Ovidius moralizatus* (an interpretation of the works of Ovid). Like the Christianizing of pagan sources in the middle ages, modern scholarship has assumed, to some extent, the medieval view of myth when the term describes a category including special kinds of figures, such as the deities in the story of Mars's love for Venus; or a class of themes, for instance, fertility in the Germanic and Celtic legends of the Fisher King; or a group of motifs, such as the quest for the Holy Grail in French and English sources.[17] But the claim that the middle ages preserved mythological interests of the ancient world involves quite a different conception of "myth" as I have been using it, one that indicates particular *habits of thinking, ordering, and remembering.* Northrop Frye, for example, has pointed to such a sense of mythology in the middle ages by remarking that "in making so functional a use of astronomical imagery, and in seeing in the sky images of law, purpose, design, the cycle of the seasons, and the order of creation, as well as of fate and the source of tragedy, Chaucer is almost closer in mental attitude to the builders of Stonehenge than he is to us."[18]

Although mythology may be reflected in certain kinds of images or narrative structures, Frye's remark indicates that it consists in a much broader perspective or "mental attitude" that may be called "mythologizing." The prehistorians Grahame Clark and Stuart Piggott have argued that such an attitude prevailed in the development of the middle ages: "It may not be extravagant to see an origin for much of medieval Europe in prehistoric societies which developed in the second millennium B.C."[19] Mircea Eliade has shown that the forms of medieval Christian belief bear striking parallels with the "cosmic structure" of prehistoric mythology. Although European peasants, Eliade argues, were Christianized for over one thousand years,

> they succeeded in incorporating into their Christianity a considerable part of their pre-Christian religious heritage which was of immemorial antiquity. It would be wrong to suppose for this reason European peasants are not Christians. But we must recognize that their religion is not confined to the historical forms of Christianity, that it still retains a cosmic structure that has been almost entirely lost in the experience of urban Christians. We may speak of a primordial, ahistorical

[17]For example, cf. Jean Seznec, *The Survival of the Pagan Gods: The Mythological Tradition and Its Place in Renaissance Humanism and Art,* trans. B. F. Sessions (1953; reprint, New York: Harper & Row, 1961); D. W. Robertson, Jr., *A Preface to Chaucer: Studies in Medieval Perspectives* (Princeton: Princeton University Press, 1962); Brian Stock, *Myth and Science in the Twelfth Century* (Princeton: Princeton University Press, 1972).

[18]*A Study of English Romanticism* (New York: Random House, 1968), p.24.

[19]*Prehistoric Soceities* (New York: Alfred A. Knopf, 1965), p. 318.

Christianity; becoming Christians, the European cultivators incorporated into their new faith the cosmic religion that they had preserved from prehistoric times.[20]

In any number of medieval books, summae, and encyclopedias like the *Etymologiarum* of Isidore of Seville, the *De universo* of Rabanus Maurus, and the *Speculum majus* of Vincent of Beauvais, we may find data that go back to prehistoric religion, such as the navel at the center of the world or the belief that the gods were once only men. But Eliade's claim that medieval Christians "incorporated" into their religion the "cosmic structure" of prehistoric myth corroborates the view that mythologizing determinations appear in the middle ages as part of the idea of the Book. The summae and encyclopedias may "contain" mythological material, but the Book itself is a sign of the mythologizing preoccupation with oneness, totality, and the presence of meaning as absolute.

Nowhere is this preoccupation clearer than in the massive classification, indexing, and subdivision of medieval encyclopedias. The following remarks in summary of Polynesian culture describe mythologizing preoccupations untouched by Christianity or writing, and yet they could stand as an introduction to the world of the great "books" of the middle ages, the Gothic cathedral, the *Repertorium morale, De universo, Historia naturalis,* the bestiaries, the Book of God's Word, and the Book of His Work.

> All things—plants, animals, tools, man's social life, his rituals and the divine beings—are linked together in an intricate system of related meanings. The linkage is both genetic and static: everything has some connection with events going back to creation; and everything is bound to a system of parallel forms, of symbols—as, for example, the village is a human body; this body is also the primordial body of the first god; the house represents man's pedigree back to the gods; even pots are images of the universe. Further, this primitive Great Design is a definition and justification of human conduct; the same elaborately integrated system of symbols defines the significance of human life.[21]

This world of mythologizing thought unmarked by the "artificial inscription" of the written word is just as much a "Book" as the

---

[20]*The Sacred and the Profane,* trans. Willard R. Trask (New York: Harper & Row, 1961), p. 164.

[21]Robert Redfield, "Thinker and Intellectual in Primitive Society," in *Culture in History: Essays in Honor of Paul Radin,* ed. Stanley Diamond (New York: Columbia University Press, 1960), p. 8.

writings that composed the medieval summa. Not only would a page of commentary from a work like the *Great Glossa* of the fourteenth century or the *Opera omnia* of Hugh of St. Cher in the thirteenth explain the linkage from past to present; exegesis would also replicate it in the process of quoting from "old authors" throughout the centuries—Augustine, Jerome, Cassiodorus, Gregorius Magnus, Bede, and others. Moreover, the repetition of this continuity in parallel forms is obvious in studies of past epochs like Peter Comestor's *Historia scholastica* and histories of the natural world like the works of Isidore, Rabanus, and Vincent of Beauvais. That the totality they attempted would eventually suggest a "house," a "city," or the "body of man" was ineluctable in imaginative writers like Augustine, who said that Eve was made from Adam so that the entire human race would be descended from the body of one man, or Hugh of St. Victor, who referred to the completeness and unity of Sacred Scripture as the *domus Dei*.[22]

What Durandus of Mende attempted in his massive thirteenth-century commentary on the liturgy and architecture of the church was an extrapolation of patterns and meanings already immanent in the structure of the building; for it embodied the great design of the universe as a system of divine truth to instruct moral conduct and reveal the eschatological pains of hell and glories of heaven. As Durandus's book attempts to mirror in its subdivision and inclusiveness the design of the church, certain items in his book, or in other summae for that matter, reflect the whole in which they are included. The image of man as the microcosmus functions in this way in many medieval books, but it is hardly unique to them. Certain images in archaic cultures serve much the same function as mirrors of the subdivision and classification that characterize a larger mythology. For example, Lévi-Strauss records the Osage myth of the "pan-symbolic function" of the elk, "whose body is a veritable *imago mundi*: its coat represents grass, its horns hills, its flanks plains, its backbone the skyline, its neck valleys and its antlers the whole hydrographic network."

This and other parallels to medieval forms, however, do not reduce them to "primitiveness," but show rather that systems of classification in myth, as Lévi-Strauss has also pointed out, are as intri-

---

[22]Augustine: "quando nec ipsam quidem feminam copulandam viro, sicut ipsum creare illi placuit, sed ex ipso, ut omne ex homine uno diffunderetur genus humanum"; *De civitate Dei* 12.21 (*PL* 41, 372D). *Didascalicon* 6.1, 2, and 4 (*PL* 176, 799, 802); Hugh's figure is based on Gregorius Magnus, *Moralium libri* (*PL* 75, 513C).

cate as any page of Bersuire or Vincent of Beauvais. For instance, primitive herbal classifications

> are evidence of thought which is experienced in all the exercises of speculation and resembles that of the naturalists and alchemists of antiquity and the middle ages: Galen, Pliny, Hermes Trismegistus, Albertus Magnus. . . . From this point of view "totemic" classifications are probably closer than they look to the plant emblem systems of the Greeks and Romans, which were expressed by means of wreaths of olive, oak, laurel, wild celery, etc., or again that practised by the medieval church where the choir was strewn with hay, rushes, ivy or sand according to the festival.[23]

This similarity between medieval and "totemic" classification is hardly coincidental; both are expressions of a common perspective that "reads" existing phenomena as connected by a preexistent design and then catalogs and indexes from a seemingly unquestioned sense of the unity and continuity of the universe: "The savage mind totalizes," Lévi-Strauss explains; it illustrates an "intransigent refusal . . . to allow anything human (or even living) to remain alien to it."[24] While obviously very different in many ways from mythology, the writing that created the idea of the Book in the middle ages did not completely sever its link with mythologizing thought, for it "totalized" when it refused to allow anything living or even dead to remain unexplained by traditional ideology.

From one point of view, the survival of mythologizing is entirely predictable in geographical areas that during the middle ages were barely touched by cultural advances. But that it survived at all and even thrived simultaneously with the study of the Bible remains clearly paradoxical in light of the opposition of scriptural writing to mythology. That opposition, biblical scholars indicate, signals the gradual shift in the ancient Near East away from mythological religions of immanentism and toward Hebrew conceptions of divine transcendence.[25] One obvious voice of that opposition is the familiar prohibitions against images heard in various biblical passages. For a divinity found through images, Jeremiah proclaims (10.14–15), is no different from the gods of the Egyptians and Mesopotamians; but before the God of the heavens, "all men stand stupefied, uncomprehending, every goldsmith blushes for the idol

---

[23]*Savage Mind*, pp. 59, 42.
[24]Ibid., p. 245.
[25]For example, see William Foxwell Albright, *Yahweh and the Gods of Canaan: An Historical Analysis of Two Contrasting Faiths* (New York: Anchor, 1969).

he has made, since his images are nothing but delusion, with no breath in them. They are Nothing, a laughable production."[26] Yet while such denunciations must have sounded from the pulpits of the middle ages, the populace was charmed by an irresistible fascination with the images created by goldsmith, sculptor, and painter. The protest stands in relation to a cathedral rich with iconography in the same way that the *écriture* of Scripture was subsumed within the system that resolved its opposition and difference. As long as the idea of the Book prevailed against its *écriture*, mythology knew no threat in medieval culture. A challenge to it could not come, so to speak, from the "inside."

However, if the idea of the Book is perpetuated in a sense of writing as a metaphor of the "system of signified truth," then what about writings that are created and read in full acknowledgement that they are only a "semblance," a self-conscious invention? Does the writing of medieval fictions replicate or oppose the Book of culture? The answers to these questions must await close study of specific works. But a beginning may be made by comparing the idea of the Book with a few basic thoughts about the nature of fiction.

4

First of all, no one would argue that Chaucer's story of the pilgrimage to the shrine of Thomas à Becket, the long theological and philosophical debates in *Le Roman de la rose,* and Dante's journey from hell to heaven challenge the moral values of the Bible and Christian interpretations of it. Instead, the comprehensiveness alone of some medieval poems, like the *Commedia,* has suggested such comparisons to the encyclopedias and summae as the comment by Ernst Curtius that "Dante's cosmic poem is such a summa too."[27] Evidence of this kind might lead one to the conclusion, which has in fact been drawn, that medieval fiction is not different from the writing in the Bible and that it too is a speculum, like the Book of God's Word and the Book of His Work.[28] The conclusion seems almost inevitable for a culture that saw sacred writing as the

---

[26]*The Jerusalem Bible,* ed. Alexander Jones (Garden City, N.Y.: Doubleday, 1966), used throughout unless otherwise noted.

[27]*European Literature,* p. 326.

[28]See D. W. Robertson, Jr., "Historical Criticism," in *English Institute Essays, 1950,* ed. Alan S. Downer (New York: Columbia University Press, 1951), pp. 3–31; idem, *Preface to Chaucer,* pp. 286–391; Robert Hollander, *Allegory in Dante's Comedy*

actual inscription of "God's finger" and nature as a "script" of his will. Furthermore, instructions for reading the images and events of the Bible according to the divisions between the "literal" and "spiritual" senses are commonly cited as the rules for reading poetry in such works as the "Letter to Can Grande della Scala," attributed to Dante, and Boccaccio's *Genealogia deorum gentilium*, books 14 and 15. Here we are told to study the obscurities in poetry according to the same rules for interpreting an event like the Exodus from Egypt—first as a historical occurrence; second as a moral deliverance of the soul from the bondage of sin; and last as a prefiguration of the passage of the soul from this life into the eternal paradise. As these intentions of the author of Holy Writ are not easily understood, neither are the meanings of poetry readily apparent; therefore, according to Boccaccio, "I repeat my advice to those who would appreciate poetry, and unwind its difficult involutions. You must read, you must persevere, you must sit up nights, you must inquire, and exert the utmost power of your mind. If one way does not lead to the desired meaning, take another; if obstacles arise, then still another; until, if your strength holds out, you will find that clear which at first looked dark. For we are forbidden by divine command to give that which is holy to dogs, or to cast pearls before swine."[29] Confronted with an obscure text in the *Commedia, The Canterbury Tales* or *Le Roman de la rose,* a medieval reader might be able to find some encouragement in these words and might even discover that the "pearls" of his author corresponded with the moral values in Sacred Scripture. But that the passage or other arguments in the *Genealogia* confirm an identity between fiction and Holy Writ is debatable.

For no matter how useful the methods of scriptural reading are for poetry—and they have been shown to be profoundly fruitful—neither Boccaccio, Dante, Chaucer, nor any other medieval poet would say that his fiction was "divine" in origin. It might be inspired by the Holy Spirit, but it certainly would have been honestly recognized as an invention of more humble origins, as is clear even in the title of Dante's *Commedia,* which was not called "Divine" until the renaissance. The literal sense of Scripture, moreover, was understood as a record of documentary fact; it was historically true.

(Princeton: Princeton University Press, 1969); John V. Fleming, *The "Roman de la Rose": A Study in Allegory and Iconography* (Princeton: Princeton University Press, 1969).

   [29]*Boccaccio on Poetry,* trans. Charles G. Osgood (New York: Liberal Arts Press, 1956), p. 62.

But does Dante ask us to believe that he actually took a journey through the afterlife and, like Lazarus, has returned from the dead to tell all? His expectations of our response must be that we will have more detachment from the illusions he has created than his own fictional creations, for example Paolo and Francesca, who were seduced into the world of adulterous love while reading the myth of Lancelot and Guinevere.[30] Such "reading episodes" are far more potent than a palinode, insofar as they suggest that Dante would have us read his *Commedia* with the full self-consciousness of its status as an invention or a semblance. As Paolo and Francesca are seduced by the Book, Amant in the *Roman* is so enthralled by his dream of a rosy maiden that he knows not lady from flower until he embraces both as a stone statue in a castle wall. For one whose assent to the power of illusions is so absolute, a palinode offers little salvation.

Because the representation of illusions may result in misguided responses, Dante and the poets of the *Roman* include in their works metapoetical arguments in the rules of adequate reading. But since even such arguments are themselves subject to interpretation, a more radical resolution may be imagined. For example, in the *Republic* Plato resolved the fear that fictions about the gods may readily distort true accounts of them by excluding from the utopia poets and poems that do not confirm public mythology. Although this decision might protect legends of the gods, it still does not solve the problem that poetry is by nature an illusion of a physical universe that is itself a copy of the world of perfect forms. Since poets present as true an "imitation and shadowy image," they are therefore "liars," and fiction is "true falsehood," which "is hated not only by the gods, but also by men."

> Although we are admirers of Homer, we shall not admire the lying dream which Zeus sends to Agamemnon; neither will we praise the verses of Aeschylus in which Thetis says that Apollo at her nuptials

---

[30]*Inferno*, 5. The departure of fiction from the myth of the Book suggested here compares, in a certain respect, with Zumthor's argument about *mouvance* in medieval French literary tradition—the inevitable variations and transformations of an *oeuvre* like the *Song of Roland* into the many *textes* of individual performances of it: "L'oeuvre est fondamentalement mouvante. . . . Le texte est la 'trace' de l'oeuvre: trace orale, fuyante, déformable," *Essai*, pp. 73, 74. Eugene Vance has also studied this departure in the *Song of Roland*; see *Reading the "Song of Roland"* (Englewood Cliffs, N.J.: Prentice-Hall, 1970); "Roland, Charlemagne, and the Poetics of Illumination," *Oliphant* 6 (1979):213–225; "Roland and the Poetics of Memory," in *Textual Strategies: Perspectives in Post-Structural Criticism*, ed. Josué Harari (Ithaca: Cornell University Press, 1979), 375–403.

"was celebrating in song her fair progeny." . . . These are the kind of sentiments about the gods which will arouse our anger; and he who utters them shall be refused a chorus; neither shall we allow teachers to make use of them in the instruction of the young, meaning, as we do, that our guardians, as far as men can be, should be god-fearing and godlike.[31]

The determination of medieval education to find the "godlike" meaning in the Bible seems to have fulfilled Plato's utopian hopes, insofar as it validated the public mythology and bound the Book of culture. But medieval poets clearly resented traditional objections to poetry, and in defending it against the charge of falsehood, apologists like Boccaccio went much further than Plato in separating fiction from truth. "The charge of falsehood," Boccaccio argues, "is without force, since poetic fiction has nothing in common with any variety of falsehood, for it is not a poet's purpose to deceive anybody with his inventions; furthermore, poetic fiction differs from a lie in that in most instances it bears not only no close resemblance to the literal truth, but no resemblance at all; on the contrary, it is quite out of harmony and agreement with the literal truth."[32] This passage grants the reader more trust in his own ability to distinguish fact from fiction than Plato ever would, perhaps because it describes the writing of the real world, not utopian writing that dares not offend known and familiar ideas, the spirits of place, and sacred lore. Such mythology is basically different from fiction, as Plato certainly feared. But poets of the middle ages, although they lived in a culture dominated by utopian ideals, assumed a more generous capacity in their audience for understanding their writing than was admitted in the system of supernatural writing that organized the Book of culture. Yet the assumption of a poet notwithstanding, one member of an audience, like the Reeve in Chaucer's *Canterbury Tales*, will inevitably rise up to confirm Plato's old fear by imagining that a fiction told by a Miller about domestic folly is a biography of his own marital embarrassments. The Reeve's "mistaken reading," like other acts in the "roadside drama," may exist not only for the values of good theater, but for the metapoetical purposes of recognizing the "facts" of fiction.[33]

[31]*Republic*, 2, in *Critical Theory since Plato*, ed. Hazard Adams (New York: Harcourt Brace Jovanovich, 1971), pp. 22–23.

[32]*Boccaccio on Poetry*, p. 63.

[33]See G. L. Kittredge, "Chaucer's Discussion of Marriage," *MP* 9 (1911–1912): 437–467; R. M. Lumiansky, *Of Sundry Folk: The Dramatic Principle in the "Canterbury Tales"* (Austin: University of Texas Press, 1955); R. M. Jordan, *Chaucer and the Shape of Creation* (Cambridge: Harvard University Press, 1967), pp. 121 ff.

Such mistakes are explainable, in one sense, because they illustrate the controlled and conscious "mistake" every reader makes in willingly suspending disbelief in order to grant credibility to the claims of fiction. But fiction begins with and encourages the awareness of its illusion making. We cannot, however, say the same about medieval response to the Book of culture. For even though a chapter in that Book, such as Plato's *Timaeus,* might be qualified by its author as only "a likely story" of the cosmos,[34] it was received with such authority in the middle ages that any sense of its "likeliness" fell away as the story grew into an elaborate mythology, lasting centuries beyond Bernard Sylvestris's thirteenth-century commentary on it. The Book of culture does not invite the sense of conjecture and hypothesis that is engaged in the reading of fiction. Rather, the Book of culture, like myth, leaves no doubt that it is a true account of the cosmos, history, nature, and the afterlife. Medieval fictions, in contrast, specialize in doubt, and while they also delight in religious values, they remain basically different from, if not opposed to, the myth of the book of culture.

The opposition consists in the recognition that Plato mentioned in the *Phaedrus* and the *Republic* and that is extended so clearly by Boccaccio: fiction creates illusions self-consciously and proceeds on the assumption that readers will not turn away complaining of its "lies." As Chaucer often described poetry, it is "pleye," and "men shall not not maken ernest of game."[35] The play of poetry took the sacrality—the "mythology"—out of writing, preventing its growth into myth. The insistence on fixed and centered structure, one of the defining properties of mythology, is obvious in many medieval notions, such as the *axis mundi,* the navel at the center of the world, the geocentric cosmos, and the New Law of Charity (maintained as the organizing principle of every chapter and book of the Bible). But the play of medieval fictional writing refuses such fixity, plays with the location of the center, and accommodates its own deficiencies by making no mistake about its difference from the natural and supernatural orders. As *écriture* opposes the "idea of the Book" (according to Derrida's argument), fiction plays with those orders

---

[34]See the commentary by F. M. Cornford, trans. *Plato's Cosmology: The "Timaeus" of Plato* (New York: Bobbs-Merrill, n.d., orig. pub. 1937), pp. 28–32.

[35]"The Miller's Prologue," in *The Works of Geoffrey Chaucer,* ed. F. N. Robinson, 2d ed. (Boston: Houghton Mifflin, 1957), p. 48. The separation between the textual tradition and Chaucer's stress on the "pleye" of literature has been argued in a related way by Glending Olson, *Literature as Recreation in the Later Middle Ages* (Ithaca: Cornell University Press, 1982).

that the Book of culture presents as absolute.[36] While the medieval and modern oppositions have little in common (*écriture* is hardly equivalent to "fiction"), their effect on structure is similar, insofar as they both initiate processes of change. The "play" of poetry, be it in Chaucer, Dante, or the poets of the *Roman,* destabilized medieval mythology, as earlier "play-factors" in the culture—according to Johan Huizinga—had changed cultural forms inherited from the ancient world.

> For the Middle Ages had inherited its great culture-forms in poetry, ritual, learning, philosophy, politics, and warfare from classical antiquity, and they were fixed forms. Medieval culture was crude and poor in many respects, but we cannot call it primitive. Its business was to work over traditional material, whether Christian or classical, and assimilate it afresh. Only where it was not rooted in antiquity, not fed by the ecclesiastical or Graeco-Roman spirit, was there room for the play-factor to "play" and create something entirely new. That was the case wherever mediaeval civilization built directly on its Celto-Germanic past or on even earlier autochthonous layers.[37]

The form least tied to antiquity or the church—the one that is the unique creation of the middle ages—is its vernacular literature. No sooner had it emerged than it needed defenses, such as Dante's *De vulgari eloquentia* and Boccaccio's *Genealogia,* books 14 and 15, not simply because it was different, but because its difference challenged the Book of culture just as other "play-factors" had changed the mythology of the Celto-Germanic past. Such a displacement was as inevitable as it was necessary, but that it was ushered in by fiction remains a paradox echoing in the nostalgia for the old world order in Sir Thomas Browne's invocation to read the "universall and publik Manuscript." For his text, like medieval fictions before it, also echoes with his own self-conscious play with

---

[36]For Derrida's comments on play (*jeu*) in relation to structure, see *The Structuralist Controversy: The Languages of Criticism and the Sciences of Man,* ed. Richard Macksey and Eugenio Donato (Baltimore: Johns Hopkins University Press, 1970), p. 268; and "La Pharmacie de Platon."

[37]*Homo Ludens: A Study of the Play-Element in Culture* (Boston: Beacon, 1955), p. 179. Cf. Eugene Vance: "We have every reason to examine [the] implicit models of communication [in the *Song of Roland*] for indications of disruption and change that might correspond to an epistemological crisis rooted in the competing cultural functions of speech and writing"; "Roland and the Poetics of Memory," in *Textual Strategies,* p. 401; Peter Haidu: "Fiction, even where intentionally established to function in subordination to an ideological superstructure, is inherently subversive of such vehiculation"; "Repetition," *MLN* 92 (1977):886.

metaphor that necessarily changes the mythology it seeks to perpetuate.

Medieval fiction may have incorporated information from the summae and encyclopedias, but it did not replicate them. The play with metaphor in poetry stands in direct opposition to the metaphor of divine or natural writing that characterizes medieval readings of the Bible and nature. Books of fiction must be separated from the Book of culture. For that Book is the creation of medieval perspectives that have less to do with the Bible itself than with the mythologizing habits of mind that the Bible sought to undermine. In its difference from mythology, fiction compares with the Bible before medieval readings created an ideology for it and turned it into a myth of homogeneous doctrine. Fiction does not mythologize. Although medieval poets were educated in inherited mythologies, they begin—not unlike the critical spokespersons in the Bible—from the vantage point of reinterpreting their culture and often challenging its myths. The effect of their writing is to see the past and present from a different perspective, and that difference compares with the objectivity sought by scholars in the renaissance who wanted to separate themselves from medieval tradition by understanding the past in its own right before time put meaning upon it. Medieval fictions certainly brought about no Copernican revolution. But the difference of myth from fiction figures prominently in the separation of "Middle Ages" from "Renaissance": that this shift was well under way in nominalism and the development of empirical methods in physical science needs no affirmation; but the degree to which medieval fiction writing became the ground for important changes in the modes of signifying meaning remains to be probed. The mythology of the Book of culture, concerned as it is with resisting change by perpetuating past models, stabilizes the conception of history as a text of organically whole "periods." Augustine's temporal language disappears into the timeless writing of an angelic intelligence. But fiction asserts its difference by inviting our challenge, by presenting us with a demand for criticism and for theories about our criticism that test and question the ways we signify meaning—even as my own are doubtless being tested now. That demand offers an approach to cultural understanding that does not indict historical inquiry, but rather promises a new and enlightened historicism.

[2]

The Semiology of Space in the Middle Ages: On Manuscript Painting, Sacred Architecture, Scholasticism, and Music

> Indeed without music no discipline can be perfect; nothing exists without it. For the world itself is said to be composed by a certain harmony of sounds and heaven revolves in harmonic modulation . . . music extends to all things.
>
> Isidore of Seville, *Etymologiarum*

1

When the term "mythological" is used to describe certain elements of medieval cultural forms, it commonly refers to vestiges that survive from archaic societies, both the legends and deities borrowed by writers of the middle ages from Greek and Roman sources and also the indigenous beliefs and practices of Europe and Britain that remained in place despite the growth of medieval traditions. But in light of recent scholarship on mythology as a form of thinking with characteristic structural properties, the view that particular features of medieval cultural forms are "vestigial" and "archaic" ought to be reexamined. On the one hand, such elements may be so regarded when they serve specifically "medieval" purposes, when the context in which they appear prevails over any recollection of an earlier time. Yet on the other hand, since a mythological survival contains *in potentia* the habits of thought that produced it, the degree to which they are completely suppressed can be determined only once they are fully recognized. If a coincidental survival turns out to be essentially tied to its past, the boundary separating "medieval" from "mythological" may be more fluid than it seems.

For example, a well-observed coincidence is the survival in the middle ages of representations of visual space that may be found in archaic societies. An obvious manifestation of this survival is the sacrality of stone, volume, and height that is illustrated by the pyramids of ancient Egypt and the sacred buildings in the Romanesque and Gothic styles of medieval Europe. While both pyramid and cathedral associate holiness with towering vertical structures and thick stone walls, these attitudes have roots in autochthonous beliefs stemming from prehistory. In the art of the caves at Lascaux, etched drawings and shades of color on the walls depict animal figures apparently less for the demands of representation than for evocation of chthonic presences still alive and moving in the stone.[1] In rites of fertility that may have been performed in ancient caves, animal ancestors of bull and bison were reunited with "mother earth" deep in her sacred spaces.[2] This sense of the life of space did not disappear, according to current studies, after the Neolithic age, but lives on in Egyptian sacred architecture, such as the mortuary temple of Queen Hatshepsut, carved far into a hillside to place the queen close to the center of her sacred origins.[3]

That these autochthonous functions of space also existed in the middle ages has been the suspicion of more than one visitor to the early churches of medieval Europe. Commenting on European sacred building of the twelfth century, one historian observes: "these were real 'mother-churches,' gravid, earth-bound, built by men of peasant stock who were conscious that mother earth and the mother of God held them equally in thrall." Con-

[1]Sigfried Giedion, *The Eternal Present*, vol. 1, *The Beginnings of Art* (New York: Bollingen Foundation, 1962), p. 3; "The animals that primeval man engraved or painted were, for him, already living in the rock. They were there: he had only to complete them. It is a fact that the natural traces of forms in the rock inspired paleolithic man to create from a fragment the so-to-speak innate form of an animal or human figure" (pp. 20–22).

[2]Giedion: "these were holy places where, with the aid of magically potent symbolic pictures, sacred rituals could be performed" (p. 525). See Georges Bataille, *Lascaux; or, The Birth of Art* (Geneva: Skira, 1955); E. Neumann, *The Great Mother: An Analysis of the Archetype*, trans. R. Manheim (New York: Pantheon, 1955); G. Rachel Levy, *The Gate of Horn: A Study of the Religious Conceptions of the Stone Age, and Their Influence upon European Thought* (London: Faber & Faber, 1948).

[3]On sacred space of Egyptian building in relation to prehistoric caves, see Sigfried Giedion, *The Eternal Present*, vol. 2, *The Beginnings of Architecture* (New York: Bollingen Foundation, 1964), p. 356; on Hatshepsut's Temple, 2:432 and plate p. 262.

cerning the decoration of these buildings, this commentator maintains that the "world of the imagination portrayed in medieval art comprehends the monsters of pre-history. . . . The sixteen stone oxen high on the towers of Laon cathedral . . . are a tribute to the nobility of the animal world."[4] And within the walls of the early churches, a sense of space is created that has many aspects in common with the sacred space of cultures predating the middle ages. For it has been argued that Romanesque churches were constructed near water because it "was holy, a direct means of communicating with the womb of the world where it lay in the depths of the earth. In the ancient world men had done the same, as the foundations of the Greek temples at Paestum still remind us. Space was essentially feminine, a sacred cave, a sacred womb —in fact the womb of 'mother church.' . . . Sacred enclosures protected the dead until the time of their rebirth, for enclosure meant security. The Romanesque church was the stronghold of God, a sure defense against all evil powers and wicked men."[5] The ancient schema linking earth, temple, and mother goddess may appear to be changed in the medieval parallel—*natura, ecclesia, mater generationis*—because of the new theology of Christianity; but theological developments did not apparently loosen the grip of autochthony on the medieval consciousness.

We may consider the persistence of a mythological presupposition as it passes through several variations in form by turning briefly to the Gothic column. It is customarily regarded as an imitation of a Corinthian prototype with capitals flowering in vines and acanthus leaves. Although highly stylized, the Greek form preserves in its motif of foliage an earlier association of the column with a living tree, such as the imitation of papyrus reeds in the columns of ancient Egyptian temples.[6] A late development of the Egyptian belief that the pillar grew out of the earth like a tree uniting it with the sky apparently informs the Corinthian column of the Greek temple of Apollo, thus providing the link between the god and the column.[7] The autochthonous roots of the Greek

[4]Friedrich Heer, *The Medieval World*, trans. Janet Sondheimer (New York: World, 1962), pp. 377, 386.

[5]Heer, *Medieval World*, pp. 380–381.

[6]The column as an imitation of the papyrus plant embodies an assumption that never disappeared from Egyptian architecture, according to Giedion: the column "always represented the power of organic growth shooting up toward the sky," *Eternal Present*, 2:287 (plates, pp. 247, 511). See also Levy, *Gate of Horn*, pp. 120–126.

[7]Discussing the Corinthian column, Vincent Scully observes: "its beginnings were with Apollo, and it was appropriate to him, because if it less specifically recalled

column as the living presence of deity or ancestor are apparently not eroded as the form passes through various styles in the middle ages. For we may still detect an aspect of autochthony in the remarks of Durandus of Mende in his thirteenth-century commentary on the architecture of the church. The columns of the cathedral, says Durandus, are the "great men" of the past, the "kings of Israel" and "bishops of the church."[8] These are conventional medieval assumptions, and occasionally their autochthonous origins have been observed: "columns housed the tree of life"; they were "hallowed things"; not only were they "lesser load bearers" but they "worked miracles"; their decorators worked in love and dread of stone that was by nature holy.[9] Insofar as these medieval attitudes have not let go of a precedent autochthony of the column as living presence, it would not be extravagant to see this mythology as the ground of the commonplace Tree of Jesse with its divine lineage and branches of great persons. The holiness with which the columns are imbued, according to Durandus, is of a piece with the sacrality of stone and mortar that composes the walls of the church: "The mortar," says Durandus, "without which there can be no stability of the walls, is made of lime, sand, and water. The lime is fervent charity, which joins to itself the sand, that is, undertakings for the temporal welfare of our brethren: because true charity takes care of the widow and the aged, the infant and the infirm."[10]

In these examples, the older mythological forms have undergone obvious mutations: mother earth has become mother church, Apollo a famous figure of ecclesiastical history, and the sanctity of stone a Christian virtue. But although the older form has been appropriated for new Christian meanings, it is still derived from fundamental ideas about space that have not changed substantially over the centuries. One way to study in finer detail how medieval representations of space may reflect a specifically mythological habit of thinking is to follow the lead of art historians who have attempted to explain the significance of the heavy emphasis on outline that distinguishes both medieval and archaic art forms. If direct historical influences seem improbable over the

---

palm leaves . . . it was clearly much more like a living tree"; it was "the god's tree symbol"; *The Earth, the Temple, and the Gods: Greek Sacred Architecture* (New Haven: Yale University Press, 1962), pp. 128, 103–105.

[8]Durandus of Mende, *Rationale divinorum officiorum* (Venice, 1568), 1.1.5^{v}B.

[9]Heer, *Medieval World*, p. 381.

[10]Durandus: "calx, charitas feruens est," *Rationale* 1.1.4^{v}A.

vast expanse of time separating the medieval from the archaic world, nonetheless, similarities in the structure of space suggest similarities in the assumptions about what space is and how it is perceived. The proposals of E. H. Gombrich may be taken up to pursue this inquiry, since he has argued a connection between medieval and ancient art on the basis of the corresponding func- of "schemata" in both forms. For example, the almost changeless forms of Egyptian paintings and sculptures reveal a heavy reli- ance on formulas and schemata, such as the circle or triangle, which craftsmen were taught for representing the human face or torso; little evidence, if any at all, can be found in the art of Egypt and prehistory that the artist tried to adjust his schema with the object perceived in the physical world in order to create a realistic image in stone or paint.[11] In the middle ages the sketchbook of Villard de Honnecourt contains a wealth of schemata and formu- las for drawing various subjects, and in them we see the reasons for the schematic form of medieval art as well as its link with the art of the mythological world. As Villard shows how to draw a hu- man face from a circle, rectangle, or star, it becomes clear that the teaching of schemata supersedes any interest in trying to adjust and match them with their corresponding forms in reality.[12] Whereas in a typically medieval drawing or painting the artist's schema is distinctly visible, in the sketch of a renaissance figure, for example by Leonardo da Vinci, the schema is barely discern- ible as it is subjected to the constant testing and adjustment that create dimensionality, movement, and background. Instructions in medieval art, Gombrich argues, contain very little illustration of the process of adjustment, correction, and testing of schemata; even where advice "to copy reality" is given, as in Villard's com- ment on the lion ("know well that it is drawn from life") we find in the animal's face, in fact in all of the animals of the album, the repetition of the same schema—human ears, mouth, teeth, lip line, eyes, and eyelashes.[13]

Despite the obvious differences in the iconography and sub- ject matter between medieval and mythological art, what has not changed over the centuries is the "projection" of the schema as

[11]E. H. Gombrich, *Art and Illusion: A Study in the Psychology of Pictorial Representa- tion,* 2d ed. (Princeton: Princeton University Press, 1969), pp. 120–125.

[12]Gombrich, "Formula and Experience," in *Art and Illusion,* pp. 146–155.

[13]Gombrich, *Art and Illusion,* pp. 78–79 and plate 55. Villard de Honnecourt, *The Sketchbook of Villard de Honnecourt,* ed. Theodore Bowie (Bloomington: Indiana University Press, 1959).

the image. Until the renaissance this process does not undergo significant alteration.

> Seen in this light, that dry psychological formula of schema and correction can tell us a good deal, not only about the essential unity between medieval and postmedieval art, but also of their vital difference. To the Middle Ages, the schema is the image; to the postmedieval artist, it is the starting point for corrections, adjustments, adaptations, the means to probe reality and to wrestle with the particular. The hallmark of the medieval artist is the firm line that testifies to the mastery of his craft. That of the postmedieval artist is not facility, which he avoids, but constant alertness. Its symptom is the sketch, or rather the many sketches which precede the finished work and, for all the skill of hand and eye that marks the master, a constant readiness to learn, to make and match and remake till the portrayal ceases to be a secondhand formula and reflects the unique and unrepeatable experience the artist wishes to seize and hold. It is this constant search, this sacred discontent, which constitutes the leaven of the Western mind since the Renaissance and pervades our art no less than our science. For it is not only the scientist . . . who can examine the schema and test its validity. Since the time of Leonardo, at least, every great artist has done the same, consciously or unconsciously.[14]

But the "leaven" of this change does not begin—as Gombrich is careful to avoid suggesting—in the renaissance. Rather, one may find versions of it, according to a recent inquiry, in the protest against mythological practices and forms mounted by the Hebrews in the ancient Near East as recorded in the Bible.[15] When renaissance artistic style was effecting changes from medieval formulaic painting, sculpture, and architecture, Luther and Calvin were finding their voices in the prophets of the Old Testament— in Hebrew rejections of alien mythologies. The "sacred discontent" heard in the Bible not only sounds its echoes from the renaissance pulpit, but also participates in the "demythologizing" movement of renaissance treatments of spatial form. The absence of this movement from medieval representations of space illustrates in yet another way that they have not become dislocated from antecedent mythological foundations.

For instance, as Villard's album illustrates the absence of correction and adjustment in rigid styles of drawing, it suggests that a

---

[14]Gombrich, *Art and Illusion*, p. 173 and plates 143, 144.
[15]Herbert N. Schneidau, *Sacred Discontent: The Bible and Western Tradition* (Berkeley: University of California Press, 1976), pp. 264–268.

Plate 3. Descent of the Heavenly Jerusalem. Apocalypse 21.9–27 (early fourteenth century). Metropolitan Museum of Art, Cloisters Collection, 1968. MS 68.174, fol. 36ᵛ.

Plate 4. The Trinity. Central triptych panel. Lucca di Tommé (mid-fourteeth century). Timken Art Gallery, Putnam Foundation Collection, San Diego, California.

similar process of "projection" may be operative in the painting of biblical manuscripts. Those habits are apparent in simple visual scenes or images that attempt to formulate a passage that is highly suggestive of spiritual reference or intended to challenge facile responses and familiar meanings. A fourteenth-century painted manuscript of the Book of Apocalypse is typical: the scriptural citation "hand of God" is depicted as a human hand reaching out of a cloud, and the descent of the celestial Jerusalem (*civitas Dei*) is a familiar walled medieval castle descending to earth gently couched on a cloud.[16] Such medieval imagery no doubt was composed in response to ordinary needs for visual illustrations of written documents in a society of limited literacy; however, the composition of "pictographs" for such references discloses an expectation that is "medieval" only by virtue of its date. To illuminate the divine inspiration of Sacred Scripture, as in a fourteenth-century painting of Saint Matthew, by depicting an angel whispering the *verbum Dei* into the ear of the evangelist captures a well-known medieval image, but it reveals the projection of the schema as the image that dates from anticipations long before the middle ages.[17] The instructions for depicting other subjects were familiar, such as the painting of "three persons in one God" of the Trinity represented, for example in an Italian painting of the thirteenth century, as three identical male figures standing behind a scene of the Crucifixion.[18] But the inspiration to mystical contemplation, if not foreclosed, is at least limited to known and familiar referents, especially when the figures are further identified by local tokens, like a crown or ring.

While these conventional examples illustrate the way rigid forms and heavy emphasis on outline in medieval art betoken the mythological projection of the schema as the image, even in a work that is noted for its variation in line, color, and iconography, such as the Lindisfarne Gospels, the representation of space remains vividly in the foreground, and the delineation of schemata prevails over all other interests. For instance, in the famous page of the cross, twelve border lines stress the framing of space within.[19] The whole area inside the border is organized accord-

---

[16]See plate 3 and Hans Holländer, *Early Medieval Art,* trans. Caroline Hillier (New York: Universe Books, 1974).

[17]See plate 2.

[18]See plate 4.

[19]See plate 5 and Janet Backhouse, *The Lindisfarne Gospels* (Ithaca: Cornell University Press, 1981).

ing to the axial symmetry of the cross, which is composed of five bell-shaped figures, four of which are also chalice figures created by the semicircle bases that compose the center of the cross. Circles and circular shapes dominate the other areas of the page, particularly the interwoven shapes of the mythological birds and serpentine animals, repeated within the last detail of the concentric circles of their eyes. In the lower two quadrants, the interlacement of birds and serpentine animals in pink and gray are in homologous relationship with the number 3. Each 3-shape is faced with an identical figure, and the pairs are repeated four times in each of the two lower quadrants. In the upper quadrants, serpents and birds are in homologous pattern with the letter C and form pairs of figures arranged back to back. The intertwining lacework of animals, birds, crosses, and circles throughout creates an effect of massive interdependence of line and figure to form a coherent, highly organized whole.

Not a corner of the framed space is left "vacant." In the upper quadrants, even the five black dots between the lateral pairs of Cs are not "empty spaces" but form an axis crossed by a horizontal line of four smaller dots between the upper and lower Cs. As the C shapes and 3-figures are not arbitrary, neither are the black spaces haphazard; they are in homologous relation to the central cross of the illumination. Furthermore, as the whole page is divided into quadrants by the main cross, both upper quadrants are subdivided again into smaller quadrants by the cross of black spaces. The figures of bell, chalice, circle, rose window, birds, serpents, the numbers three and four are radiant with theological significance. The bell and the chalice have obvious eucharistic significance, and the circle may indicate ideas about the perfection of Christ's abiding love or the unity of all men through the Crucifixion and Redemption. Neither the birds nor the serpents in the two lower quadrants have positive identity, but since the birds slay themselves (they bite their own necks), they recall common medieval mythologies about birds of self-death and new life, the pelican and the phoenix, which are certainly fitting in a painting of the cross of Christ. The serpents devour the birds in the lower quadrants but are themselves bitten in the upper sections of the page, illustrating the rivalry between serpents and birds set in motion when the serpent tempted Eve and was subsequently condemned. The serpents of evil will be devoured—as Mary was said to crush the serpent's head—by the pelican, the dove, the Christian soul, and Jesus Christ, although they will be threatened and "bitten" in that saving work.

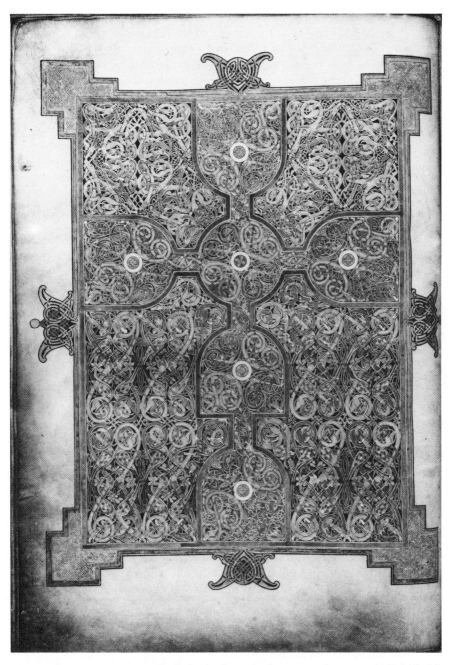

Plate 5. Cross carpet page. Lindisfarne Gospels (late seventh century). British Library. Cotton Nero MS D.iv, fol. 26b.

Since the triangle is a commonplace homologue of the Trinity, the 3-shaped figures of the sacrificial birds may serve as a homologue for any number of ideas: the Trinity, three theological virtues, three ages before the Law, three Magi. If three suggests the theological virtues, a medieval exegete would quickly suggest that a contiguous four (in the four pairs of 3s or four quadrants) includes the corresponding four cardinal virtues, especially since the total, seven, indicates the spiritual perfection of the cross that resists the Seven Deadly Sins by virtue of the other totalities present in it—seven Sacraments, seven parts of the Mass, seven petitions of the Lord's Prayer, seven tones of the scale, seven planets, seven days. From such an illuminated book, it is not difficult to follow a medieval viewer anticipating a world charged with signs, since the page is itself a sign of the immanence of meaning, like the reliefs and wall paintings in the art of the caves and pyramids. One may even be tempted to see more than a tangential link between the style of the page of the cross and the cultural context in which the Lindisfarne Gospels were painted in Northumbria about the time of the composition of *Beowulf*, bearing many of that poem's characteristics of the inlay of Christianity into a rich mythological world. But the pages of the Gospels were created by monks trained in exegesis of Scripture, however rudimentary, and their paintings reveal the coalescence of a mythology of dragons with a "mythologic" preoccupied to close all openings, establish sophisticated balances, and affirm the magnificent symmetry of the universe. The page of the cross, like the style of Homer's epics and in some measure the Old English *Beowulf* as well, bespeaks a world in which space is radiant with significance.

Medieval attempts to chart the space of known and unknown geographical areas, the making of maps, show that a schema could be asserted with so little interest in testing its validity that the space of most of Western Europe and the Near East resembles the form of a painting in illumination of a scriptural text. For example, in the late thirteenth-century map of the world hanging in Hereford cathedral, fact and fantasy, schema and projected image mingle imperceptibly.[20] A medieval pilgrim might carry a smaller version of such a map in his travels into known areas, but he would surely have to be guided by faith rather than cartography in the unknown regions. For although the places of towns

[20]See plate 6 and Malcolm Letts, "The Pictures in the Hereford *Mappa Mundi*," *Notes and Queries* 200 (1955):2–6.

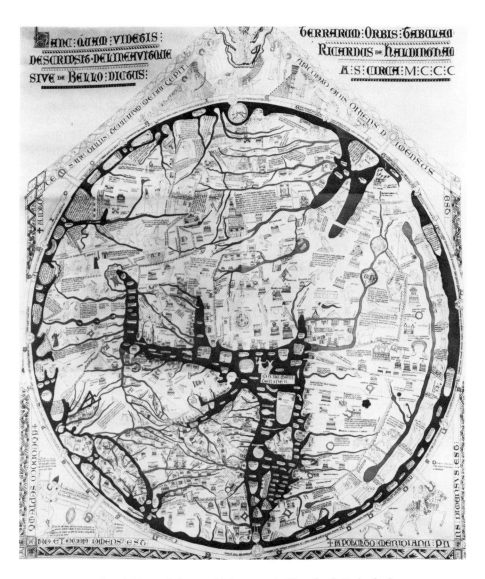

Plate 6. Map of the world (ca. 1300). Hereford Cathedral.

and rivers in the known world are vaguely represented, he would have to be wary of the regions in India where the sciopods dwelled, those popular uniped humans known to use their single foot as an umbrella. Equally suspicious were areas around the Nile, the home of the anthropophagi ("man-eaters"), beings resembling men in all ways except that their heads grew beneath their shoulders, so that they saw and ate through their chests. Travels to the "top of the world" brought one close to the origin of all life in the Garden of Eden, while the center of the round world provided the comforts of being near Jerusalem, the pivot or "navel" of this world's body. One might go off to the Black Sea—avoiding the various sea beasts—to seek the Golden Fleece by following the detailed charted course of Jason and the Argonauts. But if lost anywhere one need only remember the general rules of thumb for survival: be careful of the South, for India is a place of demons and monsters and the North has nothing but hailstorms and cold winds; do not go West, for the sun sets in that region of death; instead go East, for there the sun rises, as Christ brought the light of salvation into the world.[21]

Even with the anthropophagi, sciopods, and Grendels effectively quelled by pilgrimages to Jerusalem or Canterbury and by readings in the Bible, a mythology of another sort survived in the middle ages—the autochthony that imbues all space with meaning. The projection of cosmological notions onto geography, such as we find in medieval examples like the Hereford map, illustrates the mythology of sacred space argued, for example, by Mircea Eliade: "the cosmicization of unknown territories is always a consecration; to organize a space is to repeat the paradigmatic work of the gods."[22] Preconceived schemata, divine "paradigms," are replicated as the real order of things, dictating their nature and organization. Medieval religious conceptions that are "illuminated" in sacred painting remain tied to this sense of space. Although these art forms are conceived in the attempt to throw light on the inner nature of things, we see repeatedly that spatial representations clarify instead *their own process* of projection, and it is that "clarification" that constitutes the medieval hold on precedent ways of thinking.

[21]See Paul Shepard, *Man in the Landscape: A Historical View of the Esthetics of Nature* (New York: Alfred A. Knopf, 1967).

[22]Mircea Eliade, *The Sacred and the Profane,* trans. W. R. Trask (New York: Harper & Row, 1961), p. 33.

The separation of the means of clarifying from what is being clarified was confronted more forthrightly in the *via negativa* than in most other medieval traditions, and few writers recognized the significance of it more profoundly than Aquinas. In summarizing the purpose of human reason in the study of *sacra doctrina*, Aquinas establishes as a guiding premise the impossibility of knowing divine nature in itself—in its own *esse*: "God as an unknown is said to be the terminus of our knowledge in the following respect: that the mind is found to be most perfectly in possession of knowledge of God when it is recognized that His essence is above everything that the mind is capable of apprehending in this life: and thus, although what he is remains unknown, yet it is known that He is."[23] Recognizing the difference between human knowledge (*scientia*) and divine wisdom (*sapientia*), the study of sacred doctrine is established as an analogous mode. Analogy, Aquinas argues, is the "proper proportionality" of human knowing that does not impinge upon the purity of the divine order so long as that proportionality is maintained. In certain areas of *sacra doctrina*, such as "the names of God," we cannot separate the *quod nomen designat* from the *modus quo*—what a name designates from the way it designates—and hence must assert that, as a person may be called just or good, God must be justice or goodness itself.[24] The means of maintaining the analogous mode in such areas is possessed by the style of the argumentation, by the cue of question after question, and the repetition of such formulas as *intendet significare* ("intends to signify"). In these cues the style leads us "by the hand"—*manuductio*—realizing the clarification in each successive step.[25] Such a deliberate means of proceeding acknow-

[23]"Ad primum ergo dicendum quod secundum hoc dicimur in fine nostrae cognitionis deum tamquam ignotum cognoscere, quia tunc maxime mens in cognitione profecisse invenitur, quando cognoscit eius esse supra omne quod apprehendere potest in statu viae, et sic quamvis maneat ignotum quid est, scitur tamen quia est"; *Expositio super librum Boethii de trinitate*, ed. Bruno Decker (Leiden: E. J. Brill, 1959), 1.2.4 (p. 67); cf. *Summa* 1.12.12 (p. 40). See Victor Preller, *Divine Science and the Science of God* (Princeton: Princeton University Press, 1967).

[24]*Summa theologiae*, ed. Thomas Gilby, O.P. (New York: McGraw-Hill for Blackfriars, 1964), 1.13.2, 1.13.3 (pp. 52–58); David B. Burrell, *Analogy and Philosophical Language* (New Haven: Yale University Press, 1973), pp. 124, 136–138. See Preller, *Divine Science*, pp. 117–122.

[25]David B. Burrell, "Aquinas on Naming God," *Theological Studies* 24 (1963):195–196; idem, *Analogy*, pp. 122, 139.

ledges itself as proportionately different from an absolute conceptual system that does not proceed by names or images or analogies.

Reason, Aquinas explains, cannot describe divine mysteries like the Trinity, cannot specify their *esse*; it can only "clarify"—*manifestare*—the articles of sacred doctrine.[26] In this principle, and especially in this term, *manifestatio*, Aquinas articulates an assumption that governs his own *Summa theologiae* as well as those of other writers, such as Bonaventure's *Opera* and Peter Lombard's *Sententia*. In the summa, *manifestatio* makes no mistake about remaining on the proper human side of the divine boundary, which is protected by highly formalized principles of proceeding. However, although those principles set out to clarify an order believed to be intrinsic to the nature of things, the rigidly schematic style imitates—becomes the speculum of—the careful subdivision and order of its own procedure. And in this movement of thought, Scholasticism appears to rely on the function of schematic structure that governs various other medieval cultural forms.

The *manifestatio* of which summae are capable, first of all, is the summa itself, not only the "highest" reaches of speculation, but the "totality" or complete itemization of all aspects of an issue; such treatises must be composed of adequate *articuli*, constituent "parts" or "members," and subdivided into finer elements; the pattern of ordo of the whole is preserved by proper comparisons, *similitudines*, and sufficient contrasts, *distinctiones*; the inclusion of precise diction, harmonious sentences, and rhyme will foster mnemonic devices for rapid memorization; finally the last item in an argument must affirm the *concordantia* of the whole, the principle that no contradictions remain as all opening objections are conclusively refuted.[27] For example, within the *Summa*, Aquinas considers "The Nature and Domain of Sacred Doctrine," which he subdivides into ten constituent parts: "(1) about the need for this teaching; (2) whether it be science; (3) whether it be single or several; (4) whether it be theoretical or practical; (5) how it compares with other sciences; (6) whether it be wisdom; (7) what is its subject; (8)

[26]"Utitur tamen sacra doctrina etiam ratione humana, non quidem ad probandum fidem . . . sed ad manifestandum aliqua quae traduntur in hac doctrina"; *Summa theologiae* 1a.1.8, 2 (p. 30).

[27]See the useful appendixes in the Blackfriars' edition of the *Summa*, "The Structure of the Summa," "The Method of the Summa," "The Style of the Summa," 1:43–53; see also A. Dempf, *Die Hauptform mittelalterlicher Weltanschauung: Eine geisteswissenschaftliche Studie über die Summa* (Munich, 1925).

whether it sets out to prove anything; (9) whether it should employ metaphorical or symbolic language; (10) whether its sacred writings are to be interpreted in several senses."[28] The tenth article begins with a subdivision of "objections": *videtur* (1) that a word in Scripture cannot have several meanings, literal, allegorical, tropological, and anagogical; (2) that besides these four Augustine lists history, etiology, analogy, and allegory; (3) and that neither of these categories includes the parabolical. *Sed contra,* but on the contrary, Gregory observes that Scripture is beyond all sciences, because it reveals mystery in facts. In the *respondeo,* Aquinas supplies the traditional division of literal and spiritual senses, subdividing the latter into the allegorical, moral, and anagogical, justifying them with *auctoritas* on the figural nature of signs, and concluding that a word may have many senses in the Bible. To the first objection, *ad primum,* Aquinas denies that multiplicity produces equivocation; *ad secundum,* Augustine's four divisions correspond to the standard ones; *ad tertium,* the parabolical is not an additional category, but belongs to the literal sense, as in the image "arm of God," which signifies "operational power."[29]

If we look back at these medieval arguments through the lens of Sir Francis Bacon's *Advancement of Learning, Novum organum,* and similar renaissance critiques, we may overlook as they did—surely as Rabelais did—the important point about *manuductio* cited by Aquinas. In the progression from sign to sentence, page, chapter, book, Bible, nature, cosmos, the *manifestatio* of the summa does not validate articles of faith, but replicates in its style the divine ordo. Following that progression from a vantage point that had recently discovered infinite space, new worlds across geographical and historical horizons, and models for the universe other than the one inherited from the middle ages, Bacon, Milton, and many others denounced Scholastic argumentation as circular and confused by "webs of learning."[30] But *manifestatio* was not as "medieval" or as confused as renaissance critics claim. To be sure, the subject matter or details of content are the vital issues of writers and thinkers of the middle ages; it certainly bears, as may now be apparent, distinct parallels with commentary on Scripture and the illumination of manuscripts; and all three are the result of disciplines of learning

---

[28]*Summa* 1a (pp. 4–5).

[29]*Summa* 1a.10 (pp. 36–40).

[30]Sir Francis Bacon, *The Advancement of Learning* (1605), in *Seventeenth-Century Prose and Poetry,* ed. Alexander M. Witherspoon and Frank J. Warnke, 2d ed. (New York: Harcourt, Brace & World, 1963), p. 52.

founded on the reading of signs taught by writers like Augustine. But *manifestatio,* insofar as it compares with the mode of clarifying in the visual illuminations of the "sacred page," is not the exclusive creation of medieval Scholasticism. Rather, it is a highly formalized principle of the projection of schemata and the spatialization of thought that begins long before Aquinas, Gregory, and Augustine. The projection is obviously different in degree from Villard's replication of the schema as the image drawn with pen and ink; but *manifestatio* is not different from it in kind. For in the effort to clarify a concept or belief, *manifestatio* "clarifies" its own highly schematic form of argumentation: the *interpretans* is projected as the *interpretandum.* The means of clarifying takes the place of what is being clarified by virtue of the formalization of questioning and testing, in the same way that the artist's schema becomes his represented image when adapting, adjusting, and falsifying are minimized. For this reason, no doubt, renaissance writers and artists had little patience with medieval forms; the style of the summa simply does not conceive of falsifying an ordo maintained in *concordantia.* So long as it is maintained, the order of thought is guaranteed. But the dominance of the schematic in this order rests upon the same sense of sacred space that is evident in formulaic artistic styles of the middle ages. The sacrality of spatial arrangement controls how thinking proceeds; thought is the speculum of sacred order. Although the medieval sense of space as fraught with significance has changed considerably from earlier autochthonous cultures, it nonetheless holds on to a fundamental anticipation about sacred space that is one of the identifying characteristics of mythological thought: "to organize a space," says Eliade, "is to repeat the paradigmatic work of the gods."

The importance of "paradigmatic" structure in mythological space, for example as studied by Claude Lévi-Strauss, is that a sacred or totemic object—once thought to be significant or magical in itself—is instead a part that has the ability to recall other elements to which it compares in form, as one term in a linguistic paradigm recalls others like it or a Doric column reminds us of an Ionic or a Corinthian prototype. Thus the totemic animal or object functions as a "conceptual tool," Lévi-Strauss observes, to recall the whole classification of which it is one element: "a genuine system *by means of* a creature, and not the creature itself constitutes the object of thought and furnishes the conceptual tool."[31] With regard to

[31]Claude Lévi-Strauss, *La Pensée sauvage* (Paris: Plon, 1962); trans. George Weidenfeld as *The Savage Mind* (Chicago: University of Chicago Press, 1969), p. 149.

the medieval summa, paradigmatic structures are everywhere in evidence in the symmetrical subdivision, homologous interrelation of parts, patterned oppositions, parallel diction, syntax, rhyme, and mnemonic devices; each part has the capacity to recall the larger system, and the style of the whole is the "Scholastic memory" of the vast classificatory network of the Book of nature. In this sense, the style is an "ideograph" of the cosmos, illustrating Roland Barthes's observation that "myth is a pure ideographic system, where the forms are still motivated by the [signified] concept which they represent while not yet, by a long way, covering the sum of its possibilities for representation."[32] Aquinas and Augustine would take no issue with the "motivated" forms of things in the Bible or nature, and surely not with the infinitely rich signifiers tied mysteriously to the divine concept. Instead, by making the style of writing conform in every conceivable detail to the imago of the greater world about which they wrote, they would imitate perfection itself. But they would deny that the massive interlacement and organization of their books and of the elegant painted manuscripts they admired were the projection of a style of thinking that obeyed the expectations of mythology.

3

Recognizing that *manifestatio* involves a preoccupation to fill out and classify all space within perceptible limits suggests that verbal and visual styles have a common conceptual basis and that cultural forms that appear to have similar traits are much more than examples of the all-too-familiar "parallels." Erwin Panofsky, for example, has tried to reach behind the superficial similarities that he sees between Gothic architecture and Scholasticism by pointing to their common ground in *manifestatio*.[33] But by considering *manifestatio* as the unique invention of a style of written argumentation, his study does not directly confront how a verbal medium might "influence" an architectural style. That both Gothic architecture and Scholasticism share an obvious encyclopedic interest may

[32]Roland Barthes, "Myth Today," in *Mythologies* (1957; reprint, Paris: Seuil, 1970), trans. Annette Lavers as *Mythologies* (New York: Hill & Wang, 1972), p. 127.
[33]See Erwin Panofsky, *Gothic Architecture and Scholasticism* (Cleveland: World, 1968). An application of Panofsky's concept of Gothic form to literary style has been made by Robert M. Jordan, *Chaucer and the Shape of Creation* (Cambridge: Harvard University Press, 1967). On Gothic architecture, see also Henri Focillon, *The Art of the West in the Middle Ages*, trans. Donald King, 2d ed. (London: Phaidon Press, 1969).

have something to do, as Panofsky argues, with the historical fact that both forms reached their zenith in the areas around Paris in the twelfth and thirteenth centuries; but if a comparison is to be argued for the two forms, it may be established by considering the heritage of *manifestatio* in a style of spatializing thought.

Beginning with the centrality of *manifestatio* to Scholasticism, Panofsky argues, "the Scholastic mind demanded a maximum of explicitness. It accepted and insisted upon a gratuitous clarification of function through form just as it accepted and insisted upon a gratuitous clarification of thought through language."[34] He goes on to define *manifestatio* as "the postulate of clarification for clarification's sake," and he situates its origin in "the Scholastic mind."[35] But the Scholastic and architectural forms that are offered in illustration of this "postulate" bear striking resemblance to the patterns of organizing space and projecting inherited formulas that are operative well beyond the confines of medieval Scholasticism. For instance, the "totality" that Panofsky studies as a defining characteristic of the summa and the cathedral has several analogies in the taxonomies and classifications of mythological thought.

> Like the High Scholastic *Summa*, the High Gothic cathedral aimed, first of all, at "totality" and therefore tended to approximate, by synthesis as well as elimination, one perfect and final solution; we may therefore speak of *the* High Gothic plan or *the* High Gothic system with much more confidence than would be possible in any other period. In its imagery, the High Gothic cathedral sought to embody the whole of Christian knowledge, theological, moral, natural, and historical, with everything in its place and that which no longer found its place, suppressed. In structural design, it similarly sought to synthesize all major motifs handed down by separate channels and finally achieved an unparalleled balance between the basilica and the central plan type, suppressing all elements that might endanger this balance, such as the crypt, the galleries, and towers other than the two in front.[36]

Panofsky is hardly alone in arguing this parallel between Scholasticism and Gothic architecture.[37] But the idea of totality as it is rep-

[34]Panofsky, *Gothic Architecture*, pp. 59–60.
[35]Ibid., p. 35.
[36]Ibid., pp. 44–45.
[37]Cf. C. S. Lewis, *The Discarded Image* (Cambridge: Cambridge University Press, 1964): "At his most characteristic, medieval man was not a dreamer nor a wanderer. He was an organizer, a codifier, a builder of systems. He wanted 'a place for everything and everything in the right place.' Though full of turbulent activities, he was

resented here does not have its origin in the methodology of Scholastic argumentation, for the same kind of emphasis on the sacrality of order is to be found as a commonplace in mythological societies. In sacred structures, as Lévi-Strauss has studied them, "sacred things must have their place . . . being in their place is what makes them sacred for if they were taken out of their place, even in thought, the entire order of the universe would be destroyed. Sacred objects therefore contribute to the maintenance of order in the universe by occupying the places allocated to them."[38] By this principle, the totality of the summa and the cathedral does not consist in their gross structure, which was subject to stylistic variation and to change. What did not change from at least the time of the ancient fertility rituals performed at the sites on which some medieval cathedrals were later built is the sacrality of space in which every dark corner is charged with significance, the part an embodiment of the whole, the sign projected as the signified. The summa and cathedral have in common some of the most elemental ideas that their builders learned about the structure of space. That structure was inherited from mythology, and inheritance surely masters invention in these medieval examples.

The second characteristic of Scholastic writing, Panofsky observes, "arrangement according to a system of homologous parts," is apparent in the symmetrical divisibility of elements in architecture: "As a result of this homology we perceive what corresponds to the hierarchy of 'logical levels' in a well-organized Scholastic treatise." The customary division of the whole architectural structure—nave, transept, chevet—may itself be subdivided into high nave and side aisles opposed by apse, ambulatory, and chapels. Within these divisions, still further balances are apparent:

> first, between each central bay, the whole of the central nave, and the entire nave, transept or fore-choir, respectively; second, between each side aisle bay, the whole of each side aisle, and the entire nave, tran-

equally full of the impulse to formalize them. War was (in intention) formalized by the art of heraldry and the rules of chivalry; sexual passion (in intention), by an elaborate code of love. Highly original and soaring philosophical speculation squeezes itself into a rigid dialectical pattern copied from Aristotle. Studies like Law and Moral Theology, which demand the ordering of very diverse particulars, especially flourish. . . . The perfect examples are the *Summa* of Aquinas and Dante's *Divine Comedy*. . . . But there is a third work which we can, I think, set beside these two. This is the medieval synthesis itself, the whole organisation of their theology, science, and history into a single, complex, harmonious mental Model of the Universe" (pp. 10–11).

[38]Lévi-Strauss, *Savage Mind*, p. 10.

sept or fore-choir, respectively; third, between each sector of the apse, the whole apse, and the entire choir; fourth, between each section of the ambulatory, the whole of the ambulatory and the entire choir; and fifth, between each chapel, the whole hemicycle of chapels, and the entire choir.[39]

While the same "progressive divisibility" may be observed in a Scholastic treatise, "the principle of homology that controls the whole process" has also been noted in the much earlier example of the intricate homologies on the page of the cross in the Lindisfarne Gospels, and we find it as well in exegesis of Scripture.[40]

For instance, the preoccupation with homology found in the cathedral also informs the entry for *cathedra* in Pierre Bersuire's *Repertorium morale*:

> CATHEDRA. Nota quod CATHEDRA nomen est magisterii, et honoris. Dicam ergo, quod in scriptura reperitur
> CATHEDRA

$$
\left.\begin{array}{l} \text{Praeeminentiae,} \\ \text{Sapientiae,} \\ \text{Pestilentiae,} \end{array}\right\} \quad \text{quae est} \quad \left\{\begin{array}{l} \text{Praelatorum,} \\ \text{Magistrorum,} \\ \text{Tyrannorum.}^{41} \end{array}\right.
$$

The equation of "preeminence" with "prelates," "wisdom" with "teachers," and "pestilence" with "tyrants" is dictated not by any exclusive denotation of these terms in Scripture, but rather by a homologous "logic" that balances one generic category with its equivalent or opposite, as the first two constitute the "bona cathedra" from which the "cathedra malorum" is produced. The parallel syntax and exact genitive endings, the repetition of three singular and three plural nouns in the same gender—all balanced upon the fulcrum of "quae est" and emphasized by alliteration and rhyme achieve more than a convenient mnemonic for easy recall. The structuring of these elements reveals the composition of meaning *as to form*. The understanding of *cathedra* is "manifested" by the arrangement of parts into a visual schema in the same way as the homologue of three and four controls the composition of the Lindisfarne page of the cross or as the multiples of nave, transept, and chevet are totalized throughout the cathedral. *Manifestatio* is obvi-

---

[39]Panofsky, *Gothic Architecture*, pp. 45, 47–48.
[40]Ibid., p. 48.
[41]Pierre Bersuire, *Repertorium morale*, in *Opera omnia* (Cologne, 1731), 1.279.

ously not exclusive to Gothic architecture or Scholasticism in this summa "in miniature" from a page of fourteenth-century exegesis.

A final point about Scholastic writing, cited by Panofsky, is "distinctness and deductive cogency," the concern with adequate contrasts and clear interrelations among parts. In architecture this stylistic feature is achieved in the effort to distinguish shafts from the walls they support, columns from the several members that compose them and in turn from the ribs of the vault they maintain. "Overmembrification" is not merely gratuitous, but manifests the desire to infer the manner by which wall, pier, shaft, and arch are held together.[42] Obvious subordination makes clear the skeletal structure maintaining the whole. Although we may find this fascination with subordinating parts apparent in, for example, the nave of Canterbury cathedral, in which the membrification of columns is repeated in the ribs of the vault or in the west window composed of a massive arch subdivided distinctly into the many smaller arches supporting it, so also do we find a preoccupation with distinctness in the firm outlines of medieval drawings, the frequent use of multiple border lines sharply setting off the space between them and within the whole. The common use of bright colors for contrast carries out a similar emphasis on interrelationships. But this principle may also be perceived in scriptural commentary, in the emphasis on discriminating among the various senses of terms in a work like Alanus de Insulis's *Distinctiones,* or more broadly in the painstaking detail of demonstrating the hierarchy of four levels of reading Holy Scripture. A popular distich summarizes the familiar divisions but also tells us something about the medieval delight in *distinctiones*:

> Littera gesta docet, quid credas allegoria,
> moralis quid agas, quo tendas anagogia.

[The letter teaches the deed, the allegory what you believe, the moral what you should do, the anagogue what you strive for.][43]

The preference for "gratuitous clarification" that characterizes the function of totality, homology, and distinctness does not simply establish a parallel between two medieval cultural forms; rather,

---

[42]Panofsky, *Gothic Architecture,* pp. 49–50.
[43]For the medieval sources of this reference and a discussion of it, see Henri de Lubac, *Exégèse médiévale: Les Quatre sens de l'écriture,* 2 parts (Paris: Aubier, 1959–1964), 1:23 ff.

the experience of *manifestatio* that Panofsky claims for a Scholastic argument or the tracery of a window or wall characterizes a response to many medieval forms that are so determined to clarify their own method of construction that they reveal every joint and seam in a webbed vault, the human face of the artist's schema in the drawing of a lion, and the gloss of a word like *cathedra* structured into a visual miniature of categories and oppositions *in bono* and *in malo*. For the medieval student attentive to the visual argument of *manifestatio*

> would not have been satisfied had not the membrification of the edifice permitted him to re-experience the very processes of architectural composition just as the membrification of the *Summa* permitted him to re-experience the very processes of cogitation. To him, the panoply of hafts, ribs, buttresses, tracery, pinnacles, and crockets was a self-analysis and self-explication of architecture much as the customary apparatus of parts, distinctions, questions, and articles was, to him, a self-analysis and self-explication of reason.[44]

But the "rationalism" of this response is still centuries away from the process of correcting and adjusting in stone, paint, or words for the purposes of discovering something completely new. Instead, it is the "rationalism" of mythologizing thought: although in these medieval examples the projection of the mental order as the ordo of things to be interpreted has reached a highly sophisticated development, it remains linked in principle to the ancient practice in which an emphasis on heavy outline merely sets in relief—clarifies—a form or figure already present in nature.

4

The structuring of space in the cultural forms considered thus far has involved in various ways medieval ideas about proportion, especially proportions that were studied in terms of their numerical constituents. Although some writers concerned with numerical proportion suspected that their theories stemmed from ancient sources beyond works like Plato's *Timaeus* and Chalcidius's commentary on it, they also assumed that their own traditions were a new interpretation, a departure from antecedent notions. The Gothic cathedral stood for them, according to Otto von Simson, as

---

[44]Panofsky, *Gothic Architecture*, p. 59.

[74]

the outstanding example of what could be done with number and proportion.[45] However, we do not have to probe far in the ancient heritage of medieval tradition, to which of course they had no access, to discover that their use of proportion to organize space in sacred buildings like the cathedral does not depart from, for example, the Egyptian use of proportion to homologize the cosmos in erecting sacred structures. Giedion has demonstrated this process in studying the prehistoric inheritance of Egyptian megalithic structures:

> No architecture is more imbued with proportions than that of Egypt, which stood at the beginning. One of the reasons is that proportions were then inseparably bound up with symbolic meanings. The Egyptian demand for an embracing oneness in its conceptual image of the world could not be halted when it came to architecture. It came to the fore in the scrupulously careful cosmic orientation of the great pyramids. . . . Its close bond to the eternal presence of the cosmic is the finest bequest of Egyptian architecture. It is the most complete expression of the interconnection of cosmic and human: of eternal presence and temporal change.[46]

The "embracing oneness" and "cosmic orientation" of the Egyptian megalith suggests certain parallels with the *speculum mundi* and *domus Dei* of the medieval cathedral, but the common ground of these two forms is the similar function of numerical proportion to construct in stone a "copy" of the proportions thought to compose the greater universe. Pythagorean number theory, although formulated in Greece in the sixth century B.C., is very likely, according to Giedion, an extrapolation of systems of proportion used to construct Egyptian sacred architecture.

Pythagoras imagined that his number system could explain the proportion in all physical forms. He illustrated the theory with the tetraktys, an equilateral triangle produced from legs of four dots. In the words of one early commentator, "From this [tetraktys] all numbers proceed, as the fountain and root of ever-springing nature."[47] A perfect expression of the Pythagorean idea of the "one in the many" and the "many in the one," the tetraktys employed numbers to express the mythological view of the world as a coherent totality in which all parts had a place. The Egyptian pyramid is

[45]See Otto von Simson, *The Gothic Cathedral* (1956; reprint, New York: Bollingen Foundation,1962), pp. 3–59.

[46]Giedion, *Eternal Present,* 2:489, 506.

[47]Cited without reference by Levy, *Gate of Horn,* p. 308.

an image in stone of many of these assumptions. Its volume and surface, for instance, were exact multiples of a right triangle; the triangle itself was a multiple of a segment of one of its legs, the Pythagorean "golden section"; thus the entire megalith was an extension of the golden section.[48] Since the "cubit"—the human hand and forearm—composed a measuring grid that the Egyptians invented and used in constructing sacred buildings, the basic unit of measurement was a multiple of proportions essential to man. An element of human form served as a schema that the Egyptians saw manifested clearly—not unlike the face of Villard's lion—in the proportions of the natural world and in the heavens. What Gombrich says of the function of schemata in prerenaissance art has strong support in Giedion's study of Egypt: "Thus Egyptian architecture is a projection of the proportions of the human body transposed into a larger—but still human—scale."[49] In this process of projecting and homologizing the building to the cosmos and to the human body, Egypt never really lost, Giedion observes, the heritage of its prehistory: "The entire archaic outlook, like that of prehistory, assumed the oneness and inseparability of the world."[50] Lévi-Strauss, as we have seen, arrives at this conclusion from another point of view in remarking that mythological thought is a "logic of comprehension for which contents are indissociable from form . . . [a] systematic of finite classes, [a] universe made up of meanings."[51]

Medieval writers knew little if anything of Egyptian culture, but they had inherited a numerical theory for "the oneness and inseparability of the world" through Plato's adaptations in the *Timaeus* of Pythagorean numbers. Although Plato describes his account as only "a likely story," it was hardly received as a mere legend by the works founded on it, such as Augustine's *De musica*, Chalcidius's *Commentary on the Timaeus*, Bernard Sylvester's *Cosmographia*, and Alanus de Insulis's *De planctu naturae* and *Anticlaudianus*.[52] Like their archaic prototypes, Plato's speculations treat the proportions of nature as multiples of perfect units of measurement in man and as building blocks in the cohesive totality of the cosmic edifice. The

---

[48]Giedion, *Eternal Present*, 2:472–492.

[49]Ibid., 2:491.

[50]Ibid., 2:502.

[51]Lévi-Strauss, *Savage Mind*, p. 267.

[52]See Cornford's discussion of the "likely story," *Plato's Cosmology: The "Timaeus" of Plato*, trans. Francis M. Cornford (1937; reprint, New York: Bobbs-Merrill, n.d.), pp. 28–32; Raymond Klibansky, *The Continuity of the Platonic Tradition during the Middle Ages* (London: Warburg Institute, 1939).

Demiurge, "when he began to put together the body of the universe, set about making it of fire and earth." But to bring these two things into unity, this "builder" employed the "geometrical proportion" that governs "squares and cubes," the fundamental proportions of the Pythagorean tetrad—1:2:4:8 and 1:3:9:27.[53] These units of order account for the concord in the four building blocks of the world's body, earth, air, fire, and water, as well as the harmony of the four elements constituting the body of man. "For these reasons and from such constituents, four in number, the body of the universe was brought into being, coming into concord by means of proportion, and from these it acquired Amity, so that coming into unity with itself it became indissoluble by any other save him who bound it together."[54] The imagery and speculation have changed from the archaic world; Plato does not discuss its sacred architecture, nor does his notion of the human soul as a homology of the world's body rely on the ancient Egyptian idea of the *ka*. But the grip of the archaic outlook still persists in the projection of the mathematical schema in such a way that it determines what is perceived in man, the cosmos, or the stone monument: because the world's body consists of four elements, it is in "unity with itself" and hence is "indissoluble by any other save him who bound it together." We cannot say this is a position that asks to be challenged and doubted. On the contrary, it invites affirmation and extension, which it certainly received in the middle ages.

Although medieval writers interested in the number theory of the *Timaeus* altered some of its ideas with Christian doctrine, what they found most attractive was the use of proportion to assert "unity and concord." If Plato's schemata of proportion do not invite doubt, neither do their medieval developments. Rather, they encourage the expansion of formulas themselves, not the use of them to probe and test and question the phenomena to which they are in similitude. It is that encouragement, that insatiable extension of formulas, that constituted medieval thinking as a means of classifying and prevented a radical departure from Pythagorean number theory, geocentric cosmology, and the archaic outlook at least until the time of Galileo.

Medieval writers themselves suggest the lead in this form of thinking as classifying in theories about music, which reach far into Platonic speculation about number. Like numbers to the builders

[53]*Timaeus* 31BC, 32 (Cornford trans., p. 44); see commentary on Pythagoras, pp. 66–68.
[54]*Timaeus*, 32C (trans., pp. 44–45).

of the Pyramids, music to the builders of the cathedrals, according to von Simson, was the foundation of the aesthetics of beauty in architecture.[55] The idea that builders copied the work of the "Divine Architect" was familiar in, for example, a reference like *elegans architectus* used by Alanus de Insulis or the illustration in the *Bible Moralisée* of God bending over the universe "when he prepared the heavens . . . with a certain law and compass" (Prov. 8.27) and "ordered all things in measure, and number, and weight" (Wisd. of Sol. 11.21).[56] But these scriptural texts and many others that refer to "measure" or "number" became the basis for elaborate musical speculations. It was probably Peter Abelard in the twelfth century who first linked musical interpretation with architectural theory when he speculated on the measurements given for Solomon's temple (1 Kings 6) as musical proportions.[57] However in Abbot Suger's commentary on the consecration of Saint Denis, dedicated about 1140, we find the flowering of architectural and musical theories.[58] Suger sees Saint Denis, first of all, as the effort of builders to copy in stone and mortar the perfect architecture of God's heavenly "city" and its "church." "We made good progress with His own cooperation and *in the likeness of things divine* there was established 'to the joy of the whole earth Mount Zion, on the sides of the north, the city of the Great King.'"[59] It is apparent in several passages of the treatise that one of the ways—perhaps the most significant —Suger affirms the "likeness" of the celestial city in its earthly

[55]"The mystical contemplation of the age, no less than its philosophical speculation, seems to be under the spell of an essentially musical experience. Is not the same trend reflected in monumental art? The Gothic sanctuary . . . replaces with the graphic expression of the structural system the painted representation of heaven that adorned the Romanesque apse. . . . Whereas the Romanesque painter could but deceive the senses with the illusion of ultimate reality, the Gothic builders applied the very laws that order heaven and earth. The first Gothic, in the aesthetic, technical, and symbolic aspects of its design, is intimately connected with the metaphysics of 'measure and number and weight.' It seeks to embody the vision that the Platonists of Chartres had first unfolded, no longer content with the mere image of truth but insisting upon the realization of its laws"; von Simson, *Gothic Cathedral*, pp. 38–39.

[56]Alanus, *De planctu naturae* (PL 210, 453); for an illumination of God as architect of the universe from the *Bible Moralisée*, see von Simson, plate 6a. Douay ed. of Bible (New York: Douay Bible House, 1943).

[57]"Abelard is the first medieval writer to suggest that the proportions of the Temple were those of musical consonances and that it was this 'symphonic' perfection that made it an image of heaven"; von Simson, p. 38.

[58]See von Simson, "Suger of St.-Denis," pp. 61–90, and "The New Church," pp. 91–141, in *Gothic Cathedral*.

[59]*De consecratione ecclesiae sancti Dionysii*, trans. Erwin Panofsky as *Abbot Suger on the Abbey Church of St.-Denis and Its Art Treasures* (Princeton: Princeton University Press, 1946), pp. 104–105.

form is in the "musical" relation of nave and transept, vault and column, arch and support—in the interconnection of its many parts. For the "music" of architecture, writes Suger at the opening of his treatise, is a participation in the "eternal reason" that he says is a cosmic symphony:

> The admirable power of one unique and supreme reason equalizes by proper composition the disparity between things human and Divine; and what seems mutually to conflict by inferiority of origin and contrariety of nature is conjoined by the single, delightful concordance of one superior, well-tempered harmony. Those indeed who crave to be glorified by a participation in this supreme [*summae*] and eternal reason often devote their attention to this continual controversy of the similar and the dissimilar.[60]

This is not the prose of a writer trained to imitate the style of Scholastic argumentation, but it reveals nonetheless the form and attitude of *manifestatio* that we have seen in Scholastic writing and in Gothic architecture. Suger's style in this passage and throughout the treatise is no more or less "ornamental" than the architectural design he describes in Saint Denis. With extended subordinations, involuted appositives, sophisticated parallelisms and balances, he creates an elaborate hypotaxis that mirrors the subdivision, interconnection, and division of ribs, joints, and buttresses. Calling eternal reason the summa of *musica*, Suger identifies it not only as the "supreme" but as a "totality" that for him is imitated in the proportions of the earthly edifice. His treatise is yet another example of the summa of harmonic correspondences that Aquinas strives to render in the *concordantia* of an argument, that the masters of the Lindisfarne Gospels try to create in line and figure, and that exegetes from the time of Augustine sought to imitate in distinguishing the levels of meaning in Sacred Scripture.

When Suger turns to describe the audible song of the ceremony for the Upper Choir, he hears nothing less than the anagogic music of the afterlife: the voices of all "singing so concordantly, so close and so joyfully that their song, delightful by its consonance and unified harmony, was deemed a symphony angelic rather than human."[61] What he hears from the choir and sees in stone takes him through an experience of clarifying that seems to echo in the hypotactic style of his treatise. The "music" of Saint Denis described by

[60]Ibid., pp. 82–83.
[61]Ibid., pp. 120–121.

Suger witnesses his own vivid imagination, but also a tradition of ideas that gained initial force in Augustine's adaptations of Platonic and Pythagorean number theory in *De musica*. By comparison with other medieval traditions, this page in the medieval Book of culture is largely unread. It has been considered the development of "science" and "philosophy," when instead it is the product of *manifestatio* seeking expression in many medieval cultural forms. In its archaic and classical roots, medieval musical theory carries with it a predetermination to "musicalize" the gaps and openings in nature in the same way that illuminations "spatialized" thought. Medieval music is a "myth" not because renaissance discoveries, following Aristotle, insisted that the stars are silent, but because it is the development, perhaps the most sophisticated in late Western culture, of a form of thinking as a mimesis of the structure of sacred space.

5

"Hac [musica] etenim coelestia temperantur, mundana sive humana reguntur: haec instrumenta mores instruunt et informant" ("By music divine things are tuned, wordly and human things are governed; instrumental musics instruct and inform morals"). This comment, from John of Salisbury's twelfth-century work the *Polycraticus*, reiterates musical ideas about man, nature, and the supernatural that were traditional among writers in the middle ages, stemming from the formulas of Pythagoras.[62] Since his idea of the tetraktys contains the numerical ratio of 1:2, the basic proportion in the musical octave, writers using "numbers" (*numerus*) as a means for describing their sense of the order in nature and the cosmos were provided with an infinitely extendable vocabulary or grammar of the "music of the spheres."[63] For an imaginative writer like Augustine, the ratio of 1:2 in the musical octave is a schema that is present in man, nature, and God. Each is a speculum of the octave in the other. Augustine's theories, formulated in *De musica*,

[62]*PL* 199, 401.

[63]The importance of numbers in musical theory has been considered in part by von Simson, "Measure and Light," in *Gothic Cathedral*, pp. 21–58; Leo Spitzer, *Classical and Christian Ideas of World Harmony*, ed. A. G. Hatcher (Baltimore: Johns Hopkins University Press, 1963); Nan Cooke Carpenter, *Music in the Medieval and Renaissance Universities* (Norman: University of Oklahoma Press, 1958); see also the unpublished Ph.D. dissertation by David S. Chamberlain, "Music in Chaucer: His Knowledge and Use of Medieval Ideas about Music" (Princeton University, 1966).

were repeated throughout the middle ages. Both he and Boethius, whose *De musica* was also fundamental to medieval musical thought, were summed up comprehensively by Jacobus of Liège in his fourteenth-century work the *Speculum musicae*.[64] As described by Jacobus, audible music (*instrumentalis musica*) is composed of numerical proportions that are "heard" in the "world music" (*musica mundana*) or the "relation," "motion," and "position" of the celestial bodies, the "various relation" of the four elements (earth, water, air, fire), and the "diversity of times" in the changings from day to night, in months, years, and seasons.[65] The *concordia* of the heavenly rotations, the even proportion of nature's four elements, and the orderliness of diurnal and seasonal succession constituted a compelling example of the harmony in the physical universe and the proof of the scriptural text, "Sed omnia in mensura, et numero, et pondere disposuisti" ("Thou hast ordered all things in measure, and number, and weight"; Wisd. of Sol. 11.21).[66] *Mundana musica* was an excellent harmony for man to imitate, because it was the speculum of his own composition or "human music" (*humana musica*).[67]

That music is the harmonious "consonance" (*consonantia*) of the octave or ratio of the union of body and soul.[68] Man is composed of elements that form a musical "joining together" (*coaptatio*) accord-

---

[64]Augustine, *De musica* (PL 32, 1081–1194); Boethius, *De musica* (PL 63, 1167–1300); Jacobus of Liège, *Speculum musicae*, ed. Roger Bragard, vol. 3, *Corpus scriptorum de musica* (Rome, 1955). Important also are: Chalcidius, *Platonis Timaeus interprete Chalcidio cum eiusdem commentario*, ed. I. Wrobel (Leipzig; Teubner, 1876); Macrobius, *Commentarius in somnium Scripionis*, ed. Franciscus Eyssenhardt (Leipzig: Teubner, 1868); Martianus Capella, *De nuptiis Philologiae et Mercurii*, ed. Franciscus Eyssenhardt (Leipzig: Teubner, 1866).

[65]"Musica igitur mundana principaliter in tribus consistit; primo, in comparatione corporum coelestium, quoad motum, naturam et situm; secundo, in varia comparatione elementorum, quoad qualitates et situm eorum; tertio, in diversitate temporum, in diebus, in vicissitudinibus noctis et diei, in mensibus, in lunae crementis, in annis et eius partibus sibi succedentibus, ut hieme, vere, aestate et autumno"; *Spec. mus.* 1.13.49. The Boethian definition of world music is in *De musica* 2 (PL 63, 1171–1172).

[66]*Biblia iuxta vulgatam Clementinam nova editio* (Madrid, 1965).

[67]Like *instrumentalis* and *mundana musica*, *humana musica* was also named by Boethius (PL 63, 1171); all three were standard in medieval tradition.

[68]*De musica* 2 (PL 63, 1172): "Humanam vero musicam, quisquis in sese ipsum descendit, intelligit. Quid est enim quod illam incorpoream rationis vivacitatem corpori misceat, nisi unam consonantiam efficiens, temperatio? Quid est autem aliud quod ipsius inter se partes animae conjungat, quae . . . ex rationabili irrationabilique conjuncta est? Quid vero quod corporis elementa permisceat, aut partes sibimet rata coaptatione contineat?" For similar explanations, see Jacobus, *Spec. mus.* 1.14.50–53.

ing to the same "union" and "harmonic modulation" as that which moves the heavenly bodies.[69] Few medieval writers express as well as Alanus de Insulis the musical *concordia* uniting man and the universe. In the *De planctu naturae,* Lady Nature explains that just as the *discordia* or *dissonans* of four elements "unites" (*conciliat*) creating a *concordia* in the world, so also do the *inaequal* and *divisa* elements of the human body "join together" (*compaginat*) forming *musica* in man. The diction and syntax of Nature's comment are themselves echoes of the sense that man, like nature, is an oxymoronic harmony of opposites.

> Sicut enim quatuor elementorum concors discordia, unica pluralitas, consonantia dissonans, consensus dissentiens, mundialis regiae structuras conciliat, sic quatuor complexionum compar disparitas, inaequalis aequalitas, deformis conformitas, divisa identitas, aedificium corporis humani compaginat.

> [For just as the concordant discord, singular plurality, consonant dissonance, discordant accordance of the four elements unite into one whole the structures of the worldly kingdom, so also do the similar dissimilarity, unequal equality, deformed conformity, divided identity of the four humors join together the edifice of the human body.][70]

The literal illogic is defied by the rhetorical logic of the oxymorons that assume a level of reference to a *homologous* structure in which four parts of one entity correspond to four parts of another, and the elements of "concord" and "singularity" in nature are substituted by opposition with "equality" and "identity" in man. By multiplying its structures of similitude, its schemata for proportion, medieval musical thought does not look to nature and man to test its theory, but makes natural phenomena the example of that theory. This procedure is the logic of homology in which "contents are indissociable from form" and the universe is made up of meanings. Within the intellectual requirements of a system that expects to see congruity for its own sake, the speculum of nature reflected correspondences that in every way were perceived not as hypothetical, but as the essential bonds of things.

The homologue par excellence in medieval musical thought

---

[69] "Insuper, si proportio sive coaptatio animae humanae ad corpus suum, quod movet, ut movens coniunctum, quaedam dicitur harmonica modulatio, quare non poterit coaptatio illa vel proportio, quae est inter motores illos separatos ad orbes, quos movent, harmonica vocari modulatio?" *Spec. mus.* 1.11.38; and see 1.14.50.

[70] Alanus, *PL* 210, 443.

is *divina musica*, not so named until the fourteenth century, but clearly central in medieval tradition from the time of Augustine, who speaks of the *numeri aeterni* of divine nature. John of Salisbury's comment that "divine things" are "tuned" by music relies upon medieval opinion that the Trinity is musical because it is a perfect numerical proportion of one in three and three in one, which is homologous with numerical elements in instrumental music — 1:3, 1:2.[71] But the "divine things" John mentions refer to an idea even closer to the heart of Christianity, the Redemption. Contemplating the harmony of love set in motion in the universe by Christ, Augustine says in *De trinitate* that the "single" death of Christ accords with man's "double" death of the body and of the soul in sin. The ratio of the single to the double, or one to two (1:2), corresponds in perfect homology to the musical ratio of the octave. Man's relation to Christ is a musical "harmony, agreement, concord, or consonance" ("congruentia, sive convenientia, vel concinentia, vel consonantia").[72] Once established, the homology allows the inclusion of an entire field of terms that generate each other from the common semantic denominator, *con-*. The syllable functions as a paradigmatic part from which the semantic field of terms is totalized and limited only by the writer's versatility. For example, after the "new song," which occurs frequently in Scripture in such passages as *Cantate Domino canticum novum* (Ps. 95.1), is identified as the "New Man" (Christ) and the "New Song of Charity," then music becomes the homologue of moral life and *caritas* a "silent music of the heart."[73] Paul's exhortations to sing "spiritual hymns and canticles . . . in your hearts to the Lord" (Eph. 5.18–19) and to imitate him by singing in spirit and mind ("Psallam . . . spiritu, psallam et mente," 1 Cor. 14.15) were adjurations not to avoid loud music, but to love God in charity and, according to Wolbero of Cologne, to have "perfect knowledge" and "greatest dignity."[74]

---

[71]Augustine: "De numeris spiritualibus et aeternis" (*PL* 32, 1181–1183); Jacobus: "De quibus sit musica coelestis vel divina et quare sic vocetur"; *Spec. mus.* 1.12.40.

[72]*De trinitate* 4.2.4 (*PL* 42, 889).

[73]On *canticum novum*, for example, see: Augustine, *Sermones*, no. 10 on Psalm 144 (*PL* 46, 843); Manegold of Lautenbach, *PL* 93, 646; pseudo-Remi of Auxerre, *PL* 131, 306; Rupert of Deutz, *PL* 169, 1091–1092; Peter Lombard, *PL* 191, 1287; Wolbero of Cologne, *PL* 195, 1271–1278.

[74]"Porro qui vult perfectam habere canendi scientiam, et summam ipsius nosse dignitatem, trium istorum oportet semper habere facultatem. Quam Apostolus se nosse et habere ostendens: *Psallam*, inquit, *spiritu, psallam et mente* [1 Cor. 14.15].

The intellectual requirements of finding congruities were easily supplied in the case of the "new song," since parallels were as predictable as the semantic oppositions in *concordia* and *discordia*. As reading *in bono* created interpretation *in malo*, the practice of substituting opposite homologous parts produced from the "new song" of *caritas* the "old song" of *cupiditas*. Although the *vetus canticum* or "old song" never occurs in Scripture, it was a medieval commonplace, as we find in the commentary of the thirteenth-century exegete Hugh of St. Cher. He says that to "sing" the *canticum novum* is to "love" eternity and become new in spirit and mind with charity, whereas he who sings the old song loves the "earth" and follows the "old animosity." Each element in the homologue of the new song produces its binary opposite in a complex structural pattern.

> Qui vult hoc novum canticum cantare diligat aeterna, et fiat novus spiritus mentis suae. Hoc enim canticum est de aeternis. Nam vetus homo canticum cantat de terrenis. Novum Canticum est de pacis, et charitatis, et divinae laudis, quod cantat novus homo de spiritualibus. Quisquis enim sequitur [veterem] animositatem, non novam charitatem, novum Canticum non cantat.

> [He who wants to sing the new song loves eternity, and becomes new in the spirit of his mind. For that is the song of eternity. But the old man sings the song of the earth. The new song is of peace, and charity, and divine praise, which the new man sings concerning spiritual things. Whoever follows the old animosity, not the new charity, does not sing the new song.][75]

With a similarity between divine nature and musical concord established, separate books of Sacred Scripture become "songs," God's Word is a "melody," indeed all of Scripture is "the most excellent modulation and the most perfect music." The Bible manifests "all proportion, all concord, all consonance, all melody."[76]

The repetition of *omnis* and the *con-* prefix is not redundant but is essential to the function of a rhetoric that creates from paradigmatic parts an entire classification of moral life. The concord of the octave, like the triangular unit of the pyramid, totalizes a structure

---

Nam spiritu psallere est et verba spiritualia memoriter proferre, quod est ore cantare; et ad opera spiritu concepta procedere, quod est opere cantare; mente psallere est vitalem verborum sensum mente percipere, quod est corde cantare" (*PL* 195, 1272).

[75]Hugh on Ps. 149.1, in *Opera omnia*, 8 vols. (Venice, 1732), 2.356ᵛA; he follows Augustine almost verbatim on the same Psalm; *Enarrationes in psalmos* (*PL* 46, 843).

[76]Jacobus, *Spec. mus.* 1.12.43.

that has the potential of investing all things with meaning. Acutely aware of that structure, Isidore of Seville recommended the study of music in every curriculum, and many followed him, frequently quoting his advice:

> Itaque sine musica nulla disciplina potest esse perfecta, nihil enim est sine illa. Nam et ipse mundus quadam harmonia sonorum fertur esse compositus, et coelum ipsum sub harmoniae modulatione revolvitur . . . musica extendit se ad omnia.

> [Indeed without music no discipline can be perfect; nothing exists without it. For the world itself is said to be composed by a certain harmony of sounds and heaven revolves in harmonic modulation . . . music extends to all things.][77]

Extending music to "all things," Aelred of Rievaulx identifies charity as "world music" pervading all the elements of the physical universe by joining high to low and hot to cold with the "peace of concord."[78] As Pythagoras "played" on his monochord the music of the spheres, medieval men were instructed to "imitate" the *mundana* and *divina musica* in their moral lives and thereby become, like Christ, the summa of *musica* in the cosmic symphony, the microcosm of macrocosmic music. In the words of Jacobus, *humana* is the music of the "minor world of man" ("*humana autem de minore est mundo, id est de homine*"), while *mundana* is the music of the "major world" ("*maiore mundo*") of the universe. Those who understand and interpret Sacred Scripture or nature can possess *concordia* and *consonantia*, for they are the "best musicians" (*optimi musici*).[79] Francis of Assisi wanted his brethren to be "minstrels of the Lord" (*ioculatores Domini*), a designation probably modeled on the idea of Christ as the "new leader of the chorus" (*novus praecentor*) and the "greatest" or "total of all musicians" (*summus musicus*).[80]

The totalizing pattern of the structure of musical thought "ex-

---

[77]*Etymologiarum*, "De musica" (*PL* 82, 163); Jacobus, commenting on Isidore, *Spec. mus.* 1.11.38.

[78]Charity is "omnia continentem, omnia ambientem, omnia penetratem, ima superis conjungentem, contraria contrarii, frigida calidis, siccis humida, lenibus aspera, duris mollia, concordi quadam pace foederantem"; *Speculum charitatis* 1:21 (*PL* 195, 524). *Summa de arte praedictoria* (*PL* 210, 154).

[79]*Spec. mus.* 1.10.36; 1.13.50; 1.12.43.

[80]Cited by E. K. Chambers "Some Aspects of Medieval Lyric," in *Early English Lyrics*, ed. E. K. Chambers and F. Sidgwick (New York: Barnes and Noble, 1967), p. 288; Wolbero of Cologne, *PL* 195, 1273; Christ as *summus musicus* is cited by the musicologist Joannes Tinctoris; see Chamberlain's discussion, "Music in Chaucer," pp. 355–356.

tends to all things" irrespective of illogical identities in essential content, for there are no "illogical" similarities in homologous relationships. "What are we," asks Rupert of Deutz, "if not great musicians of God, his instruments? With harps and stringed instruments, which are truly our hearts and bodies, we are commanded to praise the Lord."[81] Because made of dried flesh stretched across wood, instruments such as the tympanum, psaltery, and cithara are glossed as Christ's body stretched across the wood of the cross. Therefore the instrument whose "flesh" must be "beaten" (*affligere*) to sound music is man when in moral acts he denies his own flesh and becomes an "organ" sounding the moral virtue of *mortificatio* and *crucifixio carnis*.[82] Medieval interpreters found no difficulty in combining the instrument and the moral idea because they were both extrapolations from the same schema, flesh upon wood. It may even be said that the medieval expansion of schemata for their own sake could not be resisted when it came to such accommodating examples as musical imagery. What is more, such an image as cithara does not "substitute" for the moral idea of self-denial (*crucifixio carnis*) but identifies it. Musical theory affirms the logic of relationships in the same manner as a structure of thought that classifies a person as a member of a certain clan because his head is shaved according to the homologous pattern for bear or beaver.[83] Like the signs in myth, the terms in medieval musical theory meet the requirements of classifying before they satisfy the demands of proof for identity.

As these examples illustrate, medieval writers in one sense did not invent theories of number and music. Students of proportion like Pythagoras, as Geoffrey Chaucer says, are "fynders" of musical harmony already "in" things.[84] The medieval emphasis on the *auctor* as the spokesman or vehicle of a tradition, not the creator of it, is illustrated throughout the history of medieval ideas about music. The absence of authorial invention protects the tradition from internal contradiction and guarantees its continuity, in the same way as the anonymity of myth in tribal cultures, as Lévi-Strauss has ob-

---

[81]*In Evangelium S. Joannis commentaria* (PL 169, 121).

[82]Following Augustine, Hugh of St. Cher on Ps. 149.3: "In tympano corium extenditur, in psalterio chordae extenduntur, in utroque organo caro crucifigitur" (*Opera omnia* 2.356^{V}B); see also Wolbero of Cologne, *PL* 195, 1245–1246; Hugh of St. Victor, *PL* 177, 626–627; Rabanus Maurus, *PL* 111, 499; *Allegoriae in sacram scripturam, PL* 112, 1067.

[83]See Lévi-Strauss, *Savage Mind*, pp. 170–172.

[84]*Book of the Duchess* (line 1168), in *The Works of Geoffrey Chaucer*, ed. F. N. Robinson, 2d ed. (Boston: Houghton Mifflin, 1957), p. 278.

served, reflects its authority. To demonstrate this point he compares myth to music, but he knows not how close he is to the massive evidence from the medieval mythology of music that supports his claim. "Music and mythology bring man face to face with potential objects of which only the shadows are actualized. . . . Myths are anonymous: from the moment they are seen as myths, and whatever their real origins, they exist only as elements embodied in a tradition. When the myth is repeated, the individual listeners are receiving a message that, properly speaking, is coming from nowhere; this is why it is credited with a supernatural origin."[85] The growth of medieval theory of music seemed as divine in origin and as natural to the real order of things as the return of day after night, the binding of hot and cold, dry and moist, heavy and light. These "musical" oppositions, predating Boethius and extending beyond Chaucer, were regarded as maintained by the "nombres proportionables" projected from a divine schema—the "sovereyn ensaumpler"—in the words of Chaucer's translation of the Timaean meter in the *Consolation of Philosophy*. The "forme of the sovereyn good" determined the form of things "in this worlde here," as Chaucer says elsewhere, and was the "caus of armonie" holding the sea in its bounds, the seasons in their order, and drawing the heart of man unto the sacred "welle of music."[86]

Medieval musical ideas proliferated, to a certain extent, because of what appears to be a "natural" congruity between, for example, the apparent regularity of celestial rotations and "world order" or the concord of voices singing in chorus, *in choro,* the antiphons and responses of the divine service and the moral music of brotherhood "sung" in the heart, *in corde,* manifesting *caritas.*[87] When the form is perceived to be motivated by order, as is obvious in the derivation of meaning from the paradigmatic progression—*in choro, in corde, in caritate*—the continuity of musical ideas is uninterrupted and the mythology is maintained. If the form cannot find its homology in a schema for proportion, it will be found in disproportion. For the anticipation that form is naturally motivated is so

---

[85]Claude Lévi-Strauss, "Overture," in *The Raw and the Cooked: Introduction to a Science of Mythology,* trans. John and Doreen Weightman (New York: Harper & Row, 1969), 1:18.

[86]*Boece* 3.m.9 (p. 350); *Parliament of Fowls,* lines 57–63 (p. 311), in Robinson.

[87]Rabanus Maurus: "Alii chorum dicerunt a concordia, quae in charitate consistit"; *De universo* (PL 111, 128). The *Interlinear Gloss* identifies singing *in choro* with "unitate charitatis" and "concordia morum"; *Bibliorum sacrorum cum glossa ordinaria,* 3.1587–1588; Amalair Metensis: "Si in choro cantamus, corde cantamus" (PL 105, 1105).

constituted in myth, as Barthes has argued, that "what the form can always give one to read is disorder itself: it can give a signification to the absurd, make the absurd itself a myth."[88] That medieval traditions mythologized disorder is illustrated by the elaborate associations of chaos and noise with sin. As paradigmatic similarities produce a theory of *concordia,* they also are extended by opposition to create theories of *discordia.* Meaning is derived through a total classification in which discord is not the absence of signification, a noise in the cosmic symphony, but rather a meaningful aspect of it and even given a place in the "semantic" field—the underworld.

"Caritas laudat Dominum, discordia blasphemat Dominum," writes Augustine in his usual imaginative manner of seeing the potentialities in any suggestive detail. Wolbero of Cologne explains that in contrast to the new song authored by Christ, the "vetus homo Adam" made the old song when he rebelled against God: "he cried out loudly [*reclamavit*] and vociferated [*vociferatus*] against the piety and justice of his Maker in pride, disobedience, and excuse of his sin." His is "the song of tearful tragedy," while Christ's is "the song of peace and of joy."[89] Gabriel, in announcing Christ's coming, proclaimed a *concordia* harmonizing man and God, a belief recalled in the iconography of music depicted frequently in paintings of the Annunciation; but sin "demusicalizes" that harmony by creating discord—*discordabat.*[90] According to the *Allegoriae in sacram scripturam,* "noise" (*clamor*) is the "cupidity of the false" who make a "tumult unto the ears of God," for "clamor [est] violenta tenatio diaboli."[91] The spatializing of the concept of noise to the underworld needs no further illustration than the "wailing," "shrill shrieks," and "fierce yells" of the damned in Dante's *Inferno.* Noteworthy also is the Chester *Harrowing of Hell* in which the infernal scene is dramatized by the explicit stage direction, "*clamor vel sonitus materalis magnus,*" perhaps rendered on stage by banging large scraps of iron.[92] Chaucer, too, must have recognized these tropol-

[88]Barthes, "Myth Today," p. 126.

[89]Augustine, *Enarrationes in psalmos* (PL 37, 1950); Wolbero of Cologne, PL 195, 1273.

[90]Absalon of Sprinkersbach, "In Annuntiatione Beatae Mariae," *Sermones* (PL 211, 131); see also Charles de Tolnay, "The Music of the Universe," *Journal of the Walters Art Gallery* 6 (1943):82–104.

[91]PL 112, 881; see Alanus, *Distinctiones,* s.v. "clamor" (PL 210, 743).

[92]See, e.g., *Inferno* 3.22–30; *La divina commedia,* ed. Natalino Sapegno, 3 vols. (Firenze: Nuova Italia, 1955–1957), 1:30; Joseph Q. Adams, ed., *Chief Pre-Shakespearean Dramas* (Cambridge: Cambridge University Press, 1924), p. 189.

Plate 7. David with beast musicians. Psalter (ca. 1300). Austrian National Library. MS 1898, fol. 66ᵛ.

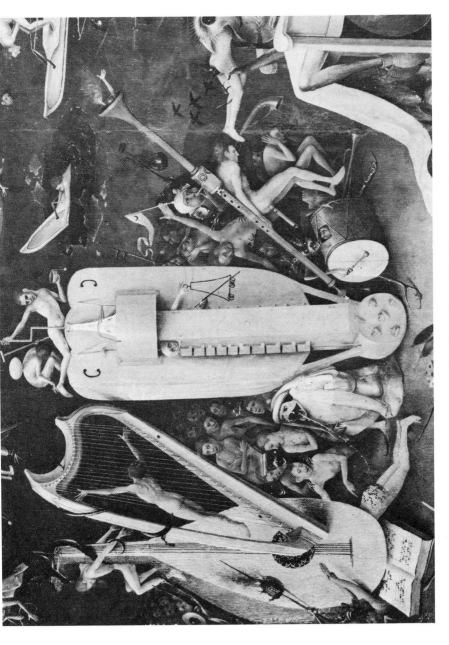

Plate 8. Harp (detail). **Right wing triptych.** *Garden of Earthly Delights.* Hieronymus Bosch (fifteenth century). The Prado Museum.

ogies of noise, for they inform the Parson's remark that Christ died "to make concord," but sinners "maken discord amonges folk" and are "likned to the devel that ever is aboute to maken discord."[93]

6

The imagery of noise in these examples does not "demythologize" the medieval tradition of music, since discordant oppositions are included within the total classification and given a fixed place in the underworld. Yet other uses of musical signs do oppose tradition, not with the noise of sin, but rather with what appears to be the *arbitrary* signification of musical imagery. For example, in manuscript illuminations depicting David playing the psalterium and singing the Psalms in the initial, musical instruments played by beasts may often be found in marginal drawings to illustrate *in malo* the bestial discord of greed and lust that is compassed by the total *musica* of praise to the Creator.[94] But the same function of signs of discord does not obtain, for instance, in Bosch's *Garden of Earthly Delights*: bestial musicians read a musical score printed on the posterior of a naked human figure who is pinned under instruments many times his size; a serpentine dragon coils around the fingerboard of a lute whose sound box is filled with briars; in the strings of a harp a naked figure is transfixed with arms outstretched and feet together.[95] Like other sections of the painting, the musical scene has provoked various conflicting interpretations. One might seek some resolution by claiming that the figure suspended in the strings of the harp suggests the medieval notion associated with gut instruments—*crucifixio carnis*. But such a reading seems arbitrary, since the scene hardly recommends for our approval the values of the *musica* of self-denial; nor is it characterized by a tone of warning for the failure to make such moral music. What we have instead is the old medieval schema of flesh in relation to wood suspended from, or in arbitrary association with, its signified meaning of *humana musica*. The metaphorical "script" of *musica* imagined by Augustine and later writers never before had such literal representation as in the notes inscribed on the naked figure. Whereas

[93]*Parson's Tale*, lines 642–643 (p. 248), in Robinson; Robinson's reference to Eph. 2.14 is questionable.

[94]See plate 7. And cf. Lilian Randall, *Images in the Margins of Gothic Manuscripts* (Berkeley: University of California Press, 1966), sections 106–108.

[95]See plate 8 and Jacques Combe, *Jérôme Bosch* (Paris: P. Tisné, 1946).

medieval musical signs were understood to be naturally present in physical things, the signs of music represented by Bosch cut that natural bond: arbitrariness is deliberate *in the form*. We might think that Bosch has mythologized chaos, but his style does not seize disorder in the same way that a motivated form gives us discord to read as myth. Rather, Bosch's musical signs provide an example of what Barthes explains as form "growing less and less motivated." It illustrates "the worn out state of myth," which "can be recognized by the arbitrariness of its signification."[96] The signs of music in Bosch, which may seem baffling and inscrutable because of their arbitrariness, on the contrary, gain their force from this very characteristic: the form is unmotivated and indicates a movement away from the long medieval traditions of the mythology of music and the sacralization of space.

While Bosch is not representative of the ways traditions were used in the middle ages, his examples nonetheless illustrate the arbitrariness of signification that was potential in medieval treatments of spatial form. Bosch maximizes that potential insofar as his style concentrates attention on the separateness of the human figure from the strings of the harp in which it is suspended. But the recognition of arbitrariness is not limited to the means Bosch employed. Other ways it may appear are suggested by the warnings against extremity observed from time to time in various medieval disciplines. For example, Hugh of St. Victor cautioned against the extravagant reading of Scripture in his demand for a return to more rigorous study of the *sensus literalis*; Bernard Sylvester demonstrates in the *Cosmographia* a qualification of excessive speculation by employing the beginnings of an empirical interest in cosmology; Geoffrey of Vinsauf in the *Poetria nova* resists deviations from generic categories by advising a respect for earlier divisions of literary style, such as high, middle, and low. But by and large, the conditions of arbitrariness in medieval traditions are suppressed by the more encompassing need to fill in and close up incomplete form. Be it an opening in a painted manuscript, the space between stars, or a gap in history, the mythological impulse is driven to affirm oneness and inseparability in its "protest against the idea that anything can be meaningless."[97] When the year 1000 A.D. passed without witnessing the Apocalypse expected to occur

[96]Barthes, "Myth Today," p. 127; cf. Lévi-Strauss, *Savage Mind*, p. 156.
[97]Lévi-Strauss, *Savage Mind*, p. 22.

at the end of the millennium, those who were disappointed simply accepted a future date.[98] What began as an allegorization of John's Book of Apocalypse was taken as a fact of documentary history in the same way that Clement of Alexandria's rhetorical charge against the pagan gods occasioned Isidore and others to locate them in specific times and places.[99] If the details are in conflict, no contradiction prevails, for ultimately time and place are not important. Any date for the arrival of Antichrist will do. More important is the compelling necessity to validate in the natural order the preexistent formulas about the past and the cosmos. Whatever was unknown and unbounded in the challenge "You know not the day nor the hour" (Matt. 25.13) became the provocation to look up the exact day and time in the complete "text" of history.

Various medieval cultural forms might be studied for the extent to which they hold on to the mythological past, like the examples I have offered here; but since the semiology of spatial forms in the middle ages assumes to some degree medieval theories of the *linguistic* sign, it will be appropriate to turn next to the grammatical and hermeneutic traditions in which those theories developed. Several questions arise from this consideration; for instance, do medieval definitions of the linguistic sign also look back, as do the practical extensions of the sign in spatial forms, to mythologizing structures? If so, how might this hold on the past be considered in view of the fact that medieval theories of the sign emerge from the effort to *depart* from the myths of precedent societies? In the next chapter, I will approach these questions with respect to the broader issue they imply: the possibility for language theory to initiate cultural change during the middle ages of Western tradition.

[98]See Norman Cohn, *The Pursuit of the Millennium* (Fairlawn, N.J.: Essential Books, 1957).

[99]A convenient review of this Euhemerist tradition is available in Jean Seznec's *The Survival of the Pagan Gods*, trans. B. F. Sessions (1953; reprint, New York: Harper & Row, 1961), pp. 12 ff.

[3]

The Language of Mythology:

On Medieval Grammar

and Hermeneutics

> The Divine Page, in its literal sense, contains many things which
> seem both to be opposed to each other and, sometimes, to impart
> something which smacks of the absurd or the impossible. But the
> spiritual meaning admits no opposition; in it, many things can be
> different from one another, but none can be opposed.
>
> Hugh of St. Victor, *Didascalicon*

1

If mythology in the middle ages is understood according to the
argument set forth so far, as a specific structure of thought rather
than simply an inherited collection of legends and characters, then
the origin and growth of medieval spatial forms appear in a new
light: the supposed displacement of pagan by Christian ideology
was not as clear-cut as those forms might suggest, and thus the hold
on the past was quite a bit tighter than medieval opinion would
have it. Although the old pagan deities were renamed or reformu-
lated for new purposes, they still figured prominently in patterns
of thought that were fixed and centered, and those structures were
not so easily called into question. Furthermore, they were an integral part of many traditions in the middle ages—from the classification of trees, animals, and stars in the study of nature to the
Gothic style in architecture, manuscript painting, and philosophical argumentation. The "mythology" of these forms consists in
their encyclopedic and totalizing structure, which has roots not in
the intellectual processes that developed to explain them—such as

the summae of Scholasticism—but in the presence of meaning in spatial form. This conception of mythology is cutomarily illustrated in the ancient world out of which Christianity emerged and the archaic societies it encountered during its movement through medieval Europe and Britain, but it is no less operative in the so-called Book of cultural forms in the middle ages. To the extent that this Text is composed of the replication of familiar schemata, such as the firm outlines dominating Romanesque and Gothic painting or the sacralization of stone and volume in church architecture, the semiology of spatial patterns is characterized by the repetition and emphasis of earlier forms, rather than by deviation from them, until the elaboration of past models gives place—by the end of the fourteenth century—to an interest in sheer ornamentation and cleverness for their own sakes (as may be noticed, for instance, in the work of Bosch).

The development of spatial forms of the sign in medieval tradition invites a certain comparison and contrast with the linguistic sign, in both its spoken and its written manifestations. If the semiology of space is characterized by elaboration and repetition over the centuries, we are led to inquire about the fate of the linguistic sign as it was treated in several medieval disciplines of learning by writers ranging from Augustine, Donatus, and Priscian in the fourth and fifth centuries to Aquinas and the speculative grammarians, or *modistae*, after the twelfth. Treatments of this subject, whether they are products of *grammatica* in the trivium or the hermeneutics of Scripture in the quadrivium, are controlled in some ways by the same repetition of *auctoritates* that determines the growth of spatial forms. However, the comparison is far from simple, not only because we cannot draw an easy equivalence between spatial and written or spoken signs, but also because medieval reflections on the linguistic sign undergo many complicated and rich variations.[1]

---

[1]For example, see: Richard W. Hunt, "Studies on Priscian in the Eleventh and Twelfth Centuries," *Medieval and Renaissance Studies* 1 (1941):194–231, reprinted with other essays as *The History of Grammar in the Middle Ages: Collected Papers*, ed. Geoffrey L. Bursill-Hall (Amsterdam: J. Benjamins, 1980); Robert H. Robins, *Ancient and Medieval Grammatical Theory in Europe* (London: Bell, 1951); Jan Pinborg, *Die Entwicklung der Sprachtheorie im Mittelalter* (Copenhagen: Frost-Hansen, 1967); Marcia L. Colish, *The Mirror of Language: A Study in the Medieval Theory of Knowledge* (New Haven: Yale University Press, 1968); Aldo D. Scaglione, *Ars Grammatica: A Bibliographic Survey* (The Hague: Mouton, 1970); Geoffrey L. Bursill-Hall, *Speculative Grammars of the Middle Ages* (The Hague: Mouton, 1971); James J. Murphy, *Rhetoric in the Middle Ages: A History of Rhetorical Theory from Saint Augustine to the Renaissance* (Berkeley and Los Angeles: University of California Press, 1974); Bernard Cer-

Whereas spatial forms are organized by an effort to contain and make present their objects of signification, some approaches to the linguistic sign appear to lead in a different direction when language is explained as a conventional, rather than a natural, representation of meaning and when the word is studied for its various "ways of signifying." The spatial sign in the middle ages is the product of the mythology of static, determinate structure, of the totalizing containment that subsumed cultural forms into a Book. Its influence, as suggested heretofore, spread well beyond visual materials, governing even the conception of writing in Scripture and the Book of nature. But it is now relevant to look in finer detail at the structure of medieval mythologizing in relation to the signs of writing and speaking. Does the linguistic sign follow a path similar to its spatial counterpart and contribute to the same mythology? A response to this question may be undertaken by considering whether the study of signs, grammar, and language became at certain points in the middle ages the ground for new departures and changes in the modes of signification.

2

We do not look far in medieval writings about verbal signs without noting the frequent reference to them as natural entities—the word as "seed," the pen as "tongue."[2] Such descriptions appear mostly commonly in comments on the hermeneutics of Scripture, and if they constitute a prevailing conception about the language of God, they exist in contrast to the understanding that linguistic meaning, whether natural or not, is never free from problems of inconsistency and misunderstanding. No one asserted this dilemma about the meaning of words more sharply than Martianus Capella. In the *Marriage of Mercury and Philology*, Martianus provides the personified figure of grammar with a knife, a stick, and a box of medicines. Each has its function, which was not forgotten in the subsequent history of grammatical studies, as is obvious in John of Salisbury's recollection, in the *Metalogicon*, of Martianus's image:

---

quiglini, *La Parole médiévale: Discours, syntaxe, texte* (Paris: Minuit, 1981); R. Howard Bloch, *Etymologies and Genealogies: A Literary Anthropology of the French Middle Ages* (Chicago: University of Chicago Press, 1983); Brian Stock, *The Implications of Literacy: Written Language and Models of Interpretation in the Eleventh and Twelfth Centuries* (Princeton: Princeton University Press, 1983).

[2] Examples are cited above, chapter 1, section 1.

Plate 9. Grammar with two children. Wooden statue. Souabe (ca. 1330). Bavarian National Museum, Munich.

grammar employs the knife, says John, to cut away linguistic errors and to purify the speech of the young; she uses the rod to suppress those who "babble in barbarisms and solecisms"; but then "with the ointment of . . . propriety and utility," she eases the pain of her patients.[3]

In her function as "nurse" of language, grammar serves Martianus, John, and other medieval commentators on the trivium as a system for controlling meaning and establishing the study of linguistics as fundamentally subservient to semantics. "If, therefore, grammar is so useful," John continues, "and the key to everything written, as well as the mother and arbiter of speech, who will [try to] exclude it from the threshold of philosophy?[4] The rhetorical question insists on the basic medieval belief that *grammatica* is the first of the seven liberal arts and absolutely indispensable for ascending the hierarchy of learning through the quadrivium, especially to the higher reaches of ethics and theology. While John's battle in the *Metalogicon* is directed immediately against detractors of the trivium, which had come under increasing attack in his time at Paris and Chartres, his enemy is not local: John writes against a general ignorance of systematic grammar. In fact, the nom de plume of his fictional adversary—one "Cornificius"—is apparently taken from Donatus's fifth-century *Vita Vergilii*, in which Cornificius is the name given to Virgil's detractor. John clearly faced the same problem as Donatus and other early medieval grammarians: linguistic signification is, to a certain extent, uncontrollable, an errant child who must be curtailed by the parental rod, or a sick body in need of grammar's medicine.

When medieval writers considered the question of signification, if they did not think of Martianus's rod, they surely had access to another story about language that was quite a bit more influential because of its scriptural authority, the account in Genesis 11 of the dissemination of languages after the destruction of Babel. Relating how God decides to "confound" (*confundamus*; Gen. 11.7) the original "one tongue" (*unum labium*; Gen. 11.5) leaving a state of linguistic chaos throughout the earth ("confusus est labium universae terrae"; Gen. 11.9), the story suggested to medieval readers the

---

[3]Martianus Capella, *De nuptiis Philologiae et Mercurii*, ed. F. Eyssenhardt (Leipzig: Teubner, 1866), 3:223. John of Salisbury, *Metalogicus* (*PL* 199, 851–852); trans. Daniel D. McGarry as *The Metalogicon of John of Salisbury* (Berkeley: University of California Press, 1955), p. 61. Also see plate 9 for an example of the popular representation of *grammatica* as "mother."
[4]*Metalogicon*, pp. 61–62.

devastating loss, like the fall of man, from the presence of God's words and thoughts—the time when meaning had no mediation and intention was undifferentiated.[5] "Why," asks John of Salisbury of the detractors of grammar, "do you not at least know Hebrew, which, as we are told, mother nature gave to our first parents and preserved for mankind until human unity [*unitatem*] was rent by impiety, and the pride which presumed to mount to heaven by physical strength and the construction of a tower, rather than by virtue, was leveled in a babbling chaos of tongues [*confusione linguarum*]?" The original language, he continues, "is more natural than the others, having been, so to speak, taught by nature herself [*natura docente loquuntur*]."[6] But in the postlapsarian world, the state of speaking and writing after Babel, only a nostalgia for an originary oneness of natural meaning survives, as readers and speakers, like the Hebrews themselves, wander in the exile of many disparate tongues. Among the medieval seven liberal arts, *grammatica* was the first bulwark against further confusion and dissemination, and the continuing appeal to the works of Priscian and Donatus, though devoted to classical Latin, provided the means for shoring up meaning against the ruin of misreading.

The unrivaled popularity of the *Ars grammatica* and the *Institutiones grammaticae* as teaching tools of grammar throughout the early middle ages (Priscian's treatise survives in over one thousand manuscripts) constitutes a paradox of linguistic history, since medieval Latin could not be pressed without strain against the matrix of classical Latin.[7] It is no surprise at all to encounter objections, such as the remark of Smaragdus of St. Michel (ninth century): "I disagree with Donatus because I hold the authority of the Scriptures to be greater."[8] The question of which has priority, classical or vulgar Latin, was a medieval commonplace, but it explains the undeveloped theory of *grammatica* less than it indicates the firm hold of the Babel story on the medieval consciousness. If an ideal state of language is assumed—as Hebrew was imagined to represent the

[5]*Biblia iuxta vulgatam Clementinam nova editio* (Madrid: Biblioteca de Autores Cristianos, 1965).

[6]*Metalogicon*, p. 28. On the Babel story, see A. Borst, *Der Turmbau von Babel*, 6 vols. (Stuttgart: Anton Hiersemann, 1957), and Bloch, *Etymologies and Genealogies*, pp. 35 ff.

[7]Margaret T. Gibson, "Priscian, 'Institutiones Grammaticae': A Handlist of Manuscripts," *Scriptorium* 26 (1972):105–124.

[8]Smaragdus of St. Michel, cited by Robins, *Ancient and Medieval Grammatical Theory*, p. 71. See also *Histoire literaire de la France*, by the Benedictine monks of St. Maur (Paris: Victor Palmé, 1866), 4.445–446.

thoughts and speech closest to God—it was inevitable that subsequent tongues would appear as rivals for priority. Now the mother tongue, Latin, has taken the place of Hebrew as the *Ursprache*, leaving the language of the Vulgate Bible in conflict with the language of Virgil and the Roman poets.

The inclination to protect signification from dissemination that is apparent in this appeal to the correct speech of God is validated by more subtle forms in medieval linguistic history, such as in the *accessus ad auctores*. Specifying the place of Priscian in the curriculum of studies, a thirteenth-century *accessus* shows the privilege granted to the spoken word before any correct appreciation of the written is possible: "praua pronunciatio quam praua copulatio." Bad *copulatio*—conjugation of noun and verb—follows from bad pronunciation, and the unavoidable mistake will be the inability to tell "domine" from "dominum."[9] Grammar's knife and rod— Priscian's firm advice on the correct syntactic functions of the eight *pars orationes,* or parts of speech—are definitely in hand in this late medieval example. A simple warning about pronunciation is controlled by a larger mythology in which the spoken is privileged as a model of the written and an ideal state of language is identified with the stabilization of signification that is always under threat of erosion by the lesser, diminished forms of speaking and writing.

The attempt to stabilize dialectical habits and solidify the flux of individual instances of language—which was surely the effect of perpetuating Donatus and Priscian in the curriculum—may be noticed as well in more rarefied and sophisticated studies, such as the reflections on the nature of the written word in Scripture. For example, in a telling page of the *Didascalicon,* Hugh of St. Victor reveals brilliantly a way out of the wandering *confusio* of the fallen state of signs by ascending back up the hierarchy to the primal word spoken by God:

> The substantial word is a sign of man's perceptions; the thing is a resemblance of the divine Idea. What, therefore, the sound of the mouth, which all in the same moment begins to subsist and fades away, is to the idea in the mind, that the whole extent of time is to eternity. The idea in the mind is the internal word, which is shown forth by the sound of the voice, that is, by the external word. And the divine Wisdom, which the Father has uttered out of his heart, invisible in It-

[9] "Accessus Prisciani," in *Accessus ad auctores,* ed. R. B. C. Huygens, Collection Latomus, vol. 15 (Brussels: Berchem, 1954), p. 42.

self, is recognized through creatures and in them. From this is most surely to be gathered how profound is the understanding to be sought in the Sacred Writings, in which we come through the word to a concept, through a concept to a thing, through the thing to its idea, and through its idea arrive at Truth.[10]

Hugh's reflections on the language of the Bible derive from his earlier concerns in the *Didascalicon* with the place of *grammatica* in the trivium and quadrivium, and he is entirely conventional in his advice. He even offers us an instance of the vertical probing back to the original source for meaning in his etymological gloss on the names "quadri*vium*" and "tri*vium*." They are so called, he says, "because by them, as by certain *ways* (*viae*), a quick mind enters into the secret places of wisdom."[11] While his immediate aim is with teaching his pupils how to read the Bible correctly, his linguistics is thoroughly informed by medieval commonplaces about language, such as those that inform Donatus and Priscian. Like them, Hugh offers an apologetics against linguistic *confusio*; language is a transparency through which meaning may be reached by ascending the hierarchy to the origin of truth; signification is identified with a parent word or an original language before the taint of differentiation and mediation; linguistic change is conceived of as a moral vice (the sin of pride in the Babel story) and a disease in the primal tongue of speaking and writing. While theoretical stability was the obvious effect of perpetuating such a "logocentric" hierarchy for medieval writers on language, the facts of linguistic usage would inevitably present an ongoing challenge to *grammatica*; but oddly enough, it was not the data of experience that brought about the next development in medieval linguistic history. It was initiated instead by the reintroduction of speculative logic and metaphysics —primarily from Aristotle—in the disciplines of study during the twelfth century.[12]

---

[10]*The Didascalicon of Hugh of St. Victor: A Medieval Guide to the Arts,* trans. Jerome Taylor (New York: Columbia University Press, 1961), pp. 121–122.

[11]Ibid., p. 87. These examples may be compared with those offered by Bloch, *Etymologies and Genealogies,* pp. 54 ff.; he has suggested that the medieval preoccupation with etymology is an extensive illustration of locating meaning in an original word or language.

[12]This point has been well established, for example, by Robins, *Ancient and Medieval Grammatical Theory,* pp. 80–90; Bursill-Hall, *Speculative Grammars,* pp. 37–113; Bloch, *Etymologies and Genealogies,* pp. 149–158; and Stock, *Implications of Literacy,* pp. 326–454.

Because of the impact of logic and dialectic on grammar after 1100, it may appear somewhat anachronistic that John of Salisbury, like the early medieval commentators, appeals to an original, natural language as a model by which subsequent languages and dialects might be described. Following the work of Peter Abelard, Anselm of Laon, and William of Conches, Peter Helias—who was John's teacher—did more than any previous commentator to establish grammar as an autonomous discipline, a "language" in itself that sought to encompass all aspects of linguistic study.[13] The "metalanguage" of *grammatica* that Peter Helias taught was the product of much innovative thinking about Donatus and Priscian, and John's *Metalogicon* shows the results. But John's book is not, finally, anachronistic, since the twelfth-century grammarians, such as Peter Helias, approach the problem of linguistic signification by reference to a model that has much in common with some of the early medieval reflections on language. Accordingly, it may not be quite accurate to divide linguistic history in the middle ages into the customary "periods"—the early teachings of grammatical commentators before 1200 and the extensive speculations that followed that date.[14] For writers like John of Salisbury show that in language theory, as in so many other medieval traditions, the continuity of *auctores* and *auctoritates* appears to prevail over radical change.

For example, with regard to the subject of the origin of words and letters, John echoes several previous disputes about whether they are natural or human.[15] Priscian had argued that they are contrived by man and yet remain tied to material things: men "pronounced letters by means of a vocabulary of elements according to a similitude with elements of the world" ("literas autem etiam elementorum vocabulo nuncupaverunt ad similitudinem mundi elementorum").[16] For John of Salisbury, "the very application of names, and the use of various expressions, although much depends on the will of man, is in a way subject to nature, which it

---

[13]See Hunt, "Studies on Priscian," in *History of Grammar*, pp. 18–38; Robins, *Ancient and Medieval Grammatical Theory*, pp. 76–80; Bursill-Hall, *Speculative Grammars*, pp. 28–31.

[14]Robins, *Ancient and Medieval Grammatical Theory*, p. 70: "It is convenient to divide the pursuit of grammar in the Middle Ages into two periods"; many have followed this lead: for example, Bursill-Hall, *Speculative Grammars*, pp. 22–23.

[15]See Bloch's attention to this distinction, *Etymologies and Genealogies*, pp. 34–53.

[16]*Institutionum grammaticarum libri XVIII*, ed. H. Keil (Hildesheim: Georg Olms, 1961), 2:6.

probably imitates." Consequently John insists that, although the grammatical study of language is "an invention of man," still it too "imitates nature, from which it derives its origin" ("naturam tamen imitatur, et pro parte ab ipsa originem ducit").[17] Because of the emphasis on the roots of names or words in their sources, letters were commonly thought to carry with them something of their origins. Isidore recognizes this representational aspect of letters when he says that they are "the indices of things, the signs of words"; but nonetheless, he also goes on to observe that in letters "there is such power that they speak to us without voice the discourse of the absent" ("dicta absentium sine voce loquantur").[18] John knew this passage from the *Etymologiarum* and inserted it almost verbatim into his *Metalogicon* (1.13).[19]

Yet in the conception of the word as an imitation of its source, John is also indebted to his language teacher. Peter Helias, in his effort to free linguistic study from questions that were not precisely grammatical, appropriates an early medieval opinion (from Priscian) when he comments that verbs were invented to signify substances *proprie*—"principally" or "properly."[20] But his excursus shows the subtle influx of dialectic; for he goes on to explain that they were created to designate the "action" and "passion" of a substance and later became extended to cover "qualities" and other "accidents." This principle allows a certain latitude in solving such problems as Priscian's *verbum substantium*, namely, that *est* as a verb designates an action or passion, and yet as a substantive it signifies things as existing. Peter argues his way out of this dilemma by claiming that, first of all, a substance unites all other things to itself ("substantia itaque unitiva est accidentium"); as derivative elements return to their source, so the verbal substantive is unitary and copulative ("omnia namque accidentia in se recipit et sibi copulat et unit").[21] Thus, though *esse* signifies a substance, it does so in the manner of an action ("quia licet substantiam significat, modo tamen actionis eam significat, ut determinatum est").[22] In Peter's solution, a certain flexibility informs the question of signification: nouns signify by naming "properly" the substances on

[17]*Metalogicon*, p. 39; *PL* 199, 840D.

[18]*PL* 82, 74–75.

[19]*Metalogicon*, p. 38; *PL* 199, 840C.

[20]The connection has been noted by Hunt, "Studies on Priscian," in *History of Grammar*, p. 19.

[21]*Summa super Priscianum*, Paris MS (Arsenal 711), Latin text in "Appendix" to Hunt's "Studies on Priscian," in *History of Grammar*, p. 37.

[22]Ibid., p. 38.

which—as John says—they are "stamped";[23] but verbs signify differently, as is apparent in the example of verbal nouns; they also signify their sources, yet do so *in modo actionis*.

However, the difference granted in this important grammatical principle of the twelfth century is not as various as it may seem, since the larger issue of derivative signification—*consignificatio*—it introduces was itself rooted in a controlling parent structure.[24] For instance, many medieval grammarians worried the question of how the word "whiteness" signifies when it is a noun (*albedo*), or a verb ("is white," *albet*), or an adjective ("white," *album*).[25] But while this example illustrates that they were touching on different "ways of signifying" in connotative functions, it would be wrong to imagine that they were unearthing a principle of linguistic indeterminancy. Terms differ manifestly in their simultaneous secondary meanings—their consignification; but they never lose possession of the primary stem from which they derive. John of Salisbury addresses this knotty problem by recalling what Bernard of Chartres used to say about it: "'Whiteness' represents an undefiled virgin; 'is white' the virgin entering the bedchamber, or lying on a couch; and 'white' the girl after she has lost her virginity."[26] If signification is gradually tainted as a word enters syntax, John goes on to explain, the linguistic state of privilege, the chastity and virginity of pure meaning (*albedo*), is a quality without "any participation of a subject [*sine omni participatione subjecti*]"; but the consignification of syntax will inevitably violate that quality through "participation by a person" until the "whiteness" of unqualified meaning is "infused" and "mixed"—"in a way still more impure [*corruptam*]."[27]

The virginity of signification remains open to the mixing of senses, but by identifying *consignificatio* with deflowering, perhaps even with sin, John and Bernard illustrate yet another strand of the many lines leading back to the natural, pristine state of meaning before Babel: signification *sine participatione subjecti* is nothing less than the unmediated language of God. While the impurity of syntax is unavoidable, the perpetuation of virginal meaning (like ecclesiastical chastity) is the preferred condition, and it was consistently

---

[23]*Metalogicon*, p. 39; *PL* 199, 841B: "impressa sunt nomina."

[24]On the category of *consignificatio* ("consignification"), see Bursill-Hall, *Speculative Grammars*, pp. 53–56.

[25]Hunt, "Studies on Priscian," in *History of Grammar*, p. 25.

[26]*Metalogicon*, pp. 151–152; *PL* 199, 893C: "sed consignificatione diversa aibat Bernardus Carnotensis, quia *albedo* significat virginem incorruptam; *albet*, eadem introeuntem thalamum aut cubantem in toro; *album* vera, eadem, sed corruptam.

[27]*PL* 199, 893C.

sought, as we will see shortly, in the discipline of ecclesiastical writing—biblical hermeneutics and exegesis. But first it will be necessary to consider a bit further whether *grammatica* remained rooted in the mimesis of nature after the twelfth century.

4

The work of Peter Helias and other twelfth-century grammarians was to have a profound impact not only immediately on treatises for teaching grammar, such as the *Doctrinale* of Alexander of Villedieu (one of the most popular texts at the end of the century), but also more remotely on the many writers who turned their attention to grammar in the thirteenth and fourteenth centuries; for example, Robert Grosseteste, Peter of Spain, Roger Bacon, and the *modistae*—Martin of Dacia, John of Dacia, Siger of Courtrai, Michel de Marabais, and Thomas of Erfurt. The contribution of twelfth-century *grammatica* was elaborated and refined in theory and terminology by each of these writers, and, as with Peter Helias, their fundamental intention was to establish grammar as a self-consistent system through the study of language per se. But it is hardly surprising, in view of the impetus to study grammar by virtue of advances in dialectic and logic, that grammarians saw their subject through the lens of philosophical categories. On the one hand, the assistance of philosophy emphasized even more an interest in *how* language signified, rather than in *what* it signified, and this direction produced many texts in "speculative grammar," *de modis significandi.* But on the other hand, in spite of an approach to the elements and functions of language as the products of convention, individual languages were not for the most part the concern of linguists in the thirteenth century or of the later *modistae.*[28] Roger Bacon, for instance, sums up much of the theoretical speculation of his age when he maintains that there really is only *one* grammar, which is subordinate to the nature of the physical world and the structure of human understanding: "grammar is one and the same according to the substance in all languages." And therefore he is led to insist that it is "not the grammarian, but the philosopher, diligently considering the proper natures of things, who sets down grammatical principles."[29] In this remark is buried the

[28]Robins, *Ancient and Medieval Grammatical Theory*, pp. 86–90; Bursill-Hall, *Speculative Grammars*, pp. 41–42.
[29]Latin text cited by Robins, *Ancient and Medieval Grammatical Theory*, p. 77.

assumption of the thirteenth century that the primary object of *grammatica* is the self-sufficiency of Latin as a metalanguage for organizing the discipline itself, rather than for describing specific linguistic instances.[30] *Vox unde vox*, the concrete occurrences of speech that illustrate conceptions about the general category of voice, was in effect a mirror image of the order of understanding, or *modus intelligendi.*

In the next century, Thomas of Erfurt, who wrote one of the most complete texts in *grammatica speculativa*, carries out Bacon's rule when he argues, with regard to sentence construction: "grammar is organic" (grammatica . . . sit organicum"); and consequently each element of the discipline must be "ordered towards some . . . necessary end or purpose."[31] Like the sentence, so also the discipline of studying it—Thomas's remark is hardly casual. The structure of thought *pars pro toto*, as it is illustrated in the many spatial forms of the sign already considered, determines as well the organization of *grammatica* among the *modistae*. We see it most clearly as they appropriate the terminology of Scholastic logic for the description of linguistic phenomena. The contrast of matter and form, which had been used by previous grammarians, is emphasized again by the *modistae*, but with new philosophical rigor—for instance, in distinguishing the material appearance of a word, or *dictio*, from a formal class of words, or *pars orationis*. Owing to a difference in form, therefore, the *dictio* denotes a meaning while the *pars orationis* has the potential of connoting derivative sense. The Scholastic interest in act and potency plays a large role in such distinctions, determining the classification of all *modi significandi* as "acts" and *modi intelligendi* and *consignificandi* as the "potencies" of those acts.[32]

Defining the parts of speech according to the modes of signifying, the *modistae* move beyond their predecessors by locating the domain of linguistics between "being" (*essens* or *ens*) and "understanding" (*intelligens*), and this situation allows it to mirror both orders simultaneously. Siger of Courtrai, for example, says that the noun "is the mode of signifying substance, permanence, rest, or being" ("modus significandi substantiae, permanentis, habitus seu entis"); but the verb is a "mode of signifying becoming or being"

[30]See Bursill-Hall, chapter 3, "Metalanguage," in *Speculative Grammars*, pp. 66–113.
[31]Thomas of Erfurt, *Grammatica speculativa*, Latin ed. and English trans., G. L. Bursill-Hall (London: Longman Group, 1972), pp. 312–313.
[32]See Bursill-Hall, *Speculative Grammars*, pp. 46–55.

("modum significandi fieri seu esse").[33] Temporality and action are the crucial distinctions in the mode of the verb for Siger, controlling his use of *ens* for the noun that may perform a certain action or *esse*. It is clear that philosphical intersts push Siger a bit further than linguistic description per se when he concludes that verbs must follow their nouns since the state of *esse* (action) obviously follows the state of *ens* (rest).[34]

In Thomas of Erfurt's *Grammatica speculativa*, the modistic determination to describe grammar in itself is again unmistakable; but the study of language as a phenomenon of convention, which had otherwise opposed medieval notions of the natural presence of meaning, reveals that language theory through the fourteenth century did not finally displace an archaic natural matrix.[35] Thomas begins his treatise with as sharp an attention to the *modus*, rather than the object, of signifying as we are likely to find in fourteenth-century grammar; he says that modes of signifying are twofold, taking their form from the active and passive modes of understanding and moods of the verb. But the priority of the source or the object determines his description: "every active mode of signifying comes from some property of the thing" ("omnis modus significandi activus est ab aliqua rei proprietate").[36] The convention of linguistic description, in this instance, remains subordinate to what is natural to the "thing," its *proprietas*. This point might not be assumed in, for example, grammatical gender, since it seems mechanically, perhaps arbitrarily, assigned by convention. Not so for Thomas, who finds in it the operation of a law of sexual differentiation: "masculine gender is the mode of signifying the thing by means of the property of acting (. . . *vir*). Feminine gender is the mode of signifying the thing by means of the property of being acted upon (. . . *mulier*)."[37] As a linguistic category has here changed places with, and even determined, a logical one (the *modus intelligendi activi* and *passivi*), grammar is imitating nature, which is in turn imitating it.

Proprietas as a determinate of meaning takes on more complex proportions in the case of the demonstrative pronoun, because it

---

[33]Siger of Courtrai, *Summa modorum significandi*, ed. G. Wallerand, in *Les Oeuvres de Siger de Courtrai*. Les Philosophes belges, 8 (Louvain, 1913), pp. 95, 108.

[34]Ibid., p. 108: "esse est proprius actus ipsius entis; cum nomen significat rem suam per modum substantiae seu entis, et verbum per modum significandi dieri seu esse, verbum immediate debet sequi ipsum nomen."

[35]Bloch has argued a similar point; *Etymologies and Genealogies*, pp. 152–156.

[36]Thomas of Erfurt, *Grammatica Speculativa*, pp. 136–137.

[37]Ibid., p. 179.

"signifies the thing by means of the property of presence" ("proprietate praesentiae").[38] The indications of presence are six for Thomas, one each for the five senses, plus one for the intellectual sense. In the example, *ille currit*, demonstration is synonymous with presence: the *dictio* makes its meaning immediate to the physical sense and is present in it. However, some demonstratives, says Thomas, are not so simple. For instance, if someone points to a bunch of grass held in the hand and observes, "This grass is growing in my garden," it is obvious that one thing "is demonstrated" (*demonstratur*) and something else "is signified" (*significatur*). In this case the grass in the hand is present to the physical sense, and the grass in the garden is conveyed to the intellectual sense; there must be different "modes of demonstrating," he continues, because of the "different modes of certainty and presence" ("diversos modos certitudinis, et praesentiae").[39] In order to take care of the separation in these examples between demonstrative elements and signification, Thomas separates the perceptual categories. But nowhere does his example, despite its suggestiveness, invite him to deviate from his first principle—the conception of spoken or written utterance as a property of the presence of meaning. Rather, he concludes, we simply move from what is "really established or present, which is demonstrated by the pronoun *ego*" to what may be "less certain and present . . . which is demonstrated by the pronoun *tu*, and so on" ("contingit enim rem esse praesentem et certam, et maxime certam vel praesentem, et sic demonstratur per hoc pronomen *ego*, vel non maxime esse certam et praesentem, et sic demonstratur per hoc pronomen *tu*, et alia similia").[40]

In this conception of relative degrees of presence that correspond to a graduating order of pronouns, we notice yet again the influential force of a precedent model, for example, Hugh of St. Victor's linguistic hierarchy that descends from the absolute *Verbum* to the lower manifestations of the written and spoken, internal and external word. The matter of which has priority—speech or writing, demonstrative utterance or signified meaning, the grass in the hand or the grass in the garden—does not really call into question Hugh's or Thomas's basic idea of the identity of discourse with presence. But this factor also means that, for Thomas and the other *modistae*, the *modus essendi* is just as much defined by as it defines its *modus significandi*. In fourteenth-century

---

[38]Ibid., pp. 200–201.
[39]Ibid.
[40]Ibid.

grammatica, many elaborate examples suggest that the modistic effort to describe linguistic phenomena in themselves remained rooted in ideas about the structure of reality and the mind. It is a discipline well aware of the separation of language from meaning, yet tied deeply to early medieval linguistic models, such as those of Donatus and Priscian, whose grammatical systems are still intact as late as Thomas of Erfurt.[41] Like the early commentators, the *modistae* created a metalanguage that mirrors its own self-sufficiency much more than it analyzes the *dictiones* of usage.[42] While this development protects signification from indeterminacy, it also forestalls the advance of distinctly new directions in thinking about the origin of language and the modes of signifying meaning.

5

If *grammatica* does not isolate the study of language from the structures of past models or other disciplines of the trivium—as the various moments in the history of the discipline considered thus far suggest—we may expect that the treatment of linguistic signs in other fields of learning illustrates a similar tendency. Such is the case, it seems, in the hermeneutic theory and practice of reading Scripture, and the reasons for it are not at all remote. Hugh of St. Victor and other grammarians have already pointed to them: signs are defined in this field of knowledge not for their own sake, but primarily and explicitly for the value of reading the Bible correctly. In view of the extensive development of medieval hermeneutics—its growth into an institution of reading after the fathers of the church and flourishing at least until the time of Denis the Carthusian—the theological force of its approach to language not only discloses how scriptural signs were defined and understood, but also indicates why the effort to study language per se in other disciplines (for example, *grammatica*) remained conditioned by the past. This situation, like the perpetuation of classical Latin as a model in *grammatica,* seems paradoxical, since hermeneutics in

---

[41]As noted, for example, by Robins, *Ancient and Medieval Grammatical Theory,* p. 86. On the situation of grammar in fourteenth-century English education, see James J. Murphy, "Literary Implications of Instruction in the Verbal Arts in Fourteenth-Century England," *Leeds Studies in English,* N.S., 1 (1967):119–135; Richard J. Schoeck, "On Rhetoric in Fourteenth-Century Oxford," *Mediaeval Studies* 30 (1968):214–225.

[42]Similar conclusions are drawn by Robins, *Ancient and Medieval Grammatical Theory,* p. 87; and Bursill-Hall, *Speculative Grammars,* pp. 330–337.

the middle ages takes its origin from vivid instances of differentiation, such as the theoretical effort to separate transcendent reference from linguistic expression, which was illustrated historically for medieval readers not only by the story of Babel, but also by the Hebrew repudiation of pagan images and habits of thought heard frequently in the prophetic books of the Old Testament.

Determined to establish a transcendent and abstract sense of divinity, a frame of reference beyond adequate representation in concrete and particular things, the Hebrew protest shows little patience with the signifying systems of the Egyptians and Sumerians, which have been characterized in the following way:

> The primitive uses symbols as much as we do; but he can no more conceive them as signifying, yet separate from, the gods or powers than he can consider a relationship established in his mind—such as resemblance—as connecting, and yet separate from, the objects compared. Hence there is coalescence of the symbol and what it signifies, as there is coalescence of two objects compared so that one may stand for the other. In a similar manner we can explain the curious figure of thought *pars pro toto,* "a part can stand for the whole"; a name, a lock of hair, or a shadow can stand for the man because at any moment the lock of hair or shadow may be felt by the primitive to be pregnant with the full significance of the man.[43]

While this form of signifying remains grounded in material substances, it would be incomplete to assume that it is incapable of becoming a basis for engaging abstract problems; and yet the Hebrew opposition demanded a capacity for reference to a transcendent order that would not be limited in any way by materiality. Medieval hermeneutic theories of the sign are conceived in that imperative, but the *signans* (or signifying means) was often described as carrying with it or within it a part of its *signatum* (or signified reference). Since this structure of the sign—*pars pro toto*—has been commonly defined in the history of semiology as an instance of "symbolic" form, it will be useful to begin hermeneutic considerations of the sign with reference to the movement toward and away from symbolic structure.[44] Thus defined, symbolic signifying has direct

[43]Henri Frankfort, "Myth and Reality," in *Before Philosophy: The Intellectual Adventure of Early Man,* by H. Frankfort, H. A. Frankfort, John A. Wilson, and Thorkild Jacobsen (Chicago, 1946; reprint, Baltimore: Penguin Books, 1973), p. 21.

[44]On symbolic signifying, see, for example Tzvetan Todorov, *Théories du symbole* (Paris: Seuil, 1977); also relevant to the question of departing from symbolic concepts of the sign is Jacques Derrida's critique of Ferdinand de Saussure in *De la grammatologie* (Paris: Minuit, 1967); see trans. by Gayatri C. Spivak, *Of Grammatology* (Baltimore: Johns Hopkins University Press, 1976), pp. 27–73.

bearing on the nature of abstraction in hermeneutics and relates more broadly to the problem of the stability of signification in the middle ages.

The question of the extent to which abstraction figures in commentaries on hermeneutics may begin with reference to Aquinas, since he explicitly takes up the problem of symbolic signification in a discussion of the place of metaphor in biblical texts. Engaging the issue "Whether Holy Scripture Should Use Metaphors and Symbols" (*De sacra doctrina*, article 9), Aquinas answers the objection, "It seems that Holy Scripture should not use metaphors," by acknowledging first the usual oppositions: similitudes are befitting only to poetic art, "the lowest of all sciences"; comparisons obscure truth; representations of the divine ought to be made from "nobler" likenesses but are frequently drawn from "lower" ones.[45] Relying on conventional ideas about Scripture, Aquinas affirms, "it is natural to man to seek intellectual truths through sensible things, because all our knowledge originates from sense. Thus in Holy Scripture spiritual truths are appropriately taught under the likeness of metaphors taken from bodily things. This is what Dionysius says: 'Divine rays cannot enlighten us unless they are covered by many sacred veils.'" Such representations only give "delight" in poetry, Aquinas continues, but in Scripture they are "both necessary and useful," since sensible imagery provokes sensitive minds not "to remain within the likenesses, but elevates them to the knowledge of intelligible truths." If Scripture employs likenesses of the divine to "less noble bodies," the intention is not to confuse but to lead the mind away from error, "for such expressions in their proper sense are not said of divine things." Furthermore such knowledge is more befitting the understanding of God proper to creatures: "for what he is not is clearer to us that what he is."[46] With that remark we are as far from equating an image with a transcendent referent as we are, for instance, in Ferdinand de Saussure's separation of the sign from the nomination of a thing.[47] But we have not left the realm of symbolic form.

In one of Aquinas's sources for article 9, Dionysius the Areopa-

---

[45]*De sacra doctrina, qualis sit et ad quae se extendat, Summa theologiae,* 1a.1.9, ed. Thomas Gilby, O.P. (New York: McGraw-Hill for Blackfriars, 1964), 1:32. On the place of Aquinas in hermeneutic tradition, see Henri de Lubac, "L'Age scholastique," in *Exégèse médiévale: Les Quatre sens de l'écriture,* 2 parts (Paris: Aubier, 1959–1964), part 2.2:285 ff.

[46]*Summa,* 1a.1.9, pp. 32–34.

[47]*Cours de linguistique générale,* ed. Charles Bally and Albert Sechehaye, in collaboration with Albert Reidlinger (Geneva, 1916; Paris: Payot, 1973); trans. Wade Baskin as *Course in General Linguistics* (New York: Philosophical Library, 1959), p. 67.

gite's *On the Celestial Hierarchy*, the argument against mistaking the similitudes in Scripture for the true nature of God respects a sacred balance that is based upon the difference between the signified and what signifies it. Beginning with the assumption that divine nature is unknowable in its essence, Dionysius affirms that between the two ways Scripture describes holy mystery—through positive similitudes and negative or "unlike" comparisons—the *via negativa* "accords more closely with that which is ineffable."[48] According to Dionysius, the danger in positive comparisons is that "we might even think that the supercelestial regions are filled with herds of lions and horses, and re-echo with roaring songs of praise, and contain flocks of birds and other creatures." "We might fall into the error of supposing that the Celestial Intelligences are some kind of golden beings, or shining men flashing like lightning, fair to behold, or clad in glittering apparel."[49] To avoid such errors, Scripture employs "unlike images" or negative comparisons that do not allow the facile identification of image and referent, appearance and reality. Since divine nature "transcends all essence and life," words and wisdom are "incomparably below it." When it is named "Invisible, Infinite and Unbounded" we are told "not what It is, but what It is not," and this "is more in accord with Its nature." Accordingly "inharmonious dissimiltidues" or negative images do not risk the identification of sign with signified because an "unseemly image" cannot be mistaken for that which surpasses all comparison.[50] In other words, the unlikeliness of the image provokes the search for spiritual truth. Since the similitude is equivalent to the whole of which it is only a part, the structure of the sign for Dionysius remains symbolic.

However, in Aquinas's other important source for article 9, Augustine's *De doctrina Christiana*, book 2, the differentiation of the sign is not so easily compromised. Augustine begins book 2 by departing from his earlier discussion of "things" (*res*) in order to take up the "sign" (*signum*), but the materiality of the *res* has left its mark on the idea of the *signum*. "Just as I began," he argues:

---

[48]*The Mystical Theology, and the Celestial Hierarchies of Dionysius the Areopagite*, trans. Editors of the Shrine of Wisdom (Fintry, England: Shrine of Wisdom, 1945), p. 25.

[49]*Mystical Theology*, pp. 24, 25.

[50]*Mystical Theology*, p. 25. For Aquinas's discussion of these distinctions, see David B. Burrell, "Aquinas on Naming God," *Theological Studies* 24 (1963):182–212; see also the same author's *Analogy and Philosophical Language* (New Haven: Yale University Press, 1973). E. H. Gombrich studies the place of Dionysius in medieval theories of signs in "*Icones Symbolicae*: Philosophies of Symbolism and Their Bearing on Art," in *Symbolic Images: Studies in the Art of the Renaissance* (New York: Phaidon Press, 1972), p. 126.

when I was writing about things, by warning that no one should consider them except as they are, without reference to what they signify beyond themselves, now when I am discussing signs [*signis*] I wish it understood that no one should consider them for what they are but rather for their value as signs which signify [*significant*] something else. A sign [*signum*] is a thing [*res*] which causes us to think of something beyond the impression the thing itself makes upon the senses. Thus if we see a track, we think of the animal that made the track.[51]

Like Dionysius, Augustine does not say that the sign is simply the nomination of something, but that it is composed of a "signified" (for example, the animal) and also of the "impression the thing itself makes upon the senses." Here we have the rudiments of a tripartite structure: the implied idea of a *signifier* is separted from a *signified,* and both are parts of a whole idea called the sign. This tridimensional pattern, like its parallel in Saussure's *Cours,* explains a conception of the "impression" that offers a clear alternative to the coalescence of image into referent that constitutes the symbolic structure of metaphor.[52]

But in the remaining pages of *De doctrina Christiana* Augustine argues for the necessity of discovering that all signs lead to one univocal meaning, and thereby he moves away from the tripartite structure of the sign and toward symbolism. Proceeding to describe "natural signs" (*signa naturalia*) as those that are not made with "any desire or intention of signifying," Augustine contrasts "conventional signs" (*signa data*), which are made for the express purpose of conveying the *intention* of whoever made them.[53] He then identifies the signs in Scripture as "conventional" because they bear the intention of the Maker conveyed through prophets and evangelists.

[51]*De doctrina Christiana* 2.1.1; trans. D. W. Robertson, Jr., as *On Christian Doctrine* (New York: Bobbs-Merril, 1958), p. 34 (*PL* 34, 35). See de Lubac, "Saint Augustin," in *Exégèse,* 1.1.177ff.; J. Engels, "La doctrine du signe chez Saint Augustin," in *Studia Patristica,* vol. 6, ed. F. L. Cross (Berlin: Akademie-Verlag, 1962), pp. 366–373; Robert A. Markus, "St. Augustine on Signs," and B. Darrell Jackson, "The Theory of Signs in St. Augustine's *De doctrina Christiana,*" both essays in *Augustine: A Collection of Critical Essays,* ed. R. A. Markus (New York: Doubleday, 1972), pp. 61–91, 93–147; Eugene Vance, "Saint Augustine: Language as Temporality," in *Mimesis: From Mirror to Method, Augustine to Descartes,* ed. John D. Lyons and Stephen G. Nichols, Jr. (Hanover, N.H.: University Press of New England, 1982), pp. 20–35.

[52]Cf. Saussure, *Course in General Linguistics,* p. 66.

[53]*De doctrina* 2.1.2, p. 34 (*PL* 34, 35). That Augustine's contrast of *signa naturalia* and *signa data* remains distinct has been maintained, for example, by Jackson, Engles, and Vance (see note 51); but the subsequent argument of this chapter suggests that, while the two categories of signs are different in theory, they are interchangeable in the practice of reading—primarily because of the theological context in which both kinds of signs function.

Conventional signs are those which living creatures show to one another for the purpose of conveying, insofar as they are able, the motion of their spirits or something which they have sensed or understood. Nor is there any other reason for signifying, or for giving signs,
except for bringing forth the transferring to another mind the action
of the mind in the person who makes up the sign. We propose to consider and to discuss this class of signs insofar as men are concerned
with it, for even signs given by God and contained in the Holy Scriptures are of this type also, since they were presented to us by the men
who wrote them.[54]

With the distinction of certain signs as intentional objects, in contrast to natural objects, Augustine involves in his argument the idea
of "use" that Aquinas referred to in article 9. The term reflects the
principle, which runs throughout the *De doctrina* and medieval exegesis as well, that the signs in Scripture are not simply to be "en-
joyed" for their own sake, but are to be "used" for the sake of un-
covering the spiritual intention of God in them. Although certain
signs, "literal" ones, are used with clear intentions, others, "figurative signs," are more difficult. "Figurative signs occur when that
thing which we designate by a literal sign is used to signify something else; thus we say 'ox' and by that syllable understand the animal which is ordinarily designated by that word, but again by that
animal we understand an evangelist, as is signified in the Scripture,
according to the interpretation of the Apostle, when it says, 'Thou
shalt not muzzle the ox that treadeth out the corn.'"[55] The ox in
this text is a conventional sign, according to Augustine's category,
because its meaning is understandable from a familiarity with the
broader intentions of Scripture. But the lack of knowledge of those
conventions leaves the figurative sign to be read either "literally" or
else in any number of arbitrary and erroneous identifications.
Furthermore, ignorance of things in the natural world is also the
potential of arbitrary interpretation, and Augustine therefore
exhorts his readers to study "the nature of animals, or stones, or
plants, or other things which are often used in the Scriptures for
purposes of constructing similitudes." Paradoxically, "natural
signs," which have no "intention of signifying," are also "conventional" because they convey the intention of signifying the universal meanings of God.

[54]*De doctrina* 2.2.3, pp. 34–35 (*PL* 34, 35).
[55]*De doctrina* 2.10.15, p. 43 (*PL* 34, 39).

Thus the well-known fact that a serpent exposes its whole body in order to protect its head from those attacking it illustrates the sense of the Lord's admonition that we be wise like serpents [Matt. 10.16]. That is, for the sake of our head, which is Christ, we should offer our bodies to persecutors lest the Christian faith be in a manner killed in us, and in an effort to save our bodies we deny God. It is also said that the serpent, having forced its way through narrow openings, sheds its skin and renews its vigor. How well this conforms to our imitation of the wisdom of the serpent when we shed the "old man," as the Apostle says, and put on the "new" [Eph. 4.22–25]; and we shed it in narrow places, for the Lord directs us, "Enter ye in at the narrow Gate" [Matt. 7.13]. Just as a knowledge of the nature of serpents illuminated the many similitudes which Scripture frequently makes with that animal, an ignorance of many other animals which are also used for comparisons is a great impediment to understanding.[56]

With this passage the tripartite structure of the sign has disappeared; for Augustine has set down the rules for reading physical things as *words* in the Book of nature: the "snake" has been transformed from the sign that began book 2 into a metaphor. The idea of the sign as an "impression" that occasions the search for truth has been replaced by an image that is an object in its own right imitating or miming a signified meaning already well known at the outset. Although Augustine is not saying that divinity is present in the snake (as we find, for instance, in Egyptian fertility myths), he is insisting that the signified precept of God—of shedding the old ways of *cupiditas* to put on the new virtue of *caritas*—is present in the image. By this move Augustine has changed the natural object, which he says has no intention, into the position of the conventional sign, which is rich with significance, and the result is the affirmation of a natural bond—a symbolic structure—between the signified and what signifies it.

The ideas about the linguistic sign that emerge from Augustine's treatise and that were to have a profound influence on subsequent theory, such as Aquinas's, compare substantially with several of the assumptions we have seen governing the tradition of *grammatica*: the conventional, rather than the natural, origin of language; its dislocation from a source or object of meaning; its inability to be the language of Adam—the mythological "one tongue" spoken before Babel. And yet hermeneutic approaches to language, like grammatical ones, attempt to reconcile these linguistic facts to a de-

---

[56]*De doctrina* 2.16.24, pp. 50–51 (*PL* 34, 46–47).

sire to preserve or recapture the natural representation of meaning, and thus they perpetuate past models by continuing appeal to
the *auctores* of linguistic history. Excursions into the various "ways
of signifying" in both grammar and hermeneutics remain committed to a more overriding interest in stabilizing signification. While
this interest may be understood to a certain extent with reference
to the symbolic reading of signs, it ought to be explored as well
through consideration of how theoretical positions inform the
practice of *writing* about signs and language. Such exploration, of
course, is not limited exclusively to exegesis, as we will see in due
course; but for now the step from theory to practice may be taken
within the tradition of hermeneutic writing—and in this case an
example is conveniently supplied again by Augustine in the *Confessions*. He began and completed the work during the span of years
when he was also laboring over the theoretical study of reading in
De doctrina Christiana. Since Augustine confronts in the *Confessions*
the problem of language as a man-made convention, it will be helpful to see how he reconciles it with God's writing in Scripture—as
well as with his own writing in the *Confessions* itself.

6

No reader leaves the text without feeling for it some of the lure
and pleasure that Augustine himself initially expresses for the seductions of pagan rhetoric and narrative, such as the oratory of
Cicero and the *Aeneid* of Virgil. The irony of this situation of reading must have been felt by Augustine, too, since he spells out rather
plainly in the early books the story of himself as a young boy first
beaten into learning *grammatica*—overcoming its various decep-
tions—and then seduced into the desire to set it and all pagan literature aside in favor of reading and writing about Scripture (the exegesis of Genesis that begins when he leaves off the story of his life,
books 10–13). As modern scholarship has become increasingly
aware, Augustine's reflections on language in the book constitute an extensive meditation on the separation of God from man.[57]

[57]See the important and provocative contributions to this issue by Eugene Vance:
"Saint Augustine: Language as Temporality" (cited above, note 51); "Augustine's
Confessions and the Grammar of Selfhood," *Genre* 6 (1973):1–28; "Augustine's *Con-
fessions* and the Poetics of the Law," *MLN* 93 (1978):618–634; also relevant are
Margaret W. Ferguson, "Saint Augustine's Region of Unlikeness: The Crossing
of Exile and Language," *Georgia Review* 29 (1975):842–864; Ulrich Duchrow, "'Sig-

The whole argument about the deception and distraction of rhetoric is an indication of the frustration the young Augustine felt in attempting to understand the transience of all earthly ventures, even intellectual exercises, in perfecting rhetorical skill; for language is a vivid instance of the temporality of worldly affairs. "Our speech," he says in book 4.10, is "accomplished by signs emitting a sound [*per signa sonantia*]; but our speech would not be whole [*totus*] unless one word pass away when it has sounded its parts [*partes suas*], so that another may succeed it [*succedat*]."[58] The necessity of temporality, illustrated here as one word or one life must succeed another, is a constant reminder of the value of seeking the *Verbum* that will not pass away.

The frustration of linguistic distraction, compared throughout the early books of the *Confessions* to the seductions of the flesh, is relentless until Augustine meets Ambrose, who teaches him how to read the Scriptures figuratively for their moral and anagogical truth. This kind of reading, an ability to see beyond the material appearance of letters to their sources of meaning, is figured for Augustine in Ambrose's "silent reading": "But while he read, his eyes passed through the pages, and his heart sought out the sense, but his voice and tongue were silent" ("vox autem et lingua quiescebant"; 6.3).[59] It is this exegetical reading *in silentio* that will ultimately capture Augustine's attention and determine the kind of writing he himself undertakes in the final three books of the *Confessions*. But for the moment and until the death of his mother (book 9), Augustine must face the mystery of the "silent writing" in the heart and in God's Book that is demanding from him some form of audible or written speech. The gap seems unbridgeable at certain points, since his own language reminds him of his difference from the divine *Verbum*. In book 7, he hears God's voice in the Psalm, "I am the food of strong men" (Ps. 39.11), but he is thrown back into renewed awareness of his own limitation in the "region of dissimilarity" of this world.[60] His utterance, his *regio dissimilitudinis*, must accept the "unlikeliness" of its own mode and find a means of "becoming like" God's Word.

num' und 'Superbia' biem jungen Augustin (386–90)," *Revue des Etudes Augustiniennes* 7 (1961):369–372.

[58]*PL* 32, 699. See also Vance's discussion, "Saint Augustine: Language as Temporality," p. 21.

[59]*PL* 32, 720, and see 721.

[60]*PL* 32, 742: "et inveni longe me esse a te in regione dissimilitudinis, tanquam audierem vocem tuam de excelso."

The death of his mother brings him closer than he had ever been to an imitation of God's silent will. In the mysterious deathbed colloquy with his mother, every "tumult of the flesh" ("tumultus carnis") is silenced—"silenced, too, the . . . fancies and imaginary revelations, every tongue, and every sign" ("sileant . . . omnis lingua et omne signum"); no "tongue of flesh" ("lingua carnis") nor even the "obscurity of a similitude" ("aenigma similitudinis") gets in the way as they "were talking thus" (9.10).[61] Confronting outright the irony of speaking and writing about silence, Augustine seeks a means of avoiding further confused wandering in the *regio dissimilitudinis*. He recognizes fully the separation between the text that the angels read "without the syllables of time" ("sine syllabis temporum") and his own noisy, distracted reading.[62] But he is led irresistibly toward that Book, toward the discourse that Ambrose, like the angels, read *in silentio* and that he now reads with Monica. As Augustine moves away from worldly excess and toward spiritual renewal following book 11, the deathbed colloquy becomes the means for solving the riddle of how he can write about God's silent Word entering his own life.

He begins book 11.2 with phrases that were to fall like potent dyes into the history of medieval writing about writing. Excess is still a powerful motion of his soul, and he is troubled by how he will ever "suffice with the tongue of my pen to express all" ("lingua calami enuntiare omnia"; 11.2).[63] To direct the passion for fulfilling desires away from fleshly ends, he requests the capacity for a new chaste and virginal utterance: "Circumcise my interior and exterior lips from every temerity and every lie. Let your Scriptures be my chaste delights" ("Circumcide ab omni temeritate omnique mendacio interiora et exteriora labia mea. Sint castae delicae meae Scripturae tuae").[64] Perhaps Bernard of Chartres was thinking of this text in the *Confessions* when he reflected on the status of pristine meaning as an undefiled virgin who is gradually corrupted when the substantive is differentiated through syntactical arrange-

---

[61]*PL* 32, 774.

[62]*PL* 32, 852. Both Bloch, *Etymologies and Genealogies* (pp. 58–63), and Vance, "Saint Augustine: Language as Temporality" (pp. 28, 33–35), have drawn attention to Augustine's sense of the temporality of language and the limitation of earthly signs; both conclude that although he seeks ways of overcoming the separation from the divine order, he does not have much hope for the capacity of words to do so. But, as this chapter argues, Augustine's view of language is not skeptical: it is full of promise for redeeming the deformity of signs and the limitations of time.

[63]*PL* 32, 809.

[64]*PL* 32, 810.

ments. We do not know for sure. But it is obvious in Augustine's passage that God's discourse is unmediated, a natural—"chaste" —state of meaning. He begins to solve the dilemma of speaking about the unspoken will of God in his own life by redirecting his attention away from himself and toward God's words in Scripture.[65] And yet, since they are the records of human writers, he must begin with a meditation on how he can get back to the paradise of the divine *Verbum* through the mediation of the created and temporal syllables of the Bible.

With "circumcised" lips and tongue, he poses the first question— the nature of God's utterance at the moment of Creation: "But how did you speak?" What was the "manner" ("modo") of it (11.6)?[66] Like the later grammarians, Augustine is motivated by fundamental questions concerning the "ways of signifying," though he has much more metaphysical weight to carry in the *Confessions*. If God spoke in Hebrew, Augustine would listen in vain since he did not know the language; yet he says that he would nevertheless understand the divine utterance "in the chamber of my thought," where it would be heard "without the organs of voice and tongue, without the sound of syllables" (11.3).[67] But the limitations of human comprehension cannot adequately reflect how God's utterance at the Creation was spoken and understood. For even the voice that said "This is my beloved Son" (Matt. 17.5) "was uttered and passed away, began and ended" until there was silence after the last syllable (11.6).[68] A creature had to say and hear these words, but the creating *Verbum* had to precede both. When it was spoken, Augustine continues, the outer ear reported the words sounding temporally to the inner ear of the understanding mind; listening to the eternal, the ear of the mind then said: "Aliud est, longe aliud est" ("It is different, it is far different"; 11.6).[69] The creating word as-

---

[65]In "Augustine's *Confessions* and the Grammar of Selfhood," pp. 17–25, Vance suggests that the question about the structure of the *Confessions*, posed by the shift from autobiography to biblical commentary beginning with book 10, may be answered specifically by reflecting on the strategy of the text to transform gradually the discourse of the "self" into a discourse about the "other" language of God, Scripture. He takes up the problem again in "Augustine's Confessions and the Poetics of the Law," esp. pp. 631–634.

[66]*PL* 32, 812.

[67]*PL* 32, 811.

[68]*PL* 32, 812.

[69]*PL* 32, 812: "Et haec ad tempus facta verba tua nuntiavit auris exterior mentis prudenti, cuius interior posita est ad aeternum Verbum tuum. At illa comparavit haec verba temporaliter sonantia, cum aeterno in silentio Verbo tuo, et dixit: Aliud est, longe aliud est." Contrast the argument of Margaret Fergusson on the topic of language in the *Confessions* and in particular on this passage in 11.6; she insists that

serts a separation between itself and the words by which it is spoken: it is self-differentiating. But so are Augustine's spoken and written words. While the "ear" is "speaking," he goes on to say that the temporal words spoken at Creation ("these words") are "below me," and God's Word is "above"—yet with this sentence, Augustine implicates the temporal words that he writes; his own utterance is self-differentiating. ("Haec longe infra me sunt; nec sunt, quia fugiant et praeterunt: Verbum autem Domini mei supra me manet in aeternum"; 11.6).[70] At the same moment as Augustine asserts the separation of divine from human discourse, he draws his own writing into parallel with the creating *Verbum*: while there is nothing similar in essence between them, the first nonetheless is profoundly involved in the second by virtue of the differentiation that both carry out. The strategy through which the text comments on itself occurs at various points when Augustine speaks of *haec verba*, but it is particularly emphatic in the interrogative mood, with which the chapter closes: "By what word of yours was it announced that a body might be created, from which these words might be created?" ("Ut ergo fieret corpus unde ista verba fierent, quo verbo a te dictum est?" 11.6).[71]

The metaphorical conjunction here between *corpus* and *verba* is hardly accidental. It suggests the parallel of his writing with the incarnational *Verbum* that "became flesh" so that saving words might be spoken. Augustine's *verba* are becoming the *corpus* explaining God's *Verbum*—an act of writing in which the presence of the word is maintained in the flesh of the letter. It is fitting, therefore, that Augustine proceeds from the question who made the words to a consideration of the continuity of the *Verbum* in the created world: "For what was spoken was not finished, and something else spoken so that all things could be spoken" ("neque enim finitur quod dicebatur, et dicitur aliud ut possint dici omnia"; 11.7).[72] Conceiving of creation as a concatenation of utterances proceeding from the first Word, Augustine links the human word—specifically his expression at the opening of book 9.8—with divine origin. "How I shall express it I do not know," he says ("sed quomodo id eloquor nescio"; 11.8), since everything begins and ends. But nothing begins or ends except as it "is known in

Augustine never gets beyond a view of language as a mode of "radical unlikeness" and "dissimilitude"—"Saint Augustine's Region of Unlikeness," esp. pp. 861–864.

[70]*PL* 32, 812.
[71]*PL* 32, 812.
[72]*PL* 32, 812.

eternal reason" ("in aeterna ratione cognoscitur"; 11.8). That *ratio* "is your Word—your Beginning—and it speaks to us" ("Ipsum est verbum tuum, quod et Principium es quia et loquitur nobis"; 11.8).[73] The *Principium*, he concludes, continues in what has been made, just as Jesus, the *Verbum*, spoken in the gospel after the creation of the world; his word was spoken as ours is—"through the flesh; and it was heard abroad by the ears of men" ("per carnem ait; et hoc insonuit foris auribus hominum"; 11.8); yet still "he is the Beginning and speaks to us" ("quia Principium est, et loquitur nobis"; 11.8).[74]

Although the primordial creation is a moment of profound differentiation, the created world and words of Augustine endure not a breach but an expansion from their origins of meaning.[75] The words of Scripture and its exegesis in the text of the *Confessions* cannot body forth the timeless presence of the *Verbum*—"no time can be totally present" ("nullum vero tempus totum esse praesens"; 11.11),[76] but the traces of that original presence are before us as Augustine turns the Word of his experience of God's will into the flesh of the words—the *corpus*—of the *Confessions*. Leaving off the story of his life in the flesh, he takes up the explication of Genesis with "circumcised" tongue as a new effort in the redemption of fallen discourse. The practice of hermeneutics is the project through which "the obscure secret of so many pages should be written" ("scribi voluisti tot paginarum opaca secreta"; 11.2); it is instituted as a recuperation of the lost origin and plentitude of God's meaning.[77] Augustine may be limited by the "syllables of time," but the project he begins is committed to seeing the Book read by the angels reflected in the Scriptures read on earth. "Your Scripture is spread abroad over the people, even to the end of the world" (13.15).[78] Although he does not dissolve all differences be-

---

[73]*PL* 32, 813.

[74]*PL* 32, 813.

[75]Compare Bloch, *Etymologies and Genealogies*, p. 60: "Augustine thus distinguishes between the undifferentiated, immaterial, divine Word which, 'engendered by the Father,' is coeternal with Him,' and corporeally articulated human speech. In some extended sense, however, words always refer to the Word. All language thus harks back to an origin synonymous with the Father who remains present in the objects of his Creation."

[76]*PL* 32, 814.

[77]*PL* 32, 810. Compare Vance, "Augustine's *Confessions* and the Grammar of Selfhood," p. 24: "language *itself* is reborn in Augustine's explication of *Genesis*." But despite this insight, Vance emphasizes the deformation of language in Augustinian theory.

[78]*PL* 32, 852.

tween the two texts, his hermeneutics is surely devoted to illuminating the dark likeness between them. By conceiving of his own interpretive writing as the gradual manifestation of an original Word—a *Principium* that has no end—Augustine illustrates in the *Confessions* what he says about reading in *De doctrina Christiana*—that signs are ultimately informed by the controlling law of *caritas*. Given the authority of Augustine for later writers, it is not difficult to see why language theory, in spite of its complexity in hermeneutics and *grammatica*, did not give birth to radical departures in the modes of signification.

7

Augustine's influence on the institution of interpreting the Bible in the middle ages must not be underestimated; but it would be wrong to assume that he was its primary *magister* controlling all later developments. Yet in view of the preoccupation with validating meaning by appeal to a source—be it an original language or text in the hermeneutic tradition or a given linguistic model in the grammatical tradition—language theory in the middle ages was fertile soil for interpretation to take root among various authors, as it does in the final books of the *Confessions*: subsequent exegesis also validates its own mode by appeal to an original text—the Bible itself, the Book in the sky, or an authoritative *auctoritas*, such as a work by Augustine. Although these medieval strategies of signifying are a long way, both in time and in composition, from Egyptian and Sumerian myth, the structure of thought *pars pro toto* has not been completely abandoned.[79] The fate of the linguistic sign

[79]This suggestion does not mean, of course, that medieval linguistic theory was primitive or naive insofar as it was rooted in mythological forms of signifying. On the contrary, such forms, as recent scholarship has shown, were capable of engaging problems at a high level of abstract speculation. For example, see Claude Lévi-Strauss, *La Pensée sauvage* (Paris: Plon, 1962), trans. George Weidenfeld as *The Savage Mind* (Chicago: University of Chicago Press, 1969); idem, "The Structural Study of Myth," in *Structural Anthropology*, trans. Claire Jacobson and Brooke G. Schoeph (New York: Basic Books, 1963), pp. 206–231; Bronislaw Malinowski, "Myth in Primitive Psychology," in *Magic, Science, and Religion and Other Essays* (1948; reprint, New York: Doubleday Anchor Books, 1954), pp. 93–148. Henri Bergson, *The Two Sources of Morality and Religion*, trans. R. A. Audra and C. Brereton (1935; reprint, New York: Doubleday Anchor, 1954); Ernst Cassirer, *The Philosophy of Symbolic Forms*, vol. 2, *Mythical Thought*, trans. R. Manheim (New Haven: Yale University Press, 1955); Mircea Eliade, *The Sacred and the Profane*, trans. Willard Trask (New York: Harper & Row, 1961). G. S. Kirk has assessed several of these theorists in *Myth: Its Meaning and Functions in Ancient and Other Cultures* (Cambridge: Cambridge University Press, 1970).

in the middle ages seems to correspond to that of its spatial counterpart: the effort to break away from precedent structures turns out to repeat or supplement some aspect of them. In this case, both the spatial and the linguistic sign function within, rather than call into question, the larger structure of medieval mythologizing that includes them. One way to consider further the nature of this mythology in medieval hermeneutics is provided by the noted argument of Erich Auerbach concerning the difference between the styles of biblical writing and the styles of myth, as represented by the Homeric poems. Auerbach's contrast is not without certain weaknesses of generalization: Homer's texts do not entirely exemplify a style "of the foreground," and the biblical documents, which were written over many centuries and which reflect different cultural influences, are not exclusively "of the background."[80] But the value of the contrast need not be judged by the application of these two categories to every detail of style in each of the two literary texts; rather, the importance may consist in the link between a particular kind of thought and the style of writing it produced: the "foregrounded" style of myth seems to be of a piece with the immanence of divinity in signs—the logocentric presence of meaning. In contrast, Hebrew writing "of the background" reflects a sense of the abstraction and transcendence of the divine order, an understanding of the essential secrecy and mystery of divine meanings, and an appreciation of their absence from the writing that tries to render them intelligible.[81] Medieval interpreters of the Bible were certainly well aware of the difference, but it is not always preserved in their own styles of writing, and where one style slides into the other, the earlier mythological form of signifying has left its mark

[80]Erich Auerbach, *Mimesis* trans. Willard Trask (1946; reprint, Garden City, N.Y.: Doubleday Anchor Books, 1957): "It would be difficult, then, to imagine styles more contrasted than those of these two equally ancient and equally epic texts. On the one hand, externalized, uniformly illuminated phenomena, at a definite time and in a definite place, connected together without lacunae in a perpetual foreground; thoughts and feelings completely expressed; events taking place in leisurely fashion and with very little suspense. On the other hand, the externalization of only so much of the phenomena as is necessary for the purpose of the narrative, all else left in obscurity; the decisive points of the narrative alone are emphasized, what lies between is nonexistent; time and place are undefined and call for interpretation; thoughts and feeling remain unexpressed, are only suggested by the silence and the fragmentary speeches; the whole, permeated with the most unrelieved suspense and directed toward a single goal . . . remains mysterious and 'fraught with background'" (pp. 7, 9).

[81]Fruitful applications of Auerbach's contrast have been made by Herbert N. Schneidau, *Sacred Discontent: The Bible and Western Tradition* (Berkeley: University of California Press, 1976), pp. 25–26, 214–216, 279–280, 301; and Robert Alter, *The Art of Biblical Narrative* (New York: Basic Books, 1981), pp. 17, 114.

on the course of the medieval hermeneutic project. This determination may be studied by taking a close look at a biblical text and then considering whether the medieval interpretation of it has anything to do with the "foregrounding" interest of mythology.

The Document of the Davidic Succession (2 Sam. 9–20; 1 Kings 2) offers a challenging test of Auerbach's view of the unmythological style of biblical narrative because it is older than the work of the Elohist and was written at a time (in Solomon's reign) when Israel was very close to her mythological neighbors. Although in this document the Hebrews first explained their sense of kingship and dynasty, they did not emulate the elaborate myths of the Egyptians and Babylonians whose kings were deities and whose monarchies replicated the kingship of the gods. Beginning with the dilemma that the queen is barren, the record raises the question of the king's successor, but it does not provide God's choice or even his will about the matter. Events proceed in the chronicle "as they occurred."

> It happened towards evening when David had arisen from his couch and was strolling on the palace roof, that he saw from the roof a woman bathing; the woman was very beautiful. David made inquiries about this woman and was told, "Why, that is Bathsheba, Eliam's daughter, the wife of Uriah the Hittite." Then David sent messengers and had her brought. She came to him, and he slept with her; now she had just been purified from her courses. She then went home again. The woman conceived and sent word to David, "I am with child." (2 Sam. 11.2–5)

Whereas in Genesis we find at least some expression of Adam's fear and hear the divine judgment upon him, the absence of subordinating information in the account of David creates a sense of the matter-of-fact about an incident that is anything but a matter of simple fact. David's predicament has vast political and religious significance, but it remains unexpressed. The one possible remedy —to send Uriah home from the battlefield to sleep with his wife— backfires when Uriah refuses out of his sense of loyalty to the king. "Are not the ark and the men of Israel, and Judah lodged in tents; and my master Joab and the bodyguard of my lord, are they not in the open fields? Am I to go to my house, then, and eat and drink and sleep with my wife? As Yahweh lives, and as you yourself live, I will do no such thing!" (2 Sam. 11.11). The impact of what is not being said in these lines creates a feeling for the unexpected that eventually results in murder. The question of Uriah has the same rhetorical effect as the famous ironic question of Isaac. And as Isaac does not know that he himself is "the lamb for the burnt offering," Uriah's innocence of heart and his simple faith in his king prevent him from ever suspecting the adultery of his wife and the dishonesty disguised behind the king's favor. At the end of the account, all we are told is: "What David had done displeased Yahweh" (2 Sam. 11.27).

The reluctance to justify David's behavior and express the divine judgment on him is evidence of the crucial difference between the Hebrew monarchy and Near Eastern mythologies of divine kingship. Studying the theology of this difference, Gerhard von Rad observes that the "Anointed" of Israel is clearly not a deity like Pharoah, nor is he especially pure, nor is his office intrinsically sacred. Unlike the monarchies of Egypt and Babylon, the Davidic dynasty did not "'come down at the beginning from heaven.' In this respect no mythic dignity of any kind attaches to it." The assumption of the presence of the divine order in myth is contrasted sharply to the premises of the Hebrew document. What Auerbach says of Genesis—"Everything remains unexpressed"—is paralleled nearly exactly by von Rad's remarks on the style of the Succession Document: "The narrator only once draws the curtain back and allows the reader for a moment to perceive the divine power at the back of what appears in the foreground. . . . This historical work was the first word spoken by Israel about Yahweh and his anointed in Jerusalem; and it is an absolutely unmythological word. This realism with which the anointed is depicted, and the secularity out of which he emerges and in which he moves, are without parallel in the ancient East."[82] By refusing to foreground the nature and reasons of the divine will, the styles of Genesis and the Succession Document do not tend toward the metaphor of writing that replicates divinity. Rather, speaking about a God who made "Darkness . . . a veil to surround him" (Ps. 18.11), the styles of biblical narratives are "demythologizing." Zeus is "comprehensible in his presence," and to touch Pharoah is to touch Ra; the Egyptian mother goddess Nutt is present in the sky, and the Mesopotamian deity Ahamash is known in the sun; Baal is immanent in the storm and Poseidon in the sea. But the Hebrew God, as Henri Frankfort has commented, "is pure being, unqualified, ineffable.

[82]Gerhard von Rad, *Old Testament Theology*, vol. 1, *The Theology of Israel's Historical Traditions*, trans. D. M. G. Stalker (New York: Harper & Row, 1962), pp. 306, 316. Auerbach, *Mimesis*, p. 9.

He is *holy* . . . all values are ultimately attributes of God alone. Hence all concrete phenomena are devalued. . . . Nowhere else do we meet this fanatical devaluation of the phenomena of nature and the achievements of man: art, virtue, social order—in view of the unique significance of the divine. . . . Only a God who transcends every phenomenon, who is not conditioned by any mode of manifestation—only an unqualified God can be the one and only ground of all existence. This conception of God represents so high a degree of abstraction that, in reaching it, the Hebrews seem to have left the realm of mythopoeic thought."[83] In contrast to deities who exist in the foreground, are *immanent,* Yahweh's nature is not revealed in the burning bush (Exod. 3.1–6) or the acts of David. The sign tells us nothing about the nature of the signified. The Hebrews speak of a God who is not known in idols but who is always "at hand" in the background—*imminent.* The signs about him do not tell us *what* he is, only *that* he is. All we hear in the episodes of Isaac and Uriah as the divine voice is an echo of a never-present totality, a sudden irruption that is only an accidental and arbitrary means by which Yahweh lets himself be known.

When we turn to the pages of medieval hermeneutic practice, the profound sense of background that characterizes such biblical texts as Abraham and Isaac or David and Bathsheba is not always maintained. Auerbach has observed this point as a general characteristic of Augustine's commentaries on Scripture, for instance, in the *Civitas Dei,* and his observations may serve as a preface to the nature of style in the many commentaries that followed Augustine. "There is visible," says Auerbach of the *Civitas Dei,*

> a constant endeavor to fill in the lacunae of the Biblical account, to supplement it by other passages from the Bible and by original considerations, to establish a continuous connection of events, and in general to give the highest measure of rational plausibility to an intrinsically irrational interpretation. Almost everything which Augustine himself adds to the Biblical account serves to explain the historical situation in rational terms and to reconcile the figural interpretation with the conception of an uninterrupted historical sequence of events. The element of classical antiquity which asserts itself here is also apparent in the language—is, indeed, more apparent there than anywhere else; the periods . . . make no impression of great art . . . but

[83]Henri Frankfort and H. A. Frankfort, "The Emancipation of Thought from Myth," chap. 8 of *Before Philosophy,* pp. 242–244. Schneidau has studied this characteristic of Hebrew thinking as a form of "demytholigizing" in several texts of the Old and New Testaments; for example, pp. 12 ff.

with their abundant display of connectives, their precise gradation of temporal, comparative, and concessive hypotaxes, their participial constructions, they still form a most striking contrast to the Biblical passage cited, with its parataxis and lack of connectives. This contrast between text and Biblical citation is very frequently to be observed in the Fathers and almost always in Augustine. . . . In such a passage as this from the *Civitas Dei,* one clearly recognizes the struggle in which two worlds were engaged in matters of language as well as in matters of fact.[84]

This insight merits careful consideration in the study of medieval hermeneutics. As forthrightly as Augustine opposed pagan habits of thinking and writing, his interpretive procedure does not finally establish a firm boundary against them. The "two worlds" that converge in his work are also two fundamentally opposed ways of signifying meaning. They are as old as Abraham's departure from the religions of Ur and as consequential as the difference between the sign that is the embodiment of its signified reference and the writing that is fraught with the background of the abstract and transcendent. If Augustine's brightly illuminated form holds on to the past, so also may the writings of many of the commentators he influenced. Perhaps they too, as Auerbach claims, "fill in the lacunae of the Biblical account" and create a form not unlike the mythologized style that stands out as a "most striking contrast to the Biblical passage cited." To examine this possibility, I would like to return to the story of David and Bathsheba and consider a typical medieval interpretation of it, for instance, one recorded in the *Glossa ordinaria.*

In this commentary, we find the record of a lengthy dialogue between the lovers that is revealed for the exegete in the mention of only one word, *concepi* (2 Kings 11.5), Bathsheba's confession that she is pregnant.

The pregnant woman goes to the king and says: "O king, I have been undone." And he says to her: "What is the matter?" "I am pregnant," she says. "The fruit of my sin grows, and inside I have the cause. In my womb I am making the betrayer. If my husband comes to me and sees, what will I say? What will I tell? What excuse will I put forward?"[85]

[84]Auerbach, *Mimesis,* pp. 65–66.
[85]*Biblia sacra cum glossa ordinaria et postilla Nicholai Lyrami,* 8 vols. (Paris, London, and Venice, 1590–1603), 2:575 AB: "Pregnans facta mulier, vadit ad regem, et dicit: O Rex, perii. Et ille: Quid habes? Pregnans (inquit) sum. Peccati mei pullulat fructus, ac cusatorem intrinsecus habeo; in ventre profero proditorem. Si venerit et viderit vir meus, quid dicam? quid loquar? qua[m] excusationem praetendam?"

Hardly an enigmatic figure, Bathsheba is almost less important than the frustrations, fears, and thoughts that are seen brightly illuminated and delineated by her. A context of motives behind David's questionable behavior is just as vividly in the foreground as the few details indicating that he was on his balcony "when kings go forth." For whatever reasons David did not go with his army to meet the enemy, exegetes saw *otiositas*, too much "idleness" or "leisure," as the explanation for his acts; the old *sententia* from elsewhere in the Bible, "the devil finds work for the idle hands," and from Seneca, "summa omnium vitiorum otiositas," are also clearly intended by the scriptural passage according to the *Glossa*, which includes them between the lines of the quoted text in the "interlinear gloss" and on all four sides of it.[86] Not only does the *Glossa* add details to the text—namely, that David was strolling about his balcony, looking out of a window and gazing eagerly at Bathsheba bathing in the nude—but further, Gregory and Rabanus take us on a virtual tour of David's internal being, pointing out the image of Bathsheba imprinted on his mind as a primary cause of the "filth of thought" (*cogitationis immunditia*) inducing *oculorum illecebra*, an "enticement of the eyes" that ineluctably provoked David's soul to *concupiscentia* and his flesh to *luxuria*.[87] The ideas "behind" the events clearly have greater reality than the events themselves. That the baby conceived by Bathsheba dies suggests that God punished David for adultery by "taking" his child, but the comment in the *Glossa* elicits from this mere suggestion an elaborate conclusion surely informed by medieval morality. "Truly, those who were born after him [the dead child] God did not kill, because David married that woman."[88] The crucial difference between the text and the comment is the generalization that the child dies *because* David and Bathsheba were not married: what is simply suggested as a result of the incident is made by the exegete into its primary cause. One implication, among many possibilities in the text, is totalized into a precept about marriage.

The biblical narrative makes no attempt to explain away the ironic aspects of events, but exegesis, like myth, refuses to tolerate irony: all events are fitted into a highly systematic and self-explanatory scheme. The overbearing irony of the entire narrative—that the king of Israel has to stoop to murder because of the devotion

---

[86]*Biblia sacra cum glossa ordinaria*, 2:573–574.

[87]*Biblia sacra cum glossa ordinaria*, 2:575; *PL* 113, 571; *PL* 109, 99.

[88]Justin Martyr, *Glossa*, 2:581B: "Qui vero post eum nati sunt, non decuit, quoniam David illam duxit uxorem."

and chastity of one of his lowly soldiers—is no contradiction in the *Glossa.* For Bathsheba is a type of the "well of living water," *puteus aquae vivae* (because she is associated with water imagery in the narrative), David is a type of Christ because he is king of Israel, and Uriah signifies the Jewish people. As a type of the well, Bathsheba is identified with *Ecclesia,* which was carried as the ark by the Jews until that "marriage" was broken by Christ. David—"appearing as the Redeemer in the flesh"—took away "by strength of hand" (*manufortis*) that "wife" from her former "husband" dedicating her to a new life of the spirit, no longer bound to the letter of the law but "conjoined" (*conjunxit*) to a new spiritual "husband."[89] The exegete is not really interested in righting David's wrongs but focuses on the apparent conflict, for it reveals that even in an event reprehensible in itself God was giving "signs" to future generations about the superiority of Christianity to Judaism. The immorality is less important than the preoccupation to see common themes illustrated in new ways. In this case the union of Christ and the Church, God and the soul of man by virtue of their unifying bond, *caritas,* is totalized in the text. While these meanings are not "literally" present, neither are they hidden in the distant background; from the medieval point of view, they were written "with Goddes fynger."[90]

In these examples, the nature of the linguistic sign is hardly arbitrary. As one commentator has observed, the sign is a "copy" that has the "magical ability to focus . . . reality and bring it into view." Another commentator, E. H. Gombrich, has argued a similar point, maintaining that such signs have their roots in the mythological cultures of prehistory; few have recognized, he argues, that "Western literature and art have preserved the peculiar habits of the ancient world to hypostasize abstract concepts."[91] As the medieval "habit" of reading is determined to reveal, clarify, and make present scriptural meanings, it too hypostasizes an imminent and transcendent order. And what is true of a sign in the Succession Document is true of the medieval sense of history in general: an

---

[89]Rabanus, *PL* 109, 100: "Sed huic David uxorem abstulit sibique conjunxit, quia videlicet *manufortis,* quod David dicitur, in carne Redemptor apparens, dum se spiritualiter loqui legem innotuit, per hoc quod juxta litteram tenebatur, hanc Judaico populo extraneam demonstravit sibique conjunxit, quia per se illam praedicare declaravit"; see also col. 99; *PL* 113, 572; *Biblia sacra cum glossa ordinaria,* 2:574–576.

[90]The reference is from Chaucer's *Summoner's Tale* (line 1890) in *The Works of Geoffrey Chaucer,* ed. F. N. Robinson, 2d ed. (Boston: Houghton Mifflin, 1957).

[91]Harry Berger, "The Ecology of the Medieval Imagination," *Centennial Review* 12 (1968):306. Gombrich, *"Icones Symbolicae,"* p. 126.

event in David's reign could be "read" in the Tree of Jesse, for instance, in the window of Chartres cathedral just as it was "written" in the past of ancient Israel. In these interpretive exercises, performed on Scripture or on nature, the organicism of mythology is in full control of the metaphor of writing.

8

For all their color and invention, the brightly illuminated glosses in the texts of Augustine or the windows of Chartres are not made explicitly in the service of advancing an order of speculative and abstract thought that might be associated with the discipline of philosophical theology. But although medieval hermeneutic practice may lack the "vocabulary" of abstract reference, it nonetheless possesses the "grammar" for it. In the determination to answer authoritatively and thoroughly the questions and doubts, the gaps and lacunae of biblical writing, exegesis carries out a function analogous with that of myth, as argued in recent theory, to *mediate* contradictions and uncertainties in a society, not to doubt things, but "to talk about them; simply, it purifies them, it makes them innocent, it gives them a natural and eternal justification, it gives them a clarity which is not that of an explanation but that of a statement of fact . . . it organizes a world which is without contradictions."[92] Such concerns may not proceed in the language of abstract inquiry, but they obviously engage problems of a very high order of thought. Turning, for example, to the sacrifice of Isaac, the background of mystery and doubt apparently did not draw the attention of the medieval exegete, from what we can tell by the popularity of the following gloss:

> Abraham ergo Deum Patrem significat, Isaac Christum. Sicut enim Abraham unicum et dilectum filium victimam Deo obtulit, sic Deus Pater unigenitum Filium pro nobis tradidit. Et sicut Isaac ligna portabat, quibus imponendus erat, sic Christus crucem, in qua figendus erat.

[92]Roland Barthes, *Mythologies* (Paris: Seuil, 1957), trans. Annette Lavers (New York: Hill & Wang, 1972), p. 143. Cf. Lévi-Strauss's view that the "savage mind totalizes" because it refuses to "allow anything human (or even living) to remain alien to it" (*Savage Mind*, pp. 10, 245) as well as his remarks on the mediation of myth in "The Structural Study of Myth," pp. 216–217, 226, 229.

[Abraham therefore signifies God the Father. Isaac signifies Christ. Just as Abraham offered to God his only beloved son as a victim, God the Father surrendered for us his only begotten Son. And just as Isaac carried the wood, on which he was to be laid, so also did Christ carry the cross on which he was to be fastened.][93]

This mode of thought is not confused by resemblances but is delighted by them, almost unwilling to separate image from referent. To the medieval interpreter, even the wood is not an extravagant parallel, as it motivates a seemingly endless chain of correspondences. The donkey that carried the instruments of the sacrifice signifies the blindness and foolishness of the Jews who bore all the sacraments in Jesus but remained blind to him. The three days' journey of Abraham to the place of the sacrifice signifies the three ages of man: before the Law, from Abraham to Moses; under the Law, from Moses to John; and thereafter under Christ. In place of Isaac, the ram caught in the thicket is sacrificed. The "ram" (*aries*) becomes Christ, the Lamb of God or his "sheep" (*ovis*). "He is the son because born, the ram because sacrificed." The ram stuck in the thicket by its two "horns" (*cornibus*) is Christ crucified by his two "arms" (*cornibus*). The "thickets" (*vepres*) are "thorns" (*spinas*) and the thorns are the "enemies" (*uniquae*) who hung the Lord. "Among the thorns of sins [*spinas peccatorum*] he is suspended." But since the head of the ram was bound in the thicket, that sign is also the crown of "thorns" (*spinas*) on Christ's head.[94]

Rather than illustrating a basic difference, as medieval theoreticians assume, *signa* and *res* are elaborately woven in these metaphorical extensions: exegesis mediates uncertainty by reading events in one part of Scripture as myth is read, according to Lévi-Strauss, as a system of "transformations": "if one aspect of a particular myth seems unintelligible, it can be legitimately dealt with . . . as a transformation of the homologous aspect of another myth, which has been linked with the same group for the sake of the argument, and which lends itelf more readily to interpretation." For example, "the episode of the jaguar's closed jaws" in one myth is the transformation of "the reverse episode of the wide-open jaws" in a myth of another geographical region. Similarly, "the episode of the genuine willingness to help shown by the vultures" in one version may be used to decipher "their false willingness" in another

---

[93]*Glossa ordinaria, PL* 113, 139.
[94]*PL* 113, 138–139.

myth.[95] This sytem of opposites that are actually bound tightly together is remarkably similar to some of the most fundamental principles of medieval exegesis taught by Augustine and later theorists.
"Quid enim quod dicitur Testamentum Vetus, nisi occultatio Novi?
Et quid est aliud quod dicitur Novum nisi Veteris revelatio?" ("Why
is the Testament called Old if it is not the concealment of the New?
And why is the other called New if it is not the revelation uncov-
ering the Old?")[96] David is a type of Christ, Abraham is God the
Father, the donkey the Jews, the wood the cross of the Crucifixion,
and the Old Law a prefiguration of the New: "Vetus Testamentum
in Novo revelatum, in Vetere Novum velatum vides" ("The Old
Testament is unveiled in the New, in the Old you see the New
veiled").[97]

In the eyes of medieval exegetes, the significance of episodes between the two testaments is not absent from the text, nor is it exactly hidden; rather, it is obscured by the veil of writing, and this
"distortion" of sense compares with Barthes's remarks on the function of myth: "However paradoxical it may seem, *myth hides nothing*:
its function is to distort, not to make disappear."[98] Or as Auerbach
puts it, myth "knows only a foreground." Like the "distortions"
between the two testaments, so are there obscured uses of terms
within individual books and chapters of Scripture, as for example,
the use of "leaven" in vituperation against the Pharisees (Matt.
16.11) and in praise of the kingdom of heaven as leavened meal
(Luke 13.20–21). Augustine's principle for this kind of reading
amounts to the "transformational law" operative in myth: "one
thing signifies another thing and still another in such a way that the
second thing signified is contrary to the first or in such a way that
the second thing is entirely different from the first. The things
signified are contrary, that is, when one thing is used as a similitude
in a good sense [*in bono*] and in another place in a evil sense [*in
malo*], like 'leaven' in the above example."[99] The development of
this principle through the major channels of exegesis is witnessed
as late as the fourteenth century in Bersuire's magnificent mine of
readings *in bono* and *in malo*, the *Repertorium morale*. Returning, for

[95]Claude Lévi-Strauss, "Overture," in *The Raw and the Cooked: Introduction to a Science of Mythology,* trans. John and Doreen Weightman (New York: Harper & Row,
1959), 1:13.
[96]*De civitate Dei* 16.26 (*PL* 41, 505). See de Lubac, "Les deux testaments," in
Exégèse, 1.1:328ff.
[97]*In psalmos* 105 (*PL* 40, 1576).
[98]Barthes, *Mythologies,* p. 121.
[99]*De doctrina* 3.25.36 (*PL* 34, 79).

instance, to *aries* ("ram") from Genesis 22, we find a medieval demonstration of the transformational rule in Bersuire's three readings *in bono*:

> *Christum Redemptorem* ("Christ the Redeemer")
> *justum praeceptorem* ("just precept")
> *Christum propugnatorem* ("Christ the Defender")

and one *in malo*:

> *carnalem peccatorem* ("carnal sinner").[100]

Opposites produce meaning just as readily as similarities in Bersuire's entry; for the transformation rests on the larger assumption that contradictions do not exist. In the *Didascalicon* Hugh of St. Victor, following Augustine, advises students in reading Scripture to interpret "the doubtful things . . . in such a way that they may not be out of harmony," for "Divine Scripture is like a building [*aedificium*]":

> The foundation is in the earth, and it does not always have smoothly fitted stones. The superstructure rises above the earth, and it demands a smoothly apportioned construction. Even so the Divine Page, in its literal sense, contains many things which seem both to be opposed to each other and, sometimes, to impart something which smacks of the absurd or the impossible. But the spiritual meaning admits no opposition; in it, many things can be different from one another, but none can be opposed.[101]

Like the idea of the Book, the image of the "building" assumes for Scripture a oneness and totality of its own method of interpreting that knows no background. The *aedificium Scripturae* has no dark corners—terms or episodes that are absent of meaning; they

---

[100]*Opera omnia*, 6 vols. (Cologne, 1730–1731), 1:210A.

[101]*Didascalicon*, p. 140. "Divinam Scripturam aedificio similem dixisse. . . . Fundamentum in terra est, nec semper politos habet lapides. Fabrica super terram, et aequalem quaerit structuram. Sic divina pagina multa secundum naturalem sensum continet, quae et sibi repugnare videntur, et nonnunquam absurditatiis aut impossibilitatis aliquid afferre. Spiritualis autem intelligentia nullam admittit repugnantiam, in qua diversa multa, adversa nulla esse possunt"; *Eruditionis didascalicae* 6.4 (*PL* 176, 802). Hugh goes on to emphasize the "totality" of the *aedificium Scripturae* in the elaborate figure of the eight "courses" of stones; this, he says, "est tota divinitas, haec est illa spiritualis fabrica" (*PL* 176, 803). See the discussion of sacred space in the previous chapter, section 3, note 38, and de Lubac, *Exégèse*, 2.2:41–60.

merely postpone the act of interpretation from eventually catching up with the total sense that is *in* the text. This hypostatization of meaning in a sequence of images, a chapter, or book constitutes a sense of the Bible as an *object* in its own right, not only the expression of the divine will, but a thing sacred in itself. Although medieval tradition perfected the idea of the Book as object, it was the bequest of mythological thinking in which the hypostatization of meaning is commonplace. The dominance of foreground is an obvious example; but the attention in recent theory to elements of transformation and contrasting features irrespective of "content" manifests the widespread evidence of the view that mythical thinking assumes the objective embodiment of meaning. Lévi-Strauss's remarks on the significance of differentiating features formulates for myth a principle that was already at work in the theory of Hugh of St. Victor: "the existence of differentiating features is of much greater importance than their content. Once in evidence, they form a system which can be employed as a grid is used to decipher a text, whose original unintelligibility gives it the appearance of an uninterrupted flow. The grid makes it possible to introduce divisions and contrasts, in other words the formal conditions necessary for a significant message to be conveyed."[102] A medieval exegete would never be convinced that his reading of an image or episode depended not on its intrinsic content but only on its structural differences. For the pearl was *in* the shell and the fruit *in* the chaff as the *Verbum* was implicit in all creation.

Although he would employ such "grids" as reading the Old Testament through the frame of the New and considering images *in bono* for their potential significance *in malo*, the results would affirm an "uninterrupted flow" that was present—for all who had eyes to see—in the bright foreground of Scripture. That signs "naturally" reflect meaning—are metaphorical—protects an assumption of *value* as intrinsic to the signification of an image or event. No matter how much the method of exegesis actually determines meaning from the structural arrangement of such clusters as the donkey, the wood, and the three days' journey, the exegete preserves his sense of the order natural to things by seeing this pattern as a *figura* of the New Testament event. It simply would not occur to him that his method does not actually proceed from what is intrinsic to a sign, that it is constituted not by what is in it, but rather

[102]Lévi-Strauss, *Savage Mind*, p. 75.

by what Saussure calls the principle of natural difference: "whatever distinguishes one sign from the other constitutes it"; the sign is not "constituted by its material substance but by the differences that separate its sound-image from all others." To think that value —as these remarks define it—does not consist in identification, but instead is a function of difference contradicts the entire medieval outlook; yet paradoxically it is operative throughout exegesis, and particularly in the grid of interpreting *in bono* and *in malo*. Although an exegete would no sooner be led to this realization than he would call Scripture a game of chess, as Saussure referred to language, his actual procedure establishes value through differential relations in the same way that Lévi-Strauss analyzes signs in myth: "the terms never have any significance," he argues. "Their meaning is one of 'position'—a function of the history and cultural context on the one hand and of the structural system in which they are called upon to appear on the other."[103] Nothing could be further from the assumptions that maintained the "building of Scripture" and Book of culture, but few insights go so far in explaining how they were constructed.

If we turn to one of the pages in the "script" of nature, for example, the entry for *castor* ("beaver") in the *De universo*, Rabanus Maurus defines the animal according to its nature: "castores a castrando dicti sunt" ("beavers are named for being castrated"). But it is clear that the signification follows from the "position" that the sign is called upon to serve in the long line of commentaries—beginning with Pliny's *Historia naturalis*. The "beaver" *in bono* may be the chaste *eunuchi Dei* in the service of the church or *in malo* the chastened heretics who, like "vices" on the pure body of Christendom, have their genital members cut off, but not a word is given to the beaver's miraculous survival of the impossibility in his name.[104]

Seemingly without limits, the *sacra pagina* in the Books of nature and Scripture affirms correspondences in a world radiant with meaning, because the signified is not limited to specific signifiers. As Barthes has commented on this aspect of myth: "There is no regular ratio between the volume of the signified and that of the signifier. . . . For instance, a whole book may be the signifier of a single [signified] concept; and conversely, a minute form (a word, a

[103]Ibid., p. 55.

[104]*PL* 111, 222; see R. P. Miller, "Chaucer's Pardoner, the Scriptural Eunuch, and the Pardoner's Tale," *Speculum* 30 (1955):180–199.

gesture . . .) can serve as signifier to a concept filled with a very rich history."[105] The order introduced into the universe by means of such systems of signifying is clearly illustrated by the great books of the later centuries, such as the *Speculum majus* of Vincent of Beauvais or the *Opera omnia* of Hugh of St. Cher. But Augustine, a leading initiator of the tradition, did not know how near he was to the mythological thinking he wrote against when he made the entire Bible the signifier of a single concept, the New Law of Charity:

> Whatever appears in the divine Word that does not literally pertain to virtuous behavior or to the truth of faith you must take to be figurative. . . . Scripture teaches nothing but charity . . . it asserts nothing except the catholic faith as it pertains to things past, future, and present. . . . Therefore in the consideration of figurative expressions a rule such as this will serve, that what is read should be subjected to diligent scrutiny until an interpretation contributing to the reign of charity is produced.[106]

The one signified concept is manifestly out of proportion to the infinitely rich signifiers in Scripture and nature; moreover, that proportion is sanctioned by Augustine's teaching that any inquiry into words or things "for their own sake" is the interest of *cupiditas* and carnal knowledge.[107] The instruction sounded throughout the middle ages like an edict against pagan attitudes, but the doctrine of using natural and scriptural phenomena was yet another guise of the mythological outlook: it too is notorious for *using* natural phenomena, instead of trying to explain them as was once assumed: "they are rather the medium through which myths seek to explain facts which are themselves not of a natural but a logical order."[108] The story of Abraham and Isaac or David and Bathsheba, the trees and beavers of the world are "used," according to Augustine's formulation, certainly not in any willful distortion, but as the proper response of making sense of the many pages in the Book of culture. Consequently the speculum created by itemizing all manifestations of the *sensus spiritualis* is a mirror of thought rather than of nature. The mirror held up to nature in the medieval centuries imitates not the phenomena reflected, but the methods of classifying and cataloging them.

[105]Barthes, *Mythologies*, p. 120.
[106]*De doctrina* 3.10.14, 15; 3.15.23; trans., pp. 88, 93 (*PL* 34, 71 and 74).
[107]*De doctrina* 3.10.15−16; trans., p. 88 (*PL* 34, 71−72).
[108]Lévi-Strauss, *Savage Mind*, p. 95.

As exegesis claims that comprehensive order for nature, it *naturalizes* the signified concept, and this principle returns us to the metaphor of writing, cited at the outset, in Sir Thomas Browne's "Letters" of nature and Isidore's observation that writers of learned commentary "turn the ploughshare upon the wax, / and plough with a point of bone." By unveiling the concept, replicating it in nature, exegesis transforms nature from a hypothetical example into the source and "revelation" of the concept itself: the beaver is called *castor* because he is castrated; trees are green because they reflect the unfading justice of God's perennial Word;[109] the human eye has seven coverings because it manifests the seven gifts of the Spirit.[110] What is true in these bits of medieval lore is of a piece with the entire sense of the past as the organization of the six ages of the world. By naturalizing their concepts, medieval habits of thought illustrate what Barthes calls the most basic mythological principle: "it transforms history into nature."[111] From the simplest reading of animals as sentences in medieval bestiaries to the vast panorama of Vincent of Beauvais's *Historia naturalis,* medieval intellectuals read nature as the validation of history, saw in natural phenomena the glowing proof of their ideas. The "mythology" of such a perspective—what allows a medieval interpreter to consume it so thoroughly—is that where only an equivalence is suggested, he sees a "causal process: the signifier and the signified have, in his eyes, a natural relationship . . . the myth-consumer takes the signification for a system of facts: myth is read as a factual system, whereas it is but a semiological system."[112] The reader is led to this involvement because the writing that composed the Book of culture is preoccupied with foreground; questioning, contradiction, and uncertainty cannot disturb the authority of traditional meanings. That the New Law of Charity organized a discipline—if not an entire intellectual tradition—for well over a millennium testifies to the strength of this principle. But it verifies less about the nature of medieval tradition than about the mythological impulse within it that controls, orders, and stabilizes culture. Augustine could no more "demythologize" a pagan tradition than could those who followed his explicit instructions for interpreting

---

[109]See Bede, *PL* 93, 12; Augustine, *PL* 37, 1179.
[110]Cited by Emile Mâle in *The Gothic Image: Religious Art in France of the Thirteenth Century,* trans. Dora Nussey (1913; reprint, New York: Harper & Row, 1958), p. 34.
[111]Barthes, *Mythologies,* p. 129.
[112]Ibid., p. 131.

it. *De doctrina Christiana,* like the theoretical treatises on exegesis that followed it, illustrates what Lévi-Strauss has said about his own analysis of mythological thought: in explaining it he "has had to conform to the requirements of that thought and respect its rhythm. It follows that this book on myths is itself a kind of myth."[113]

The link to older mythological forms of signifying that is apparent in medieval sign theory remains paradoxical in view of the biblical critique of myth and the medieval hermeneutic project that is devoted to carrying out that critique. But medieval forms are hardly a reversion to "archaic" habits, a condition of thinking in which sophisticated problems cannot be engaged. To the contrary, such problems are the primary interest of mythological thought in its prevailing commitment to close gaps and stabilize uncertainty within culture. Medieval hermeneutic theory and practice, to the extent that they are marked by myth, undertake a similar commitment, which is exemplified most apparently in the determined subordination of the several disciplines of learning as so many volumes within the encompassing Book of culture. However, insofar as medieval interpretation stands out in contrast to the biblical materials it seeks to explain, the biblical texts themselves have a noticeably different consequence for medieval signification, one that is not interested necessarily in stabilization, but in the unspecified and unbounded—in the persistent demand for change. Although hermeneutic practice, in such works as the *Glossa ordinaria,* told readers on the authority of tradition what to understand in the effort of foreclosing uncertainty and doubt, the style of biblical writing presented them with the leaven of change. The biblical challenge was controlled as long as it was absorbed within the metaphor of writing in medieval hermeneutics, but it could not be thoroughly suppressed. And where it is not, the opposition to myth is again catalyzed. The challenge is viable wherever the evidence of suppression is not effectively concealed and wherever the metaphor of writing is no longer affirmed through faithful imitation. Such contexts may be sought in various areas of the history of medieval writing, particularly those in which the Bible makes an impact that is not entirely predictable from hermeneutic convention. Medieval fiction provides one of the most obvious examples of such a context. I will turn next to it and first to Dante, since biblical writing occupies so much of his interest in the *Commedia.*

[113]Lévi-Strauss, "Overture," p. 6.

[4]

Dante's *Liber Occultorum*

and the Structure of

Allegory in the *Commedia*

Trasumanar significar per verba
non si poría; però l'essemplo basti
a cui esperienza grazia serba.
Dante, *Paradiso*

1

The survival of mythology in the middle ages received strong support from the tendency of one discipline of study to imitate another. Because learning was based on common assumptions about language—for example, the conception of the linguistic sign as a mirror of its referent—the study of pagan materials reflected the study of the natural world, and both of these imitated the means of interpreting Sacred Scripture. The old pagan gods gained new meanings, but they still figured prominently in a new mythology, the determination to study all of the past as a "text" with a prevailing plot. Among the various disciplines of learning, like so many volumes in a vast Book of culture, fictional writing too might appear—at least initially—to proceed from commonplace assumptions about language as imitation. For all Dante's interest in these issues, his *Commedia* has frequently been cited as the vernacular work that appears to "copy" the medieval idea of the Book in its various manifestations—the encyclopedias and summae. "Dante's cosmic poem," writes Ernst Curtius, "is such a summa too."[1]

[1]Ernst Robert Curtius, *European Literature and the Latin Middle Ages,* trans. Willard R. Trask (New York: Harper & Row, 1963), p. 326

If we search the *Commedia* for examples of medieval notions of language and texts, we will certainly not be disappointed. But to argue that such references illustrate the poetics dominating those medieval theories of writing that created the summa or the Book of nature involves various oversimplifications about the nature of fictive discourse and its essential difference from mythology. It is, I think, too simple to conclude—as many have—that Dante mythologized the medieval past. The crucial factors bypassed in this conclusion become apparent in those attempts, such as Charles Singleton's, to establish that the "Letter to Can Grande della Scala" is a "preface" to the *Commedia* and that the method of composition in the poem is modeled on, for example, the exegesis of a passage from Exodus. Singleton goes so far as to insist on Dante's method as "the imitation of God's way of writing" in Holy Scripture.[2] To explain the poetics of this method, Singleton appeals to Plato's concept of mimesis in the *Republic*. This choice, presumably, is more appropriate to the *Commedia* than, say, a reference to Aristotle, for whom mimesis is the imitation of the process of change and growth in nature. Whereas imitation is a form of creation for Aristotle, Dante appears to be closer to Plato. For the "allegory of the theologians" that informs the *Commedia* assumes that the visual scene is a mirror image of the transcendent order on a par with Plato's sense of imitation as a "reflection" or "copy" of what it tries to represent. When Dante abandons the "allegory of the poets" after the *Convivio,* according to Singleton, he turns to imitate God's writing, to create an image more correspondent to the divine ordo: "Dante is Plato's poet."[3] He would be welcomed into the Republic, were it a Christian utopia.

Within this view, Dante is not a mere copier of the sort whom Plato condemns in his argument against the poets in the *Republic*. Dante escapes Plato's censure of the imitator who loses the true nature of the original in the copy and who is "thrice removed" from the truth. Instead of copying mere appearances, creating "only a kind of play or sport,"[4] Dante's journey through the afterlife is "literal truth"; he gives us not an illusory world of shadows, but the "concrete reality of the world beyond";[5] his "story" lacks the quali-

<hr/>

[2]Charles S. Singleton, *Dante Studies I: "Commedia," Elements of Structure* (Cambridge: Harvard University Press, 1954), p. 15; see Singleton's "In Exitu Israel de Aegypto," *Dante Studies* 78 (1960):1–24; and Robert Hollander, *Allegory in Dante's Comedy* (Princeton: Princeton University Press, 1969), pp. 9–70.

[3]Singleton, *Dante Studies I*, p. 70.

[4]*Republic* 10.598, 602, in *The Dialogues of Plato,* trans. Benjamin Jowett, 4th ed. 4 vols. (Oxford: Clarendon Press, 1953) 2:471, 477.

[5]*Dante Studies I*, pp. 72, 73.

ties of the illusory and fictive: Singleton argues that it is a special kind of "history." "The fiction of the *Divine Comedy* is that it is not fiction. And no work ever guarded that fundamental hypothesis more carefully. Nowhere in the work is this vision of things beyond presented as a vision or a dream. These things happened, and the poet who went that way in the flesh and experienced them is, now that he has returned, a scribe who sets them down as they occurred."[6] Although this approach to imitation in the *Commedia* rescues the "copy" from the tarnished world of appearance and resemblance, it does not conceptually distinguish fiction from documentary history. Yet neither of these categories is quite right for the *Commedia*, according to Singleton; instead, the special mode of this "nonfictive" fiction is *myth*. For the *Commedia*, and this is the problem of his position, calls not for the conditional assent made to fictions, but for the absolute response that we make to myth. The poem invites this response because it "protects itself from any undermining awareness of illusion."[7] To witness how typical of myth this quality of response is, we need only compare Dante's narrative with some of Plato's dialogues, like the *Timaeus*, or for that matter with the great bulk of medieval commentaries on it. Since the renaissance, argues Singleton, we may have lost the will to respond as medievals responded to the myths of their time; yet we fail to read the *Commedia* correctly, he concludes, unless we "face the myth as myth" and believe that this is a vision not of things as we want them to be, "but as they are."[8]

While this argument rests firmly on the principle of imitation that informs many medieval disciplines and accounts for the role that response plays in perpetuating the myth of the Book, it oversimplifies the nature of response called for in Dante's *Commedia*. A distinctly contrasting approach to the poem has been argued by John Freccero. He has compared the work to a "spiritual autobiography, a novel of the self."[9] The *Commedia*, he maintains, is devoted to capturing the essence of Dante's experience of religious conversion, but it is not like a nineteenth-century autobiography

[6]Ibid., p. 62.

[7]Ibid.

[8]Ibid., pp. 78–79, 81. See also the critique of Singleton's position by Richard Hamilton Green, "Dante's 'Allegory of the Poets' and the Mediaeval Theory of Poetic Fiction," *Comparative Literature* 9 (1957):118–128; Singleton's rebuttal is in 9:129–135.

[9]John Freccero, "Dante's Novel of the Self," *Christian Century* 82 (1965):216–218. Also see Freccero's "*Medusa*: The Letter and the Spirit (*Inf.* IX)," *Yearbook of Italian Studies* (1972), pp. 1–18, and "Dante's *Medusa*: Allegory and Autobiography," in *By Things Seen: Reference and Recognition in Medieval Thought*, ed. David L. Jeffrey (Ottawa: University of Ottawa Press, 1979), pp. 33–46.

because it does not seek as its primary intention to beguile us by its realistic detail and to put us into its world. Instead, we ought to see the *Commedia* as an extended exemplum of the experience of grace.[10] In the first canto of *Paradiso*, for example, Dante himself provides a cue to understanding his poetics:

> Transumanar significar per verba
> non si poría; però l'essemplo basti
> a cui esperienza grazia serba.
>
> (*Para.* 1.70–72)

[The passing beyond humanity may not be set forth in words: therefore let the example suffice any for whom grace reserves the experience.][11]

This perspective, if applied to the poem as a whole, clearly separates the experience of the grace of conversion from the expression of that experience in the poem. For "the Dante who *is* tells the story of the Dante who *was*," and the fictional record is understood as an attempt to explain and clarify the nature of that conversion. The poem, Freccero continues, is a "confession of faith," like Augustine's famous example, and renders the conversion of the "old man" into the "new" by casting the poet's persona as a detached self who must come to understand the meaning of ascent.[12] The gap between poet and pilgrim is widest at the opening of the poem, but it slowly closes as understanding increases until the sight of the pilgrim is one with the poet's vision of light at the end of the *Paradiso*.

Freccero's idea of the *Commedia* as a "novel of the self" departs markedly from Singleton's sense of it as a "myth." As a result of this departure, we are now in a position to establish that the poetics of the poem and the response it calls for differ sharply from the Platonic aesthetics of imitation. To begin with, the medieval myth of the Book makes a claim to truth that precludes all others; it asks for unquestioned belief in its imagery, its mental picture of the beyond, its pilgrimage. By contrast, Dante's poem—and this is the unavoidable difference—does not ask us to believe in the *story* of

---

[10]John Freccero, "Introduction," in *Dante: A Collection of Critical Essays*, ed. John Freccero (Englewood Cliffs, N.J.: Prentice-Hall, 1965), pp. 3–4.

[11]*La divina commedia*, ed. Natalino Sapegno (Florence: Nuova Italia, 1955–1957): quotations from this edition are cited in the text; Charles S. Singleton, trans., *The Divine Comedy* (Princeton: Princeton University Press, 1970–1975), *Paradiso*, p. 7: unless otherwise noted, translations are Singleton's.

[12]Freccero, "Introduction," in *Dante*, pp. 4, 5–6.

the pilgrimage, but in the religious *experience* of which that journey is an illusion. The absolute assent to the illusion of the scenes of the afterlife is made only by the poet's persona. He believes profoundly in "the concrete reality of the world beyond"; for him only are the words over the hellgate—"Lasciate ogni speranza, voi ch'entrate" (*Inf.* 3.9)—"real" words.[13] But the pilgrim's point of view, like the perspective of the participants in Plato's dialogues, needs continual correction and adjustment. By means of this narrative strategy, an awareness of illusion making is inevitable. The poem therefore does not protect itself from such awareness but encourages it. Through his mistakes, the pilgrim comes to new understanding, and more broadly, as our awareness exceeds his, the illusion-making devices of the poem invite us to consider the nature of spiritual experience. The fiction of the journey is not, in effect, one among several possible "versions" of Dante's experience of conversion but a "preface" to its depth and complexity.

Because the nature of illusion in the *Commedia* is thus conditional, the Platonic poetics of imitation as copying, which informs medieval disciplines of learning, only partially explains the kind of narrative Dante has made. He includes the vast cosmos of medieval lore and learning, but rather than "imitating" that material, he uses it to "interpret" religious experience. Readers of Dante have recognized from the very beginning that the *Commedia* needs interpretation. But my point is that the language of the poem is itself an interpretation, and this claim shifts distinctly away from the view that Dante's text is a mirror copying the Book of creation. The shift may be understood by reference to a more recent development in the history of ideas about literature, the emergence—in recent departures from American formalism (New Criticism)—of a definition of language as interpretive rather than mimetic and objective.[14] Albeit in far less sophisticated philosophical moves than are familiar since Heidegger, Dante nonetheless shifted away from a similarly deep tradition of imitation and refined a similar idea of

[13]To insist that the words are "real," as do the apologists of the "allegory of theologians"—notably Hollander, *Allegory*, pp. 48, 72—is to see exclusively from the limited point of view of the poet's fictive self, the pilgrim, and to locate religious belief in the story itself, as Singleton does: *Dante Studies I*, pp. 77–81; *Comparative Literature* 9:134–135.

[14]The mot succinct argument concerning this departure is Paul de Man's "Form and Intent in the American New Criticism," in *Blindness and Insight* (New York: Oxford University Press, 1971), pp. 20–35, which is a critique of the concepts of intentionality and objectivity in formalism as represented, for example, by W. K. Wimsatt and M. C. Beardsley, "The Intentional Fallacy," in *The Verbal Icon* (1954; reprint, New York: Noonday Press, 1965), pp. 3–18.

language as a mode of interpretation. Moreover, the consequences are just as significant: although Dante was educated within a rich mythological tradition, he does not mythologize the past. His poem offers an alternative to the myth of the Book of culture. Its contents supply the materials for his story, but that is only the occasion for imagining beyond it the fullness of religious experience.

2

Among the various means through which the poetics of interpretation becomes apparent in the *Commedia,* one that readily suggests itself is the imagery of books and reading. But since such references have commonly been regarded as Dante's efforts to give us a speculum of the Book of creation and to render a portrait of the poet as a theologian, the image of the book has not been considered for the ways it creates the "textuality" of the poem, draws attention to the work as a structure conscious of its own interpretive strategy. That the textuality of the *Commedia* has been bypassed in favor of seeing it as an "object" in a mirror follows from the assumption that the poetics of the poem ought to be sought in certain theoretical texts, like the "Letter to Can Grande." When we turn, however, to the poem itself for theoretical suggestions, a passage such as *Inferno* 11 significantly qualifies the Platonic idea of art as a "copy." Lecturing on the nature of Dante's poetic composition, Virgil says:

> natura lo suo corso prende
> da divino intelletto e da sua arte;
>   e se tu ben la tua Fisica note,
>   tu troverai, non dopo molte carte,
> che l'arte vostra quella, quanto pote,
>   segue, come 'l maestro fa il discente;
>   sí che vostr'arte a Dio quasi è nepote.
> (*Inf.* 11.99–105)

[Nature takes her course from divine Intellect and from Its art; and if you note well your *Physics,* you will find, after not many pages, that your art, as far as it can, follows her, as the pupil does his master; so that your art is as it were the grandchild of God.][15]

[15]Singleton, *Inferno,* p. 115.

[144]

Although the passage speaks of nature following the divine intellect and art following nature—of art as the grandchild of God —explicit reference to Plato or Augustine on art as speculum is not present. On the contrary, Dante refers to Aristotelian "Filosophia" (line 97) and to Aristotle's text, the *Physics*. Furthermore, the whole discussion about art is not made for its own sake, but serves as an example in Virgil's answer to Dante's question of how usury is an offense to God's bounty, "la divina bontade" (line 96). It is offensive, says Virgil, because instead of true and honest labor, usury contrives "another way" ("altra via," line 109). His comparisons for honest work—nature and art—are examples of how man may legitimately earn his bread, as Genesis explains (lines 106–108). Usury offends such labors, but not because it is a poor likeness of them. Rather, usury is not a way of making and producing as the divine intellect makes nature and the poet creates his poem. It lacks the fundamental principle of labor, which is to create, and thus it scandalizes "la divina bontade."

In the context of this argument, the "imitation" of nature and art is not informed by the idea of copying. In "natura lo suo corso prende" (line 99), "course" has been made by the divine whose creative principle is ongoing in it. The reference to Aristotle's *Physics* (book 2) provides the *auctoritas* for the claim that the poet's art "follows" ("segue") nature.[16] But where Aristotle explains in book 2 of the *Physics* that art and human industry bring nature to perfection by completing nature's teleology, by making a finished form, Virgil says—not without a hint of irony—that Dante's poetry follows nature "as far as [however] it can" ("quanto pote," line 103). The stress is not on the perfected, finished thing, but on the process of generating and producing, and these ideas are carried out by the similes that art is like the "student" of the "teacher" and the "grandchild" of God. Usury violates bounty because in true work creating is always going on, as the master's teaching lives in the student and God lives in the grandchild. Shifting completely away from Platonic mimesis, *Inferno* 11 prefers Aristotle's view but qualifies his stress on the objective form of art. In the end, Dante has the last word about the poetics of his poem: he says that poetry imitates not *what* nature makes, but *as* nature makes. It carries on the process of creating and producing that is going on in nature in the

---

[16]See Aristotle, *The Physics,* trans. Philip H. Wicksteed and Francis M. Cornford (Cambridge: Harvard University Press, 1963), book 2, chap. 1, pp. 112–115.

hand of the *Deus Artifex*.[17] Instead of reflecting an object in the mirror, the passage suggests a poetics of *producing* meaning as a teacher does and the student does after him.[18] This process is in the making through the reader's interaction with the text. The form of the poem therefore is not, as it is for Aristotle, a concretized or objectified thing; rather, form is ongoing in the process of interpretation, coming into being in the dynamics of response. One of the ways Dante renders this sense of form as a continuous process is through the question of the adequacy of response. Consideration of this issue, which Dante takes up in several passages in the *Commedia*, will show further how imitation gives place to interpretation in the poetics of the poem.

While Virgil's words, "as the student follows his teacher," refer to poetic creation, they apply as well to the immediate, dramatic situation of the poem: the student Dante follows his master Virgil not to duplicate certain passages of the *Aeneid* or other books; the pilgrim's path through past texts, the book of experience, and the words of those with whom he converses on the journey are anything but arrow straight. Confusion, forgetting, dim perception, and contradiction constitute the ways of trying to understand that the pilgrim must experience: this "following" of the master is natural to the process of generating meaning in interpretation. When the journey begins, the muse of memory is invoked as a "copyist" who wrote down what the poet saw along the way:

> O muse, o alto ingegno, or m'aiutate;
> o mente che scrivesti ciò ch'io vidi.
> *(Inf.* 2.7–8)

> [O Muses, O high genius, help me now!
> O memory that wrote down what I saw.][19]

[17]The difference between Aristotle and Dante on poetic form can be further distinguished by reference to Aristotle's concept of poetic language as an imitation of the teleology of form in nature: any part is a symbolic participation in the process of the whole. But Dante's process compares with de Man's critique of the Aristotelian view of form in New Criticism: "form is never anything but a process on the way to its completion. The completed form never exists as a concrete aspect of the work that could coincide with a sensorial or semantic dimension of the language. It is constituted in the mind of the interpreter as the work discloses itself in response to his questioning." "Form and Intent," pp. 31–32.

[18]Dante's strategy illustrates Wolfgang Iser's formulation of the structure of fictive discourse as "an organization of signifiers which do not designate a signified object, but instead designate *instructions* for the *production* of the signified"; "The Reality of Fiction: A Functionalist Approach to Literature," *NLH* 7 (1975):18.

[19]Singleton, *Inferno*, p. 13.

Although the poet is trying to read from memory all that once took place, it is clear that what memory "copied" is no longer fully present to him: his knowledge is a vague and incomplete "text" that is dependent on time for its revelation. When the journey ends and memory has done its work of recall, the poet sees his experience *sub specie aeternitatis*, sees in an instant the heavens as a "volume" (*Para.* 28.13) and the universe "bound by love in one single volume" (*Para.* 33.86).[20] Between the text of dim memory at the opening of the poem and the book of the cosmos at the end, the narrator speaks directly and personally to us as readers, not to a vast public in the dramatized omniscient voice typical of epic: "O you who read" (*Inf.* 22.118); "If I had, reader, greater space for writing" (*Purg.* 33.136); "Lift then your sight with me, reader, to the lofty wheels" (*Para.* 10.7).[21]

Such direct addresses encourage the reader to treat the events of the quest as the experience of reading and to study, consider, and interpret in order to overcome the weaknesses of learning and remembering. Dante anticipates this experience for his reader by recalling at the opening of the poem his own experience of learning by long hours of study ("lungo studio") in the "volume" of Virgil, "mio maestro e 'l mio autore" (*Inf.* 1.83, 84, 85). These addresses to the reader, moreover, ask for attention in the vocabulary familiar in treatises on interpretation, thus requesting an approach to the experience of the beyond as a "text" awaiting analysis:

> lettor, prender frutto
> di tua lezione.
>
> (*Inf.* 20.19–20)

[Reader . . . take profit from your reading.]

> Aguzza qui, lettor, ben li occhi al vero,
> ché 'l velo è ora ben tanto sottile,
> certo che 'l trapassar dentro è leggero.
>
> (*Purg.* 8.19–21)

[Reader, here sharpen well your eyes to the truth, for the veil is now indeed so thin that certainly to pass within is easy.]

---

[20]Singleton, *Paradiso*, p. 377.
[21]*Inferno*, my translation; Singleton, *Purgatorio*, p. 371; *Paradiso*, p. 107.

Or ti riman, lettor, sovra 'l tuo banco,
dietro pensando a ciò che si preliba,
s'esser vuoi lieto assai prima che stanco.
(*Para.* 10.22–24)

[Now remain, reader, upon your bench, reflecting on this of which
you have a foretaste, if you would be glad far sooner than weary.][22]

While such passages serve our perspective on the poem, they are
even more critically relevant to the pilgrim who speaks them, for it
is he who, notwithstanding his own advice, forgets or misperceives
the books he has read and only slowly comes to regard his own experience as a text in need of interpretation.

A notable instance of forgetting of this sort occurs in *Inferno* 13
as the pilgrim passes through the wood of the suicides and encoun-
ters Pier delle Vigne. Had the pilgrim recalled the text concerning
the bleeding tree in the *Aeneid,* he might have been less confused in
trying to understand the source of the wailing voices among the
trees. Instead of imagining that the voices come from persons hiding behind the trees, he might have been ready to see the trees as
signs and Virgil's suggestion to break a twig from one of them as
the master's attempt to call attention to his own poem in order to
lead his student directly to the source of the text in Book 3 of the
Aeneid. But Dante follows Virgil by interpreting the original text,
not by miming it. When the tree is treated as a thing instead of a
sign, the broken branch turns into a sign pouring forth words like
sap: "sí della scheggia rotta usciva inseme / parole e sangue" ("so
from the broken twig came out words and blood together"; 13.43–
44).[23] The words speak the anguish of the wounded soul at the
same time as they behave like physical substance dripping blood
onto the ground. The bleeding tree of *Aeneid* 3 is interpreted as an
image of the suicide: he who does violence to himself treats himself
as a thing by failing to see that man is an image of the divine, a tree
of many virtues; he must endure the *contrapasso* of the thing trying
in vain to turn itself into a sign.

More broadly, as Virgil calls attention to his own poem, the textuality of the *Commedia* presents itself in a new aspect. Virgil's remark that the pilgrim has not had the text of the *Aeneid* fully in
mind compares with *Inferno* 2 in which the muse of memory is invoked as the copyist of the full text of the poet's journey. But from

[22]Singleton, *Inferno,* p. 205; *Purgatorio,* p. 77; *Paradiso,* p. 109.
[23]Singleton, *Inferno,* p. 131.

these assumptions of absence, the poet is not led to replicate the book of memory, either literary tradition (the *Aeneid*) or experience. Instead of reproducing them in their full presence, Dante is suggesting that writing cannot avoid becoming an interpretation of them and initiating change in the process. The "original" text cannot be recreated, only supplemented. Or, to put the matter another way, writing distances or alienates its sources even as it tries to retrieve them. They cannot be, so to speak, "rewritten," because a new context sets in sharp relief—it does not foreclose—the alterity of the past. Since responses that bypass this "alienation effect" of writing are incomplete, they serve Dante in various ways, one of which informs the "reading episode" of Paolo and Francesca in *Inferno* 5.

3

From the many critical responses this canto has attracted, one point has claimed central attention: the function of literature as a mediation of desire. As the lovers read one day for delight the story of Lancelot and Guinevere, the moment of their reading irrepressibly fades into the past moment about which they read; for the instant of the kiss, the illusion of the past vanishes as they are one with the glow of desire of the legendary figures. Their initial assent to the fiction is absolute, not conditional, as they enter into the world of romance and imagine themselves with Queen Guinevere and Lancelot. So complete is their assent that it is possible to explain the intensification of their desire as the result of the presence of the figures in the romance. As René Girard has described this effect: "the hero in the grip of some second-hand desire seeks to conquer the *being*, the essence, of his model by as faithful an imitation as possible."[24] In such "mimetic desire," Paolo does not really seek to take the place of Lancelot in the effort of winning Francesca; rather, Paolo desires her because of the presence of Lancelot, by linking her with him as a rival. Instead of trying to displace Lancelot, Paolo seeks to imitate him in order to desire Francesca more intensely himself. Reading is vital to this dynamic of passion, for the book itself becomes the equivalent of the go-between in *Lancelot du Lac*:

[24]René Girard, "From 'The Divine Comedy' to the Sociology of the Novel," trans. Petra Morrison, in *Sociology of Literature and Drama*, ed. Elizabeth and Thomas Barns (Baltimore: Penguin Books, 1973), p. 104.

Galetto fu il libro e chi lo scrisse.
(Inf. 5.137)

[A Gallehault was the book and he who wrote it.][25]

The lovers are "seduced" by the book. When Francesca says that they read no more "that day" ("quel giorno"; line 136), the suggestion is that they turned to the book again on other days and relived the original passion.

But Dante does not present the story without qualification as a tragedy of a love that should have been pardoned. For the French romance recapitulated by Francesca contrasts the story of her experience with Paolo on several points, so that the second text reveals itself as merely a supplement, and even a degeneration, of the original. The differences become clear in the ways that Francesca's language, as Renato Poggioli has shown, "transforms" the French text.[26] As soon as Francesca describes the kiss, for example, she realizes that she and Paolo compare not at all with the marvelous figures in the book. After Lancelot embraces the queen, Francesca refers to "this one" ("questi") by her side "who never shall be parted from me" ("che mai da me non fia diviso"; line 135).[27] She cries in desire for him, but the ambiguity of despair in being bound to him for eternity cannot be kept out of the line. Furthermore, Paolo's kiss lacks the mysterious spell of the fantasy of Lancelot's embrace: the queen's "smile" ("riso"; line 133) has been reduced to Francesca's "mouth" ("bocca"; line 136). The power of love's illusion is weakening, and the qualification is made final in the closing line in which the book and its author are named "Galeotto." The tone is a deliberate paradox of approval and disapproval, for the beauty and intoxication of the text have concealed the deception and destruction it has caused, like the grand yet cunning Galahad of the original.

The story of the lovers departs from the French romance in still more compelling ways. Francesca's speech, for instance, echoes enough of the poetry of the *dolce stil nuovo* to sound like a copy of it, but the suggestion of similarity immediately establishes that she is nothing like the ladies of that style. First of all, no woman in any of the poems in the "new sweet style" speaks in the first person. Men

[25]Singleton, *Inferno*, p. 55.
[26]Subsequent discussion of this point is based on Poggioli's essay, "Paolo and Francesca," in *Dante: A Collection of Critical Essays*, ed. John Freccero, pp. 61–77 (orig. pub. *PMLA*, vol. 72, 1957).
[27]Singleton, *Inferno*, p. 55.

take such roles. But Paolo speaks not a syllable in the entire episode. When Francesca speaks, her Provençal diction, revealed by such words as "piacer" (line 104), makes itself heard just as clearly as her Italian style.[28] She begins her "poem" with the line, "Amor, ch'al cor gentil ratto s'apprendre" (line 100), which imitates, if it does not reproduce, the famous line of Guido Guinizelli, "Al cor gentil ripara sempre amore" ("love always repairs to the gentle heart").[29] To the poets of the *dolce stil* and their admirers, such as Geoffrey Chaucer, love is identified with the gentle of heart not because of gentility of lineage, but because of gentle deeds, virtuous behavior.[30] Gentility comes from love, not birth, but Francesca does not exactly see it that way in her "lyric":

> Amor, ch'a nullo amato amar perdona,
> mi prese del costui piacer sí forte,
> che, come vedi, ancor non m'abbandona.
> (*Inf.* 5.103–105)

[Love, which absolves no loved one from loving, seized me so strongly with delight in him, that, as you see, it does not leave me even now.][31]

Although her speech echoes literary tradition, it is not by any means the poetry of Arnaut Daniel, Guinizelli, or Dante himself in *La vita nuova*. Her discourse, rather, is from the prose romances of France, the place of origin of her name, which, incidentally, means "French." Although her language sounds like an imitation, she appropriates only enough of the *dolce stil* to enunciate a difference and departure from it.

Sensitivity to these differences, however, does not characterize the response of Dante the pilgrim. He behaves, as has been noticed, rather like Paolo, who is silent, trembling, weak, and effeminate.[32] It may be imagined that he is made effeminate by love, but that trait is not Dante's invention, nor is love the only cause of it.

---

[28]Poggioli, "Paolo and Francesca," p. 67.

[29]See Sapegno's note to *Inferno* 5.100, p. 62. In *La vita nuova*, sonnet 20, line 1 is based on Guinizelli's verse: "Amore e 'l cor gentil sono una cosa, / Sì come il saggio in suo dittare pone"; the "sage" is Guinizelli—see *La vita nuova*, trans. Mark Musa (Bloomington: Indiana University Press, 1965), p. 37.

[30]See Chaucer's lyric "Gentilesse" and the disquisition on the subject in the Wife of Bath's Tale, in *The Works of Geoffrey Chaucer*, ed. F. N. Robinson, 2d ed. (Boston: Houghton Mifflin, 1957), pp. 87, 536.

[31]Singleton, *Inferno*, p. 53. The notion of the seizure of love is, of course, not a stilnovistic commonplace as these lines assume.

[32]For example, Poggioli, "Paolo and Francesca," p. 66.

The idea of male effeminacy in this context stems from a familiar medieval allegorization of the Fall, the identification of Adam with reason, Eve with sense appetite, and the fruit with delight.[33] The result of Eve's temptation and Adam's capitulation was the inversion of the proper order of masculine control over feminine desire, an "adultery" of the perfect marriage in the Eden of the soul. Dante is apparently sensitive to this commonplace understanding of the Fall in his portrait of the weakness of Paolo. In him the Eve of desire has risen up to overtake the Adam of reason through adultery and has left him effeminate in subservience for all eternity. It is this person with whom Dante the pilgrim identifies, and the consequences are startling as Dante follows Paolo and Adam in his own fall, "come corpo morte cade" ("as a dead body falls"; line 143), to the floor of hell.[34] He listens to Francesca's account of her romance with Paolo and the story within it with the same avidity and involvement as they had in responding to the French text. Like theirs, his response is immediate and absolute. He "reads" as they do, without detachment, without objectivity, and certainly without interpretation. Paolo, Francesca, and for the moment Dante too all confirm Plato's fear about response to imitation: its illusion is so powerful as to rival reality and seduce the observer.

But Dante's reference is not to Plato. In canto 5, he comments on the poetics of response through an interpretation of various medieval ideas about reading and the fall of man. On the basis of the exegetical tradition that identified spiritual blindness and sense appetite with the feminity of Eve, Dante establishes a parallel between the carnal desire and fornication of the lovers and their response to the French text. The parallel makes use of the fundamental distinction, argued by Augustine in *De doctrina Christiana*, between "enjoying" a text "for its own sake" and "using" its literal sense in order to understand spiritual truth.[35] The failure to make this distinction in reading results in "carnal" and "feminine" enjoyment, the kind we observe in Paolo and Francesca or that is illustrated by Augustine himself in his account in the *Confessions* (book 1) of reading the story of Dido.[36] Delight in the text for its own sake is so in-

---

[33]This medieval tradition developed from Augustine's allegorization of the Fall in *De trinitate* 12.12 (*PL* 42, 1007–1008). For example, see Peter Lombard, *Sententiae* 2.24.6–9 (*PL* 192, 702–705).

[34]Singleton, *Inferno*, p. 57.

[35]*De doctrina* 1.3.3–1.4.4; 3.5.9; 3.12.18 (*PL* 34, 20–21; 68–69; 72–73).

[36]Augustine identifies "literal" with "carnal" understanding in *De doctrina* (3.5.9): "For at the outset you must be very careful lest you take figurative expressions literally. What the Apostle says pertains to this problem: 'For the letter killeth, but the

tense for Augustine that he weeps for Dido when he has not yet wept for Christ. Such literal-minded reading leads away from spirituality, Augustine concludes, as a form of fornication. Dante would have seen in such reading a dramatization of Saint Paul's remark, "the letter killeth: but the spirit quickeneth" (2 Cor. 3.6), for canto 5 reflects such an interpretation in the story of the adulterers reading the story of adultery and dying in the act of their sin. The lovers read one day "per diletto" ("for delight"; line 127) "enjoying" the text for its own sake until their "literal knowledge" of it becomes their "carnal knowledge" of each other. Dante turns the book of Lancelot itself into an instrument of fornication and ends his canto in what amounts to a challenge to his readers to see the parallel between Paolo's fall and Dante's fall to the floor of hell, lest the *Inferno*, too, become an instrument of "fornication."

Dante's response to the "text" of Francesca's experience, like her own response to the French book, has precluded comment in the discourse on the many echoes in her words of texts from the past. The obvious parallel with the fall of Adam and Eve through "adulterous" reading provokes no notice. Nor do the lines that bristle with suggestions of Dido and Aeneas. The invitation to recall the *Aeneid* comes in Francesca's remark "e ciò sa 'l tuo dottore" ("and this your teacher knows"; line 123), which connects the story of lost love in Virgil's poem with Boethius's definition of tragedy. A few lines later her comment opening the story of reading, "Noi leggiavamo un giorno" ("we read one day"; line 127), balances her closing line, "quel giorno piú non vi leggemmo avante" ("that day we read no farther in it"; line 138), and both recall, as has been observed, a line from Augustine's *Confessions*, "nec ultra legere volui" ("no longer did I wish to read").[37] Augustine stops reading, he tells us, at Rom. 13.12−13 as the text converts him from wantonness to the love of God. Were Francesca's story a penitential confession, we might justify her desire to echo the words of the most famous conversion in Christian history. But since she is reminiscing about her fornication, her discourse keeps the recollection of Augustine in the background, silences it. Similarly, her description of reading parallels at a number of points Augustine's reading of the

---

spirit quickeneth.' That is, when that which is said figuratively is taken as though it were literal, it is understood carnally. Nor can anything more appropriately be called the death of the soul." *On Christian Doctrine*, trans. D. W. Robertson, Jr. (New York: Liberal Arts Press, 1958), pp. 83−84.

[37]Singleton, *Inferno*, p. 55. Hollander, *Allegory*, pp. 112−114; Guiseppe Mazzotta, *Dante, Poet of the Desert: History and Allegory in the "Divine Comedy"* (Princeton: Princeton University Press, 1979), p. 166. *Confessions* 8.12 (*PL* 32, 762).

Aeneid; and as Augustine weeps for Dido, so too does Dante cry: "Francesca, i tuoi martiri / a lacrimar mi fanno tristo e pio" ("Francesca, your torments make me weep for grief and pity"; lines 116–117).[38] But whereas Augustine repudiates himself for indulging in the *Aeneid* for its own sake, for his "adulterous" reading, Dante's text makes no such confessions. The echoes of the past do not disturb the surface of Francesca's discourse, and this effect is entirely in keeping with the poet's larger purpose. He is not imitating Augustine or Virgil, but interpreting them for the particular purposes of his poem. His text counts for its meaning on the ignorance of Francesca and the silence of the pilgrim, on the pastness and difference of the texts that they echo and even quote without realizing the significance of their own words.

4

From these responses to reading, it becomes apparent that canto 5 illustrates a rather different conception of the structure of reference than is argued in the view that Dante's *Commedia* employs a poetics of imitation as copying. The use of the term "allegory" to describe this poetics usually assumes that the structure of various "levels" of reference is essentially symbolic: the eternal is translucent in the natural, and the timeless is made present in and through the temporal;[39] medieval theory massively underwrites such a concept of structure through its insistence on the organic bond in which image and substance are part and whole—*pars pro toto*; the veil of the literal sense takes its form from the other levels of the *sensus spiritualis,* which have a simultaneous order and a simultaneous presence in the literal; diachrony no longer separates levels of sense when the "wood" Isaac carried in the Old Testament is read as the "wood" Christ carried to Calvary in the New.

But this symbolic coalescence of part into whole is not the structure of allegory in canto 5.[40] Dante the pilgrim does not see that

---

[38]Singleton, *Inferno,* p. 55.

[39]For a discussion of these points, see above chapter 3, section 5.

[40]Although most modern studies of allegory try to see (and justify) the mode as a symbolic structure (e.g., Angus Fletcher, *Allegory: The Theory of a Symbolic Mode* [Ithaca: Cornell University Press, 1964]), one sharp and provocative departure has been argued by Paul de Man, "The Rhetoric of Temporality," in *Interpretation: Theory and Practice,* ed. Charles S. Singleton (Baltimore: Johns Hopkins University Press, 1969). De Man is not concerned with medieval sources, but they prove forcefully his argument about the preoccupation of allegory with time.

Francesca is a sign of Dido, Eve, and other banished daughters, because he sees only "in the present." Nor does he see that he himself is repeating Paolo's mystified reading of Guinevere and Augustine's of Dido. Lacking a sense of the timeless in this order beyond time, he sees Francesca as "present," while she is a shade of someone who once was and who is destined to live her past always as her future. She has no present. The pilgrim illustrates ignorance of this temporal difference when, for example, he sheds tears for her, but the text is painfully aware of the demands of time: the Francesca who *speaks* can never coincide with the Francesca who *was* to relive, change, or justify her past; her pain is constituted in blindly trying to collapse the distance, close the gap, become that person again; no longer a "person," she endures a condition in which she is linked "allegorically" to other signs, which she also repeats. Allegory depersonalizes Francesca. Her loss of selfhood is her punishment and the "meaning" of the allegory.

Rather than turn to medieval theoretical treatises to understand the nature of Dante's allegory, we may reverse the procedure and find in his poem the evidence of how he understood them. The "Letter to Can Grande," which has been used to validate a poetics of imitation for the *Commedia,* is on the contrary emphatic about the distance between levels of reference, such as we find in canto 5. For we are told in the "Letter" that all the senses beyond the literal may be called "allegorical" because they are "alien" from the *sensus literalis.* This definition is justified etymologically, says the "Letter," since "allegory is derived from *alleon,* in Greek, which means the same as the Latin *alienum* or *divisum*."[41] The same point about the alienation of sense also informs Isidore's classic definition of allegory in the *Etymologiarum* as *alieniloquium*: "alien-speech"—the troping of the literal in such a way that one thing is said by the words, but something else is understood ("allegoria est alieniloquium, aliud enim sonat, aliud intelligitur").[42]

It would be difficult to offer these definitions in support of allegory as a symbolic structure, and it is impossible to establish from them a poetics of imitation as copying in canto 5. Dante's allegory insists on the division and separation of signs, on the impossibility

[41]Trans. P. H. Wicksteed in *Critical Theory since Plato,* ed. Hazard Adams (New York: Harcourt Brace, 1971), p. 122.

[42]*Etymologiarum* 1.37.22 (*PL* 82, 115). *Inferno,* canto 5, as well as other passages in the *Commedia* under discussion, suggests that the symbolic structure of the "spiritual senses" mentioned in the "Letter" cannot also apply to the "literal sense"; rather, the explanation of their difference as *alienum* indicates a clear temporal split that is essentially opposed to symbolic structure.

of the allegorical sign to erase the anteriority of its origin.[43] In contrast, because symbol, so to speak, forgets its past, Dante creates a mode so mindful of it—a gallery of figures, such as Francesca, Pier delle Vigne, and others, who are always pointing back to their past and the signs from the past whom they repeat. If symbol has no history, allegory in Dante's *Commedia* is the vehicle of it. This point, however, is not in effect a reiteration of the view that the poem is an "allegory of theologians" that insists on the literal sense of the poem as documentary history. Instead, the issue here compares with the position argued recently and provocatively by Giuseppe Mazzotta, that the *Commedia* is an "allegory of its possible readings . . . the act of reading . . . is at the same time for Dante a veritable allegory of the quest."[44] Dante, Mazzotta claims, does not attempt to render the literal sense as a mimesis of history, but rather "insinuates the oblique and shadowy path of metaphoric language in which truth and fiction have simultaneous existence."[45] The experience of reading created in the *Commedia* is not, therefore, a historian's encounter with a journey into the beyond, but an approximation of a quest for "representation adequate to its spiritual reality." Dante is a "poet of the desert" who is "away from his promised land and still in exile." He has not created a mirror of history but has dramatized the "persistent ambiguity of metaphoric language" in the form of the journey to spiritual clarification.[46]

"Ambiguity" in this discussion does not suggest that the meaning of certain passages in the *Commedia* is flawed or vague. On the contrary, Mazzotta means that various passages in the poem confront the problem that the relation between spiritual reality and its representation is by its very nature shadowy and ambiguous. The relevance of this point for my argument is that it corresponds to the concept of allegory as *alieniloquium*—a structure that designates the temporal distance between representation and its origin or end.[47] This view has little to do with the assumption that Dante at-

[43]Cf. de Man, "Rhetoric of Temporality": "the meaning constituted by the allegorical sign can then consist only in the repetition . . . of a previous sign with which it can never coincide, since it is of the essence of this previous sign to be pure anteriority" (p. 190); "in the world of allegory, time is the originary constitutive category" (p. 190).

[44]*Dante, Poet of the Desert*, p. 233.

[45]Ibid., p. 252.

[46]Ibid., pp. 256, 269.

[47]A most provocative study of allegory as a structure of desire for a lost origin has been argued recently from a basis in the psychoanalysis of Jacques Lacan by Joel Fineman, "The Structure of Allegorical Desire," in *Allegory and Representation*, ed. Stephen Greenblatt (Baltimore: Johns Hopkins University Press, 1981), pp. 26–60.

tempted to give us a mirror of the past and future. He gives us, rather, an allegory of reading, a poem about personal and public history and at the same time about the process of representing it. Recognizing Dante's allegory of reading returns us to the claim with which I began, that the poet does not copy the Book of culture but departs from it. Insofar as the allegory of reading effects this departure, my argument differs from the conclusion of Mazzotta. He maintains that the "exile" of poetry and the "desert" of reading in the *Commedia* correspond to medieval comments on reading, such as may be found in a passage from Hugh of St. Victor.[48] Although the fathers of the church may have looked back at the Hebrews in the desert and imagined intellectual processes as a sort of wandering, when they turned to the subject of reading, the bulk of tradition shows that they recalled the commonplace fourfold hierarchy of the text and looked into the speculum of nature for validation of it. Dante, on the other hand, gives us his own allegory, and it is not of nature or Scripture, but of the process of conjecturing about such readings. He does not copy old *auctores* for the allegory in the *Commedia* or the "desert" of reading. His achievement is unique because it departs from them. Rather than the exegetes, he follows the Hebrews themselves, their wandering in the wilderness and their writings that differ sharply from myths of immanence and totality. Dante was profoundly influenced by the Bible, but specifically that biblical writing so fraught with background that its traces are obvious everywhere in the deep recesses and unknown spaces of the journey into the beyond.

5

One of the ways the Bible functions as a "source" for Dante is illustrated at the end of the *Paradiso* in the image of the "book" ("volume") illuminated by "eternal light" ("etterna luce"; *Para.* 33.83).

> Nel suo profondo vidi che s'interna
> legato con amore in un volume,
> ciò che per l'universo si squaderna.
> (*Para.* 33.86–88)

[In its depth I saw ingathered, bound by love in one single volume, that which is dispersed in leaves throughout the universe.][49]

48Mazzotta, *Dante, Poet of the Desert,* pp. 256–257.
49Singleton, *Paradiso,* p. 377, and vol. 2, *Commentary* (1975), pp. 576–579.

Dante's image, according to Singleton, refers to the text beheld by Ezekiel (2.9) and to Bonaventura's remark that it is "written within" to indicate the "Dei aeterna ars et sapientia" ("the eternal art and wisdom of God") and "written without" to specify the "mundus sensibilis" ("the visible world"). Bonaventura has imposed, says Singleton, the Platonic concept of imitation on Ezekiel's image according to the conventions of medieval exegesis, and Dante has taken the book "written within" as the image for *Paradiso* 33.[50]

However, that canto 33 is based on Ezek. 2.9 is not completely clear, since that passage is concerned with the commissioning of the prophet who in the subsequent chapter is called upon to "eat that book" (Ezek. 3.1–2). Instead, *Paradiso* 33 has more in common with texts that are as celestial and visionary in setting as it is. For example, Dante's passage recalls the association of vision with words in a book that is represented vividly in Isaiah: "And the vision of all shall be unto you as the words of a book that is sealed [*libri signati*]" (Isa. 29.11).[51] The "sealed book" becomes a cosmic image in Apocalypse, where the visionary sees "in the right hand of him that sat on the throne, a book, written within and without" (Apoc. 5.1). The similarity between this scene and *Paradiso* 33, with Dante looking up at the book in the "etterna luce," is substantiated by medieval identification of Apoc. 5.1 with the *liber vitae* mentioned, for example, in Ps. 68.29: "Let them be blotted out of the book of the living [*liber vitae*] and with the just let them not be written." This verse and Apoc. 5.1, the book of life and the visionary book in the sky, are joined in Apoc. 20.12; like the closing image of the book in the *Commedia*, Apoc. 20.12, the final passage about texts in the Bible, is a vision in the presence of God and the elect. It is closer to Dante's passage than any other in Scripture.

> Et vidi mortuos magnos, et pusillos stantes in conspectu throni, et libri aperti sunt: et alius liber apertus est qui est vitae: et iudicati sunt mortui ex his, quae scripta erant in libris secundum opera ipsorum.

> [And I saw the dead, great and small, standing in the presence of the throne. And the books were opened: and another book was opened, which was the book of life. And the dead were judged by those things which were written in the books, according to their works.]

[50]"The Book of Memory," in *An Essay on the Vita Nuova* (Baltimore: Johns Hopkins University Press, 1949), pp. 38–40. Mazzotta, too, identifies Dante's allusion (p. 257) with the *liber* mentioned in Ezek. 2.9.

[51]This and subsequent Latin references to the Bible are from *Biblia iuxta vulgatam Clementinam nova editio* (Madrid: Biblioteca de Autores Cristianos, 1965); translations are from *The Holy Bible* (New York: Douay Bible House, 1943).

The reason for locating Dante's final image in these verses from Apocalypse rests on more than similarity of setting. Extensive glosses in medieval exegesis confirm it. In rendering the image for *Paradiso* 33, Dante has drawn fundamentally on a complex of ideas that appear in two seminal medieval texts, the extensive gloss on Apoc. 20.12 in Ambrose's *Expositio super septem visiones libri apocalypsis* and the equally thorough study of the passage by Augustine in the *De civitate Dei*.[52] These works provided readings of the scriptural text that were quoted so accurately and frequently by subsequent commentators that they constitute an exegetical tradition extending into Dante's own time and beyond in such works as Hugh of St. Cher's *Opera omnia* and the *Glossa ordinaria*. *Paradiso* 33 relies closely on this tradition. However, Dante does not simply follow in the footsteps of the exegetes. He adapts the image of the celestial text as a metaphor for his own personal experience of the vision of God. In contrast his own book, the story of the journey, is not a recreation of the experience once present to him but an interpretation of, or supplement to, that past "text."

That a "book" might be appropriate as a metaphor for the experience of grace is suggested by a variety of readings in exegetical tradition. To begin with, Dante's singular allusion to the book in *Paradiso* 33 is not inconsistent with the plural reference to books in Apoc. 20.12 (*libri aperti* and *alius liber*), since scriptural commentary concentrates on the oneness of the idea of the book in the passage. Augustine, for instance, says that by *libri aperti* the Bible is to be understood—"the holy books of the Old and New Testament"—because in them God revealed the commandments.[53] He goes on to clarify that one must not read the reference to the *liber vitae* "carnally" (*carnaliter*), imagining that the life of each individual is a separate book that will be read by a separate angel from beginning to end at the last judgment; rather, the *alius liber* that will be opened is singular and refers to "divine power" (*vis divina*), which will cause everyone to recall simultaneously all his own deeds. "Divine power is called a book because in it will be read all that it causes one to remember."[54] Ambrose too draws attention to "one book," the *liber vitae*, which is "the elect," in contrast to the "opened books," which are the "condemned" whose evil is now exposed ("libri multi ad

[52]Ambrose, *PL* 17, 934–935; Augustine, *PL* 41, 679–680.

[53]*PL* 41, 680. Augustine's gloss is repeated by Hugh of St. Cher, *Opera omnia*, 8 vols. (Venice, 1732), 7:422ᵛ.

[54]Augustine: "Quae nimirum vis divina, libri nomen accepit. In ea quippe quodammodo legitur, quidquid ea faciente recolitur" (*PL* 41, 680); also cited by Hugh of St. Cher, *Opera omnia* 7:422ᵛ).

reprobos: unus qui est vitae, ad electos pertinet)."[55] Although the oneness of the book is mentioned by both exegetes, Ambrose's commentary on Apoc. 20.12 has provided Dante with the centralizing image of the passage in *Paradiso* 33.86: "legato con amore in un volume." This line is close enough to be a translation of the final clause of Ambrose's gloss:

> Electi vero unum librum habent; quia unum Deum colunt, unam fidem catholicam confitentur, *uno vinculo charitatis connectuntur.*

> [The elect, however, have one book, because they worship one God, acknowledge one catholic faith, and are bound by one bond of love.][56]

The ultimate basis of Dante's closing image is Ambrose's vision of the elect in the presence of the throne of God as a "book bound by one bond of love." This line, perhaps more than all the others, provides the link between Dante's celestial image of the written object and his own personal experience of God's love.

Ambrose's comment was important enough for quotation verbatim many centuries later in the *Glossa ordinaria.*[57] It very likely inspired the reading frequently cited for the *alius liber vitae* as "Christus," because "Christ, who is our life, will appear to all in the judgment of the Jews."[58] This reading established the ground for yet another important aspect of Dante's celestial vision, the "ingathering" of all things into the "presence" of God. These ideas are contained in several glosses on Apoc. 20.12 that are summarized elegantly in Dante's own time by Hugh of St. Cher. He says that in opening the *alius liber,* "Christ is opened, because then he will appear to all showing what now is still hidden. This book, I say, is the gathering together of the living. . . the book of life is the presence of God, which is hidden from us now, but then will be opened to all, because they will see all who are being saved and all who are being damned."[59] Dante's image of the "ingathering" of all things

[55]*PL* 17, 934; Ambrose's gloss is cited later in the *Glossa*—see *Biblia sacra cum glossa ordinaria et postilla Nicholai Lyrami,* 8 vols. (Paris, London, and Venice, 1590–1603), 6:1666.

[56]*PL* 17, 934.

[57]*Biblia sacra cum glossa ordinaria,* 6:1666.

[58]*Allegoria in sacram scripturam* (*PL* 112, 987). For similar glosses, see *Glossa ordinaria* (*PL* 114, 745); Alanus de Insulis, *Distinctiones* (*PL* 210, 837); Hugh of St. Cher, *Opera omnia* 7:422ᵛ).

[59]Hugh of St. Cher: "alius liber, id est, Christus apertus est, quia tunc omnibus apparebit patens, quod modo adhuc occultum est. Liber dico qui est vitae collativus . . . vel, liber vitae, est Dei praesentia, quae modo nos latet, sed tunc erit omnibus aperta, quia videbunt omnes, qui salvandi et qui damnandi" (7:422ᵛ).

scattered has a certain parallel in Hugh's gloss on *liber* as *collativus*, which signifies *collatio* in medieval Latin, the "collating" of manu-scripts into a text.[60] That Dante's "ingathering" takes place in the light of God is also suggested by Hugh's gloss on Apoc. 20.12, for he explains the "gathering together" in the context of identifying the book as the *Dei praesentia* ("the presence of God"). In other sources, such as the *Allegoria in sacram scripturam,* the idea also ap-pears: "Liber est praesentia Dei."[61] This idea of the book as "pres-ence" subsumes all others—the "Holy Books" of Scripture, "divine power," the "elect," the "gathering" of all things scattered, "the book bound by love," "Jesus Christ." As these references coalesce symbolically to create the book as *praesentia,* it becomes a most appropriate image for signifying Dante's experience of religious grace—the ultimate *signatum* of his conversion.

But Dante's own book is not a copy of the visionary *liber.* On the contrary, his writing clearly acknowledges the difficulty—even the impossibility—of trying to recall the brilliance of God's writing once present to him. This difference is apparent, for example, in-sofar as the celestial text in *Paradiso,* like the *liber* of the exegetical tradition of Apoc. 20.12, is dominated by the imagery of closure. The pilgrim sees the book "legato" ("bound") by love; the "sustanze e accidenti . . . quasi conflati insieme" ("substance and accident as though fused"; *Para.* 33.88–89) represent a powerful action of union carried out by the verb *conflati,* whose Latin etymology, *con-flatus,* "with-wind," indicates the action of the divine "breath" blowing life into all things and creating the universe as a *Verbum;*[62] finally, Dante goes on to speak in these lines of the union as "one"—"un semplice lume" (*Para.* 33.90) and as a "knot" ("nodo"; *Para.* 33.91). However, the accumulation of images of collating and clos-ing do not give us the picture of the pilgrim as reading words in an opened book, nor is he translating from it into his own poem. Instead of copying exegetical tradition, Dante has interpreted the image of the *liber* as his own experience of religious conver-sion, which like God's book is similarly inexplicable in its full sig-nificance: as the *praesentia Dei,* the celestial text is the presence of

---

[60]*Medieval Latin Word-List,* ed. J. H. Baxter and C. Johnson (London: Oxford University Press, 1950), s.v. "collatio"; *A Latin Dictionary,* ed. C. T. Lewis and C. Short (London: Oxford University Press, 1966, s.v. "collativus" and "collatio"—"the comparison, collation of texts, manuscripts, etc." (p. 365).

[61]*PL* 112, 987; cf. *Glossa (PL* 114, 745).

[62]Singleton, *Paradiso,* p. 377. Alanus de Insulis, *Distinctiones (PL* 210, 793), identi-fies *flatus* with *ventus, Spiritus sanctus,* and *anima.* The opening of John's Gospel es-tablishes the link between "divine breath" and "word."

Dante's experience of the grace of conversion; yet as closed and bound, the book of his experience cannot be read as it is "written," according to Augustine, in the *liber* of the *vis divina*. The final image of the book in the *Commedia* reiterates the separation of the experience of grace from the story of the journey. The meaning of that experience is ultimately ineffable, and what was once brilliantly present to him is now paradoxically slipping away even in the effort to recall it.

This paradox dominates Dante's remaining commentary in *Paradiso* 33. In the line that recalls the zenith of sight, he speaks of the "depth" or "bottom" of the divine light ("Nel suo *profondo* vidi che s'interna"; *Para.* 33.85). "Speech" can no longer "show" his vision:

> Da quinci innanzi il mio veder fu maggio
> che 'l parlar mostra, ch'a tal vista cede,
> e cede la memoria a tanto oltraggio.
> *(Para.* 33.55−57)

[Thenceforward my vision was greater than speech can show, which fails at such a sight, and at such excess memory fails.][63]

Instead of recreating the fullness of his experience, the poet addresses the difficulties of writing about it: speech "fails"; his vision almost wholly fades away ("tutta cessa / mia visione"; lines 61–62); by comparison with the "supreme light" ("somma luce"; line 67), his "tongue" ("la lingua"; line 70) seeks to leave only "a single spark" ("una favilla sol"; line 71) "sounding a little in these lines" ("sonare un poco in questi versi"; line 74).[64] Time defers the memory of the Book that was once present to him and will one day be "read" again. But because his own book cannot recuperate that "presence," it draws itself into comparison with one final idea from the exegetical tradition of Apoc. 20.12, an idea that was identified by virtue of its sharp contrast with the *liber praesentiae*. This idea is the *liber occultorum*, or "book of secrets." Although the *liber occult-*

---

[63]Singleton, *Paradiso*, p. 375. The Italian follows Singleton's choice of *mostra* instead of Sapegno's *nostro*.

[64]These lines are also rich with other references that emphasize the departure of the language of the poem from the "language" of the celestial memory: Dante's "tongue" hopes only to leave a "single spark," not speak in the eloquent "tongues of fire" of the Holy Spirit (see Alanus, *Distinctiones*, *PL* 210, 838, for the link between *lingua* and *linguis igneis* of the *Spiritus Sanctus*); further, the "spark" of his "tongue" can only sound *un poco* in his verse, not imitate the full symphony of the "music of the spheres" echoing throughout the heavenly orbits.

orum is not mentioned in medieval commentary in conjunction with poetry or theories about it, Dante has applied the image as a reference for the poetics of his poem. The "book of secrets" can be traced back to Augustine's reading of the *liber* in Apoc. 20.12 as the closed book of man's *conscientia* and *memoria,* which will be "opened" (*aperti*) by divine force.[65] Repeating these readings, Alanus de Insulis says that *liber* is a similitude for *memoria,* as in the Apocalypse (1.11) when the visionary is told to "write in this book"; that is, what he sees "is commended to memory." Alanus also mentions *conscientia* as a book of things hidden in each soul that will be revealed at the last judgment.[66] Hugh of St. Cher adds to the text of *conscientia* the "book of the heart" that will be read at the end of time.[67] In the gloss on Apoc. 20.12 cited above, Hugh says that when Christ comes he will open the book of "things secret"— *occulta*—a reading he then contrasts distinctly, following other exegetes, with *praesentia.*[68] For example, the *Allegoria in sacram scripturam* identifies the *liber praesentia* with the "book of life" and the *liber* that is the *occulta hominis* with the text in Dan. 7.10: "the judgment sat and the books were opened." This "book" is the "secrets of man," says the *Allegoria,* "because what is hidden in our hearts will be manifested at the last judgment."[69] Finally, it is worth observing that, shortly after Dante's time, Pierre Bersuire separates the *liber divinus* from the *liber humanus* and divides the "human book" into man's "conscience" and the "book of the body"; he also uses the word *occultus* to describe what is hidden in the book that will one day be opened.[70]

It is this opposition between the book as "presence" and the book as "secrecy" that informs Dante's contrast between his vision of the "volume" in the heavens and his own book, the language of poetry in the *Commedia.* Even as the pilgrim looks at the heavenly book of the *praesentia Dei* illuminated by the divine intelligence itself, his poem names itself and recognizes itself in its emphasis on the limitations of language as the book of the *occulta hominis,* not only full

[65]*PL* 41, 680.

[66]Alanus, *Distinctiones* (*PL* 210, 837).

[67]Hugh of St. Cher: "videbunt sancti malorum demerita, quia libri conscientiarum, vel cordium aperti sunt" (7:422ᵛ).

[68]See note 55.

[69]*Allegoria:* "Per *librum,* occulta hominis, ut in Daniele . . . quod in judicio ultimo manifesta erunt abscondita cordis nostri" (*PL* 112, 987).

[70]Bersuire: "Liber humanus . . . liber conscientiae cordialis et liber apparentiae corporalis. . . . Liber conscientia continet bona et mala, quae fecimus. Veruntamen modo est liber signatus occultus, et involutus, sed vere in judicio omnibus erit apertus et expositus." *Repertorium morale,* in *Opera omnia* (Cologne, 1731), 2:462D.

of persons with secrets, but secretive itself, lighted poorly in hell and paradoxical in its vision in heaven. The poet's journey is his *liber occultorum*. What he sees at the end of the journey is the recollection of a book in the sky that is fading fast and always out of the reach of his words. His moment of wonder in beholding the celestial volume is finally a secret that creates as much "oblivion" ("litargo"; line 94) as twenty-five centuries wrought upon Neptune when he was startled by the shadow of Argus falling through the sea (line 96).

The contrast between the "two books" suggests a way of conceiving the "two Dantes" in relation to the structure of the poem: insofar as writing and reading are disclosed as modes of the same order—interpretation—Dante the poet and Dante the pilgrim are involved in the same activity. Consequently the "poet" is not really a being separate from the "pilgrim," one "outside" the work holding the strings of his "puppet" who is "inside" it; instead, they are one consciousness revealed *as* the language of the poem, as that process of interpreting that is striving to understand the grace of conversion. The two acts, writing and reading, differ not in kind but in temporality, since the process of interpreting is always lagging behind the full understanding of the "text" of religious experience. The desire for totality and completeness that characterizes understanding is thus not hypostatized as the language of the poem. Rather, that desire for totalization is hypostatized in an image—the visionary *liber* of *Paradiso* 33—while the language signifying the vision admits its own limitations and remains secretive. The form of the work therefore may be called "complete" not because it is imitative and objective, but because it has acknowledged, through the dialectic process of the interpreter-pilgrim and his "text," the inability to close the circle of understanding perfectly. As de Man has argued this point: "this dialogue between work and interpreter is endless. The hermeneutic understanding is always, by its very nature, lagging behind. . . . Understanding can be called complete only when it becomes aware of its own temporal predicament and realizes that the horizon within which the totalization can take place is time itself. The act of understanding is a temporal act that has its own history, but this history forever eludes totalization."[71] The mode in which this "history" is most self-disclosing is allegory. It is preoccupied with the distance between origin and end, signified meaning and the means of signifying. In the *Comme-*

---

[71]"Form and Intent," p. 32.

dia, the structure of allegory is not to be found in a signifying system seeking to represent an imaginary world; nor is its structure within the language itself, within the several "levels" of semantic sense. The allegorical sign is not symbolic, and Dante has not created a myth. On the contrary, the allegory of the *Commedia* consists in the structure of temporal distance between the originary *liber* of God, envisioned in the sky at the end of the poem, and the book of written efforts to explain the experience of its meaning. The allegorical sign is constituted not by a desire to represent its referent—to have ontology—but rather by the impossibility of the sign to coincide with the full significance of its origin or end. The understanding, therefore, that the allegorical mode occasions for Dante is the recognition of the continuing desire for recovering the *volume* with which he began—both his memory and its image of God's presence. For the determination to move through the limits of language in time, to struggle with meaning, was another medieval way of realizing the desire for God.

However totally the record of the journey has been told, the telling has never been the equivalence of living the religious experience itself. Like the secrets revealed by so many of the persons along the way—those who yearn to escape their "stories"—Dante's experience, his remembrance of time past and his desire to embrace time future, cannot be imitated or mediated by language. Canto 33 and the many other passages on reading and writing dramatize the dilemma of textuality in the *Commedia*: in the very effort to imitate the myth of the Book, a departure from it was carried out. Among Dante's sources, this departure is sharpest in biblical documents that resist the myth and metaphor of writing by leaving no doubt about the inability of language to embody the infinite and unbounded. To that realm Dante's text provides merely the glimmer of a fullness that remains beyond. Unlike myths and dreams that drop down music and light until we try to dream again, Dante's fiction follows the secrecy of the parables or the broader Gospel narrative: both conceal in the gesture of revealing, for both are devoted to the order of time and the truth of an experience that cannot be bound by time; both are texts of the *occulta hominis* whose "readings" disclose, because of what cannot be written, something about the fullness of the *praesentia Dei*.[72] By

---

[72] The discipline of exegesis in the middle ages provides massive illustration of Frank Kermode's argument in *The Genesis of Secrecy: On the Interpretation of Narrative* (Cambridge: Harvard University Press, 1979) that traditions of interpretation institutionalize the essential "secrecy" of parabolic writing and narrative discourse in

carrying out the concealing-revealing gesture of Scripture, Dante not only has created a text profoundly different from the Book of culture, but has opened it up for reconsideration and inevitably for change.

---

general; for example, in the Gospel of Mark the narrative surrounding the parables begins the process by claiming to know and even to explain their secret meaning; medieval exegesis continues and expands this institutionalization of meaning. But by making the concept of the *liber occultorum* central to his poetics, Dante unmasks the secret of the institution; he deinstitutionalizes secrecy by returning us to the radical confrontation of the secrecy of narrative.

[5]

The Origin of Language Reconsidered:

Chaucer's *House of Fame*

> "Wher Joves wol me stellyfye,
> Or what thing may this sygnifye?
> I neyther am Ennok, ne Elye,
> Ne Romulus, ne Ganymede,
> That was ybore up, as men rede,
> To heavene with daun Jupiter,
> And mad the goddys botiller."
> Loo, this was thoo my fantasye!
>
> Chaucer, *The House of Fame*

1

Dante illustrates one way fiction departs from mythology in the middle ages, and it is a conservative departure. For his writing registers its limitations by reference not, for example, to a storm or whirlwind, but to another book, the *liber praesentiae Dei,* that he sees in the heavens. His own text is set "enface" with God's as a dim or shadowy recollection of it. By continual reference to a past text that he is trying to recall but that his own language cannot transcribe, Dante's text is balanced against God's, is stabilized and in control of the potential for indeterminacy of meaning. Although Dante confesses the inadequacy of language, he never leaves us in doubt about his desire to continue to make sense out of the *sentence* from the past. And he expects as much from us. In order to suggest further the conservatism of Dante's departure, it may be compared with the approaches to language in the works of Chaucer. For instance, in *The House of Fame,* to which I will turn first, Chaucer makes more extended use of Dante than in any other poem and also includes some of the most salient ideas about writing in medieval tradition.[1] All of them are central premises of what I have called the new mythology of the middle ages, the "Book of culture." Chaucer represents the myth in an unusual way, through the fiction of the journey to Fame's house and the search for the source of new writing. However, the quest ends not with the revelation of a book or word, but with the confrontation of the abritrary Lady Fame and the whirlwind of the house of sticks. This situation poses very different consequences for the determinacy of meaning in language than does Dante's comparison of his writing to the radiance of the celestial *liber* of God.[2]

2

Chaucer's uses of past works of literature take various forms: occasionally he follows his source rather closely, as in the translation of the *Roman de la rose,* or modifies it somewhat as in the *Clerk's Tale*; at other times his source becomes a rival of the story he is trying to tell, and in *Troilus and Criseyde*; yet again, he borrows from texts with such subtlety that references may appear with the force of surprise, as in the biblical allusions of the *Miller's Tale*.[3] But in *The House of Fame* the reliance on the past takes a different form altogether. The poem appears to be less interested in subordinating and concealing the borrowings from other works of literature than in making them as obvious as possible. On the one hand, it has been customary to regard this fact of the poem's structure as a flaw and to say that in it Chaucer's materials are somehow "out of hand." It has, as a result, been called "Chaucer's most curious and

[1]F. N. Robinson, ed., *The Works of Geoffrey Chaucer,* 2d ed. (Boston: Houghton Mifflin, 1957), is used throughout for quotations from Chaucer, which will be cited hereafter in the text.

[2]The question of the indeterminacy of meaning arising from the critique of the Book of culture in the works of Dante and Chaucer is not explicitly entertained per se—to my knowledge—in medieval theoretical inquiry. However, for the implications of the question of indeterminacy one may refer to contemporary responses to the project of "deconstructing" the "text" of tradition; for instance, see the response to the work of Jacques Derrida and Paul de Man argued by Gerald Graff, *Literature against Itself: Literary Ideas in Modern Society* (Chicago: University of Chicago Press, 1979); Meyer H. Abrams, "How to Do Things with Texts," *Partisan Review* 46 (1979):566–588; Charles Altieri, "The Hemeneutics of Literary Indeterminacy: A Dissent from the new Orthodoxy," *NLH* 10 (1978):71–99.

[3]For example, see Paul A. Olson, "Poetic Justice in the *Miller's Tale*," *MLQ* 24 (1963):227–236; and my essay, "The Parody of Medieval Music in the *Miller's Tale*," *JEGP* 73 (1974):176–188.

elusive poem";[4] defying efforts to establish unity, the work is best read, according to one critic, for its "moments of new greatness."[5] On the other hand, some readers have found distinct advantages in Chaucer's style of reference to past literature, despite its fragmentary appearance. One of these advantages is that Chaucer is attempting to formulate in *The House of Fame* an ars poetica of his own. This position arises from the sense that the poem, as one critic observes, acknowledges an opposition "between what is handed down and a man's personal experience," that the work presents materials in ways that are quite "contrary to convention," and that it develops "a new critical attitude toward poetry."[6] This attitude is explicit in the narrator's wish to leave old poetic forms and search for new "tydynges"; but it is implicit elsewhere as well. "In one sense," argues another critic, "the whole work is a vindication of poetry";[7] it is a vindication, for a third critic, specifically "from the tradition which holds that poems are made out of the experience of love."[8] However "new" Chaucer's voice may be in the development of *The House of Fame,* the uses of past literature in the poem seem to have struck various readers over the years as a deliberate critique of tradition, and not the least of them is Alexander Pope, who in the *Temple of Fame* found the poem suitable for imitation as a satire against public taste during his time.[9]

Yet Pope's choice of *The House of Fame* does not assume that he considered it free from flaws, a well-unified whole, since he left out of his imitation nearly half of the original. His response is not unlike the reading of many who find the work to be an ars poetica in critique of tradition: one passage departs from dream-vision con-

---

[4]E. Talbot Donaldson, "Commentary," in *Chaucer's Poetry: An Anthology for the Modern Reader,* 2d ed. (New York: Ronald Press, 1975), p. 1117; cf. Charles Muscatine, *Chaucer and the French Tradition* (Berkeley: University of California Press, 1964), pp. 107–114; Nevill Coghill, *The Poet Chaucer,* 2d ed. (London: Oxford University Press, 1967), p. 49.

[5]Coghill, *Poet Chaucer,* p. 49.

[6]Wolfgang Clemen, *Chaucer's Early Poetry,* trans. C. A. M. Sym (London: Methuen, 1963), pp. 113–114.

[7]J. A. W. Bennett, *Chaucer's Book of Fame: An Exposition of the "House of Fame"* (Oxford: Clarendon Press, 1968), p. xi.

[8]Laurence K. Shook, "*The House of Fame,*" in *Companion to Chaucer Studies,* ed. Beryl Rowland, rev. ed. (New York: Oxford University Press, 1979), p. 418.

[9]See A. C. Cawley, "Chaucer, Pope and Fame," *REL* 3 (1962):9–19; Alfred David, "Literary Satire in the *House of Fame,*" *PMLA* 75 (1960):333–339; Donald Fry, "The Ending of the *House of Fame,*" in *Chaucer at Albany,* ed. R. H. Robbins (New York: Burt Franklin, 1975), pp. 27–40; John Leyerle, "Chaucer's Windy Eagle," *UTQ* 40 (1971):247–265; Robert B. Burlin, *Chaucerian Fiction* (Princeton: Princeton University Press, 1977), pp. 45–58.

vention, another from a French model, yet another from medieval literary theory; and the work remains curious and elusive. Nonetheless, the dilemma of appreciating *The House of Fame* only for its moments of greatness instead of for its achievement as a whole is not necessarily insurmountable. One way to confront this problem has been offered recently in the suggestion that the poem is a response not just to older literary forms, but to "tradition" in general, the bulk of both written and oral knowledge from the past.[10] This position is based, at the outset, on the meaning of the word "fame." In Middle English and Latin sources, it signifies not only rumor and reputation, but also a body of traditional knowledge. This sense of the term is current during Chaucer's time, for example, in John Trevisa's translation of Ralph Higden's *Polychronicon*, in which the conventional proof for the location of Paradise is translated as "olde fame."[11] Instead of too swiftly dismissing the form of the poem as a flawed, incomplete mélange, this approach assumes that if Chaucer wanted to conceal the obvious borrowings from sources—to hide the joints and seams of references—then he would have made more of an effort to do so. By rendering the borrowings as he has, Chaucer directs our attention to the nature of tradition (that is, "fame") itself, for one of its characteristics is the conflict or rivalry between versions of the same story. This consideration of the poem has the obvious merit of trying to explain Chaucer's use of sources not exclusively for their specific content, but rather for the way they inform the structure of the poem as a whole in relation to the theme of fame.[12] One of the most intriguing aspects of this reading is the notion of the conflict of sources, and I will summarize it here because it raises a question about Chaucer's treatment of tradition that, I think, needs reconsideration.

3

To start with, the story of Dido and Aeneas recounted in book 1 represents conflicting versions of the same legend—some material from Virgil's account in the *Aeneid*, the rest from Ovid's version in *Heroides* 7.[13] The Virgilian material in Chaucer's poem emphasizes

---

[10]Sheila Delany, *Chaucer's "House of Fame": The Poetics of Skeptical Fideism* (Chicago: University of Chicago Press, 1972).
[11]Ibid., p. 3.
[12]Ibid., p. 57.
[13]Delany, "Dido and Aeneas," in *Chaucer's "House of Fame,"* pp. 48–57; Bennett, "Venus and Virgil," in *Chaucer's Book of Fame*, pp. 1–51.

the heroism of "pius" Aeneas, his duty to family and mission. On the walls of the palace of Venus, the dreamer sees Aeneas flee burning Troy,

> and how that he
> Escaped was from al the pres,
> And took his fader, Anchises,
> And bar hym on hys bak away,
> Cryinge, "Allas! and welaway!"
> (*HF*, 166–170)

Although *The House of Fame* quickly turns to concentrate on the episode with Dido, the heroism of Aeneas is not forgotten. Rather the interest moves to love, and the source shifts to Ovid. Regarding the rejection of Dido, *The House of Fame* leaves out Virgil's rendering, in which Dido is outraged and incensed, and instead reproduces Ovid's epistle, which gives us the pathetic portrait of the unrequited lover.

> "Allas!" quod she, "my swete herte,
> Have pitee on my sorwes smerte,
> And slee mee not! goo noght awey!
> O woful Dido, wel-away!"
> Quod she to hirselve thoo.
> "O Eneas, what wol ye doo?
> O that your love, ne your bond
> That ye have sworn with your ryght hond,
> Ne my crewel deth," quod she,
> "May holde yow stille here with me!"
> (*HF*, 315–324)

But Aeneas has no response in the remaining account of *The House of Fame*. His heroism and duty are not forgotten or nullified; they exist in conflict with the portrait of him rendered by Ovid's Dido as a callous betrayer.

In this approach to the literary materials in Chaucer's poem, the oppositions are unmistakable between Virgil's text and Ovid's, Aeneas the "pius" and the traitor, Dido the shrew and the woebegone. The conflict is appropriate to the larger subject of Chaucer's poem because the ambivalence illustrates the ambiguous nature of "fame" itself.[14] What is crucial to this reading, moreover, is that Chaucer's text does not resolve the conflict of sources in order to

[14]Delany, pp. 56–57.

establish the privilege of one over the other. At one point, the question of excusing Aeneas is raised, but the narrator does not solve it:

> But to excusen Eneas
> Fullyche of al his grete trespas,
> The book seyth Mercurie, sauns fayle,
> Bad hym goo into Itayle,
> And leve Auffrikes regioun,
> And Dido and hir faire toun.
>
> (*HF*, 427–432)

Since as the appeal to the authority of the book dictates the next event to be narrated in Chaucer's poem, the opposition between the sources is bypassed. Such a strategy, according to this reading, circumvents "direct personal comment," which would presumably answer the question.[15] In the absence of a stated opinion, we are left with a view of the ambiguity of tradition rendered through the oppositions in the structure of the poem. By refusing to choose, "Chaucer grants the validity of conflicting truths and confronts the problem with no way of deciding between them." Chaucer is, in the view summarized here, a "skeptic" who knows "no rational way";[16] instead, he seeks to transcend opposition through faith. He looks forward to the uncertainty and doubt of renaissance writers and specifically to the "skeptical fideism," such as we find in Montaigne. From this position it is only one short step toward speaking of "the renaissance Chaucer," and that step has been taken by at least one critic on the premise that Chaucer is a skeptic.[17]

This position is suggestive, and its conclusion has been felt, perhaps, by many readers of *The House of Fame*. But Chaucer does not look forward to the renaissance, in my view, because he is a skeptic who opts for faith when faced with oppositions unresolved in his work. To begin with, seeing the structural ambiguity of the work as a reflection of the ambiguity of fame is a point arrived at by suspending the search for the "intention" that Chaucer may have had "in mind" and attending instead to the structural intentionality of the language of the poem. If we are to take this position fully, as we are asked to, then we really are not looking for a "direct personal comment" in the poem—be it the narrator's or "Chaucer's"—that

---

[15]Ibid., p. 54.

[16]Ibid., p. 57; her conclusion is followed by Burlin, *Chaucerian Fiction*, p. 46. Cf. John M. Fyler, *Chaucer and Ovid* (New Haven: Yale University Press, 1979), p. 57, and Fry, "The Ending of *The House of Fame*," in *Chaucer at Albany*, p. 28.

[17]See Alice Miskimin, *The Renaissance Chaucer* (New Haven: Yale University Press, 1975), esp. pp. 67–80; her debt to Delany is cited throughout.

would settle at last which strand of tradition about Aeneas and Dido is to have privilege.[18] For when we grant the language of the text its own intentionality, Chaucer's "report" of his dream is a construct in its own right, a text itself in which personal comment— even if it were given—is no less fictional than any other part of the poem. The absence of a stated or implied preference does not mean, therefore, that it should have been included. By reporting both versions of the story as he has, Chaucer has deliberately begged the question that was typically asked in the middle ages in response to tradition. I mean the determination that prompts different materials—like disparate historical events—to have special meaning, the kind of meaning conferred upon events in an encompassing narrative, where loose ends are tied up, opposing materials are subordinated, and things move toward a point of closure, particularly a moral one.

What Chaucer has accomplished by presenting the materials of Dido and Aeneas without an explicit resolution is to expose the expectation "between" the two stories, the binding, so to speak, that accommodates narrative structure to moralizing.[19] This expectation is the myth of the Book of culture finding expression in yet another form—the desire to resolve contradiction and absolve conflict that we have seen manifested in the Books of nature and Scripture and the summa of Gothic architecture and painting. By refusing to give "the answer," Chaucer has called into question the medieval preference to have events rationalized in a sequential order—"narrativized." Furthermore, he tells us as much when he does not give us the conclusion; instead, "the book seyth" that Aeneas was excused to continue his journey to Italy. The Book of traditional material about Aeneas has prefigured a response that *The House of Fame* refuses to complete.[20]

---

[18]The phrase is Delany's, p. 554.

[19]Hayden White has addressed this issue at length in "The Value of Narrativity in the Representation of Reality," *CI* 7 (1980):5–27; see also the related argument in the same volume by Frank Kermode, "Secrets and Narrative Sequence," pp. 83–101. Responses to White's essay may be found in *CI* 7 (1981):777–798.

[20]This "fracturing" of the text, the unresolved "openings" in it, are the kinds of textual properties that Kermode points to as evidence of the fundamental secrecy that cannot be suppressed by narrative; see his essay mentioned in the previous note and his book *The Genesis of Secrecy: On the Interpretation of Narrative* (Cambridge: Harvard University Press, 1979). Such textual properties, as I argue in the previous chapter, also characterize Dante's *liber occultorum,* which may well be—along with biblical writing, in Kermode's view—the most important inspirations for the secrecy of Chaucerian narrative. I will return to this point in the last section of this chapter.

The use of sources about Aeneas in Chaucer's poem is not, as a result, a confused collation of bits and pieces that ought to be appreciated only for their moments of greatness. Nor does Chaucer oppose two strands within tradition and draw a blank, leaving us with unavoidable skepticism. Rather, he has opposed his own text to the Book of the past, and this opposition has an unmistakable resolution. Chaucer has made his choice very clearly in favor of his own text, the language of poetry and its capacity to explore old books. It is through this choice, instead of through a tone of doubtfulness and skepticism, that Chaucer looks forward to the renaissance, for his choice effects an emphasis that we find quite strong in later writers—a shift away from the tradition of writing as a "copy" of the Text of the past, a "metaphor of divine perceiving," as well as a definite separation from the old view of poetry (still apparent in Boccaccio's *Genealogia deorum,* 14–15) as an embarrassed vulgar tongue of more privileged discourses.[21]

In *The House of Fame* a new appreciation for poetic writing emerges, and it is of course suggested precisely by the motif of the quest for "tydynges," for new poetic material. Although the poem relies heavily on traditional literary sources, it is not primarily concerned—as has been argued—with the nature of "tradition" as an example of the ambiguities of "fame." This position, while it has many values, depends on a more basic association in the poem—the link between "fame" and "writing." I do not refer to the argument that the poem is concerned with the "fame" of literary history or its subcategory, ars poetica, although those who have supported these approaches to the poem have added immensely to a more complete appreciation of it. I am suggesting, rather, that Chaucer is interested in "fame" as a way of studying the broader subject —also a "renaissance" one—of how language signifies, where it originates, how it is authorized, and how it is received. The dream of Venus's temple (with its walls made of painted stories), the discourse on the origin of sound, the journey to Fame's House (constructed "literally" of authors), the distribution of "fame" as the arbitrary utterance of a deity, the quest for "tydynges"—all these patterns of imagery are means of considering the signifying capacity of language. What better way to undertake such a subject than

---

[21]Cf. some of the standard renaissance defenses of the vernacular, such as Joachim du Bellay, *Défense et illustration de la langue française* (1549); Pierre Ronsard, *Abrégé de l'art poétique* (1565); William Webbe, *A Discourse of English Poetrie* (1586); George Puttenham, *The Arte of English Poesie* (1589); Richard Carew, *The Excellency of the English Tongue* (1595–1596).

to focus on "fame," which has its origin and being in the primary medium of communication, language? "Old books" in *The House of Fame* are explored, but less for their specific content than for their ability to reflect on the medium out of which they are made and through which they are represented in Chaucer's poem.

This property of language not only to designate a specific subject, such as the nature of fame, but to comment on its own order of designating—this "metalinguistic" characteristic of the poem—is one of its most noteworthy differences from the myth of the Book, which lacks this quality;[22] it is also a feature that *The House of Fame* has in common with Dante's *Commedia*, which is perhaps one of the reasons Chaucer found that poem so convenient for repeated references in his dream vision.[23] The vast question of how language signifies occupied both poets in many of their works, and Chaucer particularly confronts aspects of it in *Troilus and Criseyde* as well as in *The Canterbury Tales*.[24] In *The House of Fame* he narrows the question of writing to the study of how the poem acknowledges its difference from the myth of language that composes the Book of culture. The treatment of the sources about Aeneas in book 1 illustrates the prominence of this issue, but it is carried out in the poem by many other means as well. A salient one is Chaucer's use of the *Commedia*, to which I will turn next.

4

An extensive interpretation of Chaucer's use of Dante maintains that *The House of Fame* is largely concerned with contrasting worldly fame or reputation with eternal "fame" or God's glory.[25] For ex-

[22]On "metalanguage," see for example: Roland Barthes, *Eléments de sémiologie* (Paris: Seuil, 1964), trans. Annette Lavers and Colin Smith (Boston: Beacon Press, 1967), 4:i–iv, 89–94; Fredric Jameson, *The Prison-House of Language: A Critical Account of Structuralism and Russian Formalism* (Princeton: Princeton University Press, 1972), pp. 159–160, 203, 207–209; and Jameson's essay "Metacommentary," *PMLA* 86 (1971):9–18.

[23]See above, chapter 4.

[24]For instance, see the narrator's remarks on his writing in the prologues to each of the three books and the epilogue of *Troilus*, as well as the palinodes in the "General Prologue" (730–746), the Miller's "Prologue" (3167–3187), and the Wife of Bath's arguments against learned writing in her "Prologue." A recent account of the theme of language in *Troilus* is Eugene Vance, "Mervelous Signals: Poetics, Sign Theory, and Politics in Chaucer's *Troilus*," *NLH* 10 (1979): 293–337; on *The Canterbury Tales*, see H. Marshall Leicester, Jr., "The Art of Impersonation: A General Prologue to the *Canterbury Tales*," *PMLA* 95 (1980):213–224.

[25]B. G. Koonce, *Chaucer and the Tradition of Fame: Symbolism in "The House of Fame"* (Princeton: Princeton University Press, 1966). Scholarship on Chaucer's use

ample, Chaucer's allusions in book 1 to the underworld of Aeneas (*HF*, 439 ff.), the vanity of Venus's temple, and the "desert of Ly-bye" (*HF*, 486 ff.) represent Dante's journey through Hell with its deserts (*Inferno* 1 and 14) and many places of sensuality. In book 2, Chaucer's dream of the flight in the claws of the golden eagle (adapted from *Purgatorio* 9) is interpreted as an ironic attempt to render the second stage of Dante's journey, from the deserts of Hell to the Mountain of Purgatory. In book 3 Chaucer creates Dante's Heaven by beginning with his invocation to Apollo (bor-rowed from *Paradiso* 1) and by transporting his "pilgrim-dreamer" from the Ice Hill of Fame (the Mountain of Purgatory) to the more celestial vantages of the Houses of Fame and Rumor.[26] The argu-ment in favor of these parallels asserts that "in both poems the pro-phetic content becomes an integral part of the experience of the poet, whose need for spiritual instruction intiates a pattern of edu-cation leading to a higher stage of understanding."[27]

However, when we consider that Dante's poem is deeply con-cerned with the problem of interpreting signs and that his allegori-cal quest is in one sense understood as the ability of language to explain God's writing, then the whole subject of Chaucer's use of Dante appears in a new light. We do not look far, after all, before realizing that Chaucer's references to Dante in *The House of Fame* are by and large devoted to the meaning of "ymages," interpreting the Book of memory, and questing for "tydynges" suitable for po-etry.[28] Chaucer, it is fair to say, was one of the first to recognize the journey of the *Commedia* as an "allegory of reading," for he plays out that theme in the action of his poem.[29] Dante's journey ends with the vision of the Book in the sky, with an affirmation of the language of that *liber* as "present" in Scripture and nature. His own language, in contrast, cannot recreate God's without error; his writing is flawed by comparison with divine utterance; at most he writes a "gloss" and imagines himself a "scribe" instead of a creator

---

of Dante in *HF* has a long history: for instance, see Mario Praz, *The Flaming Heart* (New York: Doubleday Anchor 1958), pp. 29–86; Bennett, *Chaucer's Book of Fame*, passim; Miskimin, *Renaissance Chaucer*, pp. 72–88.

[26] Koonce, *Chaucer and the Tradition of Fame*, pp. 73–88.

[27] Ibid., p. 85.

[28] The subject of "memory" in *HF* has attracted some critical attention, but not in connection with Dante's use of the "book of memory"; see, for example, Beryl Row-land, "Bishop Bradwardine, the Artificial Memory, and the *House of Fame*," in *Chaucer at Albany*, pp. 41–62; Donald R. Howard, "*The Canterbury Tales:* Memory and Form," *ELH* 38 (1971):319–328.

[29] See above, chapter 4, sections 3 and 4.

like the Divine Author. His book is not a copy of the heavenly Logos, but only an effort to discover it. To that "logocentric" determination Dante aspires mightily, but he confesses throughout that his poem can never be the full equivalent of the text of memory;[30] his work cannot help hiding and concealing—like a *liber occultorum*—the divine presence. Chaucer too depicts himself in *The House of Fame* as a "student" in quest of the language emanating from a cosmic source; he too seeks the origin of that language in a heavenly "midpoint" or center; language is given various images of totality, such as a "temple," a "church," and a "house"; and finally the mysterious "auctoritee" in this world of language is introduced. That these topics enter Chaucer's poem frequently by way of Dante and especially with obvious changes in passages from the *Commedia* definitely influences the tone of *The House of Fame*. Whereas Dante emphasizes the inability of poetic language to be logocentric, Chaucer goes even further by highlighting its artificiality and rhetoricity.[31] Dante's tone is serious and stern; Chaucer's is full of play.

If *The House of Fame* borrows Dante's tripartite division, we might expect to find it confirmed, for instance, in the invocations to each of Chaucer's three books, since they echo invocations in the *Commedia*. But the borrowings are not exactly symmetrical: although book 3 relies on the invocation to Apollo from *Paradiso* 1, book 2 opens with an invocation from *Inferno* 2 not from *Purgatorio*, and the invocation of book 1 does not allude explicitly to Dante at all. Or if in book 1 Chaucer is implying a link to *Inferno* 1, it must surely be to suggest a reference from which he is departing. For example, both poets begin their poems with mention of sleep:

> But at my gynnynge, trusteth wel,
> I wol make invocacion,
> With special devocion,
> Unto the god of slep anoon,
> That duelleth in a cave of stoon
> Upon a strem that cometh fro Lete.
> (*HF*, 66–71)

The dreamer continues to pray that Morpheus will "spede / My sweven for to telle aryght" (*HF*, 78–79). But when Dante mentions

[30]"Logocentric" signifies here, as elsewhere in this book, the sense of the term that has become current since Jacques Derrida's use of it in *De la grammatologie* (Paris: Minuit, 1967).

[31]See Eugene Vance, "Chaucer's *House of Fame* and the Poetics of Inflation," *Boundary* 7 (1979):24–27; and Miskimin, *Renaissance Chaucer*, pp. 73–75.

"sleep" ("sonno") in *Inferno* 1.11, he has no hope whatever of gaining "speed," or anything else for that matter, from it;[32] on the contrary, he repudiates "sleep" as a condition of the drowsy illusions in the wood of error and turns toward Virgil, who will speed him "aright," as Morpheus never could, out of debilitating slumber. Such changes in the use of a source inform even the passages that contain direct quotations from Dante, such as the invocations to books 2 and 3.

The invocation of book 2, from *Inferno* 2, not *Purgatorio*, is another vivid example:

> O Thought, that wrot al that I mette,
> And in the tresorye hyt shette
> Of my brayn, now shal men se
> Yf any vertu in the be,
> To tellen al my drem aryght.
>
> (*HF*, 523–527)

Chaucer's source is:

> O Muse, o alto ingengno, or m'auitate;
> o mente che scrivesti ciò ch'io vidi,
> qui si parrà la tua nobilitate.
>
> (*Inf.* 2.7–9)

The Middle English carefully preserves the literal sense of the Italian, but with one significant alteration.[33] Dante extends the metaphor of "genius" as the scribe who "wrote down" past experience in the "book of memory"; Chaucer interrupts the metaphor of writing from his source by transformning it into "money" that is shut in the "treasury" of the "brain." *The House of Fame* contains many passages linking writing to money, jewels, and gold—for example, in the temple of Venus and the House of Fame—but these connections have nothing to do with Dante, who emphasizes the separation of the two media because of the potential of taint by association, as in his sharp contrast of writing and usury in *Inferno* 11.97–110. The *Commedia* is conservative in the way it identifies language as a means for talking about the experience of the supernatural; Chaucer, on the other hand, sees no risk in playing with

[32]*La divina commedia*, ed. Natalino Sapegno (Florence: Nova Italia, 1955–1957): quotations are from this edition and are cited in the text.

[33]Cf. Bennett's discussion of the Dantean parallels, pp. 49–58, and Koonce's, pp. 137–143.

associations between writing and other media of unmistakable artificiality, such as money.

A similar shift in the use of a source is carried out in the invocation to the final book of *The House of Fame*.[34] Beginning the invocation to "Appollo" for guidance in "this lytel laste bok" (*HF*, 1092–1093), Chaucer quite obviously had in mind, or on his desk, Dante's opening invocation of the *Paradiso* to "O buono Appollo" for aid in "this last labor" ("l'ultimo lavoro"; *Para*. 1.13).[35] Chaucer asks for skill in his "art poetical" (*HF*, 1095), for Apollo to "entre in my brest anoon" (*HF*, 1109) in order "to shew now / That in myn hed ymarked ys" (*HF*, 1102–1103); Dante too asks this god of poetry to "enter into my breast" ("entra nel petto mio"; *Para*. 1.19), so that he may "show forth the image of the blessed realm which is imprinted in my mind" ("l'ombra del beato regno / segnata nel mio capo io manifesti"; *Para*. 1.23–24).[36] Dante expresses his debt for whatever poetic grace he may be granted by promising to be the worthy recipient of the leaves of Apollo's tree, the laurel (*Para*. 1.24–26); Chaucer feels a similar debt, but with this image the Dantean parallel shifts drastically. Reaching high for the poetic grace that might possibly begin his homage to Apollo, the dreamer promises that if he is given the power to describe Fame's House, he will go forth, "as blyve" (*HF*, 1106) as he can, approach the first laurel tree he sees, and "kysse yt" (*HF*, 1108). The key images from Dante's invocation are here: Apollo, his descent into the poet's breast, the image in the mind, the laurel tree; but the single significant addition to the Italian source—the incredible scene of the poet communing with the divine in one breath and in the next rushing out to kiss a tree—will never allow the tone of reverence commencing Dante's paradisal journey to open Chaucer's quest for "fame."[37]

In the invocations to each of the three books of *The House of Fame*, Chaucer's deviations from his sources in the *Commedia* are not made with any striking effort to hide the joints and seams of

[34]Cf. Bennett, pp. 100–103; and Koonce, pp. 178–183.

[35]*The Divine Comedy*, trans. Charles S. Singleton (Princeton: Princeton University Press, 1970–1975); *Paradiso*, p. 3. Unless otherwise noted, modern English translations are Singleton's.

[36]Singleton, *Paradiso*, p. 5.

[37]Bennett, too, argues that Chaucer "seems deliberately to be distancing himself and his 'little book' from his great exemplar, as if to emphasize that he would never presume to essay Dante's task" (p. 102); yet he reads Chaucer's episode of kissing the tree seriously. My own sense of the ironic tone of the passage compares with Miskimin's, p. 73.

reference but rather attempt to highlight them. The effect of the invocations is far-reaching for the poem as a whole: through the treatment of tripartite division, Chaucer calls just as much attention to the mode of signifying as to the signified supernatural order. Dante's creation of this same effect in presenting his quest as an allegory of reading had an obvious influence on Chaucer. For both poets, writing affirms a structure of reference at the same time as it calls into question its own affirmation. This effect of the metalinguistic function of writing in *The House of Fame* is a mark of its principal difference from the kind of writing that composes the myth of the Book—the metaphor of divine perceiving whose structure of reference is absolute. As filled as it is with mythological materials, Chaucer's *House of Fame* does not mythologize Dante's *Commedia*. Moreover, the qualified structure of the poem is not the consequence only of the use of sources from Virgil, Ovid, and Dante; it is rendered through other aspects of *The House of Fame*, those in which Chaucer's style appears "artificial" and "ornamental." One example is Chaucer's adaptation of the genre of the dream vision.

5

Models of the convention immediately at hand for Chaucer were the French visions of Froissart, the *Paradys d'amours* and the *Temple d'onnour*, as well as Nichole de Margival's *Panthere d'amours*. But it is certain that Chaucer adapted the convention quite freely, for he also incorporates a good deal of the generic form of Macrobius's *Somnium Scripionis*.[38] As Chaucer mentions in the proem to book 2, his frame of reference for dreams draws on the "avisyon," the particular kind of dream that is divine in origin, like Scipio's, but also like the dreams mentioned in the Bible, such as Isaiah's prophetic dream or those of Nebuchadnezzar (in Daniel 1–4) and Pharaoh (in Genesis 41). These conventions, incidentally, also inform Dante's dream of the eagle's flight that carries him aloft to the Mountain of Purgatory in *Purgatorio* 9, which Chaucer adapts as a major motif in *The House of Fame*. Although the revelatory and prophetic nature of dreams becomes the basis for their function in literary conventions—to affirm belief in

[38]A fine account of this influence is available in Francis X. Newman's Ph.D. dissertation, "Somnium: Medieval Theories of Dreaming and the Form of Vision Poetry" (Princeton University, 1963), chap. 5.

the validity of the poet's experience as in *The Book of the Duchess* and *The Parliament of Fowls*—in *The House of Fame* Chaucer undermines this convention.[39]

The poem opens with the old *topos* of the *dubitatio* in which the narrator expresses his confusion about the origin and purpose of dreams;[40] the proem is a brilliant tour de force cataloging the highlights of medieval lore about dreams, and the speaker tears through it with such haste and preoccupation that his focus, we cannot help but recognize, is not going to be primarily on the documentary facts of his dream, the old convention that the poet really had the experience. This recognition is unavoidable when the speaker, after fifty or more lines of expressed ignorance and bewilderment about dreams, nonetheless assumes our unqualified belief in his claim that never has any man before him had a dream as wonderful as the one he is about to tell:

> For never, sith that I was born,
> Ne no man elles me beforn,
> Mette, I trowe steadfastly,
> So wonderful a drem as I
> The tenth day now of December.
> (*HF*, 59–63)

The sweep of the *dubitatio* in the proem suddenly runs up against the claim to fact in this passage; the inflated rhetoric hardly comes to an end in this equally inflated appeal to specificity. "The tenth day now of Decembre," although the kind of reference that might pique the scholarly itch for symbolic meanings, remains, because of the style of this context, an expression that either has a very obvious reference (such as "Mayes daye the thridde") or else signifies random choice and thus contributes to the rhetoric of exaggerated precision.[41] The tone of the proem places December tenth in the latter category as an ornamental or artificial date.[42]

Instead of encouraging the reader's conventional belief in the

---

[39]For general remarks on the dream as an authenticating device, though without attention to ironic functions of the convention, see Morton W. Bloomfield, "Authenticating Realism and the Realism of Chaucer," *Thought* 39 (1964):345.

[40]See Bennett, p. x; Delany, p. 41.

[41]Koonce does not see it this way; contrast his lengthy search for the symbolic date, pp. 57–72; nor does Leyerle in his remarks on the date in "Chaucer's Windy Eagle," pp. 249–251. See also John P. McCall, "Chaucer's May 3," *MLN* 76 (1961): 201–205.

[42]It is yet another instance of narrative secrecy that characterizes the medieval *liber occultorum*.

dream vision, the proem is a preface to our disbelief because it is so obviously concerned with invention. The poetic composition, like the dream it records, is disjoined from the authority it otherwise affirms; the tradition of the link between dreamer and listener, author and audience is deliberately interrupted.[43] A consequence of this interruption is a new understanding of the dreamer and what he "mette." Whereas the dream has been conventionally a "revelation" (as in Scripture) or a "miracle" (as in *Pearl*), Chaucer's dream has the opposite effect of emphasizing itself as pure fabrication. The dream becomes a metaphor of the poem itself.[44] Rather than authorizing the surrounding poetic composition as a historical report of an actual experience—the convention going back beyond Macrobius—the dream in this poem has the opposite effect of "de-authorizing" itself by emphasizing its own fictivity. This point is nowhere more apparent than in the content of the dream proper. It is not events past or future, but *readings* about events that the poet has undertaken in old books. The dreamer's vision is called "fantasye" (*HF,* 11) and "fantome" (*HF,* 593), and fantasies of events, as one commentator has observed, are displaced by the fictional medium that represents them.[45] This quality has been interpreted in various ways. For instance, it has been argued that Chaucer's qualified form is a result of the unresolved conflicts in his poetry, conflicts that manifest skepticism and occasion the need to transcend opposition through a "leap of faith."[46] Another suggestion is that Chaucer's emphasis on the inflation and artificiality of language draws it into comparison with the inflation of "money"; writing and money are cast as media of exchange out of control; valued for their glitter, for their "own sake" instead of for their "uses" (according to Augustine's distinction), both media are forms of idolatry.[47]

Each of these positions is a tempting way of reading the poem. But the artifice of form, I think, serves a much simpler function in the poem, one that is more fundamental to its actual *matière.* By associating writing with artificiality Chaucer is taking a step that is self-evident in theories of writing familiar to modern scholarship but not at all common in medieval tradition, especially in conven-

[43]See Delany, p. 46.
[44]Delany, too, has stressed this point (pp. 43–45), but as evidence that "neither dream theory nor literary tradition offers certain truth" (p. 44). Yet I do not see why the emphasis on fictivity and artificiality necessarily ends in skepticism for Chaucer.
[45]Vance, "Poetics of Inflation," p. 29.
[46]Delany, pp. 24, 85, 109, 113, 122.
[47]Vance, "Poetics of Inflation," p. 22.

tions of the dream as divine revelation or miracle. For the old assumption of writing as a metaphor of an order of reality transcendental or natural is set aside in preference for a direct recognition of the inability of writing to represent such an order adequately. Chaucer might have confronted this problem by offering an apologia for it, as many medieval theoreticians have attempted;[48] but on the contrary, he acknowledges outright the plain fact that writing *is* an artifice of what it represents and that it cannot change this fact without distortion. Rather than strive for a result that it can deliver only as imperfect and limited, writing—as it is studied in *The House of Fame*—begins by elevating and celebrating the artifice of form that would otherwise remain a deficiency in medieval language theory. Disclosing artifice for what it is, *The House of Fame* forestalls any threat of deficiency by presenting its imagery not in the bloodless representation of stiff forms cut out of old sources, but in a style of surprising comparisons and new energy. In a most basic sense, this poem is about the unsung fame of writing.

The dream, for instance, begins "withyn a temple ymad of glas" where the dreamer sees "ymages / Of gold," "portreytures," and other "old werk" (*HF*, 120–127). Although Venus herself is not seen in the temple, the dreamer confronts "hir figure" in a portrait provocative enough to deserve comparison with Botticelli's famous painting: she is "naked fletynge in a see" (*HF*, 132–133).[49] The story of Aeneas and Dido, which occupies the bulk of book 1, is not "in portreyture" (*HF*, 131) but is read by the dreamer from a brass wall tablet on which the text is inscribed.

> "I wol now singen, yif I kan.
> The armes, and also the man."
> (*HF*, 143–144)

After reading these opening lines of the *Aeneid*, the dreamer goes on to record what he "sawgh"—"the destruction / Of Troye," how "Ilyon assayled was," and old "kynge Priam yslayn" (*HF*, 151–159). Shortly he "hears" what Aeneas "said" and how Dido lamented. Their "fame" is already synonymous with their written story, and if the narrator's record is not sufficient evidence of it, we are told to

---

[48]Documentation of such efforts is available above in chapter 2, section 5, and chapter 3, section 2.

[49]Bennett has also noted the comparison; see *Chaucer's Book of Fame*, pp. xi, 32.

Rede Virgile in Eneydos
Or the Epistle of Ovyde.
(*HF*, 378–379)

In these passages, what the dreamer "sawgh" (*HF*, 439) is not exactly of the same order as Aeneas's experience when he "to helle wente, for to see / His fader" and "saugh" there "every turment eke" (*HF*, 441–446). The contrast is simple, but it continues Chaucer's interest throughout the poem in rendering direct perception (such as Aeneas's experience) of the supernatural order —the "vision" of it—as an elaborate metaphor of reading and writing.

When the dreamer is finally out of "this chirche" of "ymages" (*HF*, 472–473), he sees the eagle, but it too is an artifice of an eternal world, a golden form ("hyt was of gold") from a heaven that is "al newe of gold" (*HF*, 503, 506)—very likely the pages of Dante's *Purgatorio* 9 and *Paradiso* 1 that are joined as the background for the scene.[50] With the dreamer's flight in the talons of the bird, Chaucer moves close to fracturing artifice by the experience of the dreamer's fear that he will fall from the sky.

> For so astonyed and asweved
> Was every vertu in my heved,
> What with his sours and with my drede,
> That al my felynge gan to dede.
> (*HF*, 549–552)

But even here the event of flight competes with the artifice of allusion to *Purgatorio* 9 in which Dante is asleep in the talons of the golden bird conveying him to the Mountain of Purgatory, or for that matter, to the *Inferno* in which Dante swoons at various times in sadness and fear. Chaucer's passage gains its energy not because we see in it the embryo of realism developed in his later career, but because whatever strikes us as a natural reaction from the dreamer *cannot* free itself from the artifice of form that holds it. Nor is the fame of artifice rigidifying and stale. Quite the reverse: it is surprising, for instance, in the scene of Chaucer puzzling over his situation of being carried off by a bird. He declares that he is not a reincarnation of others reported to have had such experiences— "Ennok," "Elye," "Romulus," or "Ganymede" (*HF*, 588–589. "What thing," he asks, "may this sygnifye?" (*HF*, 587). But before

[50]Ibid., pp. 50–51.

the question calls for a signified, historical referent, it has more fundamental reference to its own signifying intention.[51] For "Chaucer" remains the "thing" of the question. "He" is no longer an author recording a dream of being carried off by a bird. "He" is a fiction, an integer of writing puzzling over how utterly provocative it is to think like a writer.

A similar instance in which the signs of writing call attention to their own signifying import is the discourse of the eagle. The personification of the talking bird is much more than a decorative device by which learned information relevant to the cosmic journey may be included in the poem. The ornamentality of the figure here is engaging exactly as ornament, since this bird is first Dante's golden eagle, next the scholarly guide of the voyage (Virgil), and finally an image of Beatrice.[52] But in *The House of Fame* the high style of the eagle's learned discourses, such as those concerning sound and the Milky Way, is riddled with the very different style of the everyday, the colloquialism of a figure like Pandarus or Chaunticleer.[53] After the long disquisition on sound, the eagle asks the dreamer if he has been persuaded:

> "Tell me this now feythfully,
> Have y not preved thus symply,
> Withoute any subtilite
> Of speche, or gret prolixite
> Of termes of philosophie,
> Of figures of poetrie,
> Or colours of rethorike?
> Pardee, hit oughte the to lyke!
> For hard langage and hard matere
> Ys encombrous for to here
> Attones: wost thou not wel this?"
>
> (*HF*, 853–863)

No "colours of rethorike," he insists, but the passage is effective precisely as rhetoric: for the argument does not quite leave us, "pardee," preferring colloquialism to "hard language"; nor is the

[51]Contrast Koonce's identification of the referents in exegetical history; see *Chaucer and the Tradition of Fame*, pp. 142–146.

[52]When Chaucer compares the bird to "another sonne" (*HF*, 506), he is following exactly the image Dante uses to describe the effect of following Beatrice's gesture heavenward at the beginning of *Paradiso* (1.61–63). On the conflation of these images of the bird in *Purgatorio* 9 and Beatrice in *Paradiso* 1, see Bennett, pp. 50–51.

[53]The eagle's style in this passage is studied, for instance, by Bennett (p. 70) and by Leyerle, "Chaucer's Windy Eagle," pp. 254–256.

union of styles "encombrous" unless we choose either familiarity or learning, in which case we reject the text before us since it offers the two of them "attones" as its artifice.

The poem delights in counterfeiting both learning and colloquialism, just as the music described on the way to Fame's House is a "countrefete" of the music tuning the universe heard in the famous musicians from antiquity—"Orpheus" and "Orion" (*HF*, 1201–1205).[54] Beneath these great harpers of old sit "smale harpers with her glees" who gape upward at them and "counterfete hem as an ape" (*HF*, 1209, 1212). The copy is no genuine likeness of the original; "craft" cannot imitate "kynde" without distortion. But the answer to this opposition is not to choose one or abandon both. It is rather to acknowledge the necessary artificiality of artifice: "craft" *only* "countrefeteth kynde" (*HF*, 1213), as do the small harpers and their counterpart, the talking bird. When the dreamer notices a language a little closer to "kynde," he hears the "language" of the sea, the "betynge of the see . . . ayen the roches holowe" (*HF*, 1034–1035). It is the chaos and confusion of "the grete soun,"

> "that rumbleth up and doun
> In Fames Hous, full of tydynges,
> Bothe of feir speche and chidynges,
> And of fals and soth compounded."
> (*HF*, 1025–1029)

This noisy "speche" compares with the language of nature, the sea against the cliffs, the "tempest" and the "clappe of thundring" (*HF*, 1036, 1040). It cannot be intelligibly transcribed. By contrast, artificial language, albeit "unnatural," makes no pretense of being a genuine likeness, yet at least it communicates: the language of the poem is the "craft" that "countrefeteth kynde."[55]

Approaching closer to the House of Fame, the dreamer is struck by its lush artifice. Writing here is not the signifier of concrete or abstract things; rather, things have turned into script. The dreamer sees a glistening "roche of yse" (*HF*, 1130) covered with writing: one side is melting, the side listing names of persons with little fame; the other is "conserved with the shade" (*HF*, 1160), its names "of folkes that hadden grete fames" (*HF*, 1154). The castle of Fame proper is "ful of ymageries . . . al with gold behewe" (*HF*, 1304–1306). The building is constructed of "pilers," each of which

---

[54] For the exegetical traditions of these musicians, see Koonce, pp. 196–204.

[55] Miskimin has argued a similar point; see *Renaissance Chaucer*, p. 75.

is identified with a famous author.[56] "Josephus, the olde" (*HF*, 1433),

> Upon a piler stonde on high,
> That was of led and yren fyn.
> (*HF*, 1430–1431)

He represents the enormous body of Hebrew writing—the "fame" of "Jewerye" (*HF*, 1436). On the next "yren piler strong" is Statius, who "bar of Thebes up the fame / Upon his shuldres" (*HF*, 1461–1462). Adjacent to him on a column of iron in this "house of fiction" is Homer, "and with him Dares and Tytus" (*HF*, 1466), along with others whose writings are devoted "for to bere up Troye" (*HF*, 1472). Virgil follows on a column that supports "the fame of Pius Eneas," and next to him is "Venus clerk, Ovide," whose poetry on the God of Love "bar up wel hys fame" (*HF*, 1485, 1487, 1490). Then the dreamer sees the column of Lucan, who holds up the "fame of Julius and Pompe" (*HF*, 1502) and other poets who celebrate Rome. The last piller is Claudian's, since he "bar up the fame of helle" (*HF*, 1510), notably the literature of Pluto and Proserpine. This architecture of Fame's House recalls an image from book 1 in which Venus's temple is called, for all its writing and imagery, a "chirche" (*HF*, 473). Like this image, Fame's House relies on the commonplace conception that the columns of the cathedral are the great men of ecclesiastical history.[57] Fame's House, made of the pillars of the community of "olde auctores," is a *domus auctoritatis*, a "palace of writing."

In the center of this House, Lady Fame, the image of artifice itself, sits on a throne carved from a single huge "rubee" (*HF*, 1362).[58] Although other central figures in Chaucer's works are informed by references to past literature, as "Lady Nature" in *The Parliament of Fowls* is modeled on "Natura" from Alanus de Insulis's *De planctu naturae*, the goddess Fame is an unusual conflation of

---

[56]This scene of the "hall of great authors" is typically regarded as evidence of the theme of vindicating poetry—the "fame" of literary history (e.g., Bennett, pp. xi, 138–145). But the hall is hardly a place where fame has positive value, and the dreamer must go elsewhere to find it. Despite the imagery of "pilers" and "yren," this scene contributes all the more vividly to the imagery of artifice in the poem.

[57]Various medieval sources for this commonplace are cited above, chapter 2, section 1. Koonce also recalls this idea of the house as a church, though he insists on its moral value (p. 215).

[58]See Bennett's full exposition of this complex figure: "Fortune's Sister," in *Chaucer's Book of Fame*, pp. 146–164. Cf. Koonce, pp. 206–214.

images from several old books. She is at once Philosophia and Fortuna from Boethius's *Consolation of Philosophy*, insofar as she is "wonderliche streighte," like Philosophia,

> That with her fet she erthe reighte
> And with her hed she touched hevene.
> (*HF*, 1374–1375)

Yet she occasionally behaves "ryght as her suster, dame Fortune" (*HF*, 1547), in the unpredictable and arbitrary disposition of fame that she awards to those who supplicate her, and the emphasis of Chaucer's portrait of her may be found in other famous passages about Fama and Fortuna, such as in the *Aeneid*, Petrarch's *Trionfi*, Nichole de Margival's *La Panthère d'amours*, and Alanus's *Anticlaudianus*.[59] The list of her sources is long and complex, but Chaucer has clearly not sided with one source or one emphasis that many have in common, such as Fame's betrayal of allegiances. For along with the tradition of Fama as Fortuna, Chaucer has also rendered his goddess in the iconography of the four Gospels when he says that she has as many eyes

> As fetheres upon foules be,
> Or weren on the bestes foure
> That Goddis trone gunne honoure,
> As John writ in th'Apocalips.
> (*HF*, 1382–1385)

Chaucer's Fame, as has been commonly observed, signifies the arbitrariness that is so much a part of the poem. But that significance does not include exclusively a moral category such as the irrationality of "wordly vanity" (in contrast to God's "fame") or a historical one such as the changing renown of books in literary tradition. Chaucer's "fame" has more to do with the potential for arbitrariness that is a condition of communicating in speech and writing. The idea is suggested by the goddess's function in dispensing "fame" as "speche," first her own utterance and then the clarion blast from Aeolus to announce her message to the world. A typical illustration is her response to the first company of suppliants who come before her asking for fame for their good works.

---

[59]Bennett, pp. 105–115.

> "I werne yow hit," quod she anon;
> "Ye gete of me good fame non,
> Be God! and therfore goo your wey."
> "Allas!" quod they, "and welaway!
> Telle us what may your cause be."
> <div align="right">(<i>HF</i>, 1559–1563)</div>

But she gives them none, and her disposition to other seekers is similarly unpredictable. Her utterance sometimes reflects an appeal to consistency between merit and reward, but sometimes the communication between them is lost, and the result is the reputation of her "speche" as artificial, like the mélange of images and sources composing her.

The comparison of the imagery of artifice to writing and speaking developed extensively in *The House of Fame* moves toward an inevitable and crucial question in the central image of the erratic speech of Lady Fame. Some principle of consistency ought to manifest control in speaking and in the distribution of rewards, but it is shown to be frequently arbitrary or superficial. A conventional response to this problem in the history of medieval language theory is that determinacy of meaning is controlled by appeal to authority, the authority of a source or a famous writer.[60] As we have seen, the encyclopedias of nature and Scripture are composed of elaborate extensions of such principles of authorization. In a series of examples, the last I will consider, Chaucer takes up the problem of determining meaning by appeal to authority. These examples are related to each other insofar as they all involve, in one way or another, the search for an authoritative "source," the determination to identify a primary "cause" or find a fixed "center" of reference. One of the most striking illustrations opens the poem.

6

In the *dubitatio* of book 1, the speaker's bewilderment is specifically about the *cause* of dreams: "what causeth swevenes" (*HF*, 3) confuses him, and he repeats the word "cause" seven times in the proem. "Avisioun," "revelacioun," "drem," "sweven," "fantome," "oracle," "miracle"—all seem the same because he does not know

---

[60]See above, chapter 1, section 3.

their "causes" (*HF*, 7–13). For a moment the dreamer pauses over their "signifiaunce" (*HF*, 17), their relation to points in time past and future, but the subject that dominates the proem is the search for the true origin of dreams: "why this more then that cause is" (*HF*, 20). Various origins are mentioned—"complexion," "feblenesse," "abstinence," "seknesse," "stewe," "prison," "distresse," "dysordynaunce," "curiosity," "melancholy," "drede," "devocion," "contemplacion," and others (*HF*, 21–51), but none is accepted as a primary explanation of what "causeth" dreams (*HF*, 35). Although a long history of thought on the subject echoes in the background of this *dubitatio*—for instance the distinctions drawn by Macrobius between the five species, "somnium," "visio," "oraculum," "insomnium," "visum," and their subdivisions—the tradition is surely not being discounted when the dreamer concludes, "why the cause is, noght wot I" (*HF*, 52).[61] On the contrary, the *dubitatio* serves structural purposes in the poem more than it delivers a judgment on the scholarship of dreams. It suggests that the appeal to the authority of a source, a "cause," in order to make meaning determinate in a body of knowledge, in this case about dreams, must confront the variability of that cause. An originary source may be imagined to be fixed, as a center determines a circular structure, but in the area of knowledge about dreams that center is shifting.

The point is worth attention because it bears on the concerns of the poem with the fixity and variability of structure. With regard to book 1, it is an indirect but appropriate prelude to the treatment of the sources about Dido and Aeneas that I began with: Which is to have privilege, Virgil's account or Ovid's? The questions assume a prevenient *auctoritas* that would structure the legend with an "answer," but the poem presents the relativity of differences, the absence of a "cause" that would subordinate the sources. The result in Chaucer's poem is that the traditions of Aeneas that had become subtle and complex by Chaucer's time are not oversimplified into a final word on the legend. Each tradition is represented as a version, and neither has privilege. As we have seen, the effect of this kind of treatment of sources is that they reflect on their own order of "telling" the story of Aeneas, just as their context in the encompasing "sweven" is narrating them. This metalinguistic function of writing assumes a very different sense of structure from the princi-

---

[61]The scholarship on this background has supplied much needed information (see above, notes 38–40), but it has not adequately addressed the structural function of the *dubitatio* or considered at all its relation to the quest for the origin in the poem.

ple of determinate center that organizes the myth of the past and the Book of culture. In contrast, the structure of *The House of Fame* is qualified, not fixed by an absolute center.

In book 2, the flight of the eagle and the motif of the search for "tydynges" carry out the "decentering" strategy of book 1. The quest is planned to terminate at a definite end, an image of concrete and total structure, Fame's House, where the dreamer is supposed to receive new material for his writing. But the journey is anything but arrow straight. It is, rather, composed of learned digressions on various topics, each centered in its own right; but together they are—like the mixed sources in book 1—not subordinated to a single principle. To some readers the eagle's discourse may appear "curious and elusive," yet it has a purpose entirely relevant to the subtle structure of *The House of Fame*.[62] For instance, en route to the source of "fame," the eagle's discourse on the origin of "soun" (*HF*, 753–852) sharply juxtaposes his own style of speech and the course of his flight.[63] He claims that a single source is the cause of all language; variations in speech are "broken" pieces of a primary substance, air; changes in pitch, as produced by a musical pipe, "twyst with violence" (*HF*, 775) a substance trying to remain whole. When a word is uttered, its "multiplicacioun" (*HF*, 784) into language is like a stone thrown into water:

> yf that thow
> Throwe on water now a stoon,
> Wel wost thou, hyt wol make anoon
> A litel roundell as a sercle,
> Paraunter brod as a covercle;
> And ryght anoon thow shalt see wel,
> That whel wol cause another whel.
>
> (*HF*, 788–794)

As rings of water in a pond radiate from one center, "every sercle causynge other" (*HF*, 796), so language is a structure. The rest of the lecture is replete with the imagery of centering and closing: the "sercle" becomes a "whel" that will "cause another whel / And that the thridde, and so forth" (*HF*, 794–795); the wheel suggests next a "roundel" and a "compass," each "aboute other goynge / Causeth

---

[62]Leyerle has argued this point well ("Chaucer's Windy Eagle," pp. 260–261), though without attention to the question of authority raised by the eagle's style.

[63]See Vance's remarks on the eagle's "inflating" and "deflating" rhetoric; "Poetics of Inflation," pp. 25–27.

of others sterynge," and "mytiplyinge ever moo" (*HF* 798–801). Like the First Cause itself, "every word, ywys . . . moveth first an ayr aboute" (*HF*, 809–811).

The "word" as "prime mover," as Logos, controls a conception of language as a determinate, "logocentric" structure that has deep roots in the medieval mythology of music. The lecture is informed by a long and various list of *auctoritates*, extending from Augustine's and Boethius's treatises on music and continuing through Chalcidius's commentary on Plato's *Timaeus*, Macrobius's treatise on dreams, Vincent of Beauvais's encyclopedia of nature, and Jacobus of Liège's summary of musical theory in the fourteenth century. The tradition reflected by these sources treats "number" (*numerus*) as the primary cause of audible sound (*instrumentalis musica*) and the fixed center of "music" in man (*humana musica*), in the physical world and the celestial spheres (*mundana musica*), and finally in the supernatural order (*divina musica*).[64] Informed by this rich and well-known tradition, the eagle's lecture is an elaborate application of mythological structure to language.

But the eagle is not a very effective auditor of his own lecture. In a manipulation of perspective that Chaucer employs in many later works, the eagle is unaware that the mythology of language he would "teche" (*HF*, 782) is not the language he actually speaks.[65] He reaches high for the grandeur of encyclopedic learning and frequently its style of cataloging and listing.[66] For example, regarding the tidings at Fame's House, the eagle says that the dreamer will hear:

> Mo discordes, moo jelousies,
> Mo murmures, and moo novelries,
> And moo dissymulacions,
> And feyned reparacions.
>
> (*HF*, 685–688)

But this totalizing style completes its comparison with an incongruous reference to the familiar and colloquial: "And moo berdys," he goes on,

---

[64]See the discussion of medieval musical ideas above, chapter 2, section 5.

[65]For instance, cf. the limited omniscience of the Reeve, the Wife of Bath, or the Prioress concerning their understanding of the significance of the tales they tell.

[66]Cf. the preoccupation with *manifestatio* in the summae of theological learning and Gothic architecture described above, chapter 2, sections 2 and 3.

in two houres
Withoute rasour or sisoures
Ymad, then greynes be of sondes."
(*HF*, 689–691)

Unaware of the jarring stylistic shift, the eagle again rises to the elevation of the catalog and again interrupts it, this time comparing the exchanges between lovers to the number of ears of corn stored in a barn ("loves moo eschaunges / Then ever cornes were in graunges"; *HF*, 697–698). It is this kind of shifting rhetorical style, like the arbitrary changing of subjects throughout his discourse on the way to Fame's House, that returns us to the discussion of the changing "cause" of dreams at the opening of the poem: fixity of center characterizes mythological structures, but the actual experience of dreams is far more flexible, and so is the production and reception of "speche." The discourse of *The House of Fame* acknowledges this difference, just as Dante confesses the inability of the language of his poem to imitate the myth of the *liber praesentiae Dei* at the end of the *Paradiso*. But the eagle is no imitation of Dante. Proceeding headlong to copy the "ensercled" theory of sound, the eagle continues to weave and soar, utterly unaware of the evidence in his style for the shifting center and inevitable play in the structure of language.

Book 2 closes with a passage in which this play is apparent in another way. The eagle describes what happens to words when they reach Fame's House, but he acknowledges no sense whatever of the humor of the scene he visualizes. A word uttered, he says,

wexeth lyk the same wight
Which that the word in erthe spak,
Be hyt clothed red or blak.
(*HF*, 1076–1078)

A word reaching the palace of the goddess is not merely the referent of its author's intent, claims the eagle, but has "verray hys lyknesse," indeed, even the "same body"—"man or woman, he or she" (*HF*, 1079–1082). Again the eagle's scholarship is impressive. It may even be greater than that of the learned "clerks" of the fourteenth century, since this notion of the identity of author and word goes back to a classical document unknown to them, Plato's *Cratylus*. But what is undermined by the hyperbole of the scene is the consubstantiality of utterance and reference, a position also rejected, for the most part, by medieval theoreticians.[67] For the Cratylistic notion of the "presence" of the author in his "word" obviously risked treading too heavily on sacred doctrine, although its more subtle manifestations, in such concepts as the organic bond of sign and signified, posed no apparent threat. The scene ending book 2 undermines both the Cratylistic and the organic concept of the sign: by exaggerating the bond of sound and referent to such proportions, the poem repeats the strategy of decentering structure—not only the eagle's, but also its own.

In book 3 the quest for the origin continues as the dreamer arrives at his destination expecting to hear the promised "tydynges." The palace is described in the vivid imagery of a fixed and centered place. Earlier in the journey, the dreamer was told that the House is situated:

> Ryght even in myddes of the weye
> Betwixen hevene, erthe, and see.
> (HF, 714–715)

Now arrived at that cosmic center, he sees its solidity and closure —the "walles of berile," the "castel-yate" (HF, 1288, 1294), the inside "flor, and roof, and al" that are "plated half a foote thikke / Of gold" (HF, 1344–1346). Among the "folk" present he imagines the coats of arms dispersed among so many in the crowd bound together in a single volume—"a bible / Twenty foot thykke, as y trowe" (HF, 1334–1335).[68] In the middle of the hall, high above the press on a "dees" (HF, 1360), Fame sits "in a see imperiall," installed "perpetually" on a throne (HF, 1374–1375); the songs of the muses and spheres (musica mundana and divina) circle around her, as if "tuned" by the centrality of her position:

> And, Lord! the hevenyssh melodye
> Of songes, ful of armonye,
> I herde aboute her trone ysonge,
> That al the paleys-walles ronge!
> (HF, 1395–1398)

---

[67]The medieval tradition of the via negativa, going back to Dionysius the Areopagite, is one of the more popular oppositions to the Cratylistic assumption about signs. Cf. Vance's observation about the Cratylism in the poem; "Poetics of Inflation," p. 27.

[68]This image appears to be an obvious distortion of the learned tradition of the Book as totality and authority; it turns the convention from Dante's vision of the liber praesentiae Dei to the artifice of exaggeration that could occur only in dreams.

In the context of this *concordia*, this architecture of sound, the speech of Lady Fame, like the eagle's speech earlier, echoes as a poor imitation. Her arbitrary announcement of "fame" in response to the suppliants who seek her favor is only remotely bound by the stability and value of her position in the hall. For her speech is continually sliding off the center that ties merit to reward and gives utterance determinate meaning. The blast of noise from the god of wind declaring the "fame" of each company serves all the more to emphasize the anticentric "speche" of the goddess. It is no surprise, therefore, that the dreamer does not find at this terminus of his quest the "tydynges" he has come for. The origin he seeks has been continually deferred: it is not in the poetry he has written (*HF*, 641–671); it is not in the books he has read (the sources of the poem); he has not heard it in the learned discourse of the eagle; nor is it to be found in Fame's palace. When he finally says to the anonymous escort near the end of book 3 that he has come not for the kind of tidings he has heard in Fame's hall but for "newe tydynges," "newe thinges" (*HF*, 1886–1887), he is taken elsewhere (*HF*, 1914).

It might appear that this displacement is a realization that the quest for the origin of a centered "cause" for dreams and an identifiable structure for language comes to very little. As the dreamer observes, pondering Fame's motivations:

> But thus I seye yow, trewely,
> What her cause was, y nyste.
> (*HF*, 1542–1543)

If support for Chaucer's "skepticism" is to be sought, one might look for it in these lines, or in the passage describing the house that the dreamer is taken to after leaving the goddess Fame. For this house is a labyrinth within the pale of Fame's palace:

> Under the castel, faste by,
> An hous, that Domus Dedaly,
> That Laboryntus cleped ys.
> (*HF*, 1919–1921)

Instead of solidity and closure, this house is "mad of twigges" (*HF*, 1936); it is "lyk a cage" (*HF*, 1985); sound moves in and out of its "thousand holes" (*HF*, 1949) and "dores opened wide" (*HF*, 1952); inside all things are in continual motion, "so faste hit whirleth"

[195]

(*HF*, 2006).[69] However, these contrasts to Fame's House do not necessarily signify logical oppositions, the antitheses of a meaningful order in the search for new poetic material: the poem does not stop with emptiness and nihilism. For the dreamer is escorted not into outer darkness, but into "another place" (*HF*, 1914) that is off center from the cosmic midpoint ("myddes"—*HF*, 714) of Fame's hall; he stands no longer on high, but "in a valeye" (*HF*, 1918). The house he confronts is not an image of desolation and destruction; it seems to the dreamer "founded to endure" (*HF*, 1981). And it is not "centerless," but labyrinthian, a place whose center exists as a secret; it is eccentric; the wind whirling in it is contained loosely by its wicker walls, rotating around some shifting vortex.

These patterns indicate that the search of the poem does not end in the absence of structure, the abandonment of a centerless void. The quest leads the speaker to the discovery of an "off-center" vantage, a perspective for understanding that has heretofore been confusing to him. "Soun," the most baffling image in the poem, now issues from the house of sticks: like everything else in this context, it contrasts with the splendor of Fame's palace and thus is hardly an imitation of *musica mundana* and *divina*. But the contrast is not a principle of opposition. Instead of senseless discord, language without structure, the "soun" is this time made by the dreamer himself, the writer, as the "poetry" summarizing what he heard issuing from the wicker house:

> And over alle the houses angles
> Ys ful of rounynges and of jangles
> Of werres, of pes, of mariages,
> Of reste, of labour, of viages,
> Of abood, of deeth, of lyf,
> Of love, of hate, acord, of stryf,
> Of loos, of lore, and of wynnynges,
> Of hele, of seknesse, of bildynges,
> Of faire wyndes, and of tempestes,
> Of qwalm of folk, and eke of bestes;
> Of dyvers transmutacions
> Of estats, and eke of regions;
> Of trust, of drede, of jelousye,
> Of wit, of wynnynge, of folye;
> Of plente, and of gret famyne,

[69]The image of the whirling wicker house typically serves as a reference in arguments for Chaucer's skepticism; for example, Delany, *Chaucer's "House of Fame,"* pp. 104–111.

Of chepe, of derthe, and of ruyne;
Of good or mys government,
Of fyr, and of dyvers accident.
(*HF*, 1959–1976)

This "music" is very odd. The anaphora is too long to be taken seriously as a structural principle; the *amplificatio* too inclusive; the rhyme too predictable; the syntax too repetitious; and the subject matter far too multifarious. Yet all the same it is music "off center," playing with conventions of style that announce their own overstylized preoccupations.[70] And this play with structure, like the artifice of form throughout, is a fitting vehicle for turning a most unfitting jumble of matter into amusing verse. The passage displays the kind of ingenuity that is apparent much later in Chaucer's works, such as in the lists of clutter in the *Canon's Yeoman's Tale*.[71] Even in a house of sticks, Chaucer finds a *matière* suitable for poetry, the "tydynges" that he has sought all along here being realized before us in what must remain one of the most understated discoveries in fourteenth-century poetry.

The play with literary tradition throughout the poem reflects on the theme that writing ("tydynges") proceeds, as does the quest, by virtue of its play factor. It is therefore appropriate that the poem should end with a dramatization of language at play. Book 2 closes with the personification of the "word" as the being of its speaker; book 3 ends by returning us to that figure in the animation of "lesyng" and "soth sawe" (*HF*, 2089). Uttered by different occupants of the wicker house, these two "sentences" rise up to pass "out at a wyndowe" (*HF*, 2091), but they are "achekked" when they cannot fit through the opening simultaneously. The rivalry is settled when "fals and soth" are "compounded" (*HF*, 2108) and pass through the opening as "oo tydynge" (*HF*, 2109). The scene circles back elliptically to the question that has been entertained at various points in the poem, the question of authority. As the rivalry of sources, such as between Ovid and Virgil in book 1, raises the issue of privilege and calls attention to the signifying capacity of writing,

---

[70]Insofar as Chaucer's "decentering" compares with assumptions about that term in contemporary theoretical discussion, perhaps it is fair to say that "decentering" ends not "devoid" of all options, but "off-void" or "a-centric." Cf. Derrida's remarks on structural "center" as "deficiency" recorded in *The Structuralist Controversy: The Languages of Criticism and the Sciences of Man*, ed. R. Macksey and E. Donato (Baltimore: John Hopkins University Press, 1970), p. 268.

[71]For example, lines 790–819; see the discussion of the style of this tale by Muscatine, *Chaucer and the French Tradition*, pp. 213–221.

[197]

the skirmish of the sentences in the final scenes of the poem makes the problem explicit, and it is a problem that the metalinguistic function always poses: Who has authority here? "Soth sawe" or "lesyng"? The source or the report? What writing signifies or its own signfying mode? Truth or fiction? "'Lat me go first!' 'Nay, but let me!'" (*HF*, 2097). The agreement is reached that they "wil medle us ech with other" (*HF*, 2102) and together play a game with readers who will not be able to tell them apart: "no man" shall have them separate, truth or fiction, "but bothe / At ones" (*HF*, 2104–2105).[72] The argument is ended, but what about the question of authority?

It has surely not been bypassed; nor has it been assigned by fiat to either "soth" or "fals." The ending of the poem, the recognition of the "man of gret auctorite" (*HF*, 2158), emphasizes what the foregoing argument, if not the entire journey of the dreamer, has suggested about the question of appealing to authority. When it is sought in *auctoritates,* sources, *The House of Fame* reveals the multiplicity of them and their genuine artifice; and when it is sought in *auctores,* the eagle is depicted as pedantic and Fame as utterly unpredictable. Such an appeal is the essence of the structure of mythology that was created in the middle ages out of nature and Scripture. But Chaucer's fiction repeatedly defers the attempt to identify a "source" for authority.[73] The "origin" for knowledge in the poem can only be the text itself. Its voice has replaced the *auctoritates* and *auctores* of tradition as a way of determining meaning, and its authority is the "meddling," the play, of "soth" and "fals." The play of the poem demythologizes the tradition that assumes the presence of authority by showing in the end that "he" is literally a personification, an animated word without a natural identity. The "man of gret auctorite" must be anonymous. To search for his name is to go in the wrong direction. Chaucer has led us in the last line of the poem to the "origin" that myths always lead to: they are anonymous. Fiction, on the other hand, never hides the fact of its authorship. But neither does it actually assume the authority of documentary history. Instead, it acknowledges outright, as *The House of Fame* does so elegantly, the simple point that

---

[72]The argument in the poem at this point seems to go against the intriguing study of opposition in Chaucer's poetry presented by Peter Elbow, *Oppositions in Chaucer* (Middletown, Conn.: Wesleyan University Press, 1973).

[73]In this sense the structure of reference in the poem compares with Dante's treatment of structure in the *Commedia* as the continuing desire to recover, yet simultaneously defer, a point of origin or end; see above, chapter 4.

the text itself is its own authority, its fiction our only frame of reference, and its author (notwithstanding his testimony to the "soth" of what he "sawgh") a creation of the text, a pure fiction, and even given a name—in order to sever finally the anonymous myth of the Book from the only authority the poem can have—"Geffrey" (*HF*, 729).

7

If not a poem of final conclusions, *The House of Fame* is surely a work of provocative experiments in structure, authority, and the determinacy of meaning. The dislocation of authority from the voice of the past to the play of signifying in the text, perhaps the poem's most daring move, registers a separation from the Text of tradition that is more far-reaching than anything we find in Dante's *Commedia*. Since this separation is not one that medieval theory has engaged, it is all the more conceivable that medieval readers would have been unused to it. Their expectations were conditioned—as expectations are usually shaped—by what they had read and heard, by the assumptions that disparate events and sources add up and make sense in the way that elements behave in narrative. The "myth" of the Book—its "narrativity"—was the condition of historical consciousness that authorized the truth of what happened in the physical world, and consequently it was only natural that the rules of narrative order would provide the "authenticating" realism of fictive worlds as well. Following the narrative for the purpose of understanding what the work "says" is not, of course, a medieval phenomenon, but a condition of reading in any age: narrative is the invitation of interpretation, which finds its most comfortable validation when it can appeal to sequence and subordination. We automatically make such a response in *The House of Fame* as we follow the invitation of the narrative about the quest for Fame and tidings. In this poem Chaucer uses narrative as interpretation in as plain a strategy as we will ever find in his works: we expect to follow the narrative sequence in order to discover the meaning of the poem, and it is a course exactly in the direction of locating the source and understanding the meaning of utterance. Our quest establishes its validity by continuing reference to what happens next; the authority for what the poem "says" is determined by the sequence of events: the mythology of this appeal is at work not only in the old motif of the quest for the origin, but in the structure of authority in sequentiality.

However, the narrative thread we follow does not take us very far as we wander through the labyrinth of the story trying to hold on to the argumentative line of the eagle and Lady Fame. The expectation for the rules of narrative—the formalities of connection, subordination, pattern—are quickly violated. The authority of reading can no longer make an easy appeal to story. Its authority is in conflict with other matters in the poem that will not be subordinate to it. Dante pointed to this opposition when he spoke at the end of the *Commedia* of the obscurity of his own writing (his *liber occultorum*) by comparison with the clarity of God's; similarly, one may be persuaded, as is Frank Kermode, to think of scriptural writing generally as riddled with "secret" matter that is distinctly in conflict with an interpretive inclination all too ready to read God's language as determined by familiar expectations for narrative sequence. What is true of the *Commedia* and Scripture is also true of *The House of Fame*: the resistance of the "secret matter"—the *materia occulta*—to narrative clarity is precisely what is so intriguing about it. In contrast, to maintain that the poem is out of control and elusive reveals the automatic expectation that literary works should respond to our narrative demands on them. But *The House of Fame* has much more material at odds with narrative than we are used to in Chaucer's works. When we suspend our easy access to narrative and consider the nonsequential matter of the text, as I have suggested, an argument about writing emerges that can establish itself only by its conflict with storial continuity. We expect clearness, formal purity, and authority, but along with them we receive discord and insubordination. This conflict between sequence and secrecy—the quest for the source interrupted by the errant difficulties of writing—is another way of measuring how unusual the work is in medieval literary history. But the poem is important for more compelling reasons than its moments of greatness or its difference from other literary forms. The opposition in the piece, contrasting the *muthos* of narrative to the insubordinate matter of the text, carries out the much larger preoccupation of the separation of myth from fiction, and that difference has immediate bearing on what history means after Chaucer.

The poem may be examined for the history it contains, but just as important is how it influences historical consciousness. One salient attitude is the confrontation I have been describing between the sequential order so crucial to the tradition of the Book and the *materia occulta* of the labor of composition. The poem does not move beyond this conflict to give us a form in which sequence and secrecy have come to terms with each other. To ask for such a reconciliation is perhaps the wrong question, and it may very well be that by the end of the poem Chaucer realized it. When we look to the work for narrative connectedness and closure we do not find it, no doubt because Chaucer had come to recognize through the work that too many competing factors interrupt the demand for simple clarity of sequence. Instead, the poem appeals to the poet's understanding of what is at stake in the difficulties of writing, and he does not—more remarkable still—surrender its textual properties to the audience's proprieties of unruffled, subordinate form. He runs the risk of their unfavorable response, their judgment that he may not deserve the "fame" represented by the narrative quest of the poem.

But the question of whom Chaucer wrote for, himself or his audience, is not one he treated casually. The "Prologue" to *The Legend of Good Women* takes up the question, and I will turn next to it. Through the dramatization of the poet's defense before the court of Love, Chaucer reveals that he is much less interested in himself, or the poetic imagination, than he is in his audience. Chaucer's concern in his writing, like his interest in so many other areas, is *pragmatic*; he owes a debt to Horace and the pragmatic theory of literature much more than he is a harbinger of Coleridge or Keats and Romantic preoccupations with poetic genesis. Chaucer, as the "Prologue" suggests, is concerned with being clear, with making sure that his audience recognizes certain problems and receives responses to them that make sense—good sense, not oversimplified or platitudinous opinions. Yet at the same time Chaucer assumes in the "Prologue"—as in *The House of Fame* before it and *The Canterbury Tales* after it—the play of language with meaning. He again counts on the primacy of narrative and our demand for storial sense; but he does not compromise the poet's struggle with the uncontrollable matter of writing to the reader's expectation for sequential clarity. The "Prologue" is interested in showing that this conflict is all too readily compromised and that the determinacy of meaning cannot be settled by appeal to a court of last resort. The poem takes an amusing look at those readers who demand that sort of accommodation.

[6]

Problems of Misreading:

The "Prologue" to

The Legend of Good Women

Al ne is nat gospel that is to yow pleyned;
The god of Love hereth many a tale yfeyned.
Chaucer, The Legend of Good Women

1

About the time Chaucer was at work on *The Canterbury Tales*, it is likely that he paused, perhaps in 1386, and wrote the "Prologue" to *The Legend of Good Women*. This return to the form of the dream vision, which he had abandoned before composing *Troilus and Criseyde*, has often puzzled readers—understandably—since it apparently interrupts the development of Chaucer's craft that can be traced from the early poems through *Troilus* and the *Tales*.[1] More unusual still, in 1394 or 1395, when he was well under way with the *Tales*, Chaucer probably returned again to the first version of the "Prologue" (F) and revised it. The revision (G) differs from the earlier F text in its elimination of certain personal and biographical matters, such as the directive toward the end of the poem:

"And whan this book ys maad, yive it the quene,
On my byhalf, at Eltham or at Sheene."
(PLGW, F 496–497)

---

[1]The issues involved in the return to the dream vision, including the dating of the poem, are conveniently summarized by John H. Fisher, "*The Legend of Good Women*," in *Companion to Chaucer Studies*, ed. Beryl Rowland, rev. ed. (New York: Oxford University Press, 1979), pp. 464–476.

Chaucer also excised from F some elements that seem only tertiary to storial sequence, such as the passage at the opening of the poem from Boccaccio's *Filostrato* describing the lady as a celestial light and a musician who is exhorted to play upon the poet's heartstrings and inspire his song (*PLGW*, F 84 ff.). The deletion of such figures from the F text obviously serves the formalities of narrative—concise action (unimpeded beginning, middle, and end), adequate characterization, and crisp *sentence*. Since these are the virtues of narrative in the *Tales*, it is understandable that Chaucer might wish to perfect them in the later G text; but it is not quite so easy to explain why he would leave the *Tales* in the first place and return to a form set aside many years before.

Notwithstanding the improvements of the G version, the "Prologue" has by no means satisfied its critics. That they have mostly, but not exclusively, preferred the more refined G text suggests that interpretation has taken its lead from narrative and that all elements of the poem are subordinated to it—or else they would be eliminated.[2] This assumption deserves scrutiny, insofar as one of the causes of the dissatisfaction some have had with the poem lies in the disjunction between narrative sequence and the apparent interest of the text in matters with little or no immediate bearing on it. Thus the "Prologue," not unlike *The House of Fame* before it, poses for me an interesting example of a work in which a principle of authority—either the narrator's voice or the voice of the narrative—does not prevail completely over the meaning of the text, and the question of indeterminacy is again at stake in Chaucer's game of "soth," "fals," and the reader's response. In the following pages, I will be attending to what Chaucer is playing with on the fringes of the narrative about "his" arraignment before the God of love.[3]

2

One of the first of these oblique passages occurs at the opening of the poem, the sweeping discussion about validating knowledge concerning the afterlife and believing in the claims of old books.

[2]Fisher reviews the positions taken in preference for F and G; he prefers the earlier F version because it includes biographical details; *Companion*, p. 469.

[3]It might be pointed out that my argument for the qualification of narrative in the "Prologue" compares with J. A. Burrow's view that Chaucer deviates from the "Ricardian" preference for narrative by submitting storytelling to the game of fictionalizing in *The Canterbury Tales*; see *Ricardian Poetry: Chaucer, Gower, Langland and*

The passage (*PLGW*, G 1–28) need not be quoted as an example of a typically medieval respect for *auctoritates*: without them the past would be forgotten; a book is the "keye" that will release the hasp of the closed text of "remembrance"—the Book of culture's memory, history.[4] But the exact relevance of this opening to the ensuing story is not the subject of much critical attention in early readings of the "Prologue." They are much more interested in the subsequent passage about the worship of the daisy, and consequently they prefer the elaborate extensions of this image in the F version.[5] An obvious explanation of this interest is the metaphorical extension of the image of the daisy to the imagery of Queen Alceste and the Garden of Love. Since this kind of extension is to be found in contemporary French sources—such as the marguerite poems of Deschamps and Machaut—it has been maintained that Chaucer's intention is predominantly making a model of the French allegory and that the F text, in which the daisy metaphor is more elaborate, is therefore the preferred version.

But the expectation for congruence between the story of the court of love and a presumed story about Chaucer at the court of Richard II proved to have a stronger hand on the meaning of the poem. The argument that the image of Alceste the daisy is not an allegorical image linked back to French marguerite poetry, but rather refers to Richard's queen, Anne of Bohemia, also prefers the F text, though for entirely new reasons (historical allegory), and rests its case on the exclusion of biographical details from the poem after Anne's death in 1394.[6] The appeal of this approach

---

the "*Gawain*" *Poet* (New Haven: Yale University Press, 1971), p. 88. For the conflict of "secrecy" and narrative, see my previous chapter and the two works by Frank Kermode, *The Genesis of Secrecy: On The Interpretation of Narrative* (Cambridge: Harvard University Press, 1979), and "Secrets and Narrative Sequence," *CI* 7 (1980): 83–101.

[4]The text as a "keye" may also suggest that reading will open the gate into the garden in which the dreamer finds himself in the body of the poem. But, as Robert O. Payne has indicated, books in this passage are linked to "tradition"; *The Key of Remembrance: A Study of Chaucer's Poetics* (New Haven: Yale University Press, 1963), p. 94. Thus I suggest that "remembrance" relies on the metaphor of the book of memory or the past that will be unlocked by the key of reading a book—in this case Chaucer's poem.

[5]G. L. Kittredge, "Chaucer and Some of His Friends," *MP* 1 (1903):1–18; J. L. Lowes, "The Prologue to the *Legend of Good Women* as Related to the French Marguerite Poems and to the *Filostrato*," *PMLA* 19 (1904):593–683, and the same author's "The Prologue to the *Legend of Good Women* Considered in Its Chronological Relations," *PMLA* 20 (1905):749–864.

[6]J. S. P. Tatlock, *The Development and Chronology of Chaucer's Works* (1907; reprint, Gloucester, Mass.: P. Smith, 1963); Hugo Lange, "Zur Datierung des GG-Prologs Chaucers Legende von guten Frauen: Eine heraldische Studie," *Anglia* 39 (1915):

and its long scholarly standing may be attributed to the authorization of an assumed narrative of real historical events: Chaucer may have offended women of importance in fourteenth-century society—perhaps even the queen of the realm—by composing allegedly "antifeminist" works, *Troilus and Criseyde* and the translation of the *Romance of the Rose* (both named in the poem, G 255, 265). Public reaction probably arose to protest this offense of good taste in the charges delivered by the God of Love (G 240 ff.); defenses are mounted by both a patron, Alceste (G 318 ff.), and the poet (G 446 ff.), but they cannot prevail over conventional propriety in matters of good literature, and as a result the poet must do "penaunce" by spending most of his time writing poems favorable to women, "a gloryous legende / Of goode women" (G 473–474).[7] The demand for narrative sense in the poem, ordered by the God of Love, has been answered more than adequately by modern readers of the "Prologue": their reading is "medieval" both for its claim to represent English court life in the fourteenth century and for its appeal to the custom that history should make narrative sense.

A major reinterpretation of this reading of the poem expands the reference to the defense of "bad" or "antifeminist" literature to include the much broader idea that Chaucer is writing a general defense of his poetry; although a palinode for *Troilus*, the "Prologue" to the *The Legend of Good Women* is also Chaucer's first full-fledged effort to put forth an ars poetica of all his work.[8] Setting aside the priority of historical reference, though maintaining the propriety of narrative sequence, this reading is one of the most concerted attempts to justify the obscure relationship at the opening between respect for old books and the desire for the flower.[9] It suggests that the two present a basic contrast, insofar as books stand in opposition to the experience of nature when the "source"

347–355; Viktor Langhans, "Der Prolog zu Chaucers Legende von guten Frauen," *Anglia* 41 (1917):162–181.

[7]The control of narrative on interpretation is obvious in the intricate variations that have been proposed for the assumed "story" that occasioned the poem. For instance, Margaret Galway would substitute King Richard's mother, Joan of Kent, and her husband, the Black Prince, for Alceste and the God of Love; see "Chaucer's Sovereign Lady: A Study of the Prologue to the *Legend* and Related Poems," *MLR* 33 (1938):145–199. Her view has not gone unchallenged: see Bernard F. Huppé, "Chaucer: A Criticism and a Reply," *MLR* 43 (1948):393–399; Paul G. Ruggiers, "Tyrants of Lombardy in Dante and Chaucer," *PQ* 29 (1950):445–448.

[8]In *The Key of Remembrance*, Payne examines the possibility of this project in the "Prologue." See also D. C. Baker, "Dreamer and Critic: The Poet in the *Legend of Good Women*," *UCSLL* 9 (1963):4–18.

[9]Payne, *Key*, pp. 94 ff.

for the inspiration of poetry is at issue. And that issue is precisely the theme, according to this reading, of Chaucer's "Prologue"; to document it we need only refer to the story, which is determined to probe for a satisfying resolution. But the movement back and forth between books and experience suggests that traditional and pragmatic approaches to knowledge appear to be irreconcilable opposites. Moreover, the narrator's mask of ignorance functions as a defensive strategy for not facing the problem. Nonetheless, it is acknowledged, in this view of the poem, that the story gradually moves toward harmonious resolution, for instance, in the Balade (*PLGW*, G 203–223), which celebrates Alceste as "the figurative transformation of the daisy."[10] She combines the "natural and the ideal with the traditional past"; in her the singing maidens prefigure "a possible identity of experience, vision, and books."[11] But the dreamer remains ignorant of this coalescence, which, it seems, is possible only in the ideal world of dreams.

The reconciliation imminent in the Balade does not characterize the "Prologue" as a whole, according to this argument, and that problem is set before us in the charges of the God of Love. He blames "Chaucer" not for what he has done but for what he has written, and this attack summarizes two crucial points in poetics: one, that Chaucer has not chosen the proper *sources* for composing poetry, and two, that the *intention* he had "in mynde" (*PLGW*, G 270) has not been realized in writing.[12] To these provocative problems, in the view summarized here, Chaucer has no answer. Alceste comes to the poet's defense, but she "begs the question altogether." The story seeks an answer to a comprehensive matter—"the nature and function of art and the justification of the artist"; but when the God of Love affirms "that the poet must *know* truth, must himself know *how* to select the *right* traditional means, must manage to do actually what he intended ideally—then everything stalls."[13] Instead of an answer, Chaucer retreats into "ironic evasions," and the story of the "Prologue," which had set out to "escape from the circularity of the old, compulsive, book-experience-dream pattern . . . takes Chaucer exactly nowhere."[14]

While the premise of this study of the "Prologue," which is based on what the story actually says, is entirely customary in the inter-

---

[10]Ibid., p. 98.
[11]Ibid., p. 101.
[12]Ibid., p. 102.
[13]Ibid., pp. 103–104, 105.
[14]Ibid., pp. 106, 111.

pretation of medieval literature, the argument does not entertain
the possibility that the narrative raises a problem the text is not necessarily interested in solving. Rather, the problem is treated as if
the poem minimizes or completely excludes any strategies for play.
Humor is of course observed, but it is assigned, and this point is significant, exclusively to the category of *character* in the poem—such
as the portrait of the dreamer-poet. His characterization at the
opening of the "Prologue" is one of the most vivid examples of the
Chaucerian persona as the pedantic, love-struck dreamer, not
quite capable of finding his way to the end of the next sentence.
From the assumption about the continuity of this persona in the
early poems of Chaucer, one may imagine that the G text itself is
the final "chapter" in Chaucer's "myth" about slowly making his
way into the Garden of Love and Art.[15] But just as the hyperbole
about ignorance creates a certain humor in characterization, it also
considerably qualifies the perception of the problem that the narrative begins with. We may say, as some have, that Chaucer opens
the poem with a serious question posed through the voice of an
unserious speaker, the dreamer; but the "voice" of the text, which
is separate from that speaker, is unserious too.[16]

For instance, the doubt about validating the nature of *invisibilia* is
followed by the observation that since such things cannot be
proved, one ought to believe in authorities, such as "Bernard":

> this wot I wel also,
> That there ne is non that dwelleth in this contre,
> That eyther hath in helle or hevene ybe,
> Ne may of it non other weyes witen,
> But as he hath herd seyd or founde it writen;
> For by assay there may no man it preve.
> But Goddes forbode, but men shulde leve
> Wel more thyng than men han seyn with ye!
> Men shal nat wenen every thyng a lye,
> For that he say it nat of yore ago.
> God wot, a thyng is nevere the lesse so,
> Thow every wyght ne may it nat yse.
> Bernard the monk ne say nat al, parde!
> (*PLGW*, G 4–16)

---

[15]See Robert O. Payne, "Making His Own Myth," *Chaucer Review* 9 (1975):
197–211.

[16]John M. Fyler has pointed out some of the unserious qualities of the "Prologue"
in *Chaucer and Ovid* (New Haven: Yale University Press, 1979), pp. 197–198, 118ff.
But by and large, most readings of the "Prologue" assume the questions about poetry and reception are raised in earnest.

The identity of the "Bernard" intended here is uncertain, and perhaps the obscurity is to the point, for the passage appears to question the claim to authority that it is affirming: on the one hand, the narrator seems comforted that even Bernard (the mystic of Clairvaux?) did not see all *invisibilia* in his celestial vision, and therefore one should not trifle about what less divine persons cannot see; but on the other hand, the passage also says that Bernard (whoever he was) did *not* see everything, and therefore one need not defer to him, since everyone is in the same position regarding what "in helle or hevene ybe."[17]

From such a qualified position, the imperative of the subsequent lines cannot be moved without a certain strain of logic:

> Thanne mote we to bokes that we fynde,
> Thourgh whiche that olde thynges ben in mynde.
> *(PLGW, G 17–18)*

Although the "olde thynges" constitute "doctryne" (*PLGW*, G 19) about the transcendental order, the next class of things to which we should "yeven credence" and "trowen" (*PLGW*, G 20, 21) with all of our skills is:

> olde aproved storyes
> Of holynesse, of regnes, of victoryes,
> Of love, of hate, of othere sondry thynges,
> Of which I may nat make rehersynges.
> *(PLGW, G 21–24)*

This is the stuff fictions are made of, and yet there is no acknowledgment whatever from the speaker that any difference exists between belief in the "invisible things of God" and the "invisible" illusions that fictions make. To him they are of the same order of reality. There is no "assay by preve," no experience for proof, that will validate what is in heaven and hell or how it differs from what is recorded in fictions about them, such as Dante's *Paradiso* and *Inferno*. For at least one reader of these lines, Chaucer's intent in requesting "credence" is not unlike Coleridge's remark on the "willing suspension of disbelief" that constitutes "poetic faith."[18] But

---

[17]Gabriel D. Josipovici has also observed the play in this passage; see *The World and the Book* (Stanford: Stanford University Press, 1971), pp. 56–57. But the customary response is that the passage insists seriously on believing in old books; for instance: Payne, *Key*, 94–97; Robert Worth Frank, Jr., *Chaucer and "The Legend of Good Women"* (Cambridge: Harvard University Press, 1972), pp. 19–21.

[18]Frank, *Chaucer and "The Legend,"* p. 19.

Chaucer's passage has begun with an obviously different kind of "faith"—not in the power of human illusions but in the events of history and the afterlife.

The comparison of the divine to the fictive ordo will stretch only so far before we hear the voice of the text playing with the insistence of the speaker, complaining against the way he and his narrative are inviting us to read. They are palpable, definite, and formal, while the voice of the text emanates from far less determinate properties of writing, such as the uncertain identity of "Bernard" or the shaded meaning of "trowen" when it involves "storyes." The passage, to sum up, does not simply raise a point about the "tone of voice" in which we are to take problems about the source of poetry and belief in it. Rather, the narrative carries these matters forward at the same time as the nonsequential elements of the text get in the way of their resolution. The narrative, to put the matter another way, does not act as the signifier of what the text as a whole means. The causality of storial sequence is interrupted by the play of distracting elements. An important group of such elements is the extension of the image of the daisy in the many agrarian images of the poem. They are not comfortably subordinated to storial sequence, and predictably they have gone, by and large, unremarked in readings of the poem. Before turning to them, it will be useful to note briefly that the daisy itself has seemed much more manageable to readers, because it is assimilated quite deliberately into the narrative of events.

3

One of the first explanations of the differences between the two versions of the "Prologue" maintains that the redaction in the G text of the extended language of devotion to praise a mere flower reflects a new religious conservatism in the poet. In his revisions, it has been argued, Chaucer attempts to eliminate any possibility of blaspheming religious institutions by the free mingling of sacred language and secular pleasures.[19] This explanation of editorializing is made with a firm grip on narrative sense, since it forthrightly distrusts the shaded meaning and secret sense of words. Curiously

---

[19]Dudley D. Griffith, "An Interpretation of Chaucer's *Legend of Good Women*," in *Manly Anniversary Studies* (Chicago: University of Chicago Press, 1923), pp. 32–41. See also Raymond Preston, *Chaucer* (1952; reprint, Westport, Conn.: Greenwood Press, 1969), and Marvin J. LaHood, "Chaucer's *The Legend of Lucrece*," *PQ* 43 (1964):274–276.

enough, this grip is no less firm in a reading that claims to be less moralistic and more sensitive to the play of exaggeration and parody in the text. This view turns the object of hyperbolic worship away from the religious references in the language and back toward the speaker who is doing the exaggerating. A greater degree of play is granted in this explanation of parody, which, by the way, is recognizably more medieval in its claim that parody most commonly falls back on the parodist. In this case the exaggerated praise of the flower is yet another subtle debunking of the naive dreamer: "the hyperbolic language and postures are typical for devotion to ladies, but comic for devotion to daisies."[20] The dreamer, however, knows not the difference, and in him we recognize a precursor of such figures as Absolon in *The Miller's Tale*. But while this reading attends to the play in the dreamer's speech, it nonetheless limits hyperbole to the function of character in the "Prologue" and follows the lead of narrative, claiming that the dreamer's desire to please the daisy, that is, the queen, will be fulfilled in finding the right sources for poetic praise.

This reading is clearly satisfied by the demands for narrative sense, which assimilates the daisy unmistakably into the imagery of the queen. But the story does not apologize or explain why the narrator, once the image of the flower is on his mind, cannot prevent it from playing with what he is trying to say. Words get in the way of his intention and trick him into saying what he does not mean. Before recording the dream, the narrator confesses that he lacks the tongue to praise the flower properly, and the image triggers a string of agrarian images.

> For wel I wot that folk han here-beforn
> Of makyng ropen, and lad awey the corn;
> And I come after, glenynge here and there,
> And am ful glad if I may fynde an ere
> Of any goodly word that they han left.
> And if it happe me rehersen eft
> Than they han in here freshe songes said,
> I hope that they wole nat ben evele apayd,
> Sith it is seyd in fortheryng and honour
> Of hem that eyther serven lef or flour.
> For trusteth wel, I ne have nat undertake
> As of the lef agayn the flour to make,
> Ne of the flour to make ageyn the lef,

[20]Frank, *Chaucer and "The Legend,"* p. 22.

No more than of the corn agen the shef;
For, as to me, is lefer non, ne lother.
I am witholde yit with never nother;
I not who serveth lef, ne who the flour.
That nys nothyng the entent of my labour.
For this werk is al of another tonne,
Of olde story, er swich strif was begonne.

(*PLGW*, G 61–80)

Although a redaction of the extended floral imagery in the F text, this passage is still more elaborate than the story demands. A certain quality of the style is the result of the French influence on the poem, and other aspects of it serve the characterization of the narrator's pedantry; but the rest of it has less definable purposes within the story proper. The narrator imagines himself a harvester walking through a vast "field of writing" ("makyng") after it has been "reaped" and seeking to find even a single "ere" of "corn" (or "wheat") as a suitable literary mode for praise. Confessing his inability, the narrator moves on to another metaphor, the game of the "leaf and the flower," in order to say that his own efforts have little to do with the poetry composed in the springtime game of praising the leaf or the flower as a symbol of love. His poetry is not such a game of preferences, and that disavowal clearly links the figure to the narrative as a prefiguration of his subsequent defense against the God of Love's charges that he has in fact taken sides— the wrong ones—in choosing for his poetry the stories of Amant and Criseyde.

But the text of the narrator's speech is more suggestive than he knows. While he is playing with language at the opening in the metaphor of the "field of writing" in which he finds not an "ere," it becomes evident that language is simultaneously playing with him. Initially the game is to his advantage, when the voice of the text puts words in his mouth by requesting—modestly through the pun—the attention of any "ear" in the audience who will be kind enough to listen to the "goodly word" of the poem. However, the figure of the game of writing poetry (the "leaf and the flower") does not work entirely in his favor, since the play of puns and ambiguities contradicts the disavowal he asserts. First of all, concealed in his image of the harvested "field" of literary history is the buried metaphor of nature and history as a "page" or Book, like the "Estoryal Myrour" of Vincent of Beauvais, mentioned by the God of Love (*PLGW*, G 307). The figure is surely a venerated one for establishing a claim to writing competence, but that is not exactly what our dreaming poet is trying to say. Furthermore, when the metaphor of writing is set in context with the elaborate game of the leaf and the flower, the play of references is no longer within the narrator's control. The game continues as the verb "make" (*PLGW*, G 72) echoes the earlier reference to "makyng" as "writing" (PLGW, G 62); thus if the speaker will not undertake "the lef agayn the flour to make" (*PLGW*, G 71–72), he cannot help but suggest that he will not make the "leaf" or "page" of his book of poetry into an imitation of the "flower" of literary convention—precisely the opposite meaning of his desire to find even one ear of corn in that convention.[21] Carrying on his game at the level of syntax, the narrator completes the chiastic structure of his sentence—"ne of the flour to make ageyn the lef" (*PLGW*, G 73)—but he cannot prevent the echo in it that he will not turn the flowers in nature's Book into the "leaf" of his writing, yet another contradiction of his expressed wish to venerate his special flower in the leaves of his book.

He may, as he says, have no interest in the garden game of writing poetry, but his disclaimer manifests some of the most subtle games that language can play when we hear echoes of the learned activity of reading that is a process of turning the "leaf" of the *sensus literalis* into the "flour," the *farina*, of intelligible meaning.[22] Striving to punctuate his separation from the garden game of writing, he compares it to a magician's trick of transforming the "corn" back into the "shef" (*PLGW*, G 74), but the line unmistakably extends previous images of exegetical writing, which is God's "trick" of putting the "corn" of the *sensus spiritualis* into the "shef" of the *sensus literalis* in the Books of Scripture, nature, and history. Only deafness to such echoes (which will also distinguish such other characters as Chaucer's Wife of Bath) could justify the indiscriminate echo of the next line that the "literature of the lef"—the literal meaning of things—is no different to him from the "writing of the flour"—the invisible things of God, "for, as to me, is lefer non, ne lother" (*PLGW*, G 75).[23] But as he disavows the game of the "lef," it makes a final embarrassing reappearance in "lefer," snar-

---

[21]Chaucer uses "leaf" to refer to "page," for example, in the "Prologue" to *The Miller's Tale*: "Turne over the leef and chese another tale" (3177).

[22]This commonplace is recorded, for instance, by Alanus de Insulis, *Distinctiones* (*PL* 210, 785–786), s.v. "farina."

[23]On the Wife's spiritual deafness, see D. W. Robertson, Jr., *A Preface to Chaucer: Studies in Medieval Perspectives* (Princeton: Princeton University Press, 1962), pp. 317–331.

ing him in the larger game of language. Before closing his remarks, the narrator leaves us with one more image, this time apparently moving away from the agrarian vocabulary for writing. He says that the "entent of my labour," "this werk" (*PLGW*, G 78, 79)—which is the "Prologue" to *The Legend of Good Women*—is of another kind completely, and so he chooses another metaphor, "tonne"—"kind" or "cask" (for containing water or wine). The echoes from the history of writing as a "cask of wine," or water in a cask changed into wine, are at most muted and do not carry on the play of multiple senses.[24] But the rules of another game have come into play, the rules about mixing metaphors in poetry, and they control the voice of the text, despite the narrator's ignorance of them in his continuing search for the right terms for praising his daisy.

As the narrator and his story persuade us to read for the answer to the question of poetic genesis—the proper source for poetry—the game of language protests against that invitation. The effect of this conflict is that the story about the defense of poetry as a search for the right source runs up against the plurivalent significance in writing, thereby qualifying the search as the primary "meaning" of the text. Instead of the discovery of a source in the form of a book or authority, the "Prologue" to *The Legend of Good Women*, like *The House of Fame*, reveals that the narrator's problem is in the writing itself, in the proper communication and reception of what he composes. More broadly, the development of his story in the text of the "Prologue" constitutes an exemplum of the larger issue that narrative, which seeks to determine meaning, is itself determined by its reception.[25] The introduction of the "Prologue" closes with a summary of the problem of response. To the mind of the narrator, it is a question of unqualified belief in the sincerity of authority.

[24]In the Reeve's "Prologue," "tonne" signifies the "cask" of the Reeve's life that is flowing like wine from an open tap (3891–3895). "Wine" (*vinum*) is a commonplace for "spirit" (*anima*) and "word" (*verbum*), notably the words of the Gospel; see Alanus, *Distinctiones* (PL 210, 1004–1005, s.v. "vinum"; and *Allegoriae in sacram scripturam* (PL 112, 1078–1079), s.v. "vinum."

[25]Cf. Burrow: "So the meaning of an 'ensample' depends not on its content but on the variable 'entente' of the people who use it. Alceste dismisses this very Chaucerian argument rather impatiently . . . she dictates the content of the Legends, but leaves the poet free in the critical matter of 'entente.' Chaucer quite fairly makes the most of this freedom, and produces a set of examples whose meaning, like that of *The Nun's Priest's Tale*, is extremely elusive and equivocal. Even the opening paragraph of his poem, with its unexceptionable sentiments about believing old books . . . turns out . . . to be a booby-trap"; *Ricardian Poetry*, pp. 91–92.

> But wherfore that I spak, to yeve credence
> To bokes olde and don hem reverence,
> Is for men shulde authoritees believe.
> *(PLGW,* G 81 – 83)

His own efforts have tried to respect that value, as he changes metaphors for the text—"field," "corn," "lef," "flour," "tonne"—in the well-meaning attempt to find the right one. In this search for the word that will not, presumably, be veiled by obscure senses, he finally chooses an image of the "unveiled" word itself: he is going to give us, he says, the "naked text" *(PLGW,* G 86). The "entente" is apparently to produce a text no longer bothered by ambiguous words or the dress of custom, a book whose meaning is self-disclosed and fully present, as the events in a narrative sequence make sense and add up clearly to an explicit *sentence.* However, his wish will be misspent, for his first "reader," the God of Love, imposes on him precisely those demands for the plain sense of things—the "pleyn text" *(PLGW,* G 254)—and yet the response of that deity simply will not serve as an index of adequate reading. As a result, the narrator's dream of a "naked text," an achievement so clear that words will seem like unnecessary clothes, remains only a dream, an illusion of a presence that fades out of reach behind the veil of words.[26]

4

The "Prologue" develops at great length the disjunction between the God of Love's demands on the poet and their fulfillment. If we consider only one side of this opposition, such as the argument that the God of Love's charges pose serious questions about poetic genesis, the conflicting evidence of his bias as a reader is suppressed. But it is quite apparent that the "Prologue" is interested in the conflict itself. For instance, the God of Love's demands emanate from sources of power and authority; what he will have to say about po-

---

[26]Chaucer's use of the image of "nakedness" to suggest the limited appeal of the narrative of full disclosure may be compared with Roland Barthes's observations on reading. Barthes extends the same image elaborately and playfully to suggest that the "pleasure of the text" consists not in narrative suspense, which compares with nudity, the Oedipal pleasure ("to denude, to know, to learn the origin and the end"), but in "intermittence" (like "skin flashing between two articles of clothing"), in the "staging of an appearance-as-disappearance"; *The Pleasure of the Text,* trans. Richard Miller (1973; reprint, New York: Hill and Wang, 1975), p. 10.

etry is proprietary, and we are prepared for it by the abundant attention to formality and custom in the dream. These patterns, which are rendered in the florid, dreamlike style typical of vision poetry, also serve another purpose—the preparation of the narrator's dream as the *illusion* of a revelation and the *veil* of an exposure that will remain out of reach. Birdsong prepares for the God of Love's entry, the garden is enchanted with foliage and sunlight, the lark announces the arrival of this "myghty god of Love," who with "wynges sprede" appears, accompanied by his "quene / Clothed in real habyt al of grene" (*PLGW*, G 142, 145–146). Words have the quality of elaborate clothing in the rich description of these deities; the God of Love has stepped out of the magnificently illuminated pages of such books as the *Romance of the Rose*; he is a painter's model. Formality continues in a variety of elements, for example, in the entourage of the "ladyes nyntene" (*PLGW*, G 186) who follow the King and Queen of Love, kneel in honor of them, rise, form a compass, and dance—"carole-wise" (*PLGW*, G 201)—while singing in high poetic style the Balade in praise of Alceste. For the narrator, words are the songs of visionary maidens.

Within the context of this paradisal setting, the appearance of the dreamer stands out starkly as an impropriety, and the God of Love so indicates it by his choice of imagery, which quickly returns us to earth:

> "What dost thow her
> In my presence, and that so boldely?
> For it were better worthi, trewely,
> A worm to comen in my syght than thow."
> (*PLGW*, G 241–244)

The mere presence of this poet is an offense to decorum and good taste. But it immediately becomes obvious that the God of Love's literary propriety is limited to works that favor the notion of the service of love, which means, particularly, works that avoid suggestion, innuendo, shaded meanings, and the intricate internal workings of fully wrought characters.[27] Thus he repudiates "Chaucer" for the stories of Criseyde and Amant; their "goodness" is not clear; their appreciation of love is concealed; their appearance is far too seductive; their narratives do not affirm the supremacy of this god, no matter how fully they expose themselves. Rather, their

---

[27]Fyler has called the God of Love a "literal-minded reader"; *Chaucer and Ovid*, p. 97.

exposure turns out to be an illusion of motives and causes that remain secretive, concealed behind their words. The God of Love cannot be bothered by the elements of narrative that are hidden from view, alien to sequence. All of that *materia occulta* somehow belongs to the category of "chaf," while stories that do not confuse him with cross-purposes and nonsequential elements are works of admirable "corn."

> "A ful gret neglygence
> Was it to the, to write unstedefastnesse
> Of women, sith thow knowest here goodness
> By pref, and ek by storyes herebyforn.
> Let be the chaf, and writ wel of the corn."[28]
>
> (*PLGW*, G 525–529)

The authority he stands for in this royal Court of Reading aligns itself with storial sense—the "pleyn text"; but the utterly inadequate expectations of his "reading" deauthorize his authenticating demands for narrative. As the narrator at the end of the introduction to the "Prologue" imagined a way out of the game of language by promising a book without secrets, "the naked text," the literary criticism of the God of Love leaves us wondering what the possible pleasures of such a text might be.

Readers have often turned to Alceste's defense of the narrator, hoping to find answers to his problems with the source and intention of poetry. But just as frequently they have been disappointed. She does not, it has been argued, answer the questions in poetics about proper sources and determinate meaning. At least one reader, however, has felt that despite the weakness of her defense she does unify the bifurcated matter with which the introduction to the "Prologue" begins, the division between books and experience.[29] In this view she is the synthesis of the conflict, because she becomes a figure of the unifying power of the poetic imagination.[30] As the story develops toward recognizing the identity of Alceste as the daisy, so the dreamer's spiritual development reaches fruition in the reconciliation of opposites—books and experience, tradition and individuality, art and nature. In this view, the foreshadowing of nineteenth-century concepts of the poetic

---

[28]Cf. lines 311–312: "But yit, I seye, what eyleth the to wryte / The draf of storyes, and forgete the corn?"

[29]Robert B. Burlin, *Chaucerian Fiction* (Princeton: Princeton University Press, 1977), pp. 38–44.

[30]For Burlin's discussion of imagination, see ibid., pp. 26–32.

imagination (as formulated, for example, by Coleridge) is quite deliberate. It is offered as a new solution to the problem of experience in the "Prologue." But it refers to the "experience" of the imagination, not of the physical world.[31] While it may be important to consider the concept of the imagination in Chaucer's works, the "Prologue," I think, addresses more pragmatic matters, such as the problems of writing clearly and reading adequately. Alceste is very much interested in these issues, and it will be worthwhile to take the lead of those who see a way out of the narrator's dilemmas through her defense.

To begin with, her effectiveness consists not in what she reveals, but in what her defense does not say. She is not the fulfillment of the narrator's dream of the fully self-disclosing speaker whose words, like dress or custom, fall away to expose pure intentions. On the contrary, she, like the God of Love, is depicted in the magnificent costume of royalty amid the enchanting surroundings of the garden.

> Upon the softe and sote grene gras
> They setten hem ful softely adoun,
> By order all in compas, enveroun,
> Fyrst sat the god of Love, and thanne this queene
> With the white corone, clad in grene,
> And sithen al the remenant by and by,
> As they were of degre, ful curteysly.
> (*PLGW*, G 225–231)

When she speaks to the God of Love about the poet, the narrative leads us to expect a successful defense. But readers generally have agreed that she begs the question. For instead of defending the dreamer, she throws him on the mercy of the court, observing that the God of Love, because he is a deity, should be "ryghtful" and "mercyable" (*PLGW*, G 323); some of the remarks circulated about the poet, she claims, may be just gossip or lies:

> Al ne is nat gospel that is to yow pleyned;
> The god of Love hereth many a tale yfeyned.
> For in youre court is many a losengeour.
> (*PLGW*, G 326–328)

[31]In a review of Burlin's book, Lee W. Patterson has pointed out this qualification; "Writing about Writing: The Case of Chaucer," *UTQ* 48 (1979):263–282.

Furthermore, what the poet wrote was innocent: he "nyste what he seyde" (*PLGW*, G 345); finally, the writer is a court poet and may have been ordered to compose the poems in question. When read in this way, according to the demands of the story, the defense thoroughly concedes the poet's guilt. However, the narrator remains enchanted by his apologist, and her identity is until the very end an elusive mystery that charms him. Her beauty apparently makes up for what she does not say. This concealment is a quality of attraction that also characterizes the text of her defense. It is effective, in other words, because it is *not* "the naked text" of the narrator's wish. Its motives remain cleverly concealed: through the concession of the poet's guilt, the speech establishes a most subtle defense of poetry.

She speaks to the God of Love with the aplomb of the wife who knows her husband's anger better than he does. Withholding her intentions and acknowledging his impeccable demands for propriety, she suggests that "curteysye" ought to prevail in the trial; because he is a "deite," stability should counterbalance anger. But Alceste's concealment makes itself felt in yet another way—in her veiled words. She speaks a good deal about the "lies" that the God of Love has heard, the "tale yfeyned" from "many a losengeour" and "queynte totelere accusour" (*PLGW*, G 329). These lies may well allude to false stories circulating about the poet in Richard's court. But what are "lies" in the world of fiction if not the stories that the poet himself has written—false, because that is what fictions are, not historical fact or truth, but "many a tale yfeyned." In the hypothetical, feigned realm of poetry, the God of Love has heard about "falsenesse," but specifically as it exists in the heart of Criseyde, and "jelous ymagynyng" as it fires the imagination of Amant in his pursuit of the rose (*PLGW*, G 331). Chaucer's *Troilus* and his translation of the *Romance* are blamed as the records of authors who have sought to have "som dalyaunce" (*PLGW*, G 332) with love. While one may think of them as envious writers seeking favor from the nobility, it is more likely that they are the misbegotten lovers who rival "Envye" as Troilus does thinking of Diomede, and imagine it as the "lavender" who will spread unkind gossip among his friends or in the house of Criseyde. These situations may seem to have claim to historical truth, like events in the Bible, but, says Alceste, "Al ne is nat gospel that is to yow pleyned" (*PLGW*, G 326). On the contrary, the "lies" of which the defendant is accused are his fictions—perhaps deserving comparison, as Alceste mentions, with works by "Dante" (*PLGW*, G 336). Therefore "Chaucer" has "wrongly ben acused" (*PLGW*, G 338); he wrote in "innocence," not because he was too stupid to realize what he had written (he "nyste what he seyde"; *PLGW*, G 345), but because "he" did not say it: Criseyde, Troilus, Amant, Envye, a host of others—they said it; and the text "said" it through its fictive voice, as it is now "speaking" these points in poetics. The poet is innocent of any offenses against love or truth and "oughte ben excusid" (*PLGW*, G 339). He never affirmed, and therefore he did not lie, as Boccaccio (long before Sidney) had written in his "defense of poetry," the *Genealogia deorum* (14–15).[32]

But the God of Love, we may be sure, does not read in this way. He is confused by shaded meanings and elliptical secret senses, such as we find in allegory, and prefers storial sequences, meanings that are obvious—that can be picked from the text like "corn." He is Chaucer's foil of the reader, not every reader certainly, but one who is uncomfortable with the sense of words that goes against the grain of narrative sequence. Such a reader is likely to underread poetry like Alceste's extended "allegory of reading" or overreact to it. The God of Love, especially, has overreacted; he needs the guidance of cool, rational response, and that is one reason Alceste appeals for the bulk of her speech to his "lordship." Reason, the traditional sign of the "ryghtwys lord" of thought, says Alceste, will not respond "lyk tyraunts of Lumbardye" (*PLGW*, G 353–354). The "lord" of such a reader will respond with distance and detachment to the claims of texts and will not assent to them as if they were documentary truth demanding immediate action; for the claims of fiction are "excusacyouns," "compleyntes," and "petyciouns" argued in the court of reading; they will be answered "in duewe tyme" (*PLGW*, G 362–364). This kind of disengagement, says Alceste finally, is the "sentence of the philosophre" (*PLGW*, G 365): it characterizes the rule of just courts. But it is also the "sentence" of the poet, his expectation that readers will appreciate with detachment the game of language, even when it plays with words like "sentence." The God of Love does not appreciate Alceste's language, because of his demand for the "pleyn text." Throwing out all the "draf" of words in order to grasp the "corn" of meaning, his reading assumes the utter self-disclosure of the speaker's intention; he hears only what he wants to hear: the poet is guilty. Alceste concedes this position, too. But although the secret senses of her alle-

---

[32]*Boccaccio on Poetry*, 1930, trans. Charles G. Osgood (New York: Liberal Arts Press, 1956), p. 65.

gory of reading are beyond her own grasp, they are nonetheless heard in the voice of the text controlling her discourse. Like her beguiling appearance before the dreamer, the pleasure of her discourse is that it lingers in the shadow of full disclosure as a text of much greater fascination in its play of simultaneously veiling and exposing intention than the dreamer's wish—by now forgotten —for the "naked text."

5

Yet the dreamer's fascination with Alceste, for the most part, has not characterized the general response to the "Prologue" to *The Legend of Good Women*. Not finding a solution to the problems of sources and meaning in her defense, readers have looked to the poet's own self-defense near the end of the poem (*PLGW*, G 446–464) but have not found it there either. As one commentator argues: "the 'Prologue' closes with the poet . . . no more certain than before."[33] In a qualification of this position, another reader observes that Chaucer does give us an answer to the question of sources: he is no longer interested in courtly love poetry. Chaucer's poem is a "prologue" to the problem of "choice," and he has made his in favor of a new direction in "narrative." According to this view, the choice of "story" is Chaucer's intention in the "Prologue."[34] However, the question of *intent*, which is itself a subject of study in the poem, is exposed as a principle that is not so comfortably assimilated to narrative. First of all, intention is something, according to the story, that an author has "in mind" and that is conveyed into a new container, a "tonne," the text of the poem. The narrative assumes this conception of intent, for instance, when the God of Love asks the poet: "Was there no good matere in thy mynde?" (*PLGW*, G 270). And the narrative moves ahead trying to find out just what the poet did have in mind that would motivate him to compose works as unflattering to the service of the God of Love as *Troilus* and the *Romance of the Rose*. In answer, the narrative insists on the reading of the God of Love and Alceste, that the poet had nothing good in mind at all and therefore must do "penaunce" to assuage his guilt. At long last the poet's intention is exposed, authority in narrative is reinstated, and meaning is no longer questionable.

[33]Payne, *Key*, p. 110.
[34]Frank, *Chaucer and "The Legend,"* pp. 33–35.

But from the begining of the poem other matters have continued to run counter to narrative sequence and have called into question its claim to authority in the matter of books and intention. The
narrator's opening trust in fictions conflicts with belief in *invisibilia*;
Bernard both is and is not an identifiable authority for such belief;
Alceste's defense concedes the guilt of the poet and yet vindicates
poetry. These matters gain their importance because story seeks
authority over them yet cannot quite prevail. The poem is interested in much more than its story, and Chaucer makes this point
distinct by frustrating the narrator's dream of a "naked text" of exposed intent. When the poet finally is permitted his own apologia,
all he can muster is that he is not guilty. He commences by acknowledging the supernatural wonder of the queen; he knows not
what she is, and then he utters in all simplicity:

> "Naught have agilt, ne don to love trespas.
> For-why a trewe man, withoute drede,
> Hath nat to parte with a theves dede;
> Ne a trewe lovere oghte me nat to blame,
> Thogh that I speke a fals lovere som shame.
> They oughte rathere with me for to holde,
> For that I of Criseyde wrot or tolde,
> Or of the Rose; what so myn auctour mente,
> Algate, God wot, it was myn entente
> To forthere trouthe in love and it cheryce,
> And to be war fro falsnesse and fro vice
> By swich ensaumple; this was my menynge."
> *(PLGW, G 453–464)*

This protest will be heard again, for example, in the "Prologue" to
The Miller's Tale—"blameth nat me" (3181). But before the King
and Queen of Love, the poet protests the accusations made against
him on the grounds that his "intention" was merely to follow "what
so myn auctour mente." Furthermore, readers should blame themselves, not the author, when they recognize unfavorable self-reflec-
tions in his fictions: honest persons, after all, are not implicated in
the acts of thieves, and neither are "trewe lovers" just in blaming a
poet for shaming a "fals lovere." Intention in this defense is still a
mental conveyance from the writer's mind to the vessel of the book.

However, the defense itself redefines the idea of intent by relo-
cating it from the mind of the author to the act of interpreting that
is ongoing in the process of reading and writing. For as the poet is
speaking of the "intent" in his "author's" mind, his words are carry-

ing out *their own* "entente." The appeal to the authority of the proverbial expression about the "trewe man" and the "thief" plays out its own authority on his expression, since the lines also mean that the author, like an honest man, has no more actual part in the deeds of his characters than a witness has in the deeds of a thief. The reader ought to trust the tale, not the teller, in the determination of what a text intends. More pointedly, readers should not blame the author when a "fals lovere" is shamed, for he is not recording biographical facts. But those who do impute blame to him, as the God of Love does throughout the "Prologue," have put their own purity into question by their claim to it. So does the pretense to truth in fiction become the "assay by preve" for its own assertions. Not only has the God of Love indicted himself in his protest at court, he has also exonerated Chaucer, the poet of Richard's court, who has no "parte with a theves dede" or with anyone else he may invent. The conception of intention in these lines is no longer what the author bears "in mind," for the "poet" speaking these lines clearly does not recognize their full meaning, nor does the God of Love, who has just been roundly put in his place; rather, intention comes into being through the process of discovering how the narrator's assumptions conflict with the intentions of the text. It has a determination of its own, one that shows its significance by opposing the narrative expectation for clear and simple sense.

Nowhere is this opposition more evident than in the dreamer's opening request of Alceste in his defense, to "knowe sothly what ye be" (*PLGW*, G 450). The answer is given by the God of Love a few lines before the end of the poem, and it is the kind of answer he likes to give, one in which words unveil without secrets true intentions. To the observation that Alceste makes known what she is, the God of Love responds: "That is a trewe tale" (*PLGW*, G 495). But the narrator still does not see the "entente," until the God of Love draws the parallel between daisy, queen, and Alceste and exhorts the poet to go off and look her up "in a bok, lyth in thy cheste" (*PLGW*, G 498). The reference has motivated many subsequent readers who, trusting in the authority of the God of Love and the invitation of narrative to lead interpretation in the right direction, have sought to identify—though with little success to date—what book he may have had in mind. The story moves naturally toward the end of establishing such validations for knowledge. But that is also where it began. What "assay" is there to "preve" things not seen? Which "Bernard" exactly is intended? What are the sources for authority? The narrative, as the God of Love controls it, moves us again toward the expectation that the poet is keeping something hidden in his mind about the Alceste in the "bok" in his "cheste." But since the book we have just read tells the story of the queen who is the daisy and who is named Alceste, then perhaps we ought to listen to the authority of the play of words and look her up in the "Prologue" to *The Legend of Good Women*.

6

Like *The House of Fame*, the "Prologue" to *The Legend of Good Women* holds our interest at those moments when we are uncomfortable with the direction of the story, when the poem protests against the way it invites us to find sense principally in sequence. The "Prologue," however, has not usually been read this way, and the result has been the feeling that it is one of Chaucer's least accomplished pieces, even one of his failures. Read as a preface to the subsequent legends of good women, the story concedes the writer's ineptitude as a rather bluntly ironic gesture attempting to display his ability to entertain those at court who might have accused him of antifeminism. If considered as a treatise in poetics, the poem never gives the poet enough of a chance to defend himself and explain the conflict of books and experience: the story stalls. And as a poem in the genre of the dream vision, the "Prologue" amounts to a pastiche of earlier sources, a work without refined narrative coherence or developed characterization, despite the efforts of redaction many years after the first draft. So long as the proprieties of narrative, character, and *sentence* remain the primary grounds of evaluation, the reputation of the "Prologue" to *The Legend of Good Women* will not fare well. It will be diminished by the same expectations that have been put upon *The House of Fame*, in which the demand for storial sense or no sense assumes that an indeterminate beginning, middle, or end is a violation of good form. But neither poem need be bound exclusively to such demands. For the pleasure of response arises when narrative can no longer make complete and convenient sense of what we read. From such moments of invitation, only the God of Love and readers like him would turn away. He cannot appreciate the value of indeterminate form, but Chaucer obviously does; and in *The Canterbury Tales*, it is before us again in a variety of ways, to which I will turn next.

[7]

Interpreting the "Naked Text"

in the "General Prologue"

to *The Canterbury Tales*

This storie is also trewe, I undertake,
As is the book of Lancelot de Lake.
                              Chaucer, *The Nun's Priest's Tale*

1

As Chaucer questions the nature of poetic structure in the "Prologue" to *The Legend of Good Women*, so also does he invite inquiry into it in *The Canterbury Tales* by not completing the narrative—the game of tale telling, the arrival at Canterbury Cathedral, and the return to the Tabard Inn. Among the vast and diverse scholarly efforts that have sought to confront the question of structure in the *Tales*, one assumption has been generally taken for granted—a concept of totality that rests upon the model of sequentiality illustrated by narrative.[1] At face value the *Tales* appears to be fash-

---

[1]This view is illustrated well by G. L. Kittredge's approach to the *Tales* as a continuous "drama," a "Human Comedy" in which the stories "are merely long speeches expressing, directly or indirectly, the characters of the several persons"; *Chaucer and His Poetry* (Cambridge: Harvard University Press, 1915), pp. 154–155; J. L. Lowes represents a similar sense of the work as "an organic whole, and that whole . . . essentially dramatic"; *Geoffrey Chaucer* (1934; reprint, Bloomington: Indiana University Press, 1958), p. 164. Though recent studies have criticized these early views of "organic" and "dramatic" unity, they have nonetheless maintained the primacy of narrative for an understanding of structure in the *Tales*; see Robert M. Jordan, *Chaucer and the Shape of Creation: The Aesthetic Possibilities of Inorganic Structure* (Cambridge: Harvard University Press, 1967), and the same author's review of recent scholarship on this topic—"Chaucerian Narrative," in *Companion to Chaucer Studies*, ed. Beryl Rowland, rev. ed. (New York: Oxford University Press, 1979).

ioned on such a model for structural order, and venerated traditions beginning before the time of Augustine authenticate it. Either explicitly or implicitly, narrativity is basic to the development of writing in the middle ages as well as to various other intellectual activities. From the chaos of events in the physical world, the trained reader can discern a story with a definite lesson; the natural world or the past presents itself to perception as a structure with the beginning and ending that characterize narrative. And what is true of nature is true of the lives of people. Within the confusion of personal experience is written an organizing motif or theme. One of the oldest in the medieval narrative of life—spiritual journey or quest—is reiterated by Egeus in *The Knight's Tale* (2848): "we been pilgrymes, passynge to and fro."

By writing a story about pilgrimage, Chaucer has made the structural principle of narrativity in his poem appear self-evident, and a wealth of critical investigation has attempted to establish its value. But if the critique of narrative in *The House of Fame* and the "Prologue" to *The Legend of Good Women* continued to occupy Chaucer, as the unfinished state of the journey to Canterbury appears to suggest, it will be worthwhile to take another look at structure in the *Tales*. Since assumptions about this issue are, in one way or another, tied to the "General Prologue," I will concentrate on it, turning initially to the bearing that narrativity has on the structure of the work.

2

Discussion of the place of narrative in a conception of structure may begin with an identification of the "voice" of the story, an understanding of who is speaking. It has been customary to consider the nature of this matter in *The Canterbury Tales* by comparison with Chaucer's early poetry: the journey to Thomas à Becket's shrine has replaced the dream, and the reporter narrating the trip— "Chaucer the pilgrim"—has matured somewhat from the earlier naive dreamer; neither of these personae possesses the intelligence and control of "Chaucer the poet."[2] However, insofar as the dream visions undertake penetrating insights into the nature of voice and

[2]For example, see James V. Cunningham, "Convention as Structure: The Prologue to the *Canterbury Tales*," in *Tradition and Poetic Structure* (Denver, Colo.: Alan Swallow, 1960), pp. 59–75; E. Talbot Donaldson, "Chaucer the Pilgrim," *PMLA* 49 (1954):928–936; Robert O. Payne, *The Key of Remembrance: A Study of Chaucer's Poetics* (New Haven: Yale University Press, 1963), chaps. 2–5.

the structure of poetry, the conventional conceptions of "persona" and "poet" need to be reconsidered in relation to the structure of the *Tales*. First of all, both the "Prologue" to *The Legend of Good Women* and *The House of Fame* open to us the "textual" property of writing: not only does the discourse of a text designate events or tell a story, it also discloses its own order of designating and telling. The story of a dream is assigned to a narrator-dreamer, but a "metatextual" discourse is heard in spite of what the speaker intends by his utterance. His intention differs from the order of intending carried out by his speech; try as he may, his language does not body forth his complete meaning. Thus, instead of assuming the "presence" of a speaker in his speech, it is more accurate to recognize that to a certain extent he is "absent" from his utterance.[3]

In *The House of Fame* this sense of language is represented by the imagery of artifice and by the quest of the dreamer to discover meaning in the shifting structure or play of speaking and writing. The "Prologue" to *The Legend of Good Women*, on the other hand, represents a wish for the full disclosure of intent in the image of the "naked text" (*PLGW*, G 86), in order to suggest that the lure of reading begins with the break between narrative sequence and the promise of unexpected meanings. Both poems lead to the realization that reading is a form of play at making sense; it takes its pleasure from the moves in the text, not from trying to guess what the author has "in mind." The text is not a screen of personality through which the reader seeks to perceive the author, Chaucer the poet. On the contrary, the dream visions invite our attention by representing language as a game with certain rules: as a speaker may play with the proprieties of language, so may it play with and "speak" him. The "voice" of such utterance properly belongs not to the speaker but to the text. Furthermore, the implications of these games of fictional speakers for the larger issue of authorial intent are not incidental: by playing with the principle of deferring to the poet as a means of validating meaning, the language of the text becomes a game played with the author (Chaucer), one in which he possesses no guarantee of success. The most he can hope for is the situation invented in the "Prologue" to *The Legend of Good Women*: a court of good reading may decide against the poet and in the pro-

---

[3]Consideration of the question of "absence" in current theoretical inquiry stems from such discussions in French structuralism as Jacques Derrida's *Of Grammatology*, trans. G. C. Spivak (Baltimore: John Hopkins University Press, 1976), pp. 12 ff. Structuralist premises of the speaking subject have been tested in medieval French literature by Paul Zumthor in *Langue, texte, énigme* (Paris: Seuil, 1975), esp. p. 171.

cess demonstrate unwittingly that his writing will bear much more than disapprovals of literary propriety.

These readings of the "Prologue" to *The Legend of Good Women* and *The House of Fame* present a conception of the narrator that does not differ essentially from the speaker in the "General Prologue" and the "frame" story of the journey in the *Tales*, although the later work reveals that he is more fully developed.[4] But in the dream visions the conception of voice that does not include the narrator or the other characters and that arises from indeterminate properties in their language—"the voice of the text"—is *not* another way of speaking about "Chaucer the poet." For this designation refers to the real person of fourteenth-century London. He is postulated from the position that he could not possibly be the naive bumbler depicted in the poetry, as G. L. Kittredge once protested.[5] Chaucer the man is saved from indignity and self-contradiction by the clarification (such as E. T. Donaldson's) that the persona, not the poet, is responsible for certain oversimplifications.[6] But, on the other hand, the persona could not possibly be the source for the sophistications of the poem, such as the religious echoes in unlikely places or the breaking of the dramatic illusion, or for that matter the complex narrative of the journey. Proponents of the voice of the poet in the poem explain this paradox by arguing that occasionally Chaucer drops his mask, takes over the stage directions, and speaks to us directly. At such moments he is no longer impersonating a naive self or other fictive characters. The artistry of the text in such passages, as one critic has observed, is "unimpersonated."[7] The concept of voice in this characteriza-

[4]Robert O. Payne has commented on this development in "Making His Own Myth," *Chaucer Review* 9 (1975):197–211.

[5]Kittredge: "A naif Collector of Customs would be a paradoxical monster"; *Chaucer and His Poetry*, p. 45.

[6]See Donaldson's essay "Chaucer the Pilgrim" and the reconsiderations of his view by Donald R. Howard, "Chaucer the Man," *PMLA* 80 (1965):337–343. John M. Major has offered a different opinion in "The Personality of Chaucer the Pilgrim," *PMLA* 75 (1960):1960–1962, and both sides of the question of voice are studied by H. Marshall Leicester, Jr., "The Art of Impersonation: A General Prologue to the *Canterbury Tales*," *PMLA* 95 (1980):213–224—more on this essay in the following pages. Theoretical discussion for the conception of voice that is illustrated by the naive "Chaucer the Pilgrim" is available in Wayne Booth's arguments about perspective, particularly the "unreliable narrator"; see *The Rhetoric of Fiction* (Chicago: University of Chicago Press, 1961).

[7]Donald R. Howard, *The Idea of the "Canterbury Tales"* (Berkeley: University of California Press, 1976), p. 231. Howard formulates a position that many of the critics already cited have taken either explicitly or implicitly, for example, Donaldson, Jordan, Payne, et al. Charles Muscatine is of the same opinion in *Chaucer and the*

tion, be it noted again, is identified not with a fictive construct, but with the actual *presence* of the poet; according to this view, Chaucer's presence is the "voiceness" of the text; *The Canterbury Tales* "has voiceness because the author addresses us directly and himself rehearses tales told aloud by others: we seem to hear his and the pilgrims' voices, we presume oral delivery."[8]

This conception of voice responds sensitively to properties of writing in Chaucer's poetry that cannot be comprehended by the narrator. In this respect it corresponds to what I have called the secrecy of a text, those moments when voice shifts in origin from the fictive speaker to some other source for meaning. It is at such moments, incidentally, that the God of Love and the eagle of the dream visions would lose interest, but that other readers are engaged because of the promise of unexpected discovery. However, to conceive of such instances—in the customary way—as a shift in the source of meaning from the narrator to the mind of Chaucer the poet seems to be based on a model for validating meaning that cannot be taken for granted in view of Chaucer's treatment of this subject in the dream visions. In these poems, that a speaker utters something in the full presence of an audience is no guarantee at all that he is aware of the total import of what he has said or that its meaning will be evident to others. This view of language is so unusual in medieval theory and important to the early work of Chaucer that it must have influenced the function of voice and its bearing on structure in *The Canterbury Tales*.

3

The question of voice, particularly the distinction between the voice of the narrator and that of the poet, has often been discussed with reference to the palinode at the end of the "General Prologue."

> But first I pray yow, of youre curteisye,
> That ye n'arette it nat my vileynye,
> Thogh that I pleynly speke in this mateere,
> To telle yow hir words and hir cheere,

French Tradition (Berkeley: University of California Press, 1957), pp. 264–265. In the article previously cited, Leicester carefully and admirably reconsiders this entire issue.

[8]Howard, *Idea*, p. 66.

Ne thogh I speke his wordes proprely.
For this ye knowen al so wel as I,
Whoso shall telle a tale after a man,
He moot reherce as ny as evere he kan
Everich a word, if it be in his charge,
Al speke he never so rudeliche and large,
Or ellis he moot telle his tale untrewe,
Or feyne thyng, or fynde wordes newe.
                                    (GP, 725–736)

For some readers this passage poses no difficulties at all, since—from the point of view of the story—it simply sharpens attention on the drama of unfolding events by promising to tell all.[9] But to others the palinode is an instance in which Chaucer seeks to break the dramatic illusion and make us aware of the poet behind the scenes.[10] He accomplishes this break by allowing his fictive self to become so caught up in the accuracy of reporting that he appears to lose all contact with his role as a teller of fictions, and at that point, as one critic has observed, "we recognize the presence of the poet behind the reporter. The humor of the passage arises from the play of these two viewpoints, since the excess of the reporter's earnestness in expounding the obvious is apparent only from the more knowing viewpoint of the poet, the latter, 'superior' viewpoint being the one which governs the passage."[11]

That Chaucer governs the whole and seeks at times to enter the fiction with the weight and solidity of the man behind the mask has been regarded as essential to the medieval reception of the poem. Such an opinion rests on the belief that fiction should be like history and try to authenticate its claims by realistic devices.[12] Although we are made aware, in such instances as the palinode, of

[9]This sense of the passage is taken for granted by those who approach the story of the journey as a "drama" in which the tales are long speeches expressing the personalities of the tellers. Kittredge's notion of the "Human Comedy" emphasizes this view, and R. M. Lumiansky extends it in *Of Sundry Folk: The Dramatic Principle in the "Canterbury Tales"* (Austin: University of Texas Press, 1955).

[10]This critique has been argued most fully by Jordan, *Chaucer and the Shape of Creation*, Chap. 5. Anticipations of this approach are suggested by Bertrand H. Bronson, *In Search of Chaucer* (Toronto: University of Toronto Press, 1960), esp. p. 22.

[11]Jordan, *Chaucer and the Shape of Creation*, p. 120.

[12]See Morton W. Bloomfield, "Authenticating Realism and the Realism of Chaucer," *Thought* 39 (1964):335–358; cf. Bloomfield's similar position in "Distance and Predestination in *Troilus and Criseyde*," *PMLA* 72 (1957):14–26, and Donaldson's "The Ending of Chaucer's *Troilus*," in *Speaking of Chaucer* (New York: W. W. Norton, 1970), pp. 84–101.

the inauthenticity of the fiction, Chaucer's larger plan for *The Canterbury Tales*, as illustrated by the "frame" story of the journey, is to give the poem the realism of history and thus to authenticate his work. This view and others that favor the "presence" of the poet in the palinode obviously appreciate the interruption of sequentiality by properties of writing that will not be controlled by it. But such opinions are based on an assumed preference for the realm of documentary history and the "presence" of Chaucer—"outside" the poem—that are themselves being undermined by the text. The play with this preference becomes even more striking in the parallels that may be noted between the palinode and the defenses of poetry in the "Prologue" to *The Legend of Good Women*.

The narrator not only shows the same naiveté as his counterpart in the earlier poems, he also harps on some of the dreamer's problems with writing, authority, and determinacy. Since we have heard before, in the "Prologue" to *The Legend of Good Women*, the protest of innocence and have seen that it has little to do with the prevailing intentionality of language, we might well suspect that the insistence of the narrator in the "General Prologue" to speak "pleynly" and "properly" (GP, 727, 729) may repeat the fantasy of the dreamer for the "naked text" of self-explaining significance. The God of Love would approve of the narrator's promise in the "General Prologue," since that reader vouches only for the "pleyn text" (*PLGW*, G 254). Alceste too would be pleased by the appeal to innocence and the repudiation of "lying"; but as an intentionality above her own awareness shifts her talk about lying into a commentary on the art of lying—fiction—the narrator's insistence on the accuracy of reporting begins to trip him by a broader accuracy about writing poetry. Fiction, he says, will be like history, and his reference should offend no one who is aware of the venerated convention of historical reporting that validates the story it records through the appeal to accuracy and objectivity—"historical truth." As historical witness, the narrator has in mind a familiar *topos*, but since he is a poet who is inventing the "report," the "tale untrewe" that he swears he will not tell is in fact the only tale he can tell, the "thyng" he cannot help but "feyne."[13] On this narrator the wit of the Nun's Priest's remark about his tale of a cock and fox would be totally lost:

---

[13]Chaucer was certainly not the last to apply to fiction the medieval convention of validating history; renaissance writers played the same game. See William Nelson, *Fact or Fiction: The Dilemma of the Renaissance Storyteller* (Cambridge: Harvard University Press, 1973).

This storie is also trewe, I undertake,
As is the book of Lancelot de Lake.
(*NPT*, 3211–3212)

The palinode in the "General Prologue" will not let us take seriously the ploy that a reference to a "real" order of historical events "extrinsic" to the poem can validate claims to truth. It does not deny the existence of that order, but it puts such emphasis on the fictivity of the writing that it dislocates a vantage in "reality" from which to view the "illusion." The passage is authenticating, so to speak, without authorization.[14]

Since the attempt to authorize by reference to an objective reference is the subject of play in the palinode, it is imprecise to assume that Chaucer is present before us and that the fiction, more generally, is seeking to compensate for its improverished inauthenticity, to overcome its "false" appearance. Quite the reverse seems to be the case. In *The House of Fame*, the question of authority is not settled by fiat; neither "soth sawe" nor "lesynge" prevails (*HF*, 2089); authority consists in the play of language. And in the "Prologue" to *The Legend of Good Women*, authority surely does not reside in a court of proper taste, since the intentionality of language plays itself out over the rule of the God of Love, Alceste, and the poet-dreamer. In the "General Prologue," authority is claimed in objective reporting, in the staging of the written as the oral presence of a speaker, but neither side, fictive speaker or real author, fiction or history, has privilege. As the narrator claims objectivity and accuracy in writing, it claims authority over him. Instead of the author (Chaucer), it is the language of the text that opposes the voice of the narrator at this point in the "General Prologue."

4

In spite of the narrator's wish to speak "properly," to conform to literary propriety, the meaning of what he says often has little to do with his interest in storial sense. Beyond his realization, meaning

---

[14]In light of the examples in Chaucer and those studied by Nelson, it might be more to the point to say that in fictive constructs there is no authentication without deauthorization. The problem here is not that some narrators, like the pilgrim persona, are unreliable, but that criticism has assumed—on the authority of such theoretical arguments as Wayne Booth's *Rhetoric of Fiction*—the notion of "reliable" voice; for example, "Chaucer the poet." See Frank Kermode's remarks in "Secrets and Narrative Sequence," *CI* 7 (1980):89–90.

shifts from his voice to other sources of meaning, and with this shift the structure of the poem is no longer determined simply by narrative sequentiality. If we look to one of the portraits for evidence of the shifting properties of voice, it might be imagined—as has been recently and provocatively argued—that the voice of the text is not really faced with opposition, but rather dominates the signifying gestures of language.[15] Although this conception sounds like the argument for the reliable voice of the poet, it is not. It is instead the convention of the "narrator," who is—in this formulation—not naive, but "extraordinarily sophisticated," fully aware of the range of his irony and the ramifications of what he leaves unsaid. This view recalls an earlier opinion in favor of the self-conscious narrator in the "General Prologue,"[16] but it is unique as an argument for voice in the poem as a totally fictive construct. The Monk's portrait is offered in illustration of the chief characteristic of this narrator, which is his reserve, his unwillingness to specify and draw out the implications of the religious allusions or other suggestive details of the description.

> Ther as this lord was kepere of the celle,
> The reule of seint Maure or of seint Beneit,
> By cause that it was old and somdel streit
> This ilke Monk leet olde thynges pace,
> And heeld after the newe world the space.
> He yaf nat of that text a pulled hen
> That seith that hunters ben nat hooly men,
> Ne that a monk, whan he is recchelees,
> Is likned til a fissh that is waterlees,—
> This is to seyn, a monk out of his cloystre.
> But thilke text heeld he nat worth an oystre;
> And I seyde his opinion was good.
> What sholde he studie and make hymselven wood,
> Upon a book in cloystre alwey to poure,
> Or swynken with his handes, and laboure,
> As Austyn bit? How shal the world be served?
> Lat Austyn have his swynk to hym reserved!
>
> (GP, 172–188)

[15]The essay by Leicester cited above (note 6) is the only study of this issue in the *Tales*—to my knowledge—that has been published to date.

[16]John M. Major has taken this position in the article cited in note 6. D. W. Robertson, Jr., argues the point in a different way—by maintaining that "naive" remarks of the so-called persona are instead examples of the author's antiphrasis: see *A Preface to Chaucer: Studies in Medieval Perspectives* (Princeton: Princeton University Press, 1962), p. 255.

The voice speaking these lines, to repeat, is not a naive persona, but a narrator withholding his true opinions about the Monk; all we hear are the "traces of a presence that asserts its simultaneous absence. The speaker is present as uncomprehended, as not to be seized all at once in his totality."[17] These observations essentially conform to the view I have presented in the dream visions and the "General Prologue" in support of the completely fictive status of the voice of the text and of the fallacy of identifying it or some other voice with the presence of the poet. However, the identification of the voice of the text exclusively with the narrator in the Monk's portrait and others like it seems to me to compromise some of the oppositions that the "General Prologue" counts on for its effect; moreover, it calls for an approach to the poem as an "impersonation" of its narrator rather than a study in literary portraiture.

When we ask of the Monk's portrait, Who is speaking here? the answer must include a voice that is fatuous enough to conclude, after listing the Monk's worldly and carnal appetites, "I seyde his opinion was good." It must also acknowledge that the speaker begins to imitate the voice of the Monk himself by "quoting" his opinions about religious duty: "Lat Austyn have his swynk to hym reserved!" That the impersonation here is unwitting is strongly suggested by the most crucial question of all, one that is at the heart of every monk and every pilgrimage: "How shal the world be served?" A third voice is heard, the voice of religious consciousness that recalls where the Monk should be when he is out "prikyng" and "huntyng for the hare" and what he has apparently failed to obey by regarding Benedictine rule as "somdel streit."[18] The last two qualities of voice achieve their effect because the speaker gives no evidence whatever that he is aware of the inconsistencies in his "report." Like the properties of speech in the words of Alceste, the God of Love, or the narrator in the palinode at the end of the "General Prologue," these voices emanate from language that the narrator does not fully control. We hear the voices of the text beyond what he has to say. The passage will not allow us to assign to it a single, controlling point of view. Its origin is uncertain, and it is through this kind of textual strategy that the plurality of the text establishes itself. Rather than a single speaking subject—however absent one may imagine him to be—several voices "dissolve" into each other at such points in the text as the Monk's portrait: the

---

[17]Leicester, "Art of Impersonation," p. 220.

[18]See Robertson's discussion of the iconography of the portrait, including hunting and sexuality; *Preface*, p. 253.

pilgrim-narrator is sounding like the Monk—their two voices intersect—and both of them are crossed by the voice of religious consciousness.[19] We have heard this kind of play in *The House of Fame* and the "Prologue" to *The Legend of Good Women*, and as in those poems, language itself is speaking in the Monk's portrait.

Through the play of voices, the authority of intent is no longer to be found in the "mind" of a narrator or author. Utterances shift from one point of view to another without justification or explanation. This text so full of apologies does not, finally, apologize.[20] It forestalls coming to terms with play—and for good reason. It will not compromise the reporter's shortsightedness to the Monk's worldliness or either of these to the asceticism of Benedictine and Augustinian rule. For to do so is to appeal: (1) to the narrator's expectation for "pleyn" and "proper" meanings; (2) to the Monk's errant desires; (3) to the austerity of *contemptus mundi*. None of these voices or choices has the last word about the Monk. To report his "degree" and "array" completely (GP, 40–41), as the narrator presumes, discloses motivations and expectations beyond both the Monk's and the narrator's understanding. The fiction of presence in oral voice—staging the written as oral—exposes the absence of the full revelation of the voices that are heard. The narrator is surely richer than his obtuse remarks reveal, and the voice of religious tradition is hardly given its due. Furthermore, the Monk is not given his due either, since his worldliness does not signify that he is utterly incapable of Christian virtue. To say that the poem, by leaving these issues unsettled, is incomplete and indeterminate does not mean that it is flawed; rather, the text acknowledges what it cannot articulate about people and their voices, and it establishes this knowledge in opposition to the narrative demand for speaking and writing "properly." Thus does the text outwit appeals to authority from a naive persona, a sophisticated narrator, or "Chaucer the poet." Instead of impersonating them, the poem remains committed to describing and interpreting the pilgrims and their ways of perceiving the world.[21]

[19]This approach to the several voices of the "General Prologue" responds to the shifting sources of meaning that portraits such as the Monk's set in motion; it compares with the study of voice in Roland Barthes, *S/Z: An Essay*, trans. Richard Miller (New York: Hill & Wang, 1974), esp. pp. 41–42.

[20]Cf. Barthes: "The pleasure of the text: like Bacon's simulator, it can say: *never apologize, never explain*"; *The Pleasure of the Text*, trans. Richard Miller (1973; reprint, New York: Hill & Wang, 1975), p. 3.

[21]Although Leicester relies on the argument for "absence" in Derrida and Barthes and hence assumes the indeterminacy between speaking subject and utter-

Although Chaucerian oppositions are often discussed as examples of irony, the conflicts I have been describing between narrative and nonsequential elements or the voice of the narrator and the voice of the text do not represent ironic structure. For irony commonly assumes some form of dualism that affirms one pole in preference to another, such as the superiority of judgments by Chaucer the poet in contrast to the inferiority of those by Chaucer the pilgrim. Saying one thing to mean something else, the commonplace medieval definition of irony, illustrates that a principle of identity is presumed in the opposition, a terminus that is fixed and in relation to which connotations are subordinated.[22] In such a formulation, the "play" of ironic structure is only apparent, for ultimately it is controlled by a reconciliation in which all opposites coalesce into organic unity.[23] This conception of structure does not square very well with the examples in Chaucer that I have been discussing, because the voice of the text does not have priority over the interests of the narrator, and neither of them can be correctly described as possessing the intention of the author. Moreover, the sequence of narrative events continuously determines the direction of the poem, but nonstorial elements distract and interrupt both narrative and narrator.

It may seem fitting to follow the recent approach to Chaucerian structure that has used the term "inorganic" to describe those pas-

---

ance (p. 220), nonetheless he maintains that the text is the "prologal voice" (p. 222) of one speaker, Chaucer—not the historical person, but the fiction who is constructed by the text and who seeks to "impersonate himself, to create himself as fully as he can in his work" (p. 222). We may come to discover the nature of this speaker only after we understand each of the pilgrims and their tales. This sense of the poem, although it follows the structuralist departure from notions of self-presence in voice, ultimately returns to the text as the manifestation of the consciousness of the speaker. It seems to me that this approach uses a structuralist premise to carry out what appears to be the phenomenological ambition that structuralism calls into question.

[22]For example, Isidore, *Etymologiarum* (PL 82, 115). Cf. John Speirs on the portraits of the "General Prologue": "The art is in seeing exactly what each is in relation to what each ought to be"; *Chaucer the Maker*, rev. 2d ed. (London: Faber, 1960), p. 103; also see the general survey by Vance Ramsey, "Modes of Irony in the *Canterbury Tales*," in *Companion to Chaucer Studies*, pp. 352–379.

[23]To the extent that studies of irony in Chaucer or other medieval writers are informed by formalist concepts of structure, they appear to remain indebted to Romantic theories of organicism: see the connection between irony and organic form in Cleanth Brooks's essay "Irony as a Principle of Structure" (1949), rpt. in *Critical Theory since Plato*, ed. Hazard Adams (New York: Harcourt Brace Jovanovich, 1971), 1041–1048.

sages in which a narrative stops and shifts abruptly to a new direction.[24] Chaucer's poetry differs, according to this view, from the organicism of Romantic theoreticians and poets who influenced concepts of structure in modern literature, such as the novels of Henry James or William Faulkner. In Chaucer we are aware of the discontinuity and disunity of narrative; its form is "mechanistic." But in modern fiction "the organism is the criterion of verisimilitude, and consistency of illusion is its primary requisite. Though the illusion may be complex and multileveled, as in *The Sound and the Fury*, it is never broken; the only sign of the maker's hand is in the extrinsic sectioning of the book."[25] This position is suggestive insofar as it seeks to account for the distractions of narrative sequence in Chaucer. But the claim that such breaks come from a source of authority and control extrinsic to the poem—Chaucer the poet—assumes a principle of authenticating and a reference to the "real" that are not entirely self-evident. To speak of the way Chaucer's poems call attention to themselves as written documents need not require a perspective that is imagined to be "outside" the illusion. It is less problematic to regard such events as examples of "metapoesis" or "textuality," neither of which is postulated from a ground that is asserted as "the real." Passages of this sort in *The House of Fame*, the "Prologue" to *The Legend of Good Women*, and the "General Prologue" disclose their metatextual properties by signifying events through stylistic means that put into question the status of the signifying process. Language in this conception is a means of interpreting rather than a container of information with an "inside" and an "outside."

Arguments in favor of the aesthetics of inorganic form have relied heavily on notions of the inside and outside of poetic illusions, but the model of the container assumed in this conception of language actually is deeply rooted in organic structures for construing meaning.[26] The most obvious illustrations of this linguistic model, as I have explained in previous chapters, are the organic

---

[24]Jordan, *Chaucer and the Shape of Creation*. Among those who have followed Jordan's lead in the use of this term are Howard, *Idea of the Canterbury Tales*, p. 135; and Gabriel D. Josipovici, *The World and the Book* (Stanford: Stanford University Press, 1971), pp. 31 ff.

[25]Jordan, *Chaucer and the Shape of Creation*, p. 6.

[26]Although Saussure imagined that in distinguishing *langue* from *parole* and signified from signifier he was departing from an organicist conception of language, his distinction still does not completely let go of the inside/outside dichotomy, and in this respect it holds on to an organic theory of the sign. See Derrida's study of this problem in *Of Grammatology*, part 1.

metaphors familiar in medieval theory—pearl and shell, nut and cortex, fruit and chaff.[27] Although these references may not appear in discussions of inorganic structure in Chaucer, the metaphors themselves are less important than the structure of signifying meaning that they indicate. The structure is organic because meaning is construed as the content of a specific container or form that gives it shape. Meaning is determined by the shape of the container; the bond between the signifying means and the signified sense in this structure is fixed and natural—organic.

Conceiving of narrative as an illusion of a world "inside" that is occasionally penetrated by the shaping hand of the author rests on a partial organicism. For the interruption of the narrative merely suspends its animation momentarily, until sequentiality carries the illusion to its close. In this conception, narrative serves as the signifier of what the text is attempting to establish, and thus the structure of it remains organic. But as it has been very well observed, *The Canterbury Tales* emphasizes its inauthenticity: "Chaucer induces us *unwillingly* to suspend disbelief. His is an art of the conscious mind. . . . Chaucer consciously undermines his own achievement of illusion."[28] Without saying so, these remarks point toward recognizing the textuality of intention in Chaucer's poetry. *The House of Fame* undertakes the problem of signification comprehensively; the "Prologue" to *The Legend of Good Women* rehearses the dilemmas of reading without an adequate sense of the metapoesis of fictive writing; and in the "General Prologue" Chaucer tests and tries out the issues involved in a conception of voice as oral presence. The poem suggests that the presumption of determinate meaning in the spoken word proves to have less mastery than it knows. Such a relationship of voice to meaning is indeterminate instead of inorganic, for the sanction of meaning resides not in voice or narrative, but in the play of language. While the connection between what is said and what is understood is certainly not as arbitrary as the chaotic discourse of Lady Fame, neither can the subtle structure of the "General Prologue" be explained as the inorganic speech of "Chaucer the poet."

A latent organicism informs the argument for "mechanistic" form in Chaucer, and it may be traced to the models that are offered for medieval aesthetics—cosmological theory of the late mid-

---

[27]See above, chapter 3, section 8.

[28]Jordan, *Chaucer and the Shape of Creation*, pp. 124–125; Cf. Bloomfield, "Authenticating Realism," pp. 355–358.

dle ages as it is illustrated in Gothic architecture.[29] According to this view, both these cultural traditions provide examples of order and totality that inform Chaucer's poetics. *The Canterbury Tales* is an imitation of Gothic architecture, a copy of that vast Book of stone.[30] But this analogy from the visual arts poses a problem that has not been adequately confronted: the argument claims for the poem a structural model of order that a nonorganic aesthetics would otherwise seek to undermine. The difficulty stems from assuming that the text at the foundation of medieval aesthetics and Gothic architecture—Plato's *Timaeus*—assumes a "quantitative" and "mechanistic" conception of the universe. The *Timaeus*, to be sure, explains the construction of the cosmos and nature in terms of numbers; but it is no less founded on a rich organicism: number theory for Plato is an infinitely extendable analogy for mirroring the natural bond—the common elements—between nature, man, and the universe.[31] The proportions between the human soul and body explain the concord in the physical world and ultimately the "world's body." This image, though obviously one of natural growth, is incidental—as are numbers also—to an overriding conception of nature as an intricate web of interconnected parts, any one of which may bespeak the whole. *Pars pro toto* is the structure of this massive harmony, and no tradition was more fascinated by it

[29]Jordan's extended coverage of these two cultural forms (in chap. 2, "The Elements of Medieval Aesthetic Theory," and chap. 3, "The Gothic Cathedral") compares with the very brief remarks on Gothic structure by Muscatine, *Chaucer and the French Tradition*, pp. 167–169, 245–247, rather than with Robertson's study of the Gothic form of iconography in *Preface*. It is directly to the point, however, that the same principle of Gothic form that Jordan uses to illustrate "inorganic" aesthetics—juxtaposition—serves Muscatine as evidence of the highly *organic* form of Chaucer's works. Muscatine employs juxtaposition as a species of irony perfectly in keeping with the New Critical view of this principle as fundamental to organic form (as illustrated in the essay by Brooks cited in note 23).

[30]Jordan: "Chaucer's varieties of structural unity are many. But they follow the Gothic principle of juxtaposition. . . . Characteristically, the total form is determined by the accumulation of individually complete elements. . . . In Chaucer's Gothic vision man's environment was not simply the English countryside but nature juxtaposed against supernature." Jordan's aim is to examine the tales in order "to discern something of the variety of forms attainable within the Gothic mode of 'multiple unity'"; *Chaucer and the Shape of Creation*, pp. 130–131.

[31]James A. Coulter: "The seemingly arithmetical character of Plato's formulation is probably of secondary importance, however, and we should perhaps rather emphasize its derivation from organic models. Plato clearly has in mind a normal living organism in possession of all of its natural parts and with no freakish additions, parts which are, moreover, functionally related, all of them, the one to the other and to the working whole"; *The Literary Microcosm: Theories of Interpretation of the Later Neo-Platonists* (Leiden: E. J. Brill, 1976), p. 73. The roots of Plato's number theory in the organicism of mythological forms are covered above, chapter 2, section 4.

than medieval cosmology. Various disciplines found in it something for explaining their own ideas about order. Music, for example, because of its basis in number, extended its preoccupations
with concord by elaborate applications of *musica mundana, humana,*
and *divina.*[32] Architectural theory borrowed from both disciplines
to create an exemplar of the structure of the universe, an ordo in
which there is a place for everything and everything is in its place.
Number may be the language of this universe, but its structure derives from the mythological consciousness, with its determination
to have divine and human interpenetrate. Like the pattern of metaphors in a narrative or a book, medieval disciplines radiate from a
fixed center that controls the extension of all forms.[33] In this "logocentric" cosmology, architecture is one of the most available illustrations of totalized structure: the cathedral is the Book of popular
history, just as the Bible is the *aedificium Scripturae.*[34]

Against this Book, Chaucerian structure will not compare without strain.[35] The cathedral, as Abbot Suger and other commentators never tire of repeating, is the image of the Heavenly City on
earth; in the earthly form the divine imago may be contemplated
because of a basic similitude: nature and supernature are fused in
as solid a union as man can imagine, and the narratives in the
stained glass windows, wall paintings, and statuary manifest the
history and eschatology of that union. However, in Chaucer's *Tales,*
as even an aesthetician of inorganic form argues, we recognize the
"discontinuity between fiction and experience" and above all "a
strong sense of the limitations of fiction."[36] Yet these insightful responses more clearly support the indeterminate form of voice and
narrative in Chaucer's "General Prologue" than they reflect the

---

[32]On the organicism of this tradition, see above, chapter 3, section 8.

[33]Jean Seznec: "The encyclopedic character of medieval culture, its obsession
with a *scientia universalis,* are strikingly shown, from the time of Isidore, in both
learned and popular compilations—the *Summae, trésors,* or *miroirs,* where the 'natural,' the 'moral,' and the 'historical' all have their place. From the twelfth century on,
they are apparent in the domain of scholarship. A hierarchy of the sciences does of
course exist, with Theology at their summit; but they form an organic whole, a *bloc*
which resisted disintegration for centuries"; *The Survival of the Pagan Gods,* trans.
Barbara F. Sessions (1953; reprint, New York: Harper & Row, 1961), p. 123.

[34]The phrase may be found, for instance, in Hugh of St. Victor, *Didascalicon* 6.4
(*PL* 176, 802).

[35]Jordan uses the phrase "multiple unity," borrowed from Wöfflin, to describe
what he calls the essentially "inorganic form" of Gothic. But it might be noted that
the same phrase "multeity in unity" is used by Coleridge to describe the highly organic structure of beautiful objects; see "On the Principles of Genial Criticism," 3d
essay, in *Critical Theory since Plato,* p. 464.

[36]Jordan, *Chaucer and the Shape of Creation,* pp. 6, 7.

"inorganic unity" of Gothic architecture. The God of Love, the narrator, Harry Baily, Lady Fame, and others might well imagine storial order as an imitation of the sacred architecture of the late middle ages. But the *Tales* is far too plurivalent to be a copy of such a structural model, with its fixed and centered hold on order.[37]

6

Although the *Tales* may not find its model in such mythological forms as the Gothic cathedral or the Text of the cosmos, it would be wrong to suggest that the poem is not interested in order, sequence, and closure. The insubordinate properties of the text, however, indicate that narrativity is only one among several strands of signifying; the narrative is the concern of the speaker as he tries to recreate his recollection of the journey and the stories told along the way to Canterbury Cathedral. The story of the journey is the narrator's, and his remembrance, as a recent and penetrating study has argued, has direct bearing on the structure of events.[38] But as in the argument for inorganic form just reviewed, the structure of the art of memory—the medieval book of memory—has more to do with narrative than with the structure of the entire poem. The argument for memory in the *Tales* has stressed its importance to narrative, though in this view the narrator is imagined as the foil of the real presence of the poet: "the narrator of *The Canterbury Tales*, like the narrator of *The Book of the Duchess*, remembers a past experience well enough to write it down in detail—to describe some twenty-nine pilgrims and repeat in their own words the tales they told. His memory becomes a wellspring of narrative, like the 'old book' in the *Troilus*."[39]

But what "narrator" knows this structure, if not the personality who tells the story—the teller figured by the text? It is he who ex-

---

[37]In an argument somewhat related to mine, Josipovici has maintained that Chaucer's use of "games" in conjunction with tale telling creates a pointed contrast to the medieval tradition of "the world as a book"; see "Chaucer: The Teller and the Tale," in *World and the Book*, pp. 52–99. We differ in the theoretical conception of game and play as well as in the function of the Book in Dante. My position also compares with J. A. Burrow's claim that Chaucer departs from the distinguishing characteristic of "Ricardian" poetry—"narrative"—by "fictionalizing" the conventions of telling exempla; see *Ricardian Poetry: Chaucer, Gower, Langland, and the "Gawain" Poet* (New Haven: Yale University Press, 1971), p. 88.

[38]This approach is the argument of Howard in *The Idea of the "Canterbury Tales."* The poem imitates memory "as a controlling principle of its form" (p. 139).

[39]Ibid., p. 143.

pects us to see the structure of his mnemonic process in, for example, the three groups of pilgrims in the "General Prologue," in which an "ideal" figure (such as the Knight) serves as the locus of a subdivision including seven pilgrims.[40] But the text, on the other hand, represents this structure in an arbitrary way, since it invites us to notice various alternatives for structuring the portraits in the "General Prologue."[41] While memory may include these too, because it not only stores knowledge but also records the storing process, the text acknowledges what may be called a "lapse" of memory unnoticed by the narrator and the narrative. The intention of sequence in the "General Prologue" is to recall and record, but the text has no illusions about completing that task with total success. The difference between what the narrator says and what his language actually may signify—the lapse of the text—is beyond the control of the speaker and his story. For example, an implicit parallel between the narrator's processes of recording and the Man of Law's mental habits highlights how memory is the narrator's concern rather than the exclusive structure of the text. Of this pilgrim the narrator observes, "every statut koude he pleyn by rote" (GP, 327), and the remark characterizes the narrator's own association between memorizing and writing; for he too is determined to record "pleynly" everything that he can remember—"hir wordes and hir cheer"; he will "reherce as ny as evere he kan / Everich a word" (GP, 727–733). But what may be possible "by rote" in the law is obviously not possible on the road to Canterbury, and the text recognizes by its exaggerated accuracy the narrator's ignorance of the difference, thus creating the lapse that every reader suspects in the palinode.

Such shifts in the text qualify the authority of the narrator's way of recording and occasion the process of discovering what he may have forgotten. While he seeks to imitate the record of the journey that he has memorized—to copy the book of memory—the language of the poem, by virtue of its qualifications and doubts, is more interested in commenting on him: it interprets before it imitates and records. For this reason, analogies from the visual arts that have been suggested for the poem more adequately describe the narrator's habits of seeing and recalling than they reveal the poetics of the entire work. One of these analogies is the structure of "interlace" that characterizes medieval manuscript illuminations,

---

[40]Ibid., pp. 150–151.
[41]See the convenient summary by Thomas A. Kirby, "The General Prologue," in *Companion to Chaucer Studies*, pp. 243–270.

the device by which a significant detail in a painting is explained within the context of a picture, or through which a scene is changed and a new narrative sequence begun.[42] This stylistic technique is entirely in keeping with the larger preoccupations of manuscript painting to "illuminate" or bring into the "foreground" all significant information, to leave nothing in the "background" hidden and secretive. To see a parallel, as has been argued, between the interlace structure of the manuscript page and the pages of the book of memory does not seem extravagant, for both are determined to conceive the whole in any part and find a beginning in every end—to demonstrate that "everything leads to everything else."[43] When formulated in this way, memory and illumination become two more examples of the much broader medieval determination to mythologize mental habits as the order of nature and history. Sequence and totality are the outward forms of this structure of thought, and to a certain extent they characterize the narrator's wish to recall and record. His memory also takes the form of other medieval feats of memory that are organized on the model of the journey or quest.[44] Within his record, various themes—food, money, sex, quitting—may compare with the interlace devices that end one strand of narrative and commence another. However, as the story of the journey has replaced the dream of Chaucer's early poetry, the narrator's aim to represent the complete book of memory is not unlike the dreamer's promise in the "Prologue" to *The Legend of Good Women* to compose the "naked text," that kind of writing in which speech and meaning are wedded so indissolubly that no secrets remain hidden behind the veil of words. This text is forgotten in the "Prologue"; it is replaced by a writing that is far more attractive because of the veiled meanings—for instance, in Alceste's defense—that run counter to her discourse and carry out an interpretation of it quite beyond her expectation. The "General Prologue" has much more in common with Alceste's way of speaking than it has with the pilgrim-narrator's promise to imitate the unfeigned word of recollected experience.

In the "General Prologue," the interlace of listing according to ideal types determines the narrative progress, and in this respect

[42]Howard, *Idea*, pp. 219–227. For the idea of "interlace," Howard refers to Eugène Vinaver, *The Rise of Romance* (New York: Oxford University Press, 1971); and John Leyerle, "The Interlace Structure of *Beowulf*," *UTQ* 37 (1967):1–17.

[43]Howard repeats this sentence from Lewis and Vinaver as a summary of interlaced structure; *Idea*, pp. 220, 226.

[44]Dante's works, of course, provide the most elaborate examples; see also Howard's discussion, *Idea*, pp. 144–155, 189.

the narrator is in control of his intent. But the poem begins and ends by submitting this concept of order to the play of interruptions and inconsistencies. The Knight is an ideal within the structure of social hierarchy; yet the Wife of Bath surely rivals anyone of the twenty-nine pilgrims as a figure whom readers do not forget and around whom other pilgrims may be clustered, such as the women, the married, the carnal. The Miller, too, could just as easily become the locus of a subdivision, because the details of his portrait are so indelibly drawn. Other examples might be listed in support of this point, which is simply that memory and journey do go hand in hand, but they are held by the narrator. His sense of form is objective, like the God of Love's theory of literature. For the teller of the journey to Canterbury, the form of the telling compares with memory: it is a container of some kind, a "building," a "body" (the "naked text"), the "stomach of the mind."[45] From his viewpoint experience presents itself to perception in the sequence and completeness of the well-wrought Book that can be represented in "everich a word." But conforming the entire poem to such a structuring principle is not unlike organizing the loose, discontinuous writing that is all of Scripture around one idea, such as the New Law of Charity. The narrator's intentions are perfectly in keeping with the medieval discipline of reading diverse things—the documents of the Bible or the events of the real world—as if they constitute a monolithic text. But the examples I have been concerned with in the dream visions and *The Canterbury Tales* suggest that such reading is carried out only at the expense of suppressing an opposing and basic property of writing, one that Chaucer formulates in *Troilus and Criseyde* and that applies equally well to his other works, if not also to scriptural writing: "in forme of speche is chaunge" (*T&C*, 2.22).

7

The major proposals for the structural model of *The Canterbury Tales*—narrative journey, Gothic architecture, and memory—all have an important place in the poem. But each proposal has been applied to the *Tales* under the assumption that the language of poetry is constituted by the same structural elements as the models themselves. Although an aesthetics of imitation appears to explain

---

[45]The last phrase is Augustine's, cited by Howard, *Idea*, p. 146.

the internal coherence of each of these cultural forms as well as their subordination within the medieval idea of the Book, the writing of Chaucer's book is far too interested in exploring, testing, and qualifying those and other models to establish any one of them as its structural principle. It is true that diversity and departure are accommodated by each of these models, just as they are in the *Tales*. But Chaucer's departure is more fundamental, since it involves basic differences in the structure of signifying that is rendered through poetic writing. If journey, architecture, and memory are to be studied as structural models for the *Tales*, then I suggest they be considered not as analogies by which writing may be understood, but rather as models made intelligible in and through writing—particularly through their represented forms in the writing that is so obviously concerned with each of them and that Chaucer was familiar with, Dante's *Commedia*. The influence of Dante's poem on *The House of Fame* and the ending of *Troilus* has been well acknowledged; but the importance of the *Commedia* to the structure of writing in the *Tales* may be much greater than is customarily considered. Insofar as Chaucer initiates, as I have proposed, the narrative of the quest in the "General Prologue" as a consideration of problems of reading and interpreting, he is indebted in some measure to Dante's journey as an "allegory of reading."

In its customary designation, allegory indicates the structure of multiple senses between, for instance, the story of the journey and the soul's quest for God in penance or after death; it also refers to the conventional details of literary portraiture—the iconographic imagery that is especially obvious in the first eighteen lines of the "General Prologue" or in the portraits of the Prioress and Parson. But as these traditions have been studied in earlier chapters, they manifest basically metaphoric and symbolic ways of construing meaning—structures of similitude, coalescence, and participation.[46] The Miller, for instance, not only plays the iconographic music of *discordia* with his bagpipe, but acts discordantly: he *is* his music, his signified reference. The countless examples of such symbolic forms in visual and literary art are entirely predictable within cultural traditions that were delighted with the fusion of

---

[46]Defending allegory against the charge that it lacks these stylistic preoccupations manifests a greater debt to Coleridge's critique of nonsymbolic form and its profound influence on New Criticism than to the nature of allegorical structure in Dante and Chaucer. Such a defense is illustrated by the opening arguments of Angus Fletcher in *Allegory: The Theory of a Symbolic Mode* (Ithaca: Cornell University Press, 1964).

natural and transcendent—the mythological fascination with autochthony and totalization. Chaucer certainly found such examples
in the *Commedia*. But he also must have recognized the new departure in allegorical structure that organizes those forms in the Italian poem. For Dante, the relation of representation to reference—the pilgrim's story to Francesca's book of legendary love,
the *liber occultorum* to the *liber praesentiae Dei*—is a structure of temporality, a diachronic mode, that insists on separation and departure from a source or end; it recognizes the limits of language in
time, even at the end of the journey when eternity is contemplated
and the poet laments his inability to copy what he once experienced. This structure of reference sets aside the familiar allegory
of history, with its insistence on the historicity of the literal sense,
giving preference to a writing that is about the signifying process itself, an allegory of reading. Chaucer undertakes a similar allegory
through the quest for the origin of language in *The House of Fame*
and the exploration of misreading in the "Prologue" to *The Legend
of Good Women*. The "General Prologue" continues many of these
concerns: the palinode that appeals to the historical accuracy of
writing turns around to comment not on history but on the essential fictivity of the report. The description that proceeds as an apparent imitation, for instance, of a typical fourteenth-century
monk describes instead the narrator's own commentary, revealing
the control that language has over him and his interest in reporting. Narrative asserts its authority in the "General Prologue," but as
in the dream vision, interruptions and distractions dislocate it from
remaining the primary focus of meaning. The poem begins by
marking its own mode of designating and referring; it is this allegory of signifying that instructs the concerns with historical journey and tropological ascent in the following tales. The desires,
fears, and arguments represented by the pilgrims and their tales
are first of all problems of language and reading that have been set
in motion by the "General Prologue."

In Chaucer as in Dante, the study of reading assumes a structure
that is mindful of time, not collapsed into the wish fulfillment of
the complete memory of the past or the "naked text" in which everything leads to everything else. The *Tales* is not backward looking
and anachronistic; it is radically prospective.[47] The structure of

---

[47]Lee W. Patterson has made this point in a review of *The Idea of the "Canterbury
Tales"* and other recent books on Chaucer; see "Writing about Writing: The Case of
Chaucer," *UTQ* 48 (1979):272.

this awareness is not the timelessness of symbolic and mythological dreams but the temporality of allegory. From the outset the "General Prologue" is aware of time and its conditions on the separation from the source of religious motives in the distant past of Thomas à Becket's murder. The allegory begins as pilgrims "longen" to travel to Becket's crypt (GP, 12).[48] But time immediately interrupts the quest as the narrator stops to describe each traveler— "whil I have tyme and space" (GP, 35). This first of many distractions of sequence is typical of allegorical structure: it forestalls the accommodation of closure; it is an open-ended mode; it looks like symbol and myth; it uses their characters and motifs. But it acts differently. From the opening of the "General Prologue," Chaucer's allegory proceeds in full awareness of its temporal nature, its inability to retrieve the purity and oneness of an origin—in this case before sin—or to embody an end in the confrontation of the martyr who will redeem all sin and time. The experience of the end is hardly forgotten because the pilgrims do not reach the shrine. That they will not reach it is foreshadowed often in the repeated interruptions of the sequence of events leading to it. Allegory, the discourse of signifiers that can refer to but not represent what they seek to signify, accommodates well the structure of an experience that cannot be bound by the time and space of narrative. The discourse of the poem, unlike the language of the traditions out of which it is made, remains a way of interpreting and a process for conceiving the problem that all medieval traditions ultimately returned to, the desire for God. Chaucer studied the question tirelessly in many more than his "sixty bokes olde and newe" (*PLGW*, G 273); he was schooled in an intellectual milieu that treated it as the fixed center of all knowledge. And when he undertook his last and most ambitious poem, he dramatized the question in the traditional way as a story of the journey. But after Chaucer's allegory—the form of speech that inevitably changes what it represents—the question of religious experience would never again be formulated in the language that is satisfied exclusively by plain and proper sense.

In comparison with the treatment of traditional linguistic models in the *Commedia*, Chaucer's departure is much more emphatic. But what Chaucer extended, Dante had already begun. Both poets look

---

[48]See chapter 4 above on Dante and Joel Fineman's consideration of allegory and the loss of origin in *The Canterbury Tales*—"The Structure of Allegorical Desire," in *Allegory and Representation*, ed. Stephen Greenblatt (Baltimore: Johns Hopkins University Press, 1981), pp. 26–60.

away from the medieval past in that their allegories of reading are so different from those that they read in explication of the Bible and that organized the *aedificium Scripturae* and the Book of culture. However firmly such models stabilized the institution of interpretation in the middle ages, the allegories of reading in Dante and Chaucer open the way for rereading. Both poets were profoundly influenced by linguistic tradition but even more deeply affected by the scriptural reading that inspired it. While they look away from the medieval past, they also look back to the vital commitment of their past in the reading of the Bible, in the challenge to interpretation and change that it poses. That challenge must have been felt by many readers in the middle ages, but few felt it as vividly, I think, as readers of the poetry of Dante and Chaucer.

[8]

Retrospect: On Historical Change

All mankind is of one author, and is one volume; when one man dies, one chapter is not torn out of the book, but translated into a better language; and every chapter must be so translated. God employs several translators; some pieces are translated by age, some by sickness, some by war, some by justice; but God's hand is in every translation, and his hand shall bind up all our scattered leaves again for that library where every book shall lie open to one another.

John Donne, *Devotions*

I have been considering the extent to which the idea of the Book in the middle ages consists not simply of a definitive content, but rather of specific ways of signifying, organizing, and remembering. It assumes the stability and totalization of knowledge, the belief that all learning can be contained, and the view that history is integral with nature. The metaphor of the Text was inevitably substituted for Building, Body, and Presence; predictable, too, within this tradition was the approach to the Babel story as a destruction of the building of language that was, first of all, deserved (because of self-aggrandizement) but that could nevertheless be rebuilt in the chaste pursuit of a restored discourse—the "proper" reading of the Bible, the creation of a new *aedificium Scripturae*. This view of language gained such prominence that even the challenges posed by grammar and hermeneutics were ultimately subsumed within more abiding, originary structures. Linguistic theory in the middle ages illustrates what has been called quite suggestively the "dominance of a discourse," that state of language in which analysis and reference can no longer prevail in calling into question their own conditions of signifying and thus cannot establish the grounds for discourse to move in new directions.[1]

[1] See Timothy J. Reiss, *The Discourse of Modernism* (Ithaca: Cornell University Press, 1982), pp. 22–23, 100, 170, 256, 351 ff.

The effect of such stabilization is that skepticism and doubt are suppressed within the larger interests of continuity. The circle of human knowing is maintained, along with the insistence on the geocentric cosmos, the microcosm of man, and the *musica* tuning nature in perfect harmony. To speak, as I have, of these habits of thought as "mythologizing" is no more than to suggest that their basic elements are not at all new but were well recognized in cultures predating the Christian middle ages. The animism of nature, the interpenetration of divine and human orders, the replication of the transcendent on the model of known and familiar things, the sacralization of stone and volume, and the persistence of megalithism—these forms survive in the middle ages only as vestiges. But what was not displaced was the larger "episteme" (to apply the term of Michel Foucault) in which they functioned—the taxonomic patterning of all cultural forms.[2] The metaphor of the Book or Text that has been used to characterize such a cultural episteme takes on quite literal proportions in the medieval centuries, as knowledge was collected and stored in great books or as the transcendental world was replicated in the sacred space of religious architecture. Although the mythology of the Book reaches back to precedent centuries, scholarship on historical change in the middle ages has commonly begun with a different assumption, one that was made by medieval thinkers themselves and that carries out their attempt to displace the past by creating something entirely new. Indeed, they did create new objects of knowledge, but the ways of knowing remained rooted in past habits of thought. In a most basic sense, evolving medieval cultural forms need to be examined much more closely for the archaic mythology still present in them.

But I have also been suggesting that the grounds of signifying meaning in the middle ages were shifting in another domain—the fictionalizing discourse of the poets. Literary language posed—as Plato always feared it would—a challenge to the cultural utopia. Augustine shared Plato's fear about literature, distrusting it not simply because it was pagan, but because it was literature. Its pleasures threatened the rules of proper response, raising the potential for doubt and risking the possibility of completely arbitrary conclusions. A perspective *sub specie aeternitatis*, such as Augustine assumes for himself in the *Confessions*, could no longer be guaranteed to control meaning in a discourse conceiving of boundaries as fic-

---

[2]Michel Foucault, *The Order of Things: An Archaeology of the Human Sciences* (New York: Pantheon, 1971), chap. 2, "The Prose of the World," esp. section 3.

tive. Even at this early stage in the literary theory of the Western tradition, Augustine intuits in his distrust of literature the fictivity of the so-called reliable narrator. No narrators are ultimately reliable in fictional texts, and that is one reason fiction departs from myth, the books of the poets from the ideal Book of culture. If myths have no authors and exist as the given structures within which a society lives, fictions arise from the much more limited, contingent vantage of a specific writer. Although a poet's ambition may be, as was Dante's, to copy the architecture of his universe and mirror the *auctoritas* of the past, his language, in carrying out that project, sets in motion a critique that undermines its foundation. His poem is about the dream of the medieval Book to fulfill itself and illuminate the dark secrets in the house of intellect; but like all fictions, it remains bound within the laws and limits of its own order of designating. In this way, the *Commedia* opposes the myth of the Book, which never gives up the fantasy of containing all within its sacred confines. That pursuit is powerfully sanctioned by the institution of interpreting presided over by the medieval church, whose apologists compared their proprieties of reading to the preservation of ecclesiastical chastity: only with "circumcised lips" and "tongue" will Augustine approach the "chaste delights" of the *sacra pagina*.[3] But Dante, however much he is indebted to the idea of the Book in Augustine's *Confessions*, creates a discourse that is separate from it.

The structure of this separation or departure, as I have called it, is hardly as simple as the end of one episteme and the beginning, ex nihilo, of another that is entirely new. It may be compared, instead, to the shift from oral to written discourse that was taking place at various points in time during the middle ages, including Dante's own. As this shift has been studied recently and compellingly, it may be recognized as a departure from the certainty of meaning present in the spoken word to the less certain and often ambiguous implications of the written.[4] The need for textual communities arises in order to appeal to a consensus regarding the meaning of texts and to put back the authority that is loosened when oral communication is displaced by print: the potential for indeterminacy that is on the horizon of textual signification may thereby be ruled safely out of bounds. This shift from speaking to

---

[3]Augustine, *Confessions* 11.2 (*PL* 32, 809–810).

[4]See Brian Stock, *The Implications of Literacy: Written Language and Models of Interpretation in the Eleventh and Twelfth Centuries* (Princeton: Princeton University Press, 1983).

writing may be further understood as a historical instance of the Saussurian separation of *langue* from *parole*: the metalanguage of Latin, its grammar and the logical structures that control the study of it, are distinguished from real instances of speaking and writing not only in Latin but even more emphatically in the vernacular languages as well.[5] Yet since neither of these separations is as sharp as it may appear, certainly not as clear-cut as Saussure himself imagined, they do not shed quite enough light on the nature of historical change that is catalyzed by the textuality of poetic language in the *Commedia*. For if Saussure's distinction remains finally a structure of "différence," as Derrida has argued, in which written or spoken utterance is a "marginal supplement" of the systematic *langue* to which it belongs, then the discourse of the *Commedia* establishes a ground of signification that is very different from the architectonic Text from which it derives, such as the one figured in light at the end of the *Paradiso*.[6] The glossamatics of that celestial Book remain committed to fixing and stabilizing the meaning of what is written, since the marginal commentary is imagined as a simple addition to a source that is already complete, like the dazzling illuminations of late medieval manuscripts. But insofar as Dante's poem is marginal with respect to its origin in the Book of memory, it names the incompleteness of what it supplements at the same time as it demonstrates its own inability to be complete. Its supplementary relationship to the artifice of form is no longer mystified by the assumption of complete illumination: Dante is Argus at the bottom of the infernal ocean of his quest even as he approaches the source of paradisal light in the celestial *liber* of God. That Text is the source of fascination precisely because it is the vision of perfect and definite signification; but Dante's poetic language recognizes and unveils its own limits, thereby unsettling the stability of meaning. *How* language signifies determines *what* may in fact be understood.

Medieval grammarians, especially the *modistae*, appreciated this linguistic function more deeply than most students of writing, and yet the object of language prevailed over its mode in the development of their disciplines. As linguistics remained determined by semantics, so too Scholastic logic and dialectic, although they expanded speculative grammar widely, were projected in the processes of describing linguistic phenomena per se: philosophical

[5]Ibid., pp. 88 ff., 528.

[6]See Derrida's discussion of Saussure and supplementarity in *De la grammatologie* (Paris: Seuil, 1967); also relevant is his *L'Ecriture et la différence* (Paris: Seuil, 1967).

categories were interchangeable with grammatical ones, and signification, *in nuce*, maintained its stability against the challenge of a metalinguistic analysis. A similar development is traceable in the semiology of spatial forms: as the sign is employed in the process of *manifestatio*, by which the relationship of signifier and signified is explained, the clarifying process illuminates its own signifying strategies and projects *them* as the objects of knowledge: the *interpretandum* remains an *interpretans*, as nature and history are conceived in terms of hermeneutic principles.

But the conditions of signifying change radically in the hands of the poets. For them fictional writing suspends the priority of meaning, since form asserts itself without hesitation as an object of meaning in its own right. This shift constitutes a departure in the history of signification in the middle ages that is more decisive and consequential than any corresponding movement in the disciplines of grammar and hermeneutics. New capacities for reference become possible once the structures of fixing meaning in the tradition of the Book have been suspended. It has been customary to document the unbinding of the medieval Text many centuries after Dante, in the renaissance and the seventeenth century. We see it, for instance, in John Donne's *Devotions* (*Meditation* 17 quoted above), as the feeling of loss in the face of death and its suggestion of the absence of all coherence in the macrocosm are compared to the scattered chapters and leaves of a book that will eventually be rebound by God.[7] Although typical of Donne and the spirit of an age that was witnessing the breaking up of the Ptolemaic universe, the passage carries out a play with signification that had already been in motion for centuries, and we hear it in the echoes of the conventional imagery of the Book that appears in Chaucer, Dante, and many other sources, including the last book of the Bible. The metaphor fixed by Ambrose and Augustine has been loosened, and the shift in signification may be noted long before Donne in the fictional writing of the middle ages. The boundary line separat-

---

[7]John Donne, *Devotions upon Emergent Occasions*, in *Seventeenth-Century Prose and Poetry*, ed. Alexander M. Witherspoon and Frank J. Warnke, 2d ed. (New York: Harcourt, Brace & World, 1963), p. 68. A much more pessimistic note on this subject is sounded by Donne in *The First Anniversary: An Anatomy of the World*. Related to the cosmological revolution, see for example Marjorie H. Nicolson, *The Breaking of the Circle: Studies in the Effect of the "New Science" on Seventeenth-Century Poetry*, rev. ed. (New York: Columbia University Press, 1960), and John Hollander, *The Untuning of the Sky: Ideas of Music in English Poetry, 1500–1700* (Princeton: Princeton University Press, 1961).

ing the historical "period" of the "Middle Ages" from the "Renaissance"—the revolution of an new episteme—should therefore be recognized as a far more subtle and qualified change.[8]

Insofar as this shift illustrates the function of linguistic phenomena, its structure is motivated not by the causality of Scholastic logic, but by the supplementary logic of differentiating discourse. If this way of reflecting on historical change adjusts the apparently mechanical and abrupt notion of an epistemic break, it also suggests that the ahistorical or transhistorical character of deconstruction cannot avoid confronting the facts of its own history in the medieval opposition of poetic textuality to the myth of the Text. Certainly many writers before the seventeenth century felt the grounds of signification shifting beneath them: Augustine saw the potential for arbitrary response when he meditated on language as a model for the temporality of the fallen world; Aquinas acknowledged an abiding separation between the transcendent reference of learning and the linguistic *modus quo*. But in both writers a discourse of analysis and reference is forestalled from radical departures because the governing structure within which they worked is never unsettled. In Dante, however, that structure is pointedly questioned as soon as language accepts the factors of its own impossibility, and in Chaucer this situation is before us even more provocatively. A reflection on his work invites a reconsideration of the "origins" of deconstruction as well as the unavoidable historicism it implies.

Writing about Chaucer may begin, at least provisionally, with the recognition that the sentence—despite its medieval popularity as a meditation on time—is not the model for narrative in his poetry, and that in turn narrative is not the matrix from which the larger text takes its structure. This claim, of course, does not imply that the only adequate criticism, for example, of *The Knight's Tale* is another poem, like the Miller's, or that the best critique of *The Canterbury Tales* as a whole is *The Nun's Priest's Tale*—though every reader of Chaucer suspects how perfectly appropriate such "criticism" is. My point is, rather, that models of closure (the sentence) or se-

---

[8]Foucault, in *Order of Things* (pp. 50–77) assumes this kind of sharp split between the "Classical episteme" and the seventeenth century. Reiss, in *Discourse of Modernism*, argues for a more qualified sense of historical transition in his concept of "analytico-referential discourse"; but he would situate the consolidation of this discourse between approximately 1500 and 1650, whereas I suggest it is a factor of fictional writing going back to the poets of the middle ages.

quentiality (narrative) are not quite adequate insofar as they invite conceiving of meaning as something that is complete and stable in a text. Such a conception—because it was so conventional—found its way obviously into Chaucer's poetry; but it appears, in *The House of Fame*, as a "fantasye," the timelessness of a mythological dream that is constantly submitted to the time-bound qualifications of the dreamer's understanding and the contingencies of what language can represent. The dream as a structure for the text undergoes the same criticism as the "naked text" in the "Prologue" to *The Legend of Good Women*: in itself such a figure of meaning is less interesting than the elusive dress of possible readings. The ornamentality of language in Chaucer's early poetry takes priority as a reflection on textuality because it occasions the recognition of the temporal limits of interpreting.

Regarding the later poetry, *The Canterbury Tales*, various models of the Book have been proposed as principles of structure. But each of them—the Bible, sacred architecture, and memory—rests on a premise of aesthetic imitation, whereas the properties of poetic language seem far more interested in interpreting their own rhetorical mode as well as inherited models of the Text. Literary structure (the word is finally limited by its roots in concrete things) is a process arising in response to the inevitable gaps and uncertainties of utterance. Rather than apologizing for such qualities of discourse or mystifying them with concealed, secret meaning, Chaucer's texts acknowledge them for what they are and grant the reader the authority to complete the circle of understanding. Nowhere is this self-disclosure of textuality more direct than in the confused conclusions drawn by the narrator in the "General Prologue"; but it is obvious, too, in other places, such as the remarks of the Wife of Bath and even those of the Parson, who closes the *Tales*. He, for example, asks us to reflect with him on some final matters, as we are "entering at a thropes ende" ("Pars. Prol.," 13); he refers to the outskirts of a town, but the text is inviting us to contemplate the "entering" or "beginning" now that the "thropes ende" is leading to the final "trope"—the pilgrimage as a quest to the City of God, "That highte Jerusalem Celestial" ("Pars. Prol.," 51). It is yet another image of the text as divine object, the sacred city; but it is also, contrary to the Parson's own expression, not the terminus ad quem of his discourse. Instead, his remarks before closing are the occasion for entering into questions that his discourse may have left incomplete, for he would not want to have the last word, in all humility; and so he says:

I put it ay under correccioun
Of clerkes, for I am not textuel.
("Pars. Prol.," 56–57)

Only the learned should have the right to pass judgment on what he has said. How utterly respectful of *auctores*. But his own utterance is passing judgment, too, as it appeals to an authority in itself that it is disclaiming. Speaking thus "under correccioun" is not only the Parson's style; it is also the *modus significandi* of *The Canterbury Tales* as well as the way linguistic phenomena behave generally in medieval fictional writing. Meditations on this body of literature take us back to the evidence of deconstruction that was under way many years before the "discovery" of the movement in the twentieth century, and to the recognition that poetic language in any time may offer similar evidence for writing about the relation of literature to culture. Medieval poetry has no particular privilege in this endeavor. But it does illustrate exceptionally well that historical factors are deeply embedded in language and, therefore, that efforts to separate them through critical commentary on fictional writing will bring us closer to what happened in history. Linguistic factors claim our attention first, if only because we, like the poets, assess the past primarily through language.

BIBLIOGRAPHY

Latin sources documented in this book from the *Patrologia Latina*, ed. Jacques-Paul Migne, 221 vols. (Paris, 1841–1905), have not been listed in this bibliography. See page 13 for a list of abbreviations used.

Abelard, Peter. *Dialectica*. Ed. L. M. de Rijk. Wijsgerige Teksten en Studies van het Filosofisch Instituut der Rijksuniversiteit te Utrecht. Assen: van Gorcum, 1956.

Abrams, Meyer H. "How to Do Things with Texts." *Partisan Review* 46 (1979):566–588.

Adams, John F. "The Structure of Irony in the *Summoner's Tale*." *EIC* 12 (1962):126–132.

Adams, Joseph Q., ed. *Chief Pre-Shakespearean Dramas*. Cambridge: Cambridge University Press, 1924.

Aers, David. "The *Parliament of Fowls*: Authority, the Knower and the Known." *Chaucer Review* 16 (1981):1–17.

Alanus de Insulis. *The Plaint of Nature*. Trans. James J. Sheridan. Toronto: Pontifical Institute of Medieval Studies, 1980.

Albertus Magnus (Pseudo-). *Quaestiones de modis significandi*. Ed. L. G. Kelly. SiHol, 15. Amsterdam: Benjamins, 1977.

Albright, William Foxwell. *From the Stone Age to Christianity: Monotheism and the Historical Process*. Baltimore: Johns Hopkins Press, 1940.

———. *Yahweh and the Gods of Canaan: An Historical Analysis of Two Contrasting Faiths*. New York: Anchor, 1969.

Alexander de Villa-Dei. *Doctrinale*. Ed. Dietrich Reichling. Monumenta Germaniae Paedogogica, 12. Berlin: Hofmann, 1893.

Allen, Judson Boyce. *The Ethical Poetic of the Later Middle Ages*. Toronto: University of Toronto Press, 1982.

———. *The Friar as Critic*. Nashville: Vanderbilt University Press, 1971.

Alter, Robert. *The Art of Biblical Narrative*. New York: Basic Books, 1981.

———. "Sacred History and the Beginnings of Prose Fiction." *Poetics Today* 1 (1980):143–162.

Altieri, Charles. "The Hermeneutics of Literary Indeterminacy: A Dissent from the New Orthodoxy." *NLH* 10 (1978):71–99.

Anselm of Canterbury. *De grammatico.* Ed. D. P. Henry. Notre Dame, Ind.: Notre Dame University Press, 1964.

Aquinas, Thomas. *Expositio super librum Boethii de trinitate.* Ed. Bruno Decker. Leiden: E. J. Brill, 1959.

———. *Philosophical Texts.* Ed. and trans. Thomas Gilby. New York: Oxford University Press, 1960.

———. *Summa theologiae.* Vol. 3. Trans. Michael C. Browne et al. New York: McGraw-Hill, 1964.

Aristotle. *The Physics.* Trans. Philip H. Wicksteed and Francis M. Cornford. Cambridge: Harvard University Press, 1963.

Ashworth, Earline Jeanette. *The Tradition of Medieval Logic and Speculative Grammar.* Subsidia Mediaevalia, 9. Toronto: Pontifical Institute of Medieval Studies, 1978.

Auerbach, Erich. "Dante's Addresses to the Reader." *Romance Philology* 7 (1954):268–278.

———. *Dante, Poet of the Secular World.* Trans. Ralph Manheim. Chicago: University of Chicago Press, 1961.

———. "Dante's Prayer to the Virgin (Paradiso XXXIII) and Earlier Eulogies." *Romance Philology* 3 (1949):1–26.

———. *Literary Language and Its Public in Late Latin Antiquity and in the Middle Ages.* Trans. R. Manheim. London: Routledge & Kegan Paul, 1965.

———. *Mimesis: The Representation of Reality in Western Literature.* Trans. Willard Trask. 1946. Reprint. Garden City, N.Y.: Doubleday, 1957.

Augustine. *The City of God.* Trans. Marcus Dods. New York: Random House, 1950.

———. *On Christian Doctrine.* Trans. D. W. Robertson, Jr. New York: Liberal Arts Press, 1958.

Bachofen, Johann. *Myth, Religion, and the Mother Right.* Princeton: Princeton University Press, 1967.

Backhouse, Janet. *The Illuminated Manuscript.* New York: Phaidon Press, 1979.

———. *The Lindisfarne Gospels.* Ithaca: Cornell University Press, 1981.

Bacon, Roger. *Summa grammatica.* Ed. R. Steele. Opera Hactenus Inedita Rogeri Baconi, 15. Oxford: Clarendon Press, 1940.

Bagby, Philip. *Culture and History: Prolegomena to the Comparative Study of Civilizations.* Berkeley: University of California Press, 1959.

Baker, D. C. "Dreamer and Critic: The Poet in the *Legend of Good Women.*" *UCSLL* 9 (1963):4–18.

Baker, Timothy. *Medieval London.* New York: Praeger, 1970.

Barney, Stephen A. *Allegories of History, Allegories of Love.* Hamden, Conn.: Shoe String Press, 1979.

———, ed. *Chaucer's "Troilus": Essays in Criticism.* Hamden, Conn.: Archon, 1980.

Baron, Roger, ed. *Hugonis de Sancto Victore opera propaedeutica.* Notre Dame, Ind.: Notre Dame University Press, 1966.

Barthes, Roland. *Critique et vérité*. Paris: Seuil, 1966.

————. *Le Degré zéro de l'écriture, suivi de nouveaux essais critiques*. 1953. Reprint. Paris: Seuil, 1972. Trans. Annette Lavers and Colin Smith as *Writing Degree Zero*. 1967. Reprint. Boston: Beacon, 1970.

————. *Eléments de sémiologie*. Paris: Seuil, 1964. Trans. Annette Lavers and Colin Smith as *Elements of Semiology*. Boston: Beacon, 1967.

————. *Essais Critiques*. Paris: Seuil, 1964. Trans. Richard Howard as *Critical Essays*. Evanston: Northwestern University Press, 1972.

————. *Mythologies*. 1957. Reprint. Paris: Seuil, 1970. Trans. Annette Lavers as *Mythologies*. New York: Hill & Wang, 1972.

————. *Le Plaisur du texte*. Paris: Seuil, 1973. Trans. Richard Miller as *The Pleasure of the Text*. 1973. Reprint. New York: Hill and Wang, 1975.

————. *S/Z: Essai*. Paris: Seuil, 1970. Trans. Richard Miller as *S/Z: An Essay*. New York: Hill & Wang, 1974.

Bartsch, Hans-Warner, ed. *Kerygma and Myth: A Theological Debate*. Vol. 2. Trans. Reginald H. Fuller. London: SPCK, 1962.

Bataille, Georges. *Lascaux; or, The Birth of Art*. Geneva: Skira, 1955.

Baxter, J. H., and C. Johnson, eds. *Medieval Latin Word-List*. London: Oxford University Press, 1950.

Bennett, J. A. W. *Chaucer's Book of Fame: An Exposition of the "House of Fame."* Oxford: Clarendon Press, 1968.

Benson, Larry D. "Chaucer's Historical Present: Its Meaning and Uses." *ES* 42 (1961):65–77.

————. *The Learned and the Lewed: Studies in Chaucer and Medieval Literature*. Harvard English Studies, 5. Cambridge: Harvard University Press, 1974.

Benton, John F., ed. *Self and Society in Medieval France: The Memoirs of Abbot Guibert of Nogent*. Trans. C. C. Swinton Bland. New York: Harper & Row, 1970.

Beran, Edwyn Robert. *Holy Images: An Inquiry into Idolatry and Image-Worship in Ancient Paganism and in Christianity*. London: Allen & Unwin, 1940.

Berger, Harry. "The Ecology of the Medieval Imagination." *Centennial Review* 12 (1968):279–313.

Bergson, Henri. *The Two Sources of Morality and Religion*. Trans. R. A. Audra and C. Brereton. 1935. Reprint. New York: Doubleday Anchor, 1954.

Bersuire, Pierre (Petrus Berchorius). *Opera omnia*. 6 vols. Cologne, 1730–1731.

Bethurum, Dorothy, ed. *Critical Approaches to Medieval Literature: Selected Papers from the English Institute, 1958–1959*. New York: Columbia University Press, 1960.

Beye, Charles. *The Iliad, the Odyssey and the Epic Tradition*. New York: Anchor Books, 1966.

The Holy Bible. New York: Douay Bible House, 1943.

Biblia iuxta vulgatam Clementinam nova editio. Madrid: Biblioteca de Autores Cristianos, 1965.

Bibliography

Bischoff, Bernard. "The Study of Foreign Languages in the Middle Ages." *Speculum* 36 (1961):209–224.

Blanchard, Marc Eli. *Description: Sign, Self, Desire, Critical Theory in the Wake of Semiotics.* New York: Morton, 1980.

Bloch, R. Howard. *Etymologies and Genealogies: A Literary Anthropology of the French Middle Ages.* Chicago: University of Chicago Press, 1983.

———. *Medieval French Literature and Law.* Berkeley: University of California Press, 1977.

———. "Wasteland and Round Table: The Historical Significance of Myths of Dearth and Plenty in Old French Romance." *NLH* 11 (1980):255–276.

Bloom, Harold. *The Anxiety of Influence: A Theory of Poetry.* New York: Oxford University Press, 1973.

———. *A Map of Misreading.* New York: Oxford University Press, 1975.

Bloomfield, Morton W. "Allegory as Interpretation." *NLH* 3 (1972):301–317.

———. "Authenticating Realism and the Realism of Chaucer." *Thought* 39 (1964):335–358.

———. "Chaucer's Sense of History." *JEGP* 51 (1952):301–313.

———. "Distance and Predestination in *Troilus and Criseyde*." *PMLA* 72 (1957):14–26.

———. "Generative Grammar and the Theory of Literature." In *Actes du Deuxième Congrès de Linguistes* (1967), 3:57–65. Bucharest: Rumanian Academy, 1969.

———. "Symbolism in Medieval Literature." *MP* 56 (1958):73–81.

———, ed. *Allegory, Myth, and Symbol.* Cambridge: Harvard University Press, 1981.

Boardman, John, M. A. Brown, et al., eds. *The European Community in Later Prehistory.* Totowa, N.J.: Rowman and Littlefield, 1971.

Boas, George, *Essays on Primitivism and Related Ideas in the Middle Ages.* Baltimore: Johns Hopkins Press, 1948.

Boccaccio, Giovanni. *Genealogia deorum gentilium,* Books 14 and 15. Trans. Charles G. Osgood as *Boccaccio on Poetry.* New York: Liberal Arts Press, 1956.

Boehner, Philotheus, O.F.M. *Medieval Logic.* Manchester: University Press, 1952.

Boethius de Dacia. *Modi significandi sive Quaestiones super Priscianum Maiorem.* Ed. J. Pinborg and H. Roos, S.J. CPDMA, 4. Copenhagen: Gad, 1969.

Bolgar, R. R. *The Classical Heritage and Its Beneficiaries.* Cambridge: Cambridge University Press, 1958.

Bonaventure, Brother, F.S.C. "The Teaching of Latin in Later Medieval England." *MS* 23 (1961):1–20.

Booth, Wayne. *The Rhetoric of Fiction.* Chicago: University of Chicago Press, 1961.

Botany, J. "Paradigmes lexicaux et structures littéraires, au moyen âge." *Revue d'Histoire Littéraire de la France* 70 (1970):819–835.

Boyd, Beverly. *Chaucer and the Medieval Book*. San Marino, Calif.: Huntington Library, 1973.

Branner, Robert. *Manuscript Painting in Paris during the Reign of St. Louis*. Berkeley and Los Angeles: University of California Press, 1974.

———. *St. Louis and the Court Style in Gothic Architecture*. London: A. Zwemmer, 1965.

Braunfels, Wolfgang. *Monasteries of Western Europe: The Architecture of the Orders*. Trans. Alastair Laing. London: Thames & Hudson, 1972.

Brewer, Derek. *Chaucer in His Time*. London: Thomas Nelson and Sons, 1963.

Brind'amour, Lucie, and Eugene Vance, eds. *Archéologie du signe*. Toronto: Pontifical Institute of Medieval Studies, 1983.

Bronson, Bertrand H. *In Search of Chaucer*. Toronto: University of Toronto Press, 1960.

Brooke, Christopher. *The Twelfth Century Renaissance*. New York: Harcourt, Brace & World, 1970.

Browne, R. M. "Typologie des signes littéraires." *Poétique* 7 (1971): 334–353.

Browne, Thomas. *Religio Medici and Other Works*. Ed. L. C. Martin. Oxford: Clarendon Press, 1964.

Bultmann, Rudolf. *History and Eschatology: The Presence of Eternity*. New York: Harper & Row, 1962.

———. *Jesus Christ and Mythology*. New York: Scribner, 1959.

———. *Primitive Christianity in Its Contemporary Setting*. Trans. R. H. Fuller. New York: World, 1956.

Bultmann, Rudolf, and Karl Kundsin. *Form Criticism: Two Essays on New Testament Research*. Trans. Frederick C. Grant. 1934. Reprint. New York: Harper & Brothers, 1962.

Bunim, Miriam S. *Space in Mediaeval Painting and the Forerunners of Perspective*. New York: Columbia University Press, 1940.

Burke, Kenneth. *Perspectives by Incongruity*. Bloomington: Indiana University Press, 1964.

Burlin, Robert B. *Chaucerian Fiction*. Princeton: Princeton University Press, 1977.

Burrell, David B. *Analogy and Philosophical Language*. New Haven: Yale University Press, 1973.

———. "Aquinas on Naming God." *Theological Studies* 24 (1963): 183–212.

———. "Kant and Philosophical Knowledge." *New Scholasticism* 38 (1964):189–213.

Burrow, J. A. *Ricardian Poetry: Chaucer, Gower, Langland, and the "Gawain" Poet*. New Haven: Yale University Press, 1971.

Bursill-Hall, Geoffrey L. "Aspects of Modistic Grammar." *MSLL* 17 (1966):133–148.

———. "Medieval Grammatical Theories." *CJL* 9 (1963):39–54.

———. *Speculative Grammars of the Middle Ages*. Approaches to Semiotics, 11. The Hague: Mouton, 1971.

———. "Toward a History of Linguistics in the Middle Ages (1100–1450)." In *Studies in the History of Linguistics: Traditions and Paradigms*, ed. Dell Hymes, pp. 77–92. Bloomington: Indiana University Press, 1974.

———, ed. *Thomas of Erfurt, De Modis significandi sive Grammatica speculativa*. London: Longmans, 1972.

Callas, Daniel A., O.P. "The Introduction of Aristotelean Learning to Oxford." *PBA* 20 (1943):229–281.

Campbell, Joseph. *The Masks of God: Occidental Mythology*. New York: Viking Press, 1964.

———, ed. *Pagan and Christian Mysteries: Papers from the Eranos Yearbook*. Trans. Ralph Manheim and R. F. C. Hull. New York: Harper & Row, 1963.

Caplan, Harry. *Of Eloquence: Studies in Ancient and Medieval Rhetoric*. Ithaca: Cornell University Press, 1970.

Carpenter, Nan Cooke. *Music in the Medieval and Renaissance Universities*. Norman: University of Oklahoma Press, 1958.

Carr, Edward Hallett. *What Is History?* New York: Random House, 1961.

Carroll, David. "Mimesis Reconsidered: Literature, History, Ideology." *Diacritics* 5 (1975):5–12.

Cassirer, Ernst. *An Essay on Man: An Introduction to a Philosophy of Human Culture*. Garden City, N.Y.: Doubleday, 1956.

———. *The Myth of the State*. 1946. Reprint. New Haven: Yale University Press, 1966.

———. *The Philosophy of Symbolic Forms*. Vol. 2. *Mythical Thought*. Trans. Ralph Manheim. New Haven: Yale University Press, 1955.

———. "Structuralism in Modern Linguistics." *Word* 1 (1945):99–120.

Cavell, Stanley. *Must We Mean What We Say? A Book of Essays*. New York: Charles Scribner's Sons, 1969.

Cawley, A. C. "Chaucer, Pope and Fame." *REL* 3 (1962):9–19.

———. *Chaucer's Mind and Art*. New York: Barnes & Noble, 1970.

Cerquiglini, Bernard. *La Parole médiévale: Discours, syntaxe, texte*. Paris: Minuit, 1981.

Chalcidius. *Platonis Timaeus interprete Chalcidio cum eiusdem commentario*. Ed. I. Wrobel. Leipzig: Teubner, 1876.

Chamberlain, David S. "Music in Chaucer: His Knowledge and Use of Medieval Ideas about Music." Ph.D. diss., Princeton University, 1966.

Chambers, E. K. *English Literature at the Close of the Middle Ages*. New York: Oxford University Press, 1947.

———. "Some Aspects of Medieval Lyric." In *Early English Lyrics*, ed. E. K. Chambers and F. Sidgwick, pp. 259–296. New York: Barnes & Noble, 1967.

Chaucer, Geoffrey. *The Works of Geoffrey Chaucer*. Ed. F. N. Robinson. 2d ed. Boston: Houghton Mifflin, 1957.

Chaytor, H. J. *From Script to Print: An Introduction to Medieval Vernacular Literature*. Cambridge: Cambridge University Press, 1945.

Bibliography

Chenu, Marie-Dominique, O.P. "Grammaire et théologie aux douzième et treizième siècles." *Archives d'Histoire Doctrinale et Littéraire du Moyen Âge* 10 (1935):4–28.

Cherchi, Paolo A. "Tradition and Topoi in Medieval Literature." *CI* 3 (1976):281–294.

Chew, Samuel C. *The Pilgrimage of Life*. New Haven: Yale University Press, 1962.

Clark, John Grahame Douglas. *Aspects of Prehistory*. Berkeley: University of California Press, 1970.

———. *Prehistoric Europe: The Economic Basis*. Stanford: Stanford University Press, 1966.

Clark, John Grahame Douglas, and Stuart Piggott. *Prehistoric Societies*. New York: Alfred A. Knopf, 1965.

Clemen, Wolfgang. *Chaucer's Early Poetry*. Trans. C. A. M. Sym. London: Methuen, 1963.

Clogan, Paul M., ed. *Medievalia et Humanistica: Studies in Medieval and Renaissance Culture*. New Series, 5. *Medieval Historiography*. Denton: North Texas State University, 1974.

Clover, Carol J. *The Medieval Saga*. Ithaca: Cornell University Press, 1982.

Coghill, Nevill. *The Poet Chaucer*. 2d ed. London: Oxford University Press, 1967.

Cohn, Norman. *The Pursuit of the Millennium*. Fairlawn, N.J.: Essential Books, 1957.

Colie, Rosalie. "Johan Huizinga and the Task of Cultural History." *American Historical Review* 69 (1964):607–630.

———. *Paradoxica Epidemica: The Renaissance Tradition of Paradox*. Princeton: Princeton University Press, 1966.

Colish, Marcia L. "Eleventh-Century Grammar in the Thought of S. Anselm." *Actes* 4 (1969):785–795.

———. *The Mirror of Language: A Study in the Medieval Theory of Knowledge*. New Haven: Yale University Press, 1968.

Collingwood, Robin G. *The Idea of History*. Oxford: Clarendon Press, 1946.

Combe, Jacques. *Jérôme Bosch*. Paris: P. Tisné, 1946.

Copleston, Frederick C. *A History of Medieval Philosophy*. London: Methuen, 1972.

Coulter, James A. *The Literary Microcosm: Theories of Interpretation of the Later Neo-Platonists*. Leiden: E. J. Brill, 1976.

Courcelle, Pierre. "Etude critique sur les commentaires de la 'Consolation' de Boèce." *Archives d'Histoire Doctrinale et Littéraire du Moyen Âge* 12 (1939):5–140.

Coussemaker, Edmond de. *Histoire de l'harmonie au moyen âge*. Hildesheim: G. Olms, 1966.

———, ed. *Scriptorum de musica medii aevi* Aldesheim: Georg Olms, 1963.

Crespedes, Frank V. "Chaucer's Pardoner and Preaching." *ELH* 44 (1977): 1–18.

[263]

Crombie, A. C. *Robert Grosseteste and the Origins of Experimental Science, 1100–1700.* Oxford: Clarendon Press, 1953.

Crone, G. R. *The World Map by Richard of Haldingham in Hereford Cathedral circa A.D. 1285.* London: Royal Geographical Society, 1954.

Cross, Frank Moore. *Canaanite Myth and Hebrew Epic: Essays in the History of the Religion of Israel.* Cambridge: Harvard University Press, 1973.

Culler, Jonathan. "The Linguistic Basis of Structuralism." In *Structuralism: An Introduction*, ed. D. Robey, pp. 20–36. Oxford: Oxford University Press, 1973.

——. *On Deconstruction.* Ithaca: Cornell University Press, 1982.

——. "Phenomenology and Structuralism." *Human Context* 5 (1973): 35–42.

——. *The Pursuit of Signs.* Ithaca: Cornell University Press, 1981.

——. *Structuralist Poetics: Structuralism, Linguistics and the Study of Literature.* Ithaca: Cornell University Press, 1975.

Cullman, Oscar. *Christ and Time: The Primitive Christian Conception of Time and History.* Trans. Floyd V. Filson. Philadelphia: Westminster Press, 1964.

Cunningham, James V. "Convention as Structure: The Prologue to the *Canterbury Tales*." In *Tradition and Poetic Structure*, pp. 59–75. Denver, Colo.: Alan Swallow, 1960.

Curtius, Ernst Robert. *European Literature and the Latin Middle Ages.* Trans. Willard R. Trask. New York: Harper & Row, 1963.

Damon, Phillip W. *Modes of Analogy in Ancient and Medieval Verse.* Berkeley and Los Angeles: University of California Press, 1961.

Danielou, Jean. *From Shadows to Reality: Studies in the Biblical Typology of the Fathers.* Trans. Dom Wulstan Hibberd. Westminster, Md.: Newman Press, 1960.

Dante Alighieri. *La divina commedia.* Ed. Natalino Sapegno. 3 vols. Florence: Nuova Italia, 1955–1957.

——. *The Divine Comedy.* Trans. Charles S. Singleton. Princeton: Princeton University Press, 1970–1975.

——. *La vita nuova.* In *Le opere di Dante Alighieri.* Ed. E. Moore and P. Toynbee. Oxford: Oxford University Press, 1924.

——. *La vita nuova.* Trans. Mark Musa. Bloomington: Indiana University Press, 1965.

David, Alfred. *The Strumpet Muse.* Bloomington: Indiana University Press, 1976.

Delany, Sheila. *Chaucer's "House of Fame": The Poetics of Skeptical Fideism.* Chicago: University of Chicago Press, 1972.

——. "Substructure and Superstructure: The Politics of Allegory in the Fourteenth Century." *Science and Society* 38 (1974):257–280.

Deleuze, Gilles. *Différence et répétition.* Paris: Presses Universitaires de France, 1968.

Deligiorgis, S. "Structuralism and the Study of Poetry: A Parametric Analysis of Chaucer's Shipman's Tale and Parliament of Fowls." *NM* 70 (1969):297–306.

Demetz, Peter, Thomas Greene, and Lawry Nelson, eds. *The Disciplines of Criticism*. New Haven: Yale University Press, 1970.

Dempf, A. *Die Hauptform mittelalterlicher Weltanschauung: Eine geisteswissenschaftliche Studie über die Summa*. Munich, 1925.

Denis the Carthusian. *Opera omnia*. 42 vols in 44. Montreuil, 1896–1935.

Derrida, Jacques. *De la grammatologie*. Paris: Minuit, 1967. Trans. Gayatri C. Spivak as *Of Grammatology*. Baltimore: Johns Hopkins University Press, 1976.

———. *La Dissémination*. Paris: Seuil, 1972.

———. *L'Ecriture et la différence*. Paris: Seuil, 1967.

———. *La Voix et le phénomène*. Paris: Presses Universitaires de France, 1967. Trans. David B. Allison as *Speech and Phenomena, and Other Essays on Husserl's Theory of Signs*. Evanston: Northwestern University Press, 1973.

Diamond, Stanley, ed. *Culture in History: Essays in Honor of Paul Radin*. New York: Columbia University Press, 1960.

Dineen, F. P., S.J. *An Introduction to General Linguistics*. New York: Holt, 1967.

Dionysius the Areopagite. *The Mystical Theology and the Celestial Hierarchies of Dionysius the Areopagite*. Trans. Editors of the Shrine of Wisdom. Fintry, England: Shrine of Wisdom, 1945.

———. *On the Divine Names and the Mystical Theology*. Trans. C. E. Rolt. New York: Macmillan, 1940.

Diringer, David. *The Illuminated Book: Its History and Production*. London: Faber & Faber, 1967.

Dodds, Eric Robertson. *The Greeks and the Irrational*. Berkeley: University of California Press, 1968.

Donaldson, E. Talbot. "Chaucer the Pilgrim." *PMLA* 49 (1954):928–936.

———. *Speaking of Chaucer*. New York: W. W. Norton, 1970.

———, ed. *Chaucer's Poetry: An Anthology for the Modern Reader*, 2d ed. New York: Ronald Press, 1975.

Doob, Penelope B. R. *Ego Nabugodonosor: A Study of Conventions of Madness in Middle English Literature*. Stanford: Stanford University Press, 1969.

Dorfman, Eugene. *The Narreme in the Medieval Romance Epic*. Toronto: University of Toronto Press, 1969.

Dragonetti, Roger. *Aux frontières du langage poétique: Etudes sur Dante, Mallarmé, Valéry*. Ghent: Romanica Gandensia, 1961.

Dronke, Peter. *Fabula: Explorations into the Uses of Myth in Medieval Platonism*. Leiden: E. J. Brill, 1974.

———. *Poetic Individuality in the Middle Ages: New Departures in Poetry, 1000–1150*. Oxford: Clarendon Press, 1970.

Duby, Georges. *The Early Growth of the European Economy: Warriors and Peas-*

ants from the Seventh to the Twelfth Century. Trans. Howard B. Clarke. Ithaca: Cornell University Press, 1974.

———. *The Three Orders: Feudal Society Imagined.* Trans. Arthur Goldhammer. Chicago: University of Chicago Press, 1980.

Duchrow, Ulrich. "'Signum' und 'superbia' beim jungen Augustin (386–390)." *Revue des Etudes Augustiniennes* 7 (1961):369–372.

Dumézil, Georges. *Camillus: A Study of Indo-European Religion as Roman History.* Trans. A. Aronowicz and J. Bryson. Berkeley: University of California Press, 1980.

———. *The Destiny of the Warrior.* Trans. Alf Hiltebeitel. Chicago: University of Chicago Press, 1970.

———. *From Myth to Fiction: The Sage of Hadingus.* Trans. Derek Coltman. Chicago: University of Chicago Press, 1973.

———. *L'Idéologie tripartie des Indo-Européens.* Collection Latomus, 31. Brussels: Berchem, 1958.

Durandus of Mende. *Rationale divinorum officiorum.* Venice, 1568.

Durkheim, Emile, and Marcel Mauss. "De quelques formes primitives de classification." *L'Année Sociologique* 6 (1901–1902):1–72.

Economou, George D., ed. *Geoffrey Chaucer: A Collection of Original Articles.* New York: McGraw-Hill, 1975.

———. *The Goddess Natura in Medieval Literature.* Cambridge: Harvard University, Press, 1973.

Edelstein, Ludwig. "The Function of Myth in Plato's Philosophy." *JHI* 10 (1949):463–481.

Egbert, Virginia Wylie. *The Medieval Artist at Work.* Princeton: Princeton University Press, 1967.

Ehrmann, Jacques, ed. *Structuralism.* Garden City, N.Y.: Doubleday, 1970.

Eisenstein, Elizabeth. *The Printing Press as an Agent of Change.* Cambridge: Cambridge University Press, 1979.

Elbow, Peter. *Oppositions in Chaucer.* Middletown, Conn.: Wesleyan University Press, 1973.

Eliade, Mircea. *Myth and Reality.* Trans. Willard R. Trask. New York: Harper & Row, 1963.

———. *The Sacred and the Profane: The Nature of Religion.* Trans. Willard R. Trask. New York: Harper & Row, 1961.

Engels, J. "La doctrine du signe chez Saint Augustin." In *Studia Patristica*, vol. 6, ed. F. L. Cross, 366–373. Berlin: Akademie-Verlag, 1962.

Evans, Joan. *Life in Medieval France.* New York: Phaidon Press, 1979.

Every, George. *Christian Mythology.* Feltham: Hamlyn, 1970.

Faral, Edmond, ed. *Les Arts poétiques du douzième et du treizième siècle.* Paris: Champion, 1924.

Ferguson, George Wells. *Signs and Symbols in Christian Art.* New York: Oxford University Press, 1954.

Ferguson, Margaret W. "Saint Augustine's Region of Unlikeness: The Crossing of Exile and Language." *Georgia Review* 29 (1975):842–864.

Ferrante, Joan M., and George D. Economou, eds. *In Pursuit of Perfection:*

Courtly Love in Medieval Literature. Port Washington, N.Y.: Kennikat Press, 1975.

Fineman, Joel. "The Structure of Allegorical Desire." In *Allegory and Representation,* ed. Stephen Greenblatt, pp. 26–60. Baltimore: Johns Hopkins University Press, 1981.

Fish, Stanley. *Is There a Text in This Class?: The Authority of Interpretive Communities.* Cambridge: Harvard University Press, 1980.

Fleming, John V. *The "Roman de la Rose": A Study in Allegory and Iconography.* Princeton: Princeton University Press, 1969.

Fletcher, Angus. *Allegory: The Theory of a Symbolic Mode.* Ithaca: Cornell University Press, 1964.

Focillon, Henry. *The Art of the West in the Middle Ages.* Trans. Donald King. 2d ed. London: Phaidon Press, 1969.

Fosbroke, Thomas Dudley. *British Monachism; or, Manners and Customs of the Monks and Nuns of England.* 3d ed. London: M. A. Nattali, 1843.

Foucault, Michel. *L'Archéologie du savoir.* Paris: Gallimard, 1969. Trans. as *The Archeology of Knowledge.* New York: Pantheon, 1972.

———. *Les Mots et les choses.* Paris: Gallimard, 1971. Trans. as *The Order of Things: An Archaeology of the Human Sciences.* New York: Pantheon, 1971.

Frank, Robert Worth, Jr. *Chaucer and "The Legend of Good Women."* Cambridge: Harvard University Press, 1972.

Frankfort, Henri. *Kingship and the Gods: A Study of Ancient Near Eastern Religion as the Interpretation of Society and Nature.* Chicago: University of Chicago Press, 1948.

Frankfort, Henri, H. A. Frankfort, John A. Wilson, and Thorkild Jacobsen. *Before Philosophy: The Intellectual Adventure of Ancient Man.* Baltimore: Penguin Books, 1973. (First published as *The Intellectual Adventure of Ancient Man,* Chicago: University of Chicago Press, 1946.)

Freccero, John. "*Medusa:* The Letter and the Spirit (*Inf.* IX)." *Yearbook of Italian Studies* (1972), pp. 1–18.

———, ed. *Dante: A Collection of Critical Essays.* Englewood Cliffs, N.J.: Prentice-Hall, 1965.

Fredborg, Karin M. "The Dependence of Peter Helias' *Summa super Priscianum* on William of Conches' *Glose super Priscianum.*" *CIMAGL* 11 (1973):1–57.

Freedberg, Sydney Joseph. *Painting of the High Renaissance in Rome and Florence.* New York: Harper & Row, 1972.

Friedman, John B. *The Monstrous Races in Medieval Art and Thought.* Cambridge: Harvard University Press, 1981.

Frye, Northrop. *Anatomy of Criticism, Four Essays.* Princeton: Princeton University Press, 1957.

———. *The Great Code: The Bible and Literature.* New York: Harcourt Brace Jovanovich, 1982.

———. *The Secular Scripture: A Study of the Structure of Romance.* Cambridge: Harvard University Press, 1976.

――――. *A Study of English Romanticism*. New York: Random House, 1968.

Fyler, John M. *Chaucer and Ovid*. New Haven: Yale University Press, 1979.

Galway, Margaret. "Chaucer's Sovereign Lady: A Study of the Prologue to the *Legend* and Related Poems." *MLR* 33 (1938):145–199.

Garbáty, Thomas J. "The Degradation of Chaucer's 'Geffrey.'" *PMLA* 89 (1974):97–104.

Gaylord, Alan T. "Sentence and Solaas in Fragment VII of the *Canterbury Tales*." *PMLA* 82 (1967):226–235.

Gellrich, Jesse M. "The Argument of the Book: Medieval Writing and Modern Theory." *Clio: Interdisciplinary Journal of Literature, Philosophy, and the Philosophy of History* 10 (1981):245–263.

――――. "The Parody of Medieval Music in the *Miller's Tale*." *JEGP* 73 (1974):176–188.

――――. "The Structure of Allegory." In *Analecta Husserliana*, 18:505–519. Dordrecht: Reidel, 1984.

Genette, Gérard. "Avatars du Cratylisme." *Poétique* 11 (1972):367–394; 13 (1973):111–133; 15 (1973):265–291.

Gibson, Margaret T. "The 'Artes' in the Eleventh Century." *Actes* 4 (1969):121–126.

――――. "Priscian, 'Institutiones Grammaticae': A Handlist of Manuscripts." *Scriptorium* 26 (1972):105–124.

Giedion, Sigfried. *The Eternal Present*. Vol. 1. *The Beginnings of Art*. New York: Bollingen Foundation, 1962.

――――. *The Eternal Present*. Vol. 2. *The Beginnings of Architecture*. New York: Bollingen Foundation, 1964.

Gies, Joseph, and Frances Gies. *Life in a Medieval Castle*. New York: Thomas Y. Crowell, 1974.

Gilkey, Langdon. *Naming the Whirlwind: The Renewal of God-Language*. Indianapolis: Bobbs-Merrill, 1969.

Gilson, Etienne. *A History of Christian Philosophy in the Middle Ages*. London: Sheed & Ward, 1955.

Gimbutas, Marija. *Bronze Age Cultures in Central and Eastern Europe*. The Hague: Mouton, 1965.

――――. *The Gods and Goddesses of Old Europe: Myths, Legends, and Cult Images*. Berkeley: University of California Press, 1974.

Gimpel, Jean. *The Cathedral Builders*. Trans. Carl F. Barnes, Jr. New York: Grove Press, 1961.

Ginsberg, Warren. *The Cast of Character: The Representation of Personality in Ancient and Medieval Literature*. Toronto: University of Toronto Press, 1983.

Girard, René. "From 'The Divine Comedy' to the Sociology of the Novel." Trans. Petra Morrison. In *Sociology of Literature and Drama*, ed. Elizabeth and Thomas Barns, pp. 101–108. Baltimore: Penguin Books, 1973.

――――. "Violence and Representation in the Mythic Text." *MLN* 92 (1977):922–944.

Godfrey, Robert G. "The Language Theory of Thomas of Erfurt." *SPh* 57 (1960):22–29.

———. "Late Medieval Linguistic Meta-theory and Chomsky's Syntactic Structures." *Word* 21 (1965):251–256.

Gogarten, Friedrich. *Demythologizing and History*. Trans. Neville Horton Smith. London: SCM Press, 1955.

Gombrich, E. H. *Art and Illusion: A Study in the Psychology of Pictorial Representation*. 2d ed. Princeton: Princeton University Press, 1969.

———. *Symbolic Images: Studies in the Art of the Renaissance*. New York: Phaidon Press, 1972.

Good, Edwin M. *Irony in the Old Testament*. Philadelphia: Westminster Press, 1965.

Goodrich, Norma L. *Medieval Myths*. New York: New American Library, 1961.

Gordon, Ida L. *The Double Sorrow of Troilus: A Study of Ambiguities in "Troilus and Criseyde."* Oxford: Clarendon Press, 1970.

Grabar, André. *Christian Iconography: A Study of Its Origins*. Princeton: Princeton University Press, 1968.

———. *Early Medieval Painting*. Trans. Stuart Gilbert. New York: Skira, 1957.

Grabmann, Martin. *Thomas van Erfurt und die Sprachlogik des mittelalterlichen Aristotelismus*. Munich: Bayerischen Akademie der Wissenschaften, 1943.

Graff, Gerald. *Literature against Itself: Literary Ideas in Modern Society*. Chicago: University of Chicago Press, 1979.

Grant, Edward. *Physical Science in the Middle Ages*. New York: John Wiley, 1971.

Green, Richard Hamilton. "Dante's 'Allegory of the Poets' and the Medieval Theory of Poetic Fiction." *Comparative Literature* 9 (1957):118–128.

Green, V. H. H. *Medieval Civilization in Western Europe*. London: Edward Arnold, 1971.

Greenfield, Stanley B. *The Interpretation of Old English Poems*. London: Routledge & Kegan Paul, 1972.

Griffith, Dudley D. "An Interpretation of Chaucer's *Legend of Good Women*." In *Manly Anniversary Studies*. Chicago: University of Chicago Press, 1923.

Grosseteste, Robert (Pseudo-). *Tractatus de grammatica*. Ed. K. Reichl. Veröffentlichungen des Grabmann—Institutes zur Erforschung der mittelalterlichen Theologie und Philosophie, n.s., 28. Munich: F. Schöningh, n.d.

Guillén, Claudio. *Literature as System*. Princeton: Princeton University Press, 1971.

Hadas, Moses. *Old Wine, New Bottles: A Humanist Teacher at Work*. New York: Simon & Schuster, 1962.

Haidu, Peter. "Repetition: Modern Reflections on Medieval Aesthetics." *MLN* 92 (1977):875–887.

Harari, Josué, ed. *Textual Strategies: Perspectives in Post-Structural Criticism.* Ithaca: Cornell University Press, 1979.

Hardison, O. B., Jr. "Toward a History of Medieval Criticism." *Medievalia et Humanistica* 7 (1976):1–12.

Harenberg, Werner. *Der Spiegel on the New Testament: A Guide to the Struggle between Radical and Conservative in European University and Parish.* Trans. James H. Burtness. London: Macmillan, 1970.

Haskins, Charles H. *The Renaissance of the Twelfth Century.* Cambridge: Harvard University Press, 1927.

Hatcher, Elizabeth R. "The Moon and Parchment: *Paradiso* II, 73–78." *Dante Studies* 89 (1971):55–60.

Hathaway, Ronald F. *Hierarchy and the Definition of Order in the Letters of Pseudo-Dionysius: A Study in the Form and Meaning of the Pseudo-Dionysian Writings.* The Hague: Martinus Nijhoff, 1969.

Havelock, Eric Alfred. *Preface to Plato.* New York: Grosset & Dunlap, 1963.

Hawkes, Christopher. *The Prehistoric Foundations of Europe to the Mycenean Age.* London: Methuen, 1940.

Hawkes, Christopher, and Jacquetta Hawkes. *Prehistoric Britain.* London: Chatto & Windus, 1947.

Hawkes, Jacquetta, et al. *Prehistory and the Beginnings of Civilization.* New York: Harper & Row, 1963.

Hearn, M. F. *Romanesque Sculpture: The Revival of Monumental Stone Sculpture in the Eleventh and Twelfth Centuries.* Ithaca: Cornell University Press, 1981.

Heer, Friedrich. *The Medieval World: Europe 1100–1350.* Trans. Janet Sondheimer. New York: World, 1962.

Henderson, Ian. *Myth in the New Testament.* London: SCM Press, 1963.

Henry, Desmond P. "Why 'grammaticus'?" *ALMA* 28 (1958):165–180.

———, ed. *Anselm of Canterbury, "De Grammatico."* Notre Dame, Ind.: Notre Dame University Press, 1964.

Hermann, John P., and John J. Burke, Jr., eds. *Signs and Symbols in Chaucer's Poetry.* University: University of Alabama Press, 1981.

Holenstein, Elmar. *Roman Jakobson's Approach to Language: Phenomenological Structuralism.* Trans. Catherine Schelbert and Tarcisus Schelbert. Bloomington: Indiana University Press, 1976.

Holländer, Hans. *Early Medieval Art.* Trans. Caroline Hillier. New York: Universe Books, 1974.

Hollander, John. *The Untuning of the Sky: Ideas of Music in English Poetry, 1500–1700.* Princeton: Princeton University Press, 1961.

Hollander, Robert. *Allegory in Dante's Comedy.* Princeton: Princeton University Press, 1969.

Honig, Edwin. *Dark Conceit: The Making of Allegory.* Evanston: Northwestern University Press, 1959.

Howard, Donald R. "*The Canterbury Tales*: Memory and Form." *ELH* 38 (1971):319–328.

————. "Chaucer the Man." *PMLA* 80 (1965):337–343.

————. "Fiction and Religion in Boccaccio and Chaucer." *Journal of the American Academy of Religion* 47, 2, suppl. (June 1979): H, 307–328.

————. *The Idea of the "Canterbury Tales."* Berkeley: University of California Press, 1976.

————. *Writers and Pilgrims: Medieval Pilgrimage Narratives and Their Posterity.* Berkeley: University of California Press, 1980.

Hugh of St. Cher. *Opera omnia.* 8 vols. Venice, 1732.

Hugh of St. Victor. *The Didascalicon of Hugh of St. Victor: A Medieval Guide to the Arts.* Trans. Jerome Taylor. New York: Columbia University Press, 1961.

Huizinga, Johan. *Homo Ludens: A Study of the Play-Element in Culture.* Boston: Beacon, 1955.

————. *The Waning of the Middle Ages: A Study of the Forms of Life, Thought and Art in France and the Netherlands in the Fourteenth and Fifteenth Centuries.* 1924. Reprint. New York: Doubleday, 1954.

Hunt, Richard W. *The History of Grammar in the Middle Ages: Collected Papers.* Ed. G. L. Bursill-Hall. Amsterdam: J. Benjamins, 1980.

————. "Studies on Priscian in the Eleventh and Twelfth Centuries." *Medieval and Renaissance Studies* 1 (1941):194–231.

Huppé, Bernard F. "Chaucer: A Criticism and a Reply." *MLR* 43 (1948): 393–399.

Huygens, R. B. C. *Accessus ad auctores.* Collection Latomus, 15. Brussels: Berchem, 1954.

Iser, Wolfgang. *The Implied Reader: Patterns of Communication in Prose Fiction from Bunyan to Beckett.* Baltimore: Johns Hopkins Press, 1974.

————. "The Reading Process: A Phenomenological Approach." *NLH* 3 (1972):279–299.

————. "The Reality of Fiction: A Functionalist Approach to Literature." *NLH* 7 (1975):7–38.

Jacobus of Liège. *Speculum musicae.* Ed. Roger Bragard. Vol. 3. *Corpus scriptorum de musica.* Rome, 1955–.

James, Hans Robert. *Genèse de la poésie allégorique française au moyen âge (de 1180 à 1240).* Heidelberg: C. Winter, 1968.

Jameson, Fredric. *Marxism and Form.* Princeton: Princeton University Press, 1971.

————. "Metacommentary." *PMLA* 86 (1971):9–18.

————. *The Prison-House of Language: A Critical Account of Structuralism and Russian Formalism.* Princeton: Princeton University Press, 1972.

Jeauneau, Edouard. "Deux rédactions de gloses de Guillaume de Conches sur Priscien." *Recherches de Théologies Ancienne et Médiévale* 27 (1960):212–247.

Jeffrey, David L., ed. *By Things Seen: Reference and Recognition in Medieval Thought.* Ottawa: University of Ottawa Press, 1979.

Jensen, Søren S. "Some Remarks on the Medieval Etymology of *Congruitas* and Its Background." In *Fides quaerens intellectum: Festschrift tilegnet,* ed. Heinrich Roos, S.J., pp. 60–65. Copenhagen: Frost-Hansen, 1964.

Jeremias, Joachim. *The Parables of Jesus.* Trans. S. H. Hook. Rev. ed. New York: Charles Scribner's Sons, 1963.

The Jerusalem Bible. Ed. Alexander Jones. Garden City, N.Y.: Doubleday, 1966.

Johannes de Dacia. *Summa grammatica: Divisio scientiae.* Ed. A. Otto, S.J. CPDMA, 1. Copenhagen: Gad, 1955.

John of Salisbury. *Metalogicon Libri IIII.* Ed. Clemens C. I. Webb. Oxford: Oxford University Press, 1929.

———. *The Metalogicon of John of Salisbury.* Trans. Daniel D. McGarry. Berkeley and Los Angeles: University of California Press, 1955.

Johnson, Alfred M., Jr., trans. *Structural Analysis and Biblical Exegesis: Interpretational Essays.* Pittsburgh: Pickwick Press, 1974.

Jordan, Robert M. *Chaucer and the Shape of Creation: The Aesthetic Possibilities of Inorganic Structure.* Cambridge: Harvard University Press, 1967.

Josipovici, Gabriel D. "Fiction and Game in the *Canterbury Tales.*" *Critical Quarterly* 7 (1965):193–197.

———. *The World and the Book.* Stanford: Stanford University Press, 1971.

Jung, M. R. *Etudes sur la poème allégorique en France au moyen âge.* Berne, 1971.

Kaminsky, Alice R., ed. *Chaucer's "Troilus and Criseyde" and the Critics.* Athens: Ohio University Press, 1980.

Kantorowicz, Ernst. *King's Two Bodies: A Study in Medieval Political Theology.* Princeton: Princeton University Press, 1957.

Katzenellenbogen, Adolf E. M. *Allegories of the Virtues and Vices in Medieval Art from Early Christian Times to the Twentieth Century.* 1939. Reprint. Nendeln, Liechtenstein: Kraus, 1968.

Kelly, Douglas. *Medieval Imagination: Rhetoric and the Poetry of Courtly Love.* Madison: University of Wisconsin Press, 1978.

———. "The Scope of the Treatment of Composition in the Twelfth- and Thirteenth-Century Arts of Poetry." *Speculum* 41 (1966):261–278.

Kelly, Henry A. "Aristotle-Averoes-Alemannus on Tragedy: The Influence of the *Poetics* on the Latin Middle Ages." *Viator* 10 (1979):161–209.

Kelly, Louis G., ed. *Albertus Magnus (Pseudo), Quaestiones de modis significandi.* SiHol, 15. Amsterdam: Benjamins, 1977.

———. "De modis generandi: Points of Contact between Noam Chomsky and Thomas of Erfurt." *FL* 5 (1972):225–252.

Kendrick, Thomas D., T. J. Brown, et al. *Evangelium Quattor Codex Lindisfarnensis.* 2 vols. Dietikon, Switzerland: Urs Graf Verlag, 1956.

Kermode, Frank. *The Genesis of Secrecy: On the Interpretation of Narrative.* Cambridge: Harvard University Press, 1979.

———. "Secrets and Narrative Sequence." *CI* 7 (1980):83–101.

———. *The Sense of an Ending: Studies in the Theory of Fiction.* New York: Oxford University Press, 1967.

Kirk, G. S. *Myth: Its Meaning and Functions in Ancient and Other Cultures.* Cambridge: Cambridge University Press, 1970.

Kittredge, G. L. *Chaucer and His Poetry.* Cambridge: Harvard University Press, 1915.

————. "Chaucer's Discussion of Marriage." *MP* 9 (1911–1912):437–467.

Klibansky, Raymond. *The Continuity of the Platonic Tradition during the Middle Ages.* London: Warburg Institute, 1939.

Klubertanz, George Peter. *St. Thomas Aquinas on Analogy.* Chicago: Loyola University Press, 1960.

Koerner, E. F. Konrad. *Ferdinand de Saussure: Origin and Development of His Linguistic Theory in Western Studies of Language.* Braunschweig: Vieweg, 1973.

————. *Toward a Historiography of Linguistics: Selected Essays.* SiHol, 19. Amsterdam: Benjamins, 1978.

Koonce, B. G. *Chaucer and the Tradition of Fame: Symbolism in "The House of Fame."* Princeton: Princeton University Press, 1966.

Koyre, Alexandre. *From the Closed World to the Infinite Universe.* New York: Harper & Row, 1958.

Kretzmann, Norman. *William of Sherwood's Introduction to Logic.* Minneapolis: University of Minnesota Press, 1966.

Kuhn, Thomas S. *The Structure of Scientific Revolutions.* Chicago: University of Chicago Press, 1962.

Ladner, Gerhart B. "Medieval and Modern Understanding of Symbolism." *Speculum* 54 (1979):223–256.

LaHood, Marvin J. "Chaucer's *The Legend of Lucrece.*" *PQ* 43 (1964):274–276.

Lain, Entralgo P. *The Theory of the Word in Classical Antiquity.* New Haven: Yale University Press, 1970.

Lane, Michael, ed. *Introduction to Structuralism.* New York: Basic Books, 1970.

Lange, Hugo. "Zur Datierung des GG-Prologs Chaucers Legende von guten Frauen: Eine heraldische Studie." *Anglia* 39 (1915):347–355.

Langhans, Viktor. "Der Prolog zu Chaucers Legend von guten Frauen." *Anglia* 41 (1917):162–181.

Larson, Gerald J. *Myth in Indo-European Antiquity.* Berkeley: University of California Press, 1974.

Lawlor, John. *Chaucer.* New York: Harper & Row, 1968.

Lazzeri, Gerolamo. *Antologia dei primi secoli della litteratura italiana.* Milan: U. Hoepli, 1942.

Leach, Edmund. *Genesis as Myth and Other Essays.* London: Jonathan Cape, 1969.

Leclercq, Jean. *The Love of Learning and the Desire for God: A Study of Monastic Culture.* Trans. Catherine Misrahi. New York: New American Library, 1961.

Leff, Gordon. *Medieval Thought from Saint Augustine to Ockham.* London: Penguin, 1958.

————. *Paris and Oxford Universities in the Thirteenth and Fourteenth Centuries.* New York: John Wiley, 1968.

Leicester, H. Marshall, Jr. "The Art of Impersonation: A General Prologue to the *Canterbury Tales.*" *PMLA* 95 (1980):213–224.

Lentricchia, Frank. *After the New Criticism.* Chicago: University of Chicago Press, 1980.

Letts, Malcolm. "The Pictures in the Hereford *Mappa Mundi.*" *Notes and Queries* 200 (1955):2–6.

Levinas, Emmanuel. *Totality and Infinity: An Essay on Exteriority.* Pittsburgh: Duquesne University Press, 1969.

Lévi-Strauss, Claude. *Anthropologie structurale.* Paris: Plon, 1958. Trans. Claire Jacobson and Brooke G. Schoeph as *Structural Anthropology.* New York: Basic Books, 1963.

————. *Le Cru et le cuit.* Paris: Plon, 1964. Trans. John and Doreen Weightman as *The Raw and the Cooked: Introduction to a Science of Mythology.* New York: Harper & Row, 1969.

————. *Du miel au cendres.* Paris: Plon, 1966. Trans. John and Doreen Weightman as *From Honey to Ashes.* London: Jonathan Cape, 1973.

————. *La Pensée sauvage.* Paris: Plon, 1962. Trans. George Weidenfield as *The Savage Mind.* Chicago: University of Chicago Press, 1969.

————. *Totemism.* Trans. Rodney Needham. Boston: Beacon, 1963.

————. *Tristes tropiques.* Paris: Plon, 1955. Trans. John Russell. New York: Criterion Books, 1961.

Levy, G. Rachel. *The Gate of Horn: A Study of the Religious Conceptions of the Stone Age, and Their Influence upon European Thought.* London: Faber & Faber, 1948.

Lewis, C. S. *The Discarded Image: An Introduction to Medieval and Renaissance Literature.* Cambridge: Cambridge University Press, 1964.

Leyerle, John. "Chaucer's Windy Eagle." *UTQ* 40 (1971):247–265.

————. "The Interlace Structure of *Beowulf.*" *UTQ* 37 (1967):1–17.

Lindblom, Johannes. *Prophecy in Ancient Israel.* Philadelphia: Muhlenberg Press, 1962.

Loew, Cornelius. *Myth, Sacred History, and Philosophy: The Pre-Christian Religious Heritage of the West.* New York: Harcourt, Brace & World, 1967.

Lohr, Charles H., S.J. "Aristotle in the West." *Traditio* 25 (1969):417–431.

Longran, Bernard J. *Method in Theology.* New York: Herder & Herder, 1972.

Loomis, R. S. *The Grail.* New York: Columbia University Press, 1963.

Lovejoy, Arthur O. *The Great Chain of Being: A Study of the History of an Idea.* 1936. Reprint. New York: Harper & Row, 1960.

Lowes, J. L. *Geoffrey Chaucer.* 1934. Reprint. Bloomington: Indiana University Press, 1958.

————. "The Prologue to the *Legend of Good Women* as Related to the

French Marguerite Poems and to the *Filostrato.*" *PMLA* 19 (1904):593–683.

———. "The Prologue to the *Legend of Good Women* Considered in Its Chronological Relations." *PMLA* 20 (1905):749–864.

Lubac, Henri de. *Exégèse médiévale: Les Quatre sens de l'écriture.* Vol. 1, pts. 1 and 2, vol. 2, pts. 1 and 2. Paris: Aubier, 1959–1964.

Lumiansky, R. M. *Of Sundry Folk: The Dramatic Principle in the "Canterbury Tales."* Austin: University of Texas Press, 1955.

Lyrami, Nicholai. *Biblia sacra cum glossa ordinaria et postilla.* 8 vols. Paris, London, and Venice, 1590–1603.

Lyttkens, Hampus. *The Analogy between God and the World: An Investigation of Its Background and Interpretation of Its Use by Thomas Aquinas.* Uppsala: Lundequistska Bokhandeln, 1953.

Macksey, Richard, and Eugenio Donato, eds. *The Structuralist Controversy: The Languages of Criticism and the Sciences of Man.* Baltimore: Johns Hopkins University Press, 1970.

Macrobius. *Commentarius in somnium Scipionis.* Ed. Franciscus Eyssenhardt. Leipzig: Teubner, 1868.

Magliola, Robert R. *Phenomenology and Literature: An Introduction.* West Lafayette, Ind.: Purdue University Press, 1977.

Major, John M. "The Personality of Chaucer the Pilgrim." *PMLA* 75 (1960):1960–1962.

Mâle, Emile. *The Gothic Image: Religious Art in France of the Thirteenth Century.* Trans. Dora Nussey. 1913. Reprint. New York: Harper & Row, 1958.

———. *Religious Art from the Twelfth to the Eighteenth Century.* New York: Noonday Press, 1949.

Malinowski, Bronislaw. *Magic, Science, and Religion and Other Essays.* 1948. Reprint. New York: Doubleday Anchor Books, 1954.

Man, Paul de. *Allegories of Reading, Figural Language in Rousseau, Nietzsche, Rilke, and Proust.* New Haven: Yale University Press, 1979.

———. *Blindness and Insight: Essays in the Rhetoric of Contemporary Criticism.* New York: Oxford University Press, 1971.

———. "The Rhetoric of Temporality." In *Interpretation: Theory and Practice,* ed. Charles S. Singleton, pp. 173–209. Baltimore: Johns Hopkins University Press, 1969.

Mandel, Jerome. "Other Voices in the Canterbury Tales." *Criticism* 19 (1977):338–349.

Mann, Jill. *Chaucer and Medieval Estates Satire: The Literature of Social Classes and the General Prologue to the Canterbury Tales.* Cambridge: Cambridge University Press, 1973.

Markiewicz, Henryk. "Places of Indeterminacy in a Literary Work." In *Roman Ingarden and Contemporary Polish Aesthetics,* ed. Piotr Graff and Slaw Krzemian-Ojak, pp. 159–171. Warsaw: Polish Scientific Publishers, 1975.

[275]

Markus, Robert A., ed. *Augustine: A Collection of Critical Essays*. New York: Doubleday, 1972.

Marrou, H. I. *A History of Education in Antiquity*. Trans. George Lamb. New York: New American Library, 1964.

Martianus Capella. *De nuptiis Philologiae et Mercurii*. Ed. Franciscus Eyssenhardt. Leipzig: Teubner, 1866.

Martin, Loy D. "History and Form in the General Prologue to the Canterbury Tales." *ELH* 45 (1978):1–17.

Martin, Wallace. "The Epoch of Critical Theory." *Comparative Literature* 31 (1979):321–350.

Martinus de Dacia. *De modis significandi*. Ed. H. Roos, S.J. CPDMA, 2. Copenhagen: Gad, 1961.

Mazzeo, Joseph A. *Medieval Cultural Tradition in Dante's "Comedy."* Ithaca: Cornell University Press, 1960.

Mazzotta, Giuseppe. *Dante, Poet of the Desert: History and Allegory in the "Divine Comedy."* Princeton: Princeton University Press, 1979.

McCall, John P. *Chaucer among the Gods: The Poetics of Classical Myth*. University Park: Pennsylvania State University Press, 1979.

McInerny, Ralph M. *The Logic of Analogy: An Interpretation of St. Thomas*. The Hague: Martinus Nijhoff, 1961.

McLuhan, Marshall. *The Gutenberg Galaxy: The Making of Typographic Man*. Buffalo: University of Toronto Press, 1965.

Mendenhall, George E. *The Tenth Generation: The Origins of the Biblical Tradition*. Baltimore: Johns Hopkins University Press, 1973.

Millar, E. G. *The Lindisfarne Gospels*. London: British Museum, 1923.

Miller, R. P. "Chaucer's Pardoner, the Scriptural Eunuch, and the Pardoner's Tale." *Speculum* 30 (1955):180–199.

Mink, Louis O. "Change and Causality in the History of Ideas." *Eighteenth Century Studies* 2 (1968):7–25.

Miskimin, Alice. *The Renaissance Chaucer*. New Haven: Yale University Press, 1975.

Mitchell, Sabrina. *Medieval Manuscript Painting*. New York: Viking Press, 1965.

Moir, A. L., et al. *The World Map in Hereford Cathedral*. 6th ed. illustrated. Hereford: Cathedral, 1971.

Momigliano, Arnaldo, ed. *The Conflict between Paganism and Christianity in the Fourth Century*. Oxford: Clarendon Press, 1963.

Montano, Rocco. "Dante's Aesthetic and Gothic Art." In *A Dante Symposium*, ed. William De Sua and Gino Rizzo, pp. 11–33. Chapel Hill: University of North Carolina Press, 1965.

Mortley, Paul. "Negative Theology and Abstraction in Plotinus." *American Journal of Philology* 96 (1975):363–377.

Murphy, James J. "The Arts of Discourse, 1050–1400." *MS* 23 (1961): 194–205.

———. "Literary Implications of Instruction in the Verbal Arts in Fourteenth-Century England." *Leeds Studies in English*, N.S., 1 (1967): 119–135.

———. *Rhetoric in the Middle Ages: A History of Rhetorical Theory from Saint Augustine to the Renaissance*. Berkeley and Los Angeles: University of California Press, 1974.

Murrin, Michael. *The Veil of Allegory*. Chicago: University of Chicago Press, 1969.

Muscatine, Charles. *Chaucer and the French Tradition*. Berkeley: University of California Press, 1957.

———. *Poetry and Crisis in the Age of Chaucer*. Notre Dame, Ind.: University of Notre Dame Press, 1972.

Myers, A. R. *London in the Age of Chaucer*. Norman: University of Oklahoma Press, 1972.

Nelson, William. *Fact or Fiction: The Dilemma of the Renaissance Storyteller*. Cambridge: Harvard University Press, 1973.

Neumann, E. *The Great Mother: An Analysis of the Archetype*. Trans. R. Manheim. New York: Pantheon, 1955.

Newman, Francis X. "Somnium: Medieval Theories of Dreaming and the Form of Vision Poetry." Ph.D. diss., Princeton University, 1963.

Nichols, Stephen G., Jr. "A Poetics of Historicism? Recent Trends in Medieval Literary Study." *Medievalia et Humanistica* 8 (1977):77–101.

———. "Romanesque Imitation or Imitating the Romans?" In *Mimesis: From Mirror to Method, Augustine to Descartes*, ed. John D. Lyons and Stephen G. Nichols, Jr., pp. 36–59. Hanover, N.H.: University Press of New England, 1982.

Nicolson, Marjorie H. *The Breaking of the Circle: Studies in the Effect of the "New Science" on Seventeenth-Century Poetry*. Rev. ed. New York: Columbia University Press, 1960.

Niebuhr, Reinhold. *The Nature and Destiny of Man: A Christian Interpretation*. New York: Scribner, 1941.

Nolan, Barbara. *The Gothic Visionary Perspective*. Princeton: Princeton University Press, 1977.

———. "The *Vita Nuova* and Richard of St. Victor's Phenomenology of Vision." *Dante Studies* 92 (1974):35–52.

Olson, Glending. *Literature as Recreation in the Later Middle Ages*. Ithaca: Cornell University Press, 1982.

———. "Making and Poetry in the Age of Chaucer." *CL* 31 (1979): 272–290.

Ong, Walter J. *The Presence of the Word: Some Prolegomena for Cultural and Religious History*. New York: Simon & Schuster, 1970.

Orlinsky, Harry Meyer. *Interpreting the Prophetic Tradition*. Cincinnati: Hebrew Union College Press, 1969.

Otto, Alfred, S.J., ed. *Summa grammatica: Divisio scientiae*, by Johannes de Dacia. CPDMA, 1. Copenhagen: Gad, 1955.

Owen, Charles A. *Pilgrimage and Storytelling in "The Canterbury Tales": The*

Dialectic of "Ernest" and "Game." Norman: University of Oklahoma Press, 1977.

Owst, G. R. *Literature and Pulpit in Medieval England: A Neglected Chapter in the History of English Letters and of the English People.* 2d ed. New York: Barnes & Noble, 1961.

Pächt, Otto. *The Rise of Pictorial Narrative in Twelfth-Century England.* Oxford: Clarendon Press, 1962.

Paetow, Louis J. *The Arts Course at Medieval Universities with Special Reference to Grammar and Rhetoric.* University of Illinois Studies, 3:7. Urbana: University of Illinois Press, 1909.

—————. *The Battle of the Seven Arts.* Memoirs of the University of California, 4:1. Berkeley: Univesity of California Press, 1914.

Panofsky, Erwin. *Gothic Architecture and Scholasticism.* Cleveland: World, 1968.

—————. *Renaissance and Renascences in Western Art.* Stockholm: Almquist and Wiksells, 1960.

Parker, Patricia. *Inescapable Romance*: *Studies in the Poetics of a Mode.* Princeton: Princeton University Press, 1979.

Paterson, Catherine Childs. *Medieval Gardens.* 1924. Reprint. New York: Hacker Art Books, 1966.

Patrides, C. A. *The Grand Design of God: The Literary Form of the Christian View of History.* London: Routledge & Kegan Paul, 1972.

—————. *Milton and the Christian Tradition.* Oxford: Clarendon Press, 1966.

Patterson, Lee W. "Ambiguity and Interpretation: A Fifteenth-Century Reading of *Troilus and Criseyde.*" *Speculum* 54 (1979):297–330.

—————. "Chaucerian Confession: Penitential Literature and the Pardoner." *Medievalia et Humanistica* 7 (1976):153–173.

—————. "Writing about Writing: The Case of Chaucer." *UTQ* 48 (1979): 263–282.

Payne, Robert O. *The Key of Remembrance: A Study of Chaucer's Poetics.* New Haven: Yale University Press, 1963.

—————. "Making His Own Myth." *Chaucer Review* 9 (1975):197–211.

Pearsall, D. A., ed. *The Floure and the Leafe and the Assembly of Ladies.* London and Edinburgh: Nelson, 1962.

Pépin, Jean. *Dante et la tradition de l'allégorie.* Montreal: Institute d'Etudes Médiévales, 1970.

—————. *Mythe et allégorie: Les origines grecques et les contentations judéo-chrétiennes.* Paris, 1958.

Percival, W. Keith. "The Applicability of Kuhn's Paradigms to the History of Linguistics." *LG* 52 (1976):285–294.

Petrus Helias. *Summa in Priscianum Minorem.* Ed. J. E. Tolson. CIMAGL, 27–28. Copenhagen, 1978.

Pettit, Philip. *The Concept of Structuralism: A Critical Analysis.* Berkeley and Los Angeles: University of California Press, 1975.

Piaget, Jean. *Structuralism.* Trans. Chaninah Masctler. New York: Harper & Row, 1971.

Piggott, Stuart. *Ancient Europe from the Beginnings of Agriculture to Classical Antiquity*. Chicago: Aldine, 1965.

———. *The Neolithic Cultures of the British Isles: A Study of the Stone-Using Agricultural Communities of Britain in the Second Milennium B.C.* 1954. Reprint. Cambridge: Cambridge University Press, 1970.

Pinborg, Jan. *Die Entwicklung der Sprachtheorie im Mittelalter*. Copenhagen: Frost-Hansen, 1967.

———. *Logik und Semantik im Mittelalter: Ein Uberblick*. Stuttgart: Frommann-Holzboog, 1972.

———, ed. *Siger de Courtrai, Modi significandi; Sophismata*. SiHol, 14. Amsterdam: Benjamins, 1976.

Pinborg, Jan, and H. Roos, S.J., eds. *Boethius de Dacia, Modi significandi sive Quaestiones super Priscianum Maiorem*. CPDMA, 4. Copenhagen: Gad, 1969.

Plato. *The Dialogues of Plato*. Trans. and comm. Benjamin Jowett. 4th ed. 4 vols. Oxford: Clarendon Press, 1953.

———. *Plato's Cosmology: The "Timaeus" of Plato*. Trans. Francis M. Cornford. 1937. Reprint. New York: Bobbs-Merrill, n.d.

Plumb, J. H. *The Death of the Past*. Boston: Houghton Mifflin, 1970.

———, ed. *The History of Human Society: Prehistoric Societies*. New York: Alfred A. Knopf, 1967.

Popper, Karl R. *Conjectures and Refutations: The Growth of Scientific Knowledge*. New York: Harper & Row, 1968.

Poulet, Georges. *Studies in Human Time*. Trans. Elliott Coleman. Baltimore: Johns Hopkins University Press, 1956.

Preller, Victor. *Divine Science and the Science of God: A Reformulation of Thomas Aquinas*. Princeton: Princeton University Press, 1967.

Preston, Raymond. *Chaucer*. 1952. Reprint. Westport, Conn.: Greenwood Press, 1969.

Quilligan, Maureen. *The Language of Allegory: Defining the Genre*. Ithaca: Cornell University Press, 1979.

Rabinowitz, Isaac. "'Word' and Literature in Ancient Greece." *NLH* 4 (1972):119–139.

Rad, Gerhard von. *Old Testament Theology*. Vol. 1. *The Theology of Israel's Historical Traditions*. Trans. D. M. G. Stalker from 2d German ed. New York: Harper & Row, 1962.

———. *Old Testament Theology*. Vol. 2. *The Theology of Israel's Prophetic Traditions*. Trans. D. M. G. Stalker. New York: Harper & Row, 1965.

Rand, Edward Kennard. *Founders of the Middle Ages*. 1928. Reprint. New York: Dover Publications, 1957.

Randall, Lilian. *Images in the Margins of Gothic Manuscripts*. Berkeley: University of California Press, 1966.

Ratzinger, Joseph. *Introduction to Christianity*. Trans. J. R. Foster. London: Burns & Oates, 1969.

Reeves, Marjorie. *The Influence of Prophecy in the Later Middle Ages: A Study in Joachism*. Oxford: Oxford University Press, 1969.

Reichling, Dietrich, ed. *Alexander de Villa-Dei, Doctrinale*. Monumenta Germaniae Paedogogica, 12. Berlin: Hofmann, 1893.

Reiss, Timothy J. *The Discourse of Modernism*. Ithaca: Cornell University Press, 1982.

———. "The Environment of Literature and the Imperatives of Criticism." *Europa* 4, 1 (1981):29–64.

———. "Power, Poetry, and the Resemblance of Nature." In *Mimesis: From Mirror to Method*, ed. John D. Lyons and Stephen G. Nicholas, Jr., pp. 215–247. Hanover, N.H.: University Press of New England, 1982.

Ricoeur, Paul. "Narrative Time." *NLH* 7 (1980):169–190.

Rijk, Lambertus M. *Logica Modernorum: A Contribution to the History of Early Terminist Logic*. 3 vols. Assen: van Gorcum, 1962–1967.

Rivero, Maria-Luisa. "Early Scholastic Views on Ambiguity." *HL* 2 (1975): 25–47.

Robbins, Rossell H., ed. *Chaucer at Albany*. New York: Burt Franklin, 1975.

Robertson, D. W., Jr. *Chaucer's London*. New York: John Wiley, 1968.

———. "Historical Criticism." In *English Institute Essays, 1950*, ed. Alan S. Downer, pp. 3–31. New York: Columbia University Press, 1951.

———. *A Preface to Chaucer: Studies in Medieval Perspectives*. Princeton: Princeton University Press, 1962.

Robey, David, ed. *Structuralism: An Introduction*. London: Oxford University Press, 1973.

Robins, Robert H. *Ancient and Medieval Grammatical Theory in Europe*. London: Bell, 1951.

Rollinson, Philip. *Classical Theories of Allegory and Christian Culture*. Pittsburgh: Duquesne University Press, 1981.

Roos, Heinrich, S. J., ed. *Martinus de Dacia, De modis significandi*. CPDMA, 2. Copenhagen: Gad, 1961.

Rose, Donald M., ed. *New Perspectives in Chaucer Criticism*. Norman, Okla.: Pilgrim Books, 1981.

Rowland, Beryl. *Animals with Human Faces: A Guide to Animal Symbolism*. Knoxville: University of Tennessee Press, 1973.

———, ed. *Chaucer and Middle English Studies in Honour of Rossell Hope Robbins*. Kent, Ohio: Kent State University Press, 1974.

———, ed. *Companion to Chaucer Studies*. Rev. ed. New York: Oxford University Press, 1979.

Rowlands, John. *The Garden of Earthly Delights*. New York: Phaidon, 1979.

Ruggiers, Paul G. "Tyrants of Lombardy in Dante and Chaucer." *PQ* 29 (1950):445–448.

Ryding, William W. *Structure in Medieval Narrative*. The Hague: Mouton, 1971.

Said, Edward. *Abecedarium Culturae: Structuralism, Absence, Writing, Modern French Criticism*. Chicago: University of Chicago Press, 1972.

———. *Literature and Society: Selected Papers from the English Institute, 1978*. Baltimore: Johns Hopkins University Press, 1980.

Saintsbury, George. *The Flourishing of Romance and the Rise of Allegory.* New York: Scribner, 1897.

Salman, Phillips. "Instruction and Delight in Medieval and Renaissance Criticism." *Renaissance Quarterly* 32 (1979):303–332.

Salu, Mary B., ed. *Essays on "Troilus and Criseyde."* Totowa, N.J.: Rowman and Littlefield, 1979.

Sammons, Jeffrey L. *Literary Sociology and Practical Criticism.* Bloomington: Indiana University Press, 1978.

Sandler, Lucy Freeman. *The Psalter of Robert de Lisle in the British Library.* New York: Oxford University Press, 1983.

Saussure, Ferdinand de. *Cours de linguistique générale.* Ed. Charles Bally and Albert Sechehaye, in collaboration with Albert Riedlinger. Geneva, 1916. Reprint. Paris: Payot, 1973. Trans. Wade Baskin as *Course in General Linguistics.* New York: Philosophical Library, 1959.

Scaglione, Aldo D. *Ars Grammatica: A Bibliographic Survey.* Janua Linguarum, 77. The Hague: Mouton, 1970.

Schapiro, Norman R., trans. *The Comedy of Eros: Medieval French Guides to the Art of Love.* Urbana: University of Illinois Press, 1971.

Schiwy, Günther. *Structuralism and Christianity.* Trans. Henry J. Koren. Pittsburgh: Duquesne University Press, 1971.

Schneidau, Herbert N. *Sacred Discontent: The Bible and Western Tradition.* Berkeley: University of California Press, 1976.

Schoeck, Richard J. "On Rhetoric in Fourteenth-Century Oxford." *Mediaeval Studies* 30 (1968):214–225.

Scully, Vincent. *The Earth, the Temple, and the Gods: Greek Sacred Architecture.* New Haven: Yale University Press, 1962.

Seznec, Jean. *The Survival of the Pagan Gods: The Mythological Tradition and Its Place in Renaissance Humanism and Art.* French ed., 1940. Trans. Barbara F. Sessions. 1953. Reprint. New York: Harper & Row, 1961.

Shepard, Paul. *Man in the Landscape: A Historical View of the Esthetics of Nature.* New York: Alfred A. Knopf, 1967.

Shoaf, Richard A. *Dante, Chaucer, and the Currency of the Word: Money, Images, and Reference in Late Medieval Poetry.* Norman, Okla.: Pilgrim Books, 1983.

Shroder, Maurice Z. "The Novel as a Genre." *Massachusetts Review* 4 (1963): 291–308.

Siger of Courtrai. *Summa modorum significandi.* Ed. G. Wallerand. In *Les Oeuvres de Siger de Courtrai.* Les Philosophes Belges, 8. Louvain, 1913.

———. *Summa modorum significandi: Sophismata.* Ed. J. Oinborg. SiHol, 14. Amsterdam: Benjamins, 1976.

Simon de Dacia. *Opera.* Ed. A. Otto, S.J. CPDMA, 3. Copenhagen: Gad, 1963.

Simpson, William K. *The Literature of Ancient Egypt: An Anthology.* New Haven: Yale University Press, 1972.

Simson, Otto von. *The Gothic Cathedral.* 1956. Reprint. New York: Bollingen Foundation, 1962.

Singleton, Charles S. *Dante Studies I: "Commedia," Elements of Structure.* Cambridge: Harvard University Press, 1954.
———. *An Essay on the Vita Nuova.* Baltimore: Johns Hopkins University Press, 1949.
———. "In Exitu Israel de Aegypto." *Dante Studies* 78 (1960):1–24.
———. "The Irreducible Dove." *Comparative Literature,* 9 (1957):129–135.
Smalley, Beryl. *The Study of the Bible in the Middle Ages.* Notre Dame, Ind.: University of Notre Dame Press, 1964.
Smith, Barbara H. *Poetic Closure: A Study of How Poems End.* Chicago: University of Chicago Press, 1968.
Snell, Bruno. *The Discovery of the Mind: The Greek Origin of European Thought.* Cambridge: Harvard University Press, 1963.
Southern, R. W. *The Making of the Middle Ages.* New Haven: Yale University Press, 1953.
———. *Medieval Humanism and Other Studies.* Oxford: Basil Blackwell, 1970.
Speirs, John. *Chaucer the Maker.* Rev. 2d ed. London: Faber, 1960.
Spicq, Ceslaus. *Esquisse d'une histoire de l'exégèse latine au moyen âge.* Bibliothèque Thomiste, 26. Paris: J. Vrin, 1944.
Spitzer, Leo. "The Addresses to the Reader in the *Commedia.*" In *Romanische Literaturstudien* 1936–1956, pp. 574–595. Tübingen: Niemeyer, 1959.
———. *Classical and Christian Ideas of World Harmony.* Ed. Anna G. Hatcher. Baltimore: Johns Hopkins Press, 1963.
———. "Note on the Poetic and the Empirical 'I' in Medieval Authors." *Traditio* 4 (1946):414–422.
Stace, W. I. *Religion and the Modern Mind.* New York: J. B. Lippincott, 1952.
Stacy, R. H. *Defamiliarization in Language and Literature.* Syracuse: Syracuse University Press, 1977.
Stegmuller, Frederick. *Repertorium biblicum medii aevi.* 7 vols. Madrid: Matriti, 1950–1961.
Stephenson, Carl, ed. *Mediaeval Institutions: Selected Essays.* Ithaca: Cornell University Press, 1954.
Stewart, Stanley. *The Enclosed Garden: The Tradition and the Image in Seventeenth-Century Poetry.* Madison: University of Wisconsin Press, 1966.
Stock, Brian. *The Implications of Literacy: Written Language and Models of Interpretation in the Eleventh and Twelfth Centuries.* Princeton: Princeton University Press, 1983.
———. "The Middle Ages as Subject and Object: Romantic Attitudes and Academic Medievalism." *NLH* 5 (1973):527–547.
———. *Myth and Science in the Twelfth Century.* Princeton: Princeton University Press, 1972.
Streuver, Nancy S. *The Language of History in the Renaissance.* Princeton: Princeton University Press, 1970.

Suger, Abbot of St.-Denis. *De consecratione ecclesiae sancti Dionysii*. Trans. Erwin Panofsky as *Abbot Suger on the Abbey Church of St.-Denis and Its Art Treasures*. Princeton: Princeton University Press, 1946.

Sullivan, Sheila. *Critics on Chaucer*. Coral Gables: University Of Miami Press, 1970.

Tatlock, J. S. P. *The Development and Chronology of Chaucer's Works*. 1907. Reprint. Gloucester, Mass.: Peter Smith, 1963.

Thomas of Celano. "Dies irae." In *Hymns of the Roman Liturgy*, ed. Joseph Connelly, pp. 252–256. Westminster, Md.: Newman Press, 1957.

———. *S. Francisci Assisiensis vita et miracula*. Rome: Desclée, Lefebure, 1906.

Thomas of Erfurt. *Grammatica speculativa*. Latin ed. and English trans., G. L. Bursill-Hall. London: Longman Group, 1972.

Thomson, David. *A Descriptive Catalogue of Middle English Grammatical Texts*. New York: Garland, 1979.

Thomson, Harrison. *The Writings of Robert Grosseteste, Bishop of Lincoln 1235–1253*. Cambridge: Cambridge University Press, 1940.

Thrupp, Sylvia. *Millennial Dreams in Action: Essays in Comparative Study*. The Hague: Mouton, 1962.

Thurot, Charles. *Notices et extraits de divers manuscrits latins pour servir à l'histoire des doctrines grammaticales au moyen âge*. Notices et Extraits des Manuscrits de la Bibliothèque Impériale, 22. Paris: Imprimerie Impériale, 1868. Reprint. Frankfurt: Minerva, 1964.

Thurston, Paul T. *Artistic Ambivalence in Chaucer's Knight's Tale*. Coral Gables: University of Florida Press, 1968.

Todorov, Tzvetan. *Grammaire du Décaméron*. The Hague: Mouton, 1969.

———. *Littérature et signification*. Paris: Larousse, 1967.

———. *Théories du symbole*. Paris: Seuil, 1977.

Toliver, Harold. *Animate Illusions: Explorations of Narrative Structure*. Lincoln: University of Nebraska Press, 1974.

Tolnay, Charles de. *Hieronymus Bosch*. Trans. M. Bullock and H. Mins, 1965. London: Methuen, 1966.

———. "The Music of the Universe." *Journal of the Walters Art Gallery* 6 (1943):82–104.

Trentman, John A. "Extraordinary Language and Medieval Logic." *Dialogue* 7 (1968):286–291.

Trimpi, Wesley. "The Quality of Fiction: The Rhetorical Transmission of Literary Theory." *Traditio* 30 (1974):1–118.

Tuve, Rosemond. *Allegorical Imagery: Some Medieval Books and Their Posterity*. Princeton: Princeton University Press, 1966.

Unterkircher, Franz. *A Treasury of Illuminated Manuscripts: A Selection of Miniatures from Manuscripts in the Austrian National Library*. New York: Putnam, 1967.

Vance, Eugene. "Augustine's *Confessions* and the Grammar of Selfhood." *Genre* 6 (1973):1–28.

———. "Augustine's *Confessions* and the Poetics of the Law." *MLN* 93 (1978):618–634.

———. "Chaucer's *House of Fame* and the Poetics of Inflation." *Boundary* 7 (1979):17–37.

———. "Désir, rhétorique et texte—Semences de la différence: Brunet Latin chez Dante." *Poétique* 42 (1980):137–155.

———. "Love's Concordance: The Poetics of Desire and the Joy of the Text." *Diacritics* 5 (1975):40–52.

———. "Mervelous Signals: Poetics, Sign Theory and Politics in Chaucer's *Troilus.*" *NLH* 10 (1979):293–337.

———. *Reading the "Song of Roland."* Englewood Cliffs, N.J.: Prentice-Hall, 1970.

———. "Roland and the Poetics of Memory." In *Textual Strategies: Perspectives in Post-Structuralist Criticism*, ed. Josué Harari, pp. 374–403. Ithaca: Cornell University Press, 1979.

———. "Roland, Charlemagne, and the Poetics of Illumination." *Oliphant* 6 (1979):213–225.

———. "Saint Augustine: Language as Temporality." In *Mimesis: From Mirror to Method, Augustine to Descartes*, ed. John D. Lyons and Stephen G. Nichols, Jr., pp. 20–35. Hanover, N.H.: University Press of New England, 1982.

———. "Signs of the City: Medieval Poetry as Detour." *NLH* 4 (1973): 557–574.

Vickery, John B., ed. *Myth and Literature: Contemporary Theory and Practice.* Lincoln: University of Nebraska Press, 1966.

Villard de Honnecourt. *The Sketchbook of Villard de Honnecourt.* Ed. Theodore Bowie. Bloomington: Indiana University Press, 1959.

Vinaver, Eugène. *The Rise of Romance.* New York: Oxford University Press, 1971.

Vincent of Beauvais. *Speculum quadruplex.* Graz: Akademische Druk-U. Verlaganstalt, 1964–1965.

Watts, Ann Chalmers. *The Lyre and the Harp.* New Haven: Yale University Press, 1969.

Weinrich, Harald. "Structures narratives du mythe." *Poétique* 1 (1970):25–34.

Weisheipl, James A., O.P. "Curriculum of the Faculty of Arts at Oxford in the Early Fourteenth Century." *MS* 26 (1964):143–185.

———. "Developments in the Arts Curriculum at Oxford in the Early Fourteenth Century." *MS* 28 (1966):151–175.

Weston, Jessie L. *From Ritual to Romance.* 1920. Reprint. New York: Peter Smith, 1941.

Wetherbee, Winthrop. *Platonism and Poetry in the Twelfth Century: The Literary Influence of the School of Chartres.* Princeton: Princeton University Press, 1972.

Wheelwright, Philip. *Metaphor and Reality.* Bloomington: University of Indiana Press, 1962.

White, Hayden. *Metahistory: The Historical Imagination in Nineteenth-Century Europe*. Baltimore: Johns Hopkins University Press, 1973.

———. *Tropics of Discourse: Essays in Cultural Criticism*. Baltimore: Johns Hopkins University Press, 1978.

———. "The Value of Narrativity in the Representation of Reality." *CI* 7 (1980):5–27.

William of Thierry. *The Works of William of St. Thierry*. Vol. 3. *The Enigma of Faith*. Trans. John D. Anderson. Washington: Cistercian, Consortium Press, 1974.

Wimsatt, James I. *Allegory and Mirror: Dominant Modes in Middle English Literature*. New York: Pegasus, 1970.

Wimsatt, W. K., and M. C. Beardsley. *The Verbal Icon*. 1954. Reprint. New York: Noonday Press, 1965.

Wittig, Susan. *Stylistic and Narrative Structures in the Middle English Romances*. Austin: University of Texas Press, 1978.

Wood, Chauncey. *Chaucer and the Country of the Stars: Poetic Uses of Astrological Imagery*. Princeton: Princeton University Press, 1970.

Woolf, Rosemary. "Chaucer as Satirist in the General Prologue to the Canterbury Tales." *Critical Quarterly* 1 (1959):150–157.

Wright, Thomas. *The Worship of the Generative Powers during the Middle Ages* (London, 1866), bound with *A Discourse on the Worship of Priapus*, by Richard Payne Knight (London, 1786). In *Sexual Symbolism: A History of Phallic Worship*, intro. Ashley Montague. New York: Julian Press, 1957.

Yates, Francis. *The Art of Memory*. Chicago: University of Chicago Press, 1966.

Zacher, Christian K. *Curiosity and Pilgrimage: The Literature of Discovery in Fourteenth-Century England*. Baltimore: Johns Hopkins University Press, 1976.

Zumthor, Paul. *Essai de poétique médiévale*. Paris: Seuil, 1972.

———. "From Hi(story) to Poem, or the Paths of Pun: The Grands Rhétoriqueurs of Fifteenth-Century France." *NLH* 10 (1979):231–263.

———. *Langue, texte, énigme*. Paris: Seuil, 1975.

INDEX

Library of Congress Cataloging in Publication Data

Gellrich, Jesse M., 1942–
  The idea of the book in the Middle Ages.

  Bibliography: p.
  Includes index.
  1. Books—History—400–1400.   2. Literature, Medieval—History and criticism.
3. Transmission of texts.   4. Civilization, Medieval.   5. Learning and scholarship—
History—Medieval, 500–1500.   6. Chaucer, Geoffrey, d. 1400—Criticism and
interpretation.   I. Title.
Z6.G44   1985   002   84-23814
ISBN 0-8014-1722-8